PEACEMAKER

ALSO BY THANT MYINT-U

The Hidden History of Burma: Race, Capitalism, and the Crisis of Democracy in the 21st Century

Where China Meets India: Burma and the New Crossroads of Asia

The River of Lost Footsteps: A Personal History of Burma

The Making of Modern Burma

PEACEMAKER

U THANT AND THE FORGOTTEN QUEST FOR A JUST WORLD

THANT MYINT-U

W. W. NORTON & COMPANY

Independent Publishers Since 1923

Copyright © 2025 by Thant Myint-U

All rights reserved
Printed in the United States of America
First Edition

For information about permission to reproduce selections from this book, write to
Permissions, W. W. Norton & Company, Inc., 500 Fifth Avenue, New York, NY 10110

For information about special discounts for bulk purchases, please contact
W. W. Norton Special Sales at specialsales@wwnorton.com or 800-233-4830

Manufacturing by Lakeside Book Company
Book design by Dana Sloan
Production manager: Louise Mattarelliano

Library of Congress Cataloging-in-Publication Data is available.

ISBN 978-1-324-05197-8

W. W. Norton & Company, Inc., 500 Fifth Avenue, New York, NY 10110
www.wwnorton.com

W. W. Norton & Company Ltd., 15 Carlisle Street, London W1D 3BS

10 9 8 7 6 5 4 3 2 1

For BG

CONTENTS

	Note to Readers	xi
	Prologue	1
1	New World	7
2	Congo	25
3	Missile Crisis	45
4	Havana	65
5	Grand Slam	77
6	Turn! Turn! Turn!	95
7	Vietnam	111
8	Rolling Thunder	129
9	Kashmir	147
10	The Sound of Silence	165
11	Eve of Destruction	185
12	Gaza and the Sinai	197
13	The Six-Day War	211
14	Revolution	235
15	Bad Moon Rising	255
16	One World	273
17	Both Sides Now	289
	Epilogue	305
	Author's Note	311
	Acknowledgments	313
	Notes	317
	Image Credits	349
	Index	351

NOTE TO READERS

This book follows the usage of proper names as they were commonly rendered in English from the late 1950s through the early 1970s. For example, "Peking" is used instead of "Beijing." I have also used terms prevalent at the time, such as "Third World" rather than the more recent "Global South." Additionally, Vietnamese names appear without diacritics for readability and consistency with most English-language sources of the era. While this simplifies presentation, it does not reflect the full accuracy of Vietnamese orthography.

Through these choices, I have tried to maintain historical authenticity while avoiding unnecessary distractions.

PEACEMAKER

PROLOGUE

THE FORMER BEATLE WAS wearing a brown polka-dot jacket with a black turtleneck, and little round sunglasses. "Say, could you tell me how to get a ticket to this lunch? Nobody sent me one and I don't know where to sit."

It was around noon on a cold and rainy mid-December day in 1971 and John Lennon had just arrived with Yoko Ono at the Pierre Hotel in New York for a luncheon. "We're not snobs," said Lennon. "We don't mind mixing with the straights." A startled young woman at the reception desk quickly replied that the couple would be seated on the dais with U Thant, Governor Rockefeller, Pete Seeger, Senator Frank Church, Arthur Goldberg, and Jacques Cousteau. No ticket was required.[1]

The lunch was a farewell tribute to Thant, who was about to step down after more than a decade as Secretary-General of the United Nations. Thant, who was Burmese, had, like many of his compatriots, only a single personal name; the "U" was an honorific roughly meaning "mister."

Dorothy Hammerstein, wife of the Broadway lyricist Oscar Hammerstein, had organized funding for the event, attracting contributions from dozens of Thant's friends, including Jacqueline Kennedy Onassis, Walter Lippmann, John D. Rockefeller, and a mix of corporate and union donors, such as the Woolworth Company and the Amalgamated Laundry Workers.

Lennon and Ono were ushered into the chandeliered ballroom where they and nearly six hundred other guests sipped wine, ate canapés, and chatted amiably: American congressmen, bankers and captains of industry, Hollywood moguls, peace activists, ambassadors, and top UN officials. There was Myrna Loy, star of the silver screen, Jacqueline Wexler, a former nun who had fought against Vatican authority, Robert Wagner, the three-term mayor of New York, Barbara Ward, a distinguished economist and early campaigner for sustainable development, and Burgess Meredith, who had recently played the Penguin in the TV series *Batman*.

Also in the crowd was Victor Lessiovski, a KGB agent (codename: Fedora) and one of Thant's special assistants. The FBI believed they had turned the spy years ago. In fact, the supposed double agent was still working for Moscow and feeding disinformation about the UN directly to the White House.[2]

"U Thant works for peace and so do we," Lennon told Sally Quinn, a reporter for *The Washington Post*. "Besides, if we want to take over the establishment, we have to find out how it works."

Lennon and Ono were introduced to Thant, the world's preeminent diplomat and the first non-European to head an international organization.

"I've been following your activities. You've got a hard job," Lennon said respectfully.

"I've been following your activities too," replied the jovial sixty-two-year-old as he puffed on a Cuban Partagas cigar. Thant, a regular watcher of *The Ed Sullivan Show* on Sunday nights, explained that he had seen the Beatles on television and had been delighted to find Lennon's name on the guest list.

The event had been organized by the World Federalist Movement, founded in the 1930s by suffragists and now directed by Norman Cousins—the influential former editor of the *Saturday Review*, a staunch opponent of the Vietnam War, and an ally of Thant's. The World Federalists were committed to what they called a "Human Manifesto" and pledged themselves "Planetary Citizens." They wanted a world free of "divisions and wars between men" and believed that only a stronger United Nations was "capable of governing our planet in the common human interest." Distinguished men and women from many fields joined together to support this vision of a closer human community, including Coretta Scott King, the composer Leonard Bernstein, the architect Buckminster Fuller, the mountaineer Edmund Hillary, the musician Yehudi Menuhin, the playwright Arthur Miller, the writer Kurt Vonnegut, the scientist C. P. Snow, the historian Arnold Toynbee, the explorer Thor Heyerdahl, and even the Dalai Lama.[3]

Over a hundred people, including scores of presidents and prime ministers who could not attend the event in person, sent telegrams, and these were printed out and stapled together for each guest.[4] A message from the Nobel laureate Linus Pauling described the Secretary-General as "one of the greatest men of the Twentieth Century." The folk singer Joan Baez sent a simple missive: "Love and gratitude to you and wishing you and all of us strength for the struggle which seems to continually lie ahead of us and let there be joy in that struggle."

Lunch was followed by a dessert of Strawberry Delight and a musical tribute by Pete Seeger, who sang "Where Have All the Flowers Gone?" and "Jacob's Ladder," during which he encouraged everybody to sing along. New York governor Nelson Rockefeller, Norman Cousins, Barbara Ward, and Jacques Cousteau made brief remarks before Thant took a final puff on his cigar and walked to the podium.

In a charcoal pinstripe suit, the diplomat from Burma explained how he had worked to "harmonize" the attitudes of governments around the world and give priority to "the human factor." He was, he said, a conservative Buddhist who valued "modesty, humility, love, a live-and-let-live attitude," and, most of all, "understanding the other man's point of view." Over his decade at the helm, the spirit of internationalism had been kept alive, Thant declared. But global crises were now coming in "dangerously rapid succession." Patriotism was fine, but an additional allegiance, to the entire world community, was now essential.

Warming to his theme, he put aside his notes and said, "We have to learn a great deal . . . but far more importantly, we have to *unlearn* a great

Thant with John Lennon and Yoko Ono at his retirement party, December 1971.

deal. We have to unlearn a lot of dogma ... to get rid of that very bad concept of 'my country, right or wrong.'"

As the assembled guests applauded and rose to their feet, Norman Cousins handed Thant a copy of the "Human Manifesto" and declared Thant "Planetary Citizen Number One."

During Thant's speech, Lennon was seen whispering to Ono before handing a little note to Seeger. When the speech was over, Seeger passed Lennon his guitar. Lennon sang a song he had recently written about peace and which, he said, he had never performed before in America: "It's called 'Imagine.'"

A beaming Thant said the event was the most moving in his career.

Until he was nearly forty years old, Thant was a schoolteacher in a small backwater town in Burma, then part of the British Empire. When his country became independent in 1948, he joined government service, initially as a spokesman, and in less than a decade found himself at the very center of global politics as Burma's ambassador to the UN, living in midtown Manhattan. In 1961, during the coldest years of the Cold War, with the UN on the edge of collapse, he emerged as the only person in the world acceptable to both Moscow and Washington as Secretary-General. He would be on the front lines of nearly every major global conflict until 1972—often caught on the horns of an impossible decision.

In 1967, a Gallup poll ranked Thant the sixth most admired man in the world, just behind Martin Luther King Jr. and Robert Kennedy and ahead of Richard Nixon and Ronald Reagan. In the early 1960s he had pulled the UN back from bankruptcy, battled white supremacist mercenaries in the Congo, and, in 1962, mediated a peaceful end to the Cuban Missile Crisis. All this had won him widespread acclaim (except from some on the British and American right), as did his success in securing a ceasefire during the 1965 India–Pakistan War.

But Thant was also an intensely controversial figure. In the years following that poll, his unrelenting efforts to end the fighting in Vietnam, on terms very different from those desired by Lyndon Johnson's White House, made him an enemy of many in the American national security establishment. His decision to withdraw UN peacekeepers from Gaza and the Sinai on the eve of the Six-Day War and his later diplomacy, aimed at a peace based on an Israeli withdrawal from the recently occupied territories, drew further ire, even from those in the US and the UK who had been sympathetic to his stance on Vietnam. The UN's inability to address the Soviet invasion of Czechoslovakia or the famines and bloodshed in Biafra and Bangladesh, together with its admission of Communist China, further sapped support for Thant and the world organization.

In much of the rest of the world, Thant was seen as a tireless champion for the rights of the newly independent states of Africa and Asia. From the mid-1950s, their leaders had transformed the UN, fighting for a global peace based on racial equality and the equality of nations. Thant doggedly stood up for their hard-won sovereignty and pushed for the rapid economic development he believed was the best antidote to future instability. His tough rhetoric against apartheid and white domination across southern Africa, disparaged by many in Western countries, was universally applauded in what was then known as the Third World. Toward the end of his tenure, he became a strident advocate for environmental protection and a critic of what he considered unsustainable consumerism. In one of his last acts, he helped prepare the groundwork for the first Earth Summit in Stockholm.

Two weeks after the lunch at the Pierre, Thant retired, then virtually disappeared from history. A central figure in averting nuclear catastrophe during the Cuban Missile Crisis, Thant is almost nowhere to be found in popular or even scholarly accounts of those pivotal events. There is no Hollywood film featuring the Burmese Secretary-General and his Indian and Egyptian deputies mediating between John F. Kennedy, Nikita Khrushchev, and Fidel Castro. This first generation of nonwhite peacemakers on the world stage has been almost entirely forgotten.

There was once a faith in a new internationalism, which could remake the world after empire, bring about a permanent peace, and create a fairer global economy.

This book is the story of a man and a portrait of that time.

1 | NEW WORLD

IN A RENTED FIFTH-FLOOR apartment in Manhattan's well-heeled Lenox Hill neighborhood, the heavy beige curtains partly drawn to let in the morning light, the slim, middle-aged Burmese diplomat, dressed in a crisp white shirt and gray wool trousers, sat down to his usual morning meal of scrambled eggs, bacon, and toast. Just a few years before, in the shaded calm of his ocher-colored bungalow in Rangoon, breakfast would have been a bowl of piping hot fish soup, fragrant with ginger, turmeric, and lemongrass. On this morning, September 18, 1961, his Zenith radio crackled with troubling news—of Soviet atomic tests in the deserts of central Asia and simmering tensions in a divided Berlin. Outside, the hum of traffic rose steadily along 72nd Street, punctuated by bursts of car horns and the occasional wail of a siren, the city already in full swing. Thant could feel the pace of change accelerating, for himself and for the planet.[1]

For much of his life, Thant had been a teacher and later the headmaster of a school in his hometown of Pantanaw, a sprawl of muddy streets, mango trees, and teak houses in Burma's steamy and mosquito-infested Irrawaddy delta. Yet he dreamed of an existence beyond his remote little town. He mastered English on his own, read everything he could on British and world history, and penned a steady stream of essays for the local papers on the politics of the time. Once, when he was probably in his late thirties and aspiring to a more cosmopolitan life, he had a studio photograph taken, wearing a dark English suit as he sat at a polished wooden table, with a painted background intended to look as if he were in a grand European parlor. When Burma gained independence from Britain in 1948, he moved with his family to the capital, Rangoon, where he joined the new administration and rose quickly to become a senior civil servant.

It wasn't an easy path. When Thant was fifteen, his father died and the once well-to-do family found itself suddenly impoverished, which limited educational prospects for the bookish young man. The other top mandarins, nearly all educated at Oxford or Cambridge, looked down on him for his lack of even a provincial university degree. He had to prove himself, and this meant working twice as hard as the others—without making enemies.

His wife, Thein Tin, wanted him to succeed. She kept him on an even keel and, as a devout Buddhist, frequently reminded him of the value of equanimity and the impermanence of all things. When they had first met, Thant was in his early twenties and Thein Tin eleven years older. Originally from a town near Mandalay, in Upper Burma, she had moved to Pantanaw with her mother several years before, after the death of her father, and was managing her own successful cigar factory. Burma at the time was a male-dominated colonial society where men often married women far younger, but the young Thant was attracted to the experienced, independent businesswoman. Thein Tin had little interest in marrying and had rejected at least a couple of previous suitors. But Thant persisted, stopping by the house she shared with her mother, making conversation, often with his future mother-in-law, nearly every evening for years before Thein Tin finally agreed to be his wife. Their first child, a boy named Maung Bo, died from a respiratory ailment when he was a toddler. Two more children soon followed: a daughter, Aye Aye Thant, and a son, Tin Maung Thant, or Timmy.

In the mid-1950s, Thant, as chief advisor, began to travel with Burma's prime minister U Nu on official trips around the world. For both, the travels were an education in global politics. In discussions with Mao Tse-tung and Chou En-lai in Peking, they learned about China's fear of Western encirclement. In Moscow, they were hosted by Khrushchev, whom they found "down-to-earth" and "with a good sense of humor." In London, they heartily agreed with a recently retired Winston Churchill that Burma and Britain should "bury old animosities." And in Hanoi, they found Ho Chi Minh friendly and "contagiously enthusiastic" about the "excellent" French food served.[2]

In 1955, Thant accompanied his prime minister on an official two-week tour across America. They watched a baseball game at Yankee Stadium, visited a Ford factory in Detroit, enjoyed a Hopi dance in Arizona, and met Alfred Hitchcock, Jimmy Stewart, and Doris Day on the set of *The Man Who Knew Too Much*.

When Thant moved to New York in 1957, as Burma's ambassador to the United Nations, his wife and children had never before been abroad. They first stayed at the Adams Hotel on 86th Street and regularly ate at a Chinese restaurant several blocks away, the only place where they could find anything remotely similar to Burmese cuisine. For six months, Thant tried to find a place to live, only to be turned down by ten buildings, "because I am an Asian," he supposed.[3]

Thant and his family were part of a wave of people coming from Asia and Africa to represent their countries at the UN. Nearly all faced housing challenges, as did the organization's own non-white staff. When the UN headquarters was being built in the late 1940s, the new Peter Cooper Village downtown was considered a possible solution. But the residential development was owned by the Metropolitan Life Insurance Company, which effectively barred non-whites—its president, Frederick Ecker, stated publicly that "negroes and whites don't mix."[4] The UN then made a deal with Parkway Village in Queens, offering housing to any staff or diplomats facing discrimination.

Parkway Village was not an option for Thant. As an ambassador, he needed to be reasonably close to his office, the Burmese diplomatic mission at 888 Madison Avenue, as well as to the UN. Eventually, he found an apartment in a building at the corner of 72nd Street and Park Avenue, which was also home to diplomats from Iran and Niger. His friend Mongi Slim, the Tunisian ambassador, lived downstairs.

Thein Tin spoke no English. In New York, she tried English lessons but soon gave up. Still, she was happy in the city, hosting Burmese friends for overnight stays, and relieved to be far away from Burma's increasingly feverish politics and armed rebellions. In cat eye glasses, her graying hair in a tight bun, and always in Burmese dress, she explored fabric shops for material to make Burmese-style clothes and bought shirts for her husband at Macy's and Alexander's. On weekends, Thant made sure to limit social events to ones in which Thein Tin could participate—not swanky cocktail parties on the UN circuit, but informal meals at the homes of American acquaintances who had lived in Burma.

Thant relished the UN's vibrant social scene. Back in Pantanaw, he and Thein Tin rarely got past the corner of their little street when taking an evening stroll, as Thant stopped to chat with every neighbor they saw. Now it was an endless round of cocktail parties and black-tie receptions, and lunches with journalists as well as diplomats, often at Danny's Hideaway, a steakhouse on Lexington and 45th Street adorned with photos of John Wayne and other Hollywood celebrities who had eaten there.

Still, Thant preferred to be home for dinner. First thing every morning, as if it was a Burmese open-air market, Thein Tin shopped for food at the grocery store on 86th Street, and then prepared elaborate meals of beef or chicken curry, usually cooked with a paste of onions, garlic, ginger, and cayenne pepper, together with rice, sour soups, and spicy salads. Ingredients not readily available on the Upper East Side or even Chinatown, such as pickled tea, were brought by a steady stream of visitors from Rangoon.[5]

Now fifty-three years old and a rising star at the UN, Thant hoped to be a bridge between a West he had long admired and countries like Burma, newly independent and eager to carve out a place in the world. He had little desire to return to Rangoon anytime soon, where festering political tensions fed into rumors of an imminent army coup. A keen swimmer, he had recently signed up for a five-year membership at the nearest branch of Vic Tanny's fitness chain, where there was a pool.[6]

On that overcast morning of September 18, 1961, as Thant and his family were starting their day, a familiar voice from WNYC reported on the Yankees' dramatic twelfth-inning victory over the Detroit Tigers. Thant preferred to watch boxing on television; baseball was a game he barely understood. But then came the news that froze him: several hours earlier, the *Albertina*, a DC-6 transport plane carrying United Nations Secretary-General Dag Hammarskjöld together with his aides and crew, had gone missing somewhere over the forests of central Africa.

Hammarskjöld was on a mission to end brutal fighting in the newly independent Congo. The big powers—the Americans, the Soviets, the British, and the French—were backing different sides in what was becoming a complex struggle. All wanted a piece of the Congo pie and had wildly divergent ideas on what the UN should do. The Soviets supported Patrice Lumumba, the lanky, bespectacled, thirty-five-year-old head of the new Congo government—but opposed the peacekeeping operation he had requested, for which the United Nations had already deployed thousands of blue-helmeted troops, soldiers from as far afield as Morocco and Malaya, into the country. The Americans, while supporting the peacekeepers, had helped overthrow Lumumba in late 1960, judging the Congolese leader to have drifted too close to Moscow. The British and the French, meanwhile, were conspiring with the Belgians—who for decades had ruled the vast central African nation, nearly equal in size to all of Western Europe, with almost unimaginable cruelty—to keep the southern region of Katanga, with its fabulously lucrative copper mines, under de facto European control.[7]

For the past four years, Thant had been representing his country on a range of issues, from nuclear disarmament to decolonization. The Congo was his biggest concern. The Burmese ambassador knew that the crisis in the heart of Africa was pulling the UN apart and might soon leave it weak and irrelevant on the international stage. That would be disastrous, especially for the smaller countries like Burma that saw the global body as their best, perhaps their only, hope for a peaceful and prosperous future.

Within minutes, Thant was in his official navy blue Buick, the "DPL" plates marking him as a diplomat. Herman, his wiry young driver from

Brooklyn, navigated rush hour traffic with practiced precision, weaving past the tenement buildings along Second Avenue and cutting across 45th Street. Soon, the gleaming concrete and glass towers of United Nations headquarters came into view. The Buick glided past the fluttering flags of over a hundred nations, their colors vivid under the gray sky, before descending into the building's vast subterranean parking garage along the East River.

In times of crisis, the best place to go was the Delegates' Lounge. There was the gently sloping General Assembly Hall, where presidents and prime ministers delivered their speeches every autumn, and the Security Council chamber, where ambassadors, sometimes in emergency sessions, convened around a horseshoe-shaped table to debate and decide on pressing matters of war and peace. The Delegates' Lounge was where the informal action took place: the nerve center for gossip, off-the-record conversations, and, sometimes, secret deals. With its well-stocked bar, Danish designer chairs and Finnish standing lamps, an enormous world map, and floor-to-ceiling windows, the lounge looked the perfect location for a Hollywood spy thriller. It had been the setting, just three years before, for an early scene in Alfred Hitchcock's *North by Northwest*.

When Thant arrived, the vast room, about seventy yards long, was already crowded with men in flannel suits of every nationality, cigarette smoke drifting through the air and a loudspeaker gently paging diplomats in different languages. The Americans tended to monopolize two sofas at one end. The Soviets and their Communist satellites huddled a comfortable distance away. A bank of wooden telephone booths stood ready nearby.

With his browline glasses and dark hair slicked back from a high forehead, Thant was a familiar face in the lounge. His closest colleagues were the other Afro-Asian ambassadors, including the Oxford-educated, jazz-loving Ghanaian Alex Quaison-Sackey, the rotund Egyptian lawyer Omar Loutfi, who had helped draft the UN's Universal Declaration of Human Rights, and the pencil-mustached Tunisian Mongi Slim, whose accomplishments included the installation of the Delegates' Lounge espresso machine, one of the few in Manhattan at the time.[8]

Toward the end of the Second World War, Franklin D. Roosevelt imagined a United Nations at the center of a new international order, one in which five allies—the United States, the United Kingdom, France, the Soviet Union, and China—would together police the world. Then, the Cold War turned allies into adversaries and within a few years of the UN's establishment in 1945, commentators were predicting its early death.

There were, however, other ideas, linked to visions of rejuvenated European empires, about what the world body might achieve. Jan Christian Smuts, the longtime prime minister of South Africa and one of the drafters of the UN Charter, was both a committed imperialist and a staunch supporter of apartheid. During the drafting of the charter in San Francisco, he praised the UK as the greatest colonial power in the world and imagined a future in which the British Empire would be remade as the British Commonwealth with its white dominions, such as South Africa and Australia, at its core. The non-white colonies would take their places further down the racial hierarchy, Communism would be contained, and existing networks of trade and profits reinforced.[9] The UN would set an overall framework within which a racially ordered Commonwealth could thrive. "Men and women everywhere," he said, "including dependent peoples, still unable to look after themselves, are thus drawn into the vast plan to prevent war."[10]

India's representative, Vijaya Lakshmi Pandit, the sister of prime minister and independence leader Jawaharlal Nehru, denounced Smuts's "Nazi doctrine" and warned that a race-based "new world order" could lead only to "conflict and ultimate disaster." Though at the time, fewer than a dozen of the UN's members were from Asia and Africa, they managed to push through the UN's General Assembly (in which each country has one vote and no state has a veto) a resolution challenging Smuts's contention that racial segregation was a path to stability. Many in London, Paris, and Brussels, as well as Pretoria, were appalled.

Pandit's intervention against racism was a taste of what was to come.

In April 1955, over three hundred delegates from twenty-nine Asian and African governments, representing half the world's population, gathered in Bandung, a hill town in Indonesia. No such meeting had ever happened before. The conference was organized by Burma, India, Pakistan, and Ceylon (now Sri Lanka) along with Indonesia, which a few years before had won a bloody war of independence against the Netherlands. The delegates present, Communists and anti-Communists, republicans and monarchists, had little in common except a shared experience of racial humiliation. The Mau Mau massacres in Kenya were fresh in the minds of many, as well as the recent bloody crackdown in Nyasaland (now known as Malawi) and the vicious subjugation of the black majority in South Africa.

By late 1960, UN membership had ballooned to nearly a hundred, with seventeen new African nations admitted in that year alone. Until then, the US and Western European governments had held sway in the General Assembly, where Washington could usually count on the backing of pliant Latin American regimes. The Afro-Asians were now close to a majority, and they regularly joined forces with countries like Yugoslavia, Ireland, and Sweden that were similarly "neutral" in the Cold War. As the Americans and Soviets competed for their votes, the Afro-Asians came to believe that the future of the UN was increasingly in their hands. They saw no reason for a Cold War and the buildup of atomic arsenals. They were impatient and ambitious and envisaged a post-imperial age that would see the rapid economic development of the poorer nations. Their prime targets were colonialism and white supremacy.

In December 1960, after weeks of high-level negotiation, the Afro-Asians, including Thant and his Burmese delegation, managed to secure overwhelming support for a declaration calling for "the transfer of all powers" from the colonizers to the colonized "without any conditions or reservations." There was a mood of celebration and anticipation as they put forth their demand for the end of empire. What they wanted first and foremost was an international system which ensured that their hard-won independence was real and irreversible: at its heart would be a United Nations that would belong not just to the white nations but to the entire world.

Thant had been an organizer of the Bandung conference, and from 1957, in his speeches as Burma's ambassador to the UN, he dismissed the notion that a "balance of terror" between the superpowers could bring about a lasting peace. Instead, he pushed for an end to atomic testing, challenging not just the Soviets and the Americans but also the French, who had just exploded their first nuclear weapon in the Sahara Desert. "To the peoples of Asia and Africa," he said at the UN, "the atomic bomb is something more than a fearsome instrument of terror . . . it represents the white man's instrument of terror, having only been used once in war, by whites against a non-white race."[11]

His view, like that of many of his Afro-Asian colleagues, was that the

Afro-Asian leaders at the UN, October 1960 (left to right): Prime Minister Saeb Salaam of Lebanon, President Gamal Abdel Nasser of Egypt, President Kwame Nkrumah of Ghana, (then Ambassador) Thant of Burma, Prime Minister Jawaharlal Nehru of India, and President Sukarno of Indonesia.

arms race should be replaced by a single-minded focus on economic development. He reasoned that "the means and the knowledge" now existed to industrialize the poorer ex-colonial nations and that this would be "the most constructive and exciting venture of all time."

Thant also focused on Algeria, where hundreds of thousands had died and millions were forcibly displaced in fighting between the National Liberation Front (FLN) and French colonial troops.[12] Burma had no historic relationship with Algeria, but Thant accepted the chairmanship of the Afro-Asian committee working in solidarity with the FLN, in addition to that of the Congo Conciliation Commission, a similar grouping of Afro-Asian ambassadors. He carefully negotiated resolutions affirming Algeria's right to independence and labeling French atrocities against Algerian civilians a clear breach of the Universal Declaration of Human Rights and the Genocide Convention.[13] The choice, Thant stated, was between negotiations and an "intensification of the war." Lakhdar Brahimi, a young FLN diplomat, believed that Thant's efforts provided an all-important morale boost at a pivotal moment in his country's fight for freedom.[14]

Thant identified as an Afro-Asian neutralist but prided himself on not being a radical. In negotiating for Algeria, he did not see himself as anti-French. On the contrary, he felt certain that it was in France's own interest to end colonial rule. His intention, he explained, was "to help France by helping the Algerian cause."[15] He vigorously supported decolonization but equally supported the best possible relations between the newly independent states and the Western democracies. In this, he found common cause with the European diplomats whose governments were most committed to the UN, such as the Irish ambassador Patrick Boland and Sweden's Agda Rössel, the first woman representative at the world body. They too were habitués of the Delegates' Lounge.

Dag Hammarskjöld, an economist from an aristocratic Swedish family, had been the UN's Secretary-General for eight years—the organization's chief administrative officer, the head of its Secretariat. The big powers had expected him to be a bland technocrat, a safe pair of hands, but the UN Charter gave the Secretary-General the power not only to mediate disputes but to engage the Security Council on "any matter which in his opinion may threaten the maintenance of international peace and security." Exactly where the Secretary-General's powers begin and end is unclear. Hammarskjöld pushed the limits and proved himself a virtuoso innovator, intervening in conflicts from Laos to Lebanon, and in the process transforming the Secretary-Generalship into one of the most important jobs in the world. At the end of the Suez Crisis, he was instrumental in creating a peacekeeping force between Egypt and Israel. The Americans cheered him on, as his efforts aligned well with their aims.

In September 1960, Hammarskjöld's aide Andrew Cordier, a former State Department official, had conspired in the US-backed ousting of Congolese prime minister Patrice Lumumba, possibly with Hammarskjöld's knowledge.[16] Lumumba was flown to Katanga where, in January 1961, he was tortured over many weeks and then killed. The Soviets began to view Hammarskjöld as a tool of Western interests and demanded his resignation. French president Charles de Gaulle lambasted his "ambition and vanity."[17] There was growing speculation that Hammarskjöld might resign in the not-too-distant future and that his trip to the Congo was a last-ditch effort to secure a truce before he stepped down.

In the Delegates' Lounge, Thant and his fellow ambassadors exchanged greetings in the practiced manner of diplomats—broad smiles, firm handshakes, and convivial murmurs—but beneath the surface, a somberness settled, one heavier than any he could recall.[18] On most days, he liked to lighten the mood with a witty pun or a well-rehearsed schoolboyish joke, but not now. The lounge was buzzing with speculation. Was there a chance that Hammarskjöld's plane had simply gone elsewhere or been forcibly diverted? Belgian mercenaries supporting the Katanga secession had fighter aircraft known to harass UN flights. Hammarskjöld was on his way to meet with Katanga's rebel leader, Moïse Tshombe. Perhaps these mercenaries (and their shadowy backers overseas) didn't want the meeting to happen?

Before long, news that the wreckage of the plane had been found ricocheted through the room. The DC-6 had crashed in the forests of Northern Rhodesia (now Zambia), killing everyone on board. By early afternoon, the blue and white United Nations flag was flying at half-staff. In theory, Hammarskjöld's successor could be anyone in the world. But with the UN an increasingly byzantine realm of its own, all eyes were on the ambassadors already serving in New York.

Two weeks before the crash, Thant had been in Belgrade for the inaugural conference of the Non-Aligned Movement. The gathering brought two dozen African and Asian governments together with Yugoslavia, a Communist state that had broken out of the Kremlin's orbit. The assembled neutralists, seeing themselves as a growing force in international relations, resolved to de-escalate Cold War tensions. Privately, they also traded ideas on who might replace Hammarskjöld. A journalist for the London *Observer*, perhaps picking up gossip among the delegates, speculated about Thant as a possible future Secretary-General, describing him as "a cool civil servant, a charmer, a man of infinite discretion, and the embodiment of non-alignment."[19]

Cold War tensions were approaching their peak. In Europe, American and Soviet forces confronted each other across a divided Berlin. Both sides were prepared for battle. Over these same weeks, the USSR resumed nuclear testing, exploding atomic bombs high in the atmosphere almost every day. The Afro-Asians came away from Belgrade determined to save the UN and place one of their own at its helm. Only a strong United Nations, they were certain, could prevent another world war. And a strong United Nations required an adept Secretary-General. They had presumed they would have until the end of Hammarskjöld's term in two years to come up with a name. Even if he resigned, they would at least have a few weeks', if not a few months', notice. Now Hammarskjöld was dead, killed in mysterious circumstances, and the Afro-Asians knew they needed to act fast.

Thant was a clear candidate and, partly due to his efforts, Burma had become an influential nation on the global stage. Sandwiched between China and India and about the size of France and England combined, it had joined the UN immediately upon winning independence from Britain in 1948. Whereas some postcolonial governments swayed toward the capitalist West and others toward the Communist East, Burma had remained resolute in cultivating friendships with everyone. On all issues, the Burmese ambassador adopted what he considered an impartial stance while quietly nudging competing states toward a pragmatic outcome. Over the past year, as the Congo slid into chaos, Thant had teamed up with his Irish and Swedish counterparts to steer a path between the West and the more strident Afro-Asian position, led by Ghana. Yet Thant was not afraid to challenge the big powers, often telling American audiences, for example, that the US should allow Communist China a seat at the UN as an isolated China was more dangerous to the world. Many walked out of these speeches in protest.

The Americans had been discreetly following Thant's progress since his early days as a civil servant. When Thant became ambassador in New York, the US embassy in Rangoon reported to Washington that the one-time schoolteacher had always been "a strong anti-Communist," "known for his integrity, loyalty, and courageous advocacy of moderate solutions," and "the most potent friend of the United States in the Burmese government."[20] As Burma's UN ambassador, Thant had tried to be helpful to the Americans. When, in September 1960, the leaders of India, Ghana, and Egypt put forward a resolution calling for a meeting between President Eisenhower and Chairman Khrushchev, the Soviets eagerly accepted while the Americans, opposed to the idea, were uncertain how to respond. They told Thant they feared the meeting would be a volatile one and would inflame already tense relations. Thant then met privately with Indian prime minister Jawaharlal Nehru and suggested withdrawing the draft, but Nehru refused, telling Thant that he believed in "personal diplomacy" and asking him to co-sponsor the resolution. Thant politely declined. In the end, the Americans mustered a slim majority against the resolution and noted Thant's efforts.[21]

In early 1961, the new administration of John F. Kennedy appointed Adlai Stevenson as UN ambassador. Stevenson, formerly governor of Illinois, had lost two presidential elections, both to Eisenhower, and then lost the Democratic nomination to Kennedy. Thant and Stevenson immediately struck up a friendly relationship, reflecting the administration's desire to work with the more moderate Afro-Asians as well as Stevenson's own pro-UN views. Thant approvingly reported back to Rangoon a "change in atmosphere" at the UN following the youthful Irish American's election to the presidency.[22]

Thant also enjoyed unusually close ties with the Israelis. In 1955, when he circled the globe with the Burmese prime minister, Egypt and several other Afro-Asian states had cautioned the delegation against visiting Israel. But the prime minister, who had been deeply affected by the accounts he had read of the Holocaust, instead canceled a planned stop in Cairo. Tens of thousands lined the streets of Haifa and Tel Aviv to give a rapturous welcome to their new Burmese friends. They met David Ben-Gurion, Golda Meir, and other political figures, toured kibbutzim, and met the scientists working to further Israel's industrial abilities. Thant was so impressed by what he saw that on his return he wrote a booklet for Burma's foreign ministry, later translated and published by the Israeli government, titled "Israel Through Burmese Eyes."[23]

When Thant became UN ambassador, he attended Israeli diplomatic functions and spoke frequently at Jewish American events, from Springfield, Massachusetts, to Miami, Florida. He became friends with Israel's representative at the UN, Abba Eban, and attended Eban's farewell dinner in 1959, the only Afro-Asian ambassador to do so. Sitting next to Eleanor Roosevelt, he lavished praise on the scholarly Eban for "his dignity and grace matched only by his extraordinary eloquence." He called for other states to recognize Israel and help bring about "peaceful co-existence" between Jews and Arabs.[24] At the same time, he nurtured close ties with the Arab envoys, including Adnan Pachachi of Iraq and Omar Loutfi of Egypt.

Under the UN Charter, the Secretary-General is appointed by the General Assembly, but the candidate must first be recommended by the Security Council, where the big powers each wield a veto. Big and small powers alike understood what was at stake: not just the future of the world organization but global peace itself. A deadlock in the choice of successor could easily strain superpower tensions beyond the breaking point.

The Secretary-General should be replaced, Soviet leader Nikita Khrushchev had declared the year before, by not one person but three: two representing the Western and Eastern blocs and one drawn from the "uncommitted states." He termed this arrangement a troika, from the Russian word for a carriage pulled by three horses, arguing that "while there are neutral countries, there are no neutral men." The Soviets now revived this idea, sensing an opportunity to enfeeble an organization they considered more useful to the Americans than to themselves.

Into the vacuum left by Hammarskjöld's death had stepped one of the UN's most senior bureaucrats, Andrew Cordier (the ex-State Department official who had been in Leopoldville during the overthrow of Lumumba); at a press conference, the Soviet ambassador charged Cordier with "usurping" the powers of the Secretary-General. On September 20, two days after Hammarskjöld's death, the Soviets, anxious and looking to compromise, sent a foreign official to ask Thant if he might consider being an interim Secretary-General at the head of a group that would include three "under secretaries." This was a variation on the "troika" formula that Khrushchev had unsuccessfully trotted out the previous year. Thant replied that he was not interested and that his government was against the idea "at any level."[25] The Americans, meanwhile, declared they would fight the troika idea "tooth and nail."[26]

That same day, Thant attended a meeting of Afro-Asians and other non-aligned nations, at which Ghana and Algeria pressed for a united front behind a single candidate. Thant knew he was one of several candidates, and spent the day with other ambassadors and international journalists, trying to get a feel for what everyone was thinking. He was also in close touch by cable (a confidential diplomatic telegram) with the Burmese government in Rangoon, to report what he learned and to ask what they wanted him to do. The prime minister instructed him to make himself available but not on an interim basis. They didn't want him taking the job in a "confused situation" or in the face of Soviet opposition.

Two names were mentioned in the press. One was Thant. The other was the Tunisian Mongi Slim, Thant's downstairs neighbor, a Paris-educated lawyer of mixed Greek and Turkish heritage who had just been elected president of the General Assembly.

Over the next days there was much scheming in smoke-filled rooms in and around UN headquarters as well as frantic discussions in capitals around the world. The Afro-Asian leaders worked to break the impasse. Kwame Nkrumah, Ghana's visionary prime minister and a strident proponent of both African unity and Afro-Asian solidarity, messaged President Nasser of Egypt, President Sukarno of Indonesia, and Prime Minister Nu of Burma to say that the next UN chief should be "a candidate from Burma." Nkrumah, Nasser, and Sukarno were nationalist heroes and giants in the Non-Aligned Movement. Thant asked his prime minister not to issue any statement of support, wanting to work behind the scenes. On September 28, Rangoon replied with a cable saying they would be "happy to see you fill the top post" as long the arrangement was "acceptable by East and West." They would leave all tactics to Thant and signed off, "All the best of luck."[27]

By the end of September, there was a groundswell of support for Thant. The Soviets made it known that he was acceptable, and enthusiastic support came from Nehru, Sukarno, and other Afro-Asians, including Cambodia's ruler, Prince Norodom Sihanouk. Only the French were resistant; Thant's relentless advocacy of Algerian independence was an irritant, and his lack of French was a hindrance. A French source reportedly complained that Thant was "too short" for the role (he was just under 5 feet 8 inches tall). Thant responded to the Associated Press, "You can tell them that I am taller than Napoleon, who did not speak English."[28] The French ambassador, Armand Bérard, a friend who understood the Burmese diplomat's popularity at the UN, advised his government not to stand in Thant's way.

Israel's foreign minister Golda Meir sent a cable to Thant saying that he was Tel Aviv's sole choice as Mongi Slim was unacceptable to the Jewish state.[29] The Arab delegations stated that they valued Thant's work on Algeria and his "stand on colonialism and imperialism." As a way of signaling to the Soviets that Thant was acceptable to the Arab nations despite his friendship with Israel, a smiling Egyptian foreign minister Mohammed Fawzi told Thant, in front of the Soviet foreign minister Andrei Gromyko, that Egypt "sees eye to eye with Burma on all issues except one"—by which he meant Rangoon's friendship with Israel.[30] Thant was the sole candidate agreeable to both the Arabs and the Israelis.

By early October there was a consensus that Thant should be the next head of the UN, though the Soviets stipulated that he should be appointed only as Acting Secretary-General for a single year. This was accepted, including by Thant and his government. Moscow also insisted on knowing the exact number and nationality of the senior officials Thant would appoint; this was a way of circumscribing his authority. For another few weeks, there was a tedious and unsuccessful back-and-forth about possible combinations. On October 26, at a lunch at Danny's Hideaway, Thant told reporters he would come up with his own formula as a way of breaking the deadlock. Exhausted diplomats began murmuring, "Leave it to U Thant."

A few days later, Thant appeared on the bi-monthly television program *Adlai Stevenson Reports*. Stevenson had become a fervent advocate for Thant, and the interview was a way of showcasing him to the American public. Thant stated his admiration for Hammarskjöld's concept of a Secretary-General who was independent and would act "vigorously" in pursuit of peaceful solutions. He said he would be "impartial" but "not necessarily neutral."

The French made a last-minute effort to ensure that Thant appointed one of their own as his *chef de cabinet*, or chief of staff. Thant pushed back, saying he would not be dictated to by any government on any of his appointments and that Paris was free to veto him if they wished. The French backed off.[31]

At 11 a.m. on November 3, the Security Council met in a closed session. Egypt's Omar Loutfi was the Council's president that month. Within minutes, Loutfi emerged and told Ramses Nassif, a young Egyptian UN official, "It's our friend, U Thant—unanimous decision." Nassif found Thant chatting with other diplomats in the nearby North Lounge. "Congratulations are in order!" he said. Thant beamed and replied, "I hope your source is a good one!"[32] A few hours later, the General Assembly, also unanimously, elected Thant Acting Secretary-General.

The Congo was in chaos. In Berlin, the Cold War was heating up, with Soviet and American tanks facing off at Checkpoint Charlie. The very survival of the UN was uncertain. And in this moment of crisis, the governments of the world put what faith they had in a little-known schoolteacher-turned-diplomat from Burma. Thant was chosen because of his tact and the respect he demonstrated for all points of view. At least as importantly, he was chosen because he was an Afro-Asian and because Burma was neutral between East and West. Thant had a year to prove himself. No one knew then of the extraordinary challenges to come.

2 | CONGO

NEW YORK WASN'T THE obvious choice for the headquarters of the United Nations. It was initially seen as too vast, too frenetic a city, and likely to subsume the identity of the fledgling organization. Toward the end of the war various European cities were considered, with Geneva, site of the old League of Nations, a strong contender, but a consensus developed that the world organization should be located in the United States, as a way of preventing the Americans from abandoning their own project, as they had done with the League a quarter century earlier. In any case, much of Europe was in ruins. San Francisco, Boston, and Philadelphia vied for selection, as did South Dakota, which proposed the construction of an entirely new city of giant concentric circles in the Black Hills.[1] Then the Rockefeller family offered to buy and donate an 18-acre site of slaughterhouses and tenement buildings at Turtle Bay in Manhattan, along the East River. The United Nations readily accepted.

New York's fast-paced, no-nonsense ethos soon energized the organization in a way that a Swiss lakeside town or a mountain idyll never could. And the thousands of men and women who came to New York from every corner of the world to serve the UN changed the city forever. The UN made New York the capital of the world.

An international team of architects, led by Oscar Niemeyer of Brazil and Le Corbusier of France, swiftly went to work and in October 1952 unveiled a modernist masterpiece of manicured lawns and interlocking structures, designed to seem to as though it was floating on water. At the one side rose an imposing thirty-nine-story Secretariat of steel, green glass, and Vermont marble.

The Secretary-General's office occupied a commanding perch on the thirty-eighth floor of the tower, its row of picture windows framing a sweeping view of the East River and the quilt of low-rise buildings stretching across Queens and Brooklyn. A small private apartment was hidden away to the side. The rest of the floor housed the offices of senior UN officials and their assistants and secretaries, everything in a mid-century modern décor, with Finnish ceiling lights casting a soft glow over the curved amber glass ashtrays, Swedish elmwood desks, and Danish teak chairs upholstered in blue.

Thant took his oath of office in the General Assembly on November 30, 1961, with family members and his driver, Herman, watching from the visitor's gallery. He took up his position the next morning, turning the thermostat to nearly 80 degrees Fahrenheit but otherwise keeping the office as it was. He knew he was on probation. He also flew in five hundred Burmese cigars from Rangoon and kept a supply handy in a box near his desk.[2]

Thant was the first non-European to head any international body and also the first from a poor, ex-colonial country. He couldn't be sure how others saw him. With the big powers circling, the new Secretary-General had to be decisive; he must not seem weak but at the same time not appear presumptuous. He had to build on Hammarskjöld's successes but avoid the dynamics that under Hammarskjöld had brought the organization to the verge of collapse.

He assembled his top team—all men of color, a sea change in a century of white-dominated international diplomacy. As his peacekeeping chief, Thant chose Ralph Bunche, an already world-famous African American mediator who had won a Nobel Peace Prize for brokering the 1949 Arab–Israeli armistice. Born in Detroit, the fifty-seven-year-old Bunche, light-skinned with graying wavy hair, had been raised by his grandmother, the daughter of an Irish American plantation owner and his slave. He was an early scholar of colonialism in Africa, a prominent voice on civil rights in America, and had served as a close aide to Hammarskjöld in the Congo and in New York.

To direct his office as *chef de cabinet*, Thant selected forty-six-year-old C. V. Narasimhan, a Madras-born, Oxford-educated former member of the British-era Indian Civil Service. Stocky, with a long, rectangular face and suits that seemed a size too big, Narasimhan had already spent several years in senior UN posts. He would manage an international bureaucracy of over 3,500 staff in New York and 14,500 elsewhere in the world and would be the Secretary-General's gatekeeper, the man who saw him first and last at the office every day. Thant also persuaded his friend Omar Loutfi to leave his position as Egypt's ambassador and join him as chief political advisor.

Thant believed that the loyalty of these men would be to the world organization above all. Over his time as ambassador, he had come to know all three well, Loutfi especially. All were given the rank of under secretary, as was the Soviet Georgy Arkadev. Thant assured Moscow that Arkadev would be included in weekly cabinet-style meetings, but after he'd gone through the motions a few times those meetings were quietly shelved.

When Hammarskjöld became Secretary-General in 1953, he had more than two years to settle into the job before being confronted with a major crisis. Thant didn't even have two days. First, he had to rescue the organization from insolvency. The UN was about $100 million in debt, primarily because the Soviet bloc governments, together with the French and the Belgians, were refusing to pay for peacekeeping.

Thant immediately proposed issuing bonds as a way of borrowing money from friendly governments while seeking a longer-term solution. Though the idea originated in Washington, Thant not only made it his own but sought to make as many governments as possible feel it was their idea as well. US secretary of state Dean Rusk reported to Kennedy that Thant, "in a remarkable series of interviews with every delegation, concentrated in six successful evenings," gained the needed support.[3] The bonds were sold and financial collapse was postponed, at least for a while.

His second priority was to resolve the escalating crisis in the Congo. The Katanga secession was still in full swing, with its leader, forty-one-year-old Brussels-educated Moïse Tshombe, backed by a well-armed and Belgian-trained *gendarmerie* of over three thousand men as well as hundreds of European and South African mercenaries. The mercenaries and their supporters overseas were white supremacists (with a core of French fascists) who believed that an independent, white-dominated Katanga was the key to ensuring continued white domination across southern and eastern Africa.

There were also vast profits to protect. Katanga supplied 69 percent of the world's industrial diamonds, 49 percent of its cobalt, and 9 percent of its copper, and it was one of the few sources of the uranium needed to make atomic bombs. Much of Katanga's mining was in the hands of a single Belgian company: Union Minière du Haut Katanga. Union Minière, in turn, was partly owned by the UK company Tanganyika Concessions, directed by Captain Charles Waterhouse, a Conservative member of Parliament. Over just the past five years, Belgian and British shareholders had received nearly £464 million in profits.[4] Cash from Union Minière and Tanganyika Concessions kept the Katanga rebellion going.

With Lumumba dead and a pro-American regime in charge in Leopoldville, Washington wanted to see the Congo reunited but in a measured and negotiated way, so as not stir up feelings in Britain and Belgium and among America's own pro-Katanga right wing. The United States hoped Thant would be a man of "prudence and restraint" who wouldn't act rashly.[5]

From the start, however, the Burmese diplomat took a more aggressive stance than Hammarskjöld, who, to the very end, had tried to accommodate the Katanga secessionists. The new Acting Secretary-General was guided by his military and civilian staff in the Congo, many of whom had been shocked by Hammarskjöld's killing. He was also influenced by his background in Burma. Like the Congo, Burma had descended into civil war immediately after becoming independent. At one point, the government, which Thant served, held only Rangoon, with the rest of the country a sea of warlords, Communist insurgents, and ethnic minority rebels. Thant's formative political experience was as part of a government desperately trying to hold together a multiethnic country that had been patchworked together under colonial rule.

For Thant and his Afro-Asian colleagues, Katanga was the fulcrum on which the future depended: either it would be free of white supremacy and foreign domination worldwide, or it would be one in which the ex-imperial powers could still intervene as they wished. Most of the world was now comprised of nominally independent states. But what sovereignty really meant would be determined by what the United Nations now did.

On November 24, 1961, with Thant's behind-the-scenes encouragement, the Security Council passed a resolution condemning the secession of Katanga and authorizing the use of "the requisite measure of force" to remove foreign soldiers. Two days later, at the stadium in his capital, Elizabethville, an angry Moïse Tshombe told thousands of supporters that Thant was preparing for war against Katanga. Tshombe lambasted the blue-helmeted Indian peacekeepers as "the mercenaries of

Thant at the Security Council with top aides Inderjit Rikhye and Ralph Bunche just after becoming Acting Secretary-General in November 1961.

Khrushchev" and called on the Irish and Swedes to switch sides as it was Katanga that was on the side of "Christian and Occidental civilization."[6]

A few days later, soldiers loyal to Tshombe dragged two British UN officials from a black-tie party in Elizabethville for the visiting American senator Chris Dodd, a major fundraiser for the secessionists. They were both severely beaten up, with broken noses and fractured ribs, before being released. An Indian officer who went looking for them disappeared and was never found. A soldier who accompanied the officer was discovered dead.

Thant was incensed. On December 1, in his first press briefing, the Acting Secretary-General called Tshombe "a very unstable man" and stated that the United Nations peacekeeping operation in the Congo (ONUC, from its French initials) would "act vigorously to reestablish law and order." The share price of Union Minière immediately sank.[7]

A combat-experienced Indian brigade, recently stationed by the UN in the breakaway province, began fighting to seize positions from white mercenary-led units. At the Acting Secretary-General's request, extra battalions of Swedish, Irish, and Nigerian troops were rushed into place, along with a column of armored cars.[8] ONUC's recently assembled air force, comprised of Swedish Saab fighters and Indian Canberra bombers, took to the skies. The Kennedy administration supplied the UN with twenty-one transport planes but was nervous that Thant would go too far. The UN's own military officers advised that despite the military buildup, a decisive victory at this point remained unlikely.[9] Over the following fortnight, nearly two dozen UN soldiers were killed in battle and nearly a hundred wounded.

Politically, the UN's situation was even more tenuous. The hard-line Afro-Asians led by Ghana's president Kwame Nkrumah called for ever tougher action, while the UK, France, and Belgium were determined to halt any UN offensive. Meanwhile, in the US, the pro-Katanga lobby was gaining ground due to the efforts of Markpress, a Swiss-based public relations firm.

The British media in particular were scathing, with the *Sunday Telegraph* warning that the UN Secretariat had "tasted blood." European-friendly Katanga was portrayed as the hapless victim of Afro-Asian belligerence. Viscount Hinchingbrooke, writing in the *Sunday Express*, described Thant's organization as a "charging rhinoceros, tearing up the earth," a "monster of iniquity," a "juggernaut which is rolling down upon us." The British establishment were no less critical in private. The Marquess of Salisbury, a former cabinet member and enthusiastic champion of white supremacy in Africa, wrote in a letter to the foreign secretary, Lord Home, "What an awful body the UN have become!"[10]

The new UN chief pressed London for the thousand-pound British-made bombs needed for ONUC's Canberra jets. Prime minister Harold MacMillan first stalled, then, after "strong encouragement from Washington," agreed. The UK government couldn't appear entirely opposed to the world organization's efforts. MacMillan, however, soon found himself having to backpedal in the face of attacks from the many Katanga supporters within his own Conservative Party.[11] He appealed to the Acting Secretary-General, proposing a ceasefire. Thant stated publicly that any ceasefire before his troops had gained full freedom of movement would be a "setback." He wanted the promised bombs. Shortly afterward, eighty Conservative members of Parliament put forward a motion condemning the government over what they saw as its fecklessness in the face of "UN aggression" against Katanga. When MacMillan telephoned Kennedy and begged for help, he found his transatlantic ally noncommittal.

MacMillan then deployed David Ormsby-Gore, the UK's ambassador in Washington, who was scheduled to dine at the White House that evening and who had been close friends with the president since both were at university. MacMillan told Ormsby-Gore that the Conservative government could fall within the next twenty-four hours. The diplomat's influence worked. Kennedy at once phoned the State Department and said, "I have David Gore sitting beside me here, and he will explain what it is the British government wants done and I want it done."[12]

Adlai Stevenson, Kennedy's ambassador to the UN, sat down with Thant the next morning. Thant bowed to the pressure, withdrawing his request for the bombs because of "British anxiety."[13] The fighting then ended, without conclusion.

Thant realized he wasn't going to get much further with the British. He needed to concentrate on the Americans, building on the rapport he already enjoyed with Stevenson. The gregarious sixty-two-year-old Stevenson was a regular on the UN and Upper East Side party circuit, often staying up until the early hours to drink and dance; he described diplomacy as a mix of "protocol, alcohol, and Geritol." Back in October, he and Thant had attended the premiere of *West Side Story* together with the film's star, Natalie Wood. Though Stevenson could no longer convince the much busier Thant to join him at the movies, the two still saw each other almost every day.

On January 19, 1962, President Kennedy met the Acting Secretary-General over lunch at Stevenson's official residence on the top floor of the Waldorf Astoria hotel. A State Department memo informed the president that Thant's "bearing and behavior on assuming a difficult task has been exemplary."[14] A few days before, the historian and presidential advisor Arthur Schlesinger had written to Kennedy that there was a "crisis of confidence" in the UN, in no small part because of worries that the world body would soon be dominated by "untried people from young and unsophisticated countries." Thant represented "a reasoned and responsible group of statesmen" from these same countries and should therefore be encouraged.

Schlesinger also noted speculation that Thant was finding the job "burdensome." The speculation could have come from various quarters; it may also have stemmed from a Thanksgiving meal the previous November, at the home of a mutual friend, when Thant had turned away from Schlesinger and other distinguished guests, preferring to spend the evening questioning and sharing jokes with the teenagers present.[15]

In the opulent surroundings of the Waldorf Astoria suite, Kennedy, Thant, and Stevenson first sat side by side on a plush sofa, the picture of urbane camaraderie. Clad in dark, fashionably slim suits and ties, they smiled and chatted easily as the flashes of dozens of cameras lit the room, reporters and television crews capturing every moment. After the public show of unity, they retreated to the dining table to tackle weightier matters over an artichoke and shrimp casserole. They exchanged thoughts on the Congo and on escalating tensions between the Netherlands and Indonesia over the western half of New Guinea.[16] The new Indonesian state had, in the late 1940s, defeated the Netherlands to win control over all of what had been the Dutch East Indies except for western New Guinea, at the eastern edge of the archipelago, which remained under Dutch rule. Washington was keen to avert a war between a rising Afro-Asian power and an important NATO ally. Kennedy asked Thant's help in convincing Jakarta not to invade the contested island, "as they were going to get Papua in the long run anyway."[17]

Toward the end of the lunch, Thant offered Kennedy a Burmese cigar. Kennedy, taken aback by the formidable-looking black cigar, asked if it was extremely strong. Thant assured the president that it was actually quite mild and after a few puffs Kennedy agreed it was "very good."[18] Thant soon sent a batch, fresh from Burma, as a souvenir of their first meeting and a satisfied president wrote back that the cigars had arrived "at a particularly opportune moment" and he had assured his associates that they were "less deadly than they might appear at first glance."[19] Thant also thanked Stevenson for the lunch, informing him that he was sending an assistant to obtain the recipe for the casserole from the ambassador's housekeeper. Stevenson replied that his flattered housekeeper "will never be the same again."[20]

Eleanor Roosevelt was also pleased. In her diary that week, she wrote that President Kennedy had made a "very significant gesture" by making a special trip to New York to see Thant and giving "the country the feeling of how important he considered the UN."[21] The world was at a unique moment, when a young American president and a generation of leaders from the newly independent states of Asia and Africa shared a desire to see the global organization succeed.

With Washington reasonably friendly, Thant was eager to move ahead in the Congo. He deployed Ralph Bunche to work with the Americans in brokering a deal, however unlikely, between Tshombe and the government in Leopoldville. He also sent the scholarly and soft-spoken Robert Gardiner, a Cambridge-educated economist from Ghana who was then the highest-ranking black African in the UN, to Leopoldville to head the entire UN Congo operation, as a check on Western influence.

At the same time, Thant tasked his new chief military advisor, the Indian general Indar Jit Rikhye, with bolstering ONUC's military force into one capable of defeating the white mercenaries in Katanga once and for all. Thant also stationed the Swede Sture Linner, Hammarskjöld's close aide, in Brussels to meet with businessmen and political leaders both there and in London to discuss ways to tighten sanctions against Katanga. Thant wanted to give the impression that military force was a last resort, and also to keep a close watch on European thinking and calm fears while preparing his next move.[22]

As Thant settled into his new role, he brought to the office an entirely different style from his predecessor. Brian Urquhart, a former assistant to Hammarskjöld (and one of the UN officials who had been kidnapped from the party in the Congo), remembered that when Thant became Secretary-General, "between breakfast and lunch one day ... the messages from New York assumed a completely new tone." Whereas Hammarskjöld was fond of linguistic gymnastics, Thant's cables "were very no-nonsense, saying you were responsible for the security of our people there, so you'd better get on with it, take whatever measures you think fit, and we'll support you."[23] The wife of an American diplomat suggested that "Hammarskjöld generated electricity: one vibrated in his presence like a tight wire in a high wind." Thant, on the other hand, tended "to defuse people when they are wound up."[24]

In an interview with Alistair Cooke for the BBC, the new UN chief talked about his personal philosophy.[25] "We try to get at the truth by contemplation and meditation ... and explore what is happening inside of us," he told Cooke. He had been raised in the Burmese Buddhist tradition, a variant of neoconservative Buddhism that encouraged a cheerful acceptance of life's vicissitudes. Central was mindfulness of one's own emotional states and a continuing effort to avoid negative emotions, such as anger, and boost the positive ones, such as happiness for other people's good fortune. A calm disposition and a playful sense of humor were highly valued. Thant often said that he was tolerant of all things except intolerance.[26]

The new Secretary-General's relationship with the press was also entirely different. Hammarskjöld avoided reporters as much as he could, steering clear of them in the hallways. Thant, who had written hundreds of articles for Rangoon papers and magazines over the past two decades, embraced the media, regularly giving briefings and often inviting correspondents to lunch. Journalists, in turn, gave him a honeymoon of positive coverage. *Newsweek* told its readers that "everything about U Thant radiates a kind of mellow reasonableness and composure," from his "immaculately tailored Western suits" to his "soft Oxford-accented tones," as he "moved through two or three cocktail parties a night."[27] The news service UPI quoted an American diplomat describing Thant as "a blooming miracle."[28]

There was also hostile media coverage. Thant was embroiled in a dispute with his landlord, William Wholey, who was charging him three times the legal amount for the rent-controlled apartment. Wholey had also demanded $3,000 for an air conditioner even though Mongi Slim, downstairs, had just had one installed for free. When Thant discovered the price-gouging, he had informed Wholey that he would pay only $400 a month, the correct sum, or he would leave; Wholey responded by charging him over $6,000 for damages to the curtains and furniture.[29] The New York Housing Commission had begun investigating William Wholey for overcharging Thant and the case was scheduled to be heard by the state supreme court. In response, Wholey had gone public with his claim that the family cat was responsible for extensive damages. "U Thant and His $6,447 Cat," blared the *Herald Tribune*'s headline on May 17. The Burmese feline, Wholey told reporters, "tore the damask curtains, ripped up the carpets and upholstery."[30] The landlord also painted a lurid picture of wild excess, accusing the diplomat of "entertaining great numbers of guests, at which functions a great amount of liquor, food, and tobacco was dropped, permitting upwards of twenty persons to sleep on the floor, food be thrown about from the windows, and animals to sit and sleep on the carpets..." Thant countered that this was complete fabrication, adding fuel to the media fire.

Thant soon suffered a far more devastating blow. His son, Timmy, had left for Burma, thinking he might study at Rangoon University. Timmy had experienced problems adjusting to life in America, often skipping school without his parents' knowledge, but over the past couple of years he had seemed happier. His mother was anxious about her son going back to Burma alone, but Thant thought that reconnecting with his country was a good idea and made sure the university would give Timmy a place. After several weeks, Timmy decided that Burma, or at least the university, wasn't for him and planned to return to New York.

On a rain-soaked afternoon, Timmy boarded a crowded bus in a leafy residential neighborhood to cable his parents from the Telegraph Office, a few miles away in downtown Rangoon. There were not enough seats and Timmy, in a Burmese sarong and flip-flops, was standing on the footboard when the vehicle turned a sharp corner. The lanky twenty-year-old fell, hitting his head on the pavement and fracturing his skull. The

Thant with his wife, Thein Tin, and son, Timmy, at their home in Rangoon in 1952.

panicked driver first drove Timmy to the bus company's clinic; staff there insisted the young man be rushed to the hospital. Timmy was in and out of consciousness and losing a lot of blood. Shortly after reaching Rangoon General Hospital, he was pronounced dead.

May 21 was a sunny spring day in New York. Thant was in his office, discussing the New Guinea situation with the Dutch foreign minister. A little before 3 p.m., a reporter informed the Secretary-General's press aide, Ramses Nassif, of Timmy's death, which had just come over the wires, wanting to make sure Thant didn't hear the news first on the radio. Nassif dashed over to Thant's *chef de cabinet* Narasimhan, who had the office next door to the Secretary-General, and the two men waited till the meeting was over. Narasimhan remembers those few minutes as being the most difficult in his life. Thant's first words were, "What will I say to my poor wife?"[31]

Grief stricken, Thant and Thein Tin arranged a Buddhist ceremony at a monastery in Rangoon. Thein Tin was too distraught to make the long trip, and Thant, who wept when shown the coroner's photographs, told colleagues he was too pressed by work to go. In the Burmese tradition, the ceremony, which takes place exactly a month after a death, is more important than the next-day burial or cremation and is a way for the family to seek the best possible afterlife for their loved one. In Timmy's honor, relatives donated alms to monks, including the revered Buddhist abbot Mahasi Sayadaw, and dedicated a sanctuary for fish and goats. In a message to mourners, Thant and Thein Tin expressed their hope that Timmy would "rejoice" and "reap the benefits of these merits in whatever plane of existence he now is. May he be happy therein."[32]

A few weeks later, Thant received some of Timmy's paintings from his old art teacher, June Steingart. In a long letter to both parents, she described Timmy's discovery of painting and conveyed her hope that these "simple lovely works will brighten your lives a little and bring to you again the warmth of your boy."[33] Thant could not bear to take them home to his wife, so he hung them in the private apartment next to his office.

In July 1962, Thant flew to London and had his first audience with

Queen Elizabeth. It was meant to be a brief call, but the queen kept him for nearly an hour. The first thing she said was, "As a mother I know how much you must have suffered when you heard the terrible news of the death of your son. I thought of you and I thought of your wife when the news was brought to my attention." There were tears in her eyes and in Thant's, too.[34]

Thant was in London as part of a European tour. In Uppsala, Sweden, he paid his respects at Hammarskjöld's grave. In Norway, he sailed on a yacht with King Olav. And in Dublin, he was hosted by the Irish revolutionary and president Éamon de Valera, whom he had admired since his youth. On Irish television, he was asked whether, as Secretary-General, "certainly the greatest and most prestigious post in the world today," he found "that the very heavy responsibilities of the post are too much."

"It all depends on the interpretation of the words 'too much,'" was Thant's answer. "It is a relative term. Perhaps when I was headmaster, I thought that my responsibilities were too much."[35]

Thant was trying to ensure that Europeans saw him not as an angry radical from the Third World but as a moderate statesman with whom they could feel at ease. Harold MacMillan and Thant disagreed on the way forward in the Congo, but the British leader, after their meetings in both New York and London, came away finding the Secretary-General "very pleasant" and "sensible enough."[36]

Over these months, Thant developed what became known as the U Thant Plan for the Congo, in which Katanga would renounce its secession and integrate into a federal arrangement. Thant tried to get Moïse Tshombe to agree—which Brian Urquhart, now Bunche's deputy, compared to "trying to get an eel into a bottle."[37] The UN team worked in tandem with the Kennedy administration and consulted the Afro-Asian delegations closely, too. They knew that without progress soon, the whole Congo operation could still result in ignominious failure.

To turn up the pressure, Thant began to hit out specifically at the Belgian mining giant Union Minière. At a press conference in London, he said flatly that "The problem of the Congo is Katanga, and the problem of Katanga is finance, and the problem of finance is Union Minière." He pointed out that over the past year Tshombe had received $65 million in mining revenue, of which $59 million came from Union Minière. "This," he declared, "is the crux of the problem."[38]

While on a visit to Finland, he was told that Tshombe had organized thousands of women and children to abuse the Indian UN troops at a roadblock outside Elizabethville, and that the troops showed "remarkable restraint" despite being cursed at and spat on. To reporters in Helsinki, Thant derided Tshombe and his men as "a bunch of clowns." Back in New York, he stated that all sides had to accept his plan in its entirety. There would be, he declared, no further negotiations.[39]

That summer, Thant was proving useful to the Americans. On the Congo, the UN and the US were now traveling in a similar direction. In August, the Netherlands and Indonesia agreed to a compromise brokered by Thant on the future of Dutch-controlled Papua New Guinea. There would be an interim UN Executive Authority and a promise that the Papuans would be allowed to decide their own future. For Thant and the Americans, the priority was avoiding a Dutch–Indonesian war. For the Secretary-General, there was also an ingrained antipathy to the breakup of former colonial possessions, as well as a desire to build goodwill in the Kennedy administration. Following the Dutch–Indonesian accord, President Kennedy wrote to Thant, "Once again the world organization has become under your leadership, a center for harmonizing the actions of nations on behalf of peace."[40]

The missing piece, now, was a more solid relationship with the Soviets. They were demanding that the UN use force against Katanga, in line with the position of the more hard-line Afro-Asian countries, but at the same time they refused to pay a single ruble toward the costs of the operation. Thant would need Moscow's active consent if he were to continue beyond the expiration of his yearlong appointment as Acting Secretary-General in November. And so, in late August, Thant flew to Yalta to spend a day with Nikita Khrushchev at the Soviet chairman's summer home. The dacha, named Wisteria, complete with two saltwater swimming pools, had been built a few years before along the southern coast of Crimea, less than twenty miles from where Roosevelt, Churchill, and Stalin had set the contours of the world organization in February 1945.

As the car rolled up the drive to the secluded dacha, Thant found the short, bald sixty-eight-year-old Khrushchev waiting for him at the gate, dressed in a rumpled, light-colored suit and holding a baby. A cluster of other grandchildren darted about nearby. He shook hands with the Kremlin leader, exchanged a few greetings through an interpreter, then merrily scooped up one of the little boys. In the rustic, familial surroundings, the summer air hot and thick, Thant immediately felt much more relaxed than he had in the marbled palaces of Western Europe.[41] Back in Burma, he had been an ardent anti-Communist, but he was inclined to see Khrushchev's Russia as fundamentally different from Stalin's and not the evil empire portrayed in the American media.

Khrushchev was then at the apex of his power. Officially the Chairman of the Council of Ministers as well as First Secretary of the Communist Party, he had outfoxed his opponents in the years following the death of Joseph Stalin. From the start of his tenure in 1956 he moved the USSR in a reformist direction, loosening restrictions on daily life as well as on the economy. Soviet science and technology advanced by leaps and bounds, symbolized by the launch of Sputnik, the world's first artificial satellite. Khrushchev was keen to prove the Communist system superior to capitalism and, like Kennedy, was eager to make friends in the Third World.

Thant and Khrushchev discussed events in the Congo and the UN's financial difficulties, Khrushchev doing most of the talking as his grandchildren played around the men's chairs. Thant asked for a "voluntary contribution" to keep UN peacekeeping afloat, to which Khrushchev replied, "Don't worry. The Americans will pay. They pushed the United Nations into the Congo and the Congo is shaping up according to their wish. At the last moment, they will pay."

The talk then turned to Berlin. Germany had been divided after the war between a capitalist West and a Communist East; its former capital city was divided as well. Since 1958 Moscow had been demanding the withdrawal of NATO troops from an encircled West Berlin. The Americans refused. Thant agreed with Khrushchev that a peace treaty should be signed to end the Berlin crisis and draw a curtain on the "last vestiges" of the Second World War. But he also counseled patience. President Kennedy was well-intentioned and had a good sense of the rest of the world, he tried to persuade Khrushchev, but needed to manage an "extremely ill-informed" American public.

At this mention of America, Khrushchev became more animated. "Semi-pornography is broadcast or some sort of sports competition is shown where they beat a man almost to death.... There is no opera house in America; it is a very rich country and it doesn't have an opera house! Here capitalism, you know, shows its savage side. Everything is done in order to steal and squeeze out resources from the people and poison the consciousness of the people!"

Thant couldn't help himself and related the story of his landlord. "He said I was holding wild parties!" "He made a statement to the Hearst newspapers!" "Of course, I filed a slander suit against him but I don't want any trouble and so am moving to another apartment."

"There's your freedom of the press for you!" said Khrushchev, and suggested the UN move to Berlin. "Personal expenses would be more reasonable, the climate more acceptable..."

Thant indulged his host, saying that "an ever-growing number of Asian and African countries are losing any illusions with respect to New York, particularly the African delegations. Delegates from various countries come to me literally almost every day and say that discrimination is exhibited toward them almost everywhere: in the elevator, in the restaurant—everywhere!"

Thant enjoyed a big lunch beside the sea with Khrushchev's entire family, after which the Soviet leader insisted on a swim. Thant loved swimming, but protested that swimming after a meal leads to indigestion. "Nonsense!" declared the Soviet. The argument that he had no swimsuit with him was equally of no avail: "Take one of mine!" The Soviet leader's girth was considerably greater than Thant's, so Thant wrapped the suit around him like a Burmese sarong. For thirty minutes the two bobbed around together in the Black Sea, Khrushchev using inflatable rings, as Soviet and UN officials, photographers, and security men watched from the shore. They had no language in common, having spoken all day through a translator. Thant thought Khrushchev "hummed what seemed a Russian tune." Though he got little of what he'd wanted from Khrushchev, he felt he had a better measure of the man. And, he hoped, the Soviet leader had a better measure of him.

Before leaving the USSR, Thant accepted an invitation to speak on air and gambled that he could speak bluntly without endangering his new relationship. On Moscow Radio, he said that if the Soviet people knew the truth about the situation in the Congo, they would change their minds about the UN's role and "shoulder their share of the heavy responsibilities now being undertaken by the world organization." His remarks stating his "gratitude to the people and the government of this great country" were broadcast; the rest was censored.[42]

Shortly after Thant returned to New York, he terminated the lease on his Lenox Hill apartment and found an expansive new home in Riverdale, an upscale neighborhood at the western end of the Bronx about thirty minutes by car from midtown Manhattan: a big redbrick ivy-covered house with a long gravel driveway, with copper beech, pine, and red silk trees and bushes of rhododendron, all on five acres of land sloping down to the Hudson River. There was a heated swimming pool as well.

In November 1960, their daughter Aye Aye Thant had married a Burmese student she had met in New York, Tyn Myint-U, who was working on his PhD in aeronautics at New York University. After a couple of months in an apartment nearby, the newlyweds moved in with Thant and Thein Tin. The whole family now relocated together to Riverdale.

Thein Tin loved the house, with its spare rooms in the attic for guests and a big kitchen for preparing Burmese meals. After Timmy's death, she stopped attending functions at the UN, preferring the company of old friends. Thirty years before, in Pantanaw, soon after their first son died, she and Thant had fostered a boy, Saw Lwin, who was now in his thirties and married with two young children of his own. Thein Tin asked that the family come to stay and they did, first at the house, and then in an apartment nearby.

On September 13, 1962, Thant traveled to Washington at the invitation of the president. Kennedy had recently proposed a mission to the moon and the two chatted about future global cooperation in outer space—a particular interest of Thant's. A few months back, he had organized a private reception with sandwiches and champagne in his office for the astronaut John Glenn, the first American to orbit the Earth, with Vice President Lyndon Johnson in attendance.

The president and the Secretary-General also discussed the Congo. Thant believed he now had the Americans as well as the Afro-Asians solidly behind him. The Soviets would not undermine him if he was careful. The British seemed to understand that he had been as patient as possible. He had to end the Katanga secession, see the Congo unified, and withdraw the UN before he ran out of money or troops or both.[43] Over the following weeks he prepared for a showdown with Tshombe and the white mercenaries.[44]

Around this time, Thant, echoing the sentiments of other Afro-Asian leaders, spoke often and publicly of "the shadow of the hydrogen bomb" and the urgent need to reduce tensions between "the two giants." The Cold War was nearing its climax and Berlin was the center of attention. Thant worried that even a minor skirmish could spin out of control. In a note to himself, Thant wrote, "President Kennedy, Mr. Khrushchev, Mr. Macmillan, and President De Gaulle are not masters of the world, even in the sense that Stalin, Churchill, and Roosevelt were at Yalta. They cannot settle by themselves the fate of Asia, Africa, and the Middle East. Perhaps they cannot even decide in any positive way the future of Europe."[45]

Unknown to Thant, not long before his swim with Nikita Khrushchev, ships carrying nuclear warheads had sailed close to the Crimean coast. They were bound for Cuba.

3 | MISSILE CRISIS

WHEN HIS SCHEDULE ALLOWED, Thant liked to spend a few minutes in meditation first thing in the morning. This didn't mean sitting cross-legged on the floor or even following a fixed method. Instead, before getting out of bed, he simply kept his eyes closed and tried to think positively about the day ahead.

Today, though, he was in a hurry, and after a quick shower and coffee he headed straight to the city. As his driver took him along the tree-lined Henry Hudson Parkway, across Harlem, then down through the tunnels of FDR Drive, Thant scanned the papers. It was Monday, October 22, 1962; the *New York Times* front page featured a piece about his peacekeeping chief Ralph Bunche's upcoming mission to the Congo. There were also articles on the Berlin crisis and the nascent war between India and China. The lead, however, was Cuba, and speculation that President Kennedy would soon give a televised speech.

Several days before, on October 16, Kennedy had been informed that the Soviets were building atomic missile bases in Cuba. Kennedy and Khrushchev had met once, in Vienna in June 1961. Kennedy fretted afterward that he had come across as "young and inexperienced." His fears may have had some substance, as Khrushchev concluded from the encounter that he could push the "immature" US leader around.[1] The president also read in the press that his predecessor, Dwight Eisenhower, who had been Allied Supreme Commander during the Second World War, was calling him "weak on foreign policy." Whatever the military threat, with midterm elections around the corner, Kennedy needed to show he was tough.

The focus then and since had been Berlin. Now Khrushchev was turning his attention to America's backyard. Cuba, a hundred miles off the coast of Florida, had recently come under the rule of Fidel Castro's revolutionary government. At the start of 1959, Castro had overthrown a US-backed military dictatorship and the US, in turn, had been trying repeatedly to oust him. In the early months of the Kennedy administration, the CIA had organized a botched invasion by armed exiles at the Bay of Pigs on Cuba's south coast. Kennedy, embarrassed as well as angered, felt he had been railroaded by his own military and intelligence establishment into approving the operation. After the Bay of Pigs, Castro, a keen baseball player who had once applied to study at Harvard, declared himself a Marxist-Leninist and asked the Soviets for massive military assistance.

Khrushchev sensed an opportunity. In 1962, the Soviets had few missiles capable of reaching the continental United States. At the same time, the Americans were developing intercontinental Minuteman missiles that could be launched before the Soviets had time to respond. The US had also deployed medium-range missiles in Italy and Turkey.

While visiting the Varna Seaside Park in Bulgaria and raging against the missiles just a stone's throw away in Turkey, Khrushchev realized he could do to the Americans what they were doing to him: he could install medium-range missiles in Cuba that could hit targets in the US with atomic warheads. He would sneak them in. When they were in place, it would be too late for the Americans to do anything about them; their choice would be to accept the presence of the missiles or risk nuclear war. At the same time, he could take credit for defending the revolution in Cuba. He told his defense chief, Marshal Rodion Malinovsky, that Moscow would be stuffing a hedgehog down Uncle Sam's pants.[2]

Over the following week, the president's men huddled in secret to debate their response. Kennedy considered bombing the missile sites and following up with a land invasion, removing Castro once and for all. The Joint Chiefs of Staff raised the armed forces alert status to Defense Readiness Condition (or DEFCON) 3, midway between normal readiness and war. Yet as the specter of all-out nuclear conflict came into sharper focus, Kennedy hesitated. Secretary of State Dean Rusk reminded the president of Thant's observation that Berlin was Khrushchev's "obsession,"[3] and Kennedy understood that an attack on Cuba carried the risk of Soviet retaliation against American troops there. He did not want to risk Armageddon. And so, instead, he ordered the US Navy to establish a blockade around Cuba and stop any "offensive weapons" from reaching the island nation.

At this point, more than three dozen Soviet ships were steaming toward Cuba loaded with atomic missiles and warheads, together with four Foxtrot diesel submarines armed with nuclear-tipped torpedoes.[4] Unknown to Washington, virtually the entire Soviet strategic arsenal was already in or on its way to the Caribbean.

The Americans had seen reconnaissance photos of the Soviet missile sites on the island, but had no idea that thirty-six missiles were already fitted with nuclear warheads. They were also oblivious to the stationing of short-range Luna missiles that could explode battlefield atomic weapons, each equal in explosive power to the bombs dropped at Hiroshima and Nagasaki. Just one could wipe out an American invasion force. These were under the tactical control of the Soviet commander in Cuba.[5] There were also over forty thousand Soviet troops on the island—far more than the American estimate of several thousand.

By the time he readied his speech for national television, President Kennedy was preparing for the US to talk tough at the UN. But he was also open to compromise. If the UN proposed a swap of the missiles in Turkey and Italy for the ones in Cuba, he might accept.[6] After initially leaning toward an invasion, Kennedy was now looking for a diplomatic way out.

As soon as Thant reached the UN on Monday, October 22, he took the elevator up to the thirty-eighth floor where General Indar Jit Rikhye was waiting for him, together with *chef de cabinet* C. V. Narasimhan.

Rikhye, a forty-one-year-old Indian army general, had fought in Iraq and Italy during the Second World War before commanding the UN's force in the Congo. He had just returned from a Pentagon briefing with Admiral John McCain, who was attached to Ambassador Adlai Stevenson's staff. The Americans wanted Thant to be prepared. Rikhye handed his boss an album of aerial photographs showing the Soviet missile sites in Cuba and told him that the president would deliver his television speech that evening.[7]

Thant spent the early evening at a reception hosted by Ghana's ambassador, Alex Quaison-Sackey, before returning to his office to watch Kennedy's speech. At 7 p.m., a glum-faced Kennedy told the world about the Soviet "offensive weapons in Cuba," which he said posed a "clandestine, reckless, and provocative threat to world peace." He demanded their "dismantling and withdrawal" and called for an emergency meeting of the UN Security Council. He also announced the imminent establishment of a "quarantine" of Cuba, meaning the naval blockade.

Thant could scarcely believe what he was hearing. Was it the president's intention to corner Khrushchev? And would Khrushchev, "with his back to the wall, hold up his hands and give in?" At the same time, he thought the Soviet leader must have been "out of his mind" to think he could sneak the missiles into Cuba, given that American reconnaissance planes were flying worldwide.[8]

Thant spent the next couple of hours with Rikhye, Narasimhan, and his Egyptian advisor Omar Loutfi. He felt he had to insert himself into the crisis, but in a way that would not exceed his authority and scupper a role in any future diplomacy. Hammarskjöld had never tried to mediate between the superpowers; the Acting Secretary-General was in uncharted waters.

Rikhye warned that approximately thirty Soviet missiles would be ready soon, half of them able to strike almost any part of the United States. American cities might have three minutes' notice before being obliterated. Thant believed they had to try anything they could to avert a "nuclear showdown."[9]

At about 10 p.m., Thant received an official request from Stevenson for an emergency meeting. Over the coming hours, he received a similar request from the Soviet ambassador, the bow-tied Valerian Zorin, who declared that the US was driving the world toward thermonuclear war by arrogating to itself the right to stop and search foreign vessels on the high seas. The Cubans also asked for an emergency meeting, to consider "the act of war unilaterally committed by the United States in ordering a naval blockade."

Meanwhile, in Moscow, Khrushchev summoned his party's presidium, the highest policy-making body, to report that he had authorized the use of battlefield atomic weapons to repel what he believed was an impending American invasion of Cuba, though they would be launched only on direct orders from the Kremlin. "The point is that we do not want to unleash a war," the chairman told his colleagues. "We want to intimidate and restrain the USA."

In fact, when Khrushchev had learned of the blockade, he ordered nearly all Soviet ships carrying nuclear weapons to turn back.[10] Khrushchev may already have sensed the need to find a way out. For now, though, he was feeling the need to rattle his sword. A massive 300-kiloton hydrogen bomb was launched from the Kapustin Yar rocket complex near Volgograd and exploded high over the deserts of central Asia as a demonstration of Moscow's capabilities. In Havana, Castro ordered full mobilization for war.

Thant knew he had no time to lose. He also had no mandate to act. Normal procedure was for the Security Council to request the Secretary-General to intercede in a conflict, but there was no chance this would happen given that it was the veto-wielding superpowers themselves at the center of the crisis. But Thant couldn't just sit on his hands and wait.

Beginning early in the morning of the next day, October 23, he met with diplomats from around the world, including the ambassadors from Egypt, Ghana, Yugoslavia, and India. He wanted their ideas and would also need their explicit support. Omar Loutfi met with the Afro-Asian delegations Thant was unable to see himself. In the absence of a Security Council mandate, the Acting Secretary-General decided he would leverage his position as a representative of the Afro-Asians and the broader Non-Aligned Movement.

By late afternoon, Thant and his aides agreed that he should issue a public appeal to all parties. Zanon Rossides, the ambassador from Cyprus, came up to the thirty-eighth floor to inform Thant that the representatives of all forty-four non-aligned governments had just met and decided to urge the Secretary-General to take immediate steps to defuse the crisis. The Cypriot saw Thant's eyes light up as he exclaimed, "I now have the needed backing for action!"[11]

That evening, Thant began drafting messages to Kennedy and Khrushchev. "At the request of a large number of Member Governments," he asked the Americans to suspend their blockade and the Soviets to suspend further arms shipments to Cuba, in order to de-escalate tensions and create a window for diplomacy. His message made clear that his aim was a "peaceful resolution" of the crisis.

The following morning, October 24, the Acting Secretary-General arrived at his office to be told that more than three dozen ambassadors were waiting to see him. When he met Adlai Stevenson at 2:30 p.m. and told him what he was intending to do, the American ambassador expressed disappointment that Thant's appeal would not include any mention of the missiles already in Cuba. Stevenson asked Thant to postpone sending his messages for twenty-four hours. Thant refused, but agreed to see the ambassador again at 5 o'clock.

That same morning, Kennedy was meeting with his Executive Committee, or ExComm, a group of cabinet members, military chiefs, and trusted advisors set up specially to deal with the Cuban crisis. Dean Rusk reported that Thant was about to send a message with "vague references to verification, and no reference to the actual missiles in Cuba." Kennedy was not pleased and ordered that Stevenson press Thant harder.

Thant would not budge. He knew that if he opened his messages up for negotiation with either side, his initiative would be doomed from the start. When Stevenson returned at 5 p.m., Thant notified him that the messages had been sent as they were. He would, however, call for a halt to the construction of the missile sites when he addressed the Security Council that night.[12]

October 24 was, coincidentally, United Nations Day, marking the founding of the organization sixteen years before. At 6 p.m., Thant attended a long-planned concert by the Leningrad Symphony Orchestra and the renowned violinist David Oistrakh, while Kennedy was again meeting with ExComm. Thant's message had just been received, and the president read it aloud. National Security Advisor McGeorge Bundy asked, "Do you want to answer it tonight? Stevenson thinks it an advantage to make a quick answer."

"Yeah, so do it. We ought to welcome his efforts."[13]

The Security Council resumed discussions at 8 p.m. Fourteen men sat around the horseshoe-shaped table: the Secretary-General, one of his lieutenants, the representative of Cuba, and the eleven ambassadors whose governments were Council members. Behind them was a giant painting by the Norwegian artist Per Krohg of a phoenix rising from a world in ashes, flanked by floor-to-ceiling windows showcasing the dark flowing waters of the East River at night. Dozens of aides sat behind their respective ambassadors. Loutfi, Narasimhan, and Rikhye sat behind Thant. Facing the council were seats for diplomats from governments who were not Council members, as well as public galleries. Other places were reserved for press and staff. The room was filled to the brim, with scores of diplomats standing. From their booths above the chamber, translators provided simultaneous translation into all of the UN's official languages: English, French, Spanish, Russian, and Chinese.

The air was thick with tension. As Thant prepared to speak, all cameras zoomed in on his face. There was absolute silence, except for the momentary sounds of papers shuffling or a throat being cleared.[14] "What is at stake is not just the interests of the parties directly involved, nor just the interests of all Member States, but the very fate of mankind," he began. "If today the United Nations should prove itself ineffective, it may have proved itself so for all time."[15]

He was taking action, he said in his deep, accented voice, not only as the UN's Acting Secretary-General but "as a human being" who hoped "that moderation, self-restraint, and good sense would prevail over all other considerations." After reading out the messages he had sent to the American and Soviet leaders, he continued: "All conflicts have more than two sides, those of the two antagonists and that of the rest of the world."

He then laid out what he believed could be the framework for a resolution of the crisis: an end to the construction of "major military facilities" in Cuba in return for an American pledge not to invade the island. He was, he said, drawing inspiration from the remarks of the Cuban president at the UN two weeks before, that "weapons" in Cuba would be unnecessary if the US were to "give us proof, by word and deed" that it would not "carry out aggression against our country."

Since the Second World War "there has never been a more dangerous or closer confrontation of the major powers," argued Thant. Only negotiations, "good sense and understanding" placed above "the anger of the moment or the pride of nations," he concluded, could secure "the peace of the world."[16] The Council was then adjourned. No further measures would be taken on the various draft resolutions that were meant to be debated, and delegates instead lined up to congratulate him. "Let's leave it to Thant," said many. Or, as one ambassadorial wit put it, "Over to U."

The Soviet ambassador, Valerian Zorin, however, was fuming. He took Thant aside and told him he should have criticized the United States, as both Ghana and Egypt (members of the Council that year) had done. Thant replied calmly that he was no longer speaking as Burma's representative but as Acting Secretary-General. "My conscience is very clear," he said before cutting off the conversation and departing the chamber.

That same evening, Kennedy telephoned Harold MacMillan and read out Thant's message. MacMillan thought it "rather tiresome" as "it looks sensible and yet it's very bad," since it mentioned nothing about the missile sites already constructed. Stevenson worried that Kennedy was being advised by some, including MacMillan, to go against his instincts and react negatively. "Kicking like a steer," he urged the White House to give Thant a chance. Secretary of State Dean Rusk likewise advocated using UN diplomacy.

In the Kremlin, Khrushchev raged. A blockade suggested no American military action, but at the same time it wasn't the climb-down he had expected from his inexperienced young opponent. He let fly at the visiting Romanian leader Gheorghe Gheorghiu-Dej, "cursing like a bargeman" and calling Kennedy "a millionaire's whore." The Romanian thought that if Kennedy had actually been in the room, "the lunatic would have strangled him dead on the spot."[17] In contrast, Khrushchev's public response was tough but controlled. He called the blockade "an act of aggression" and said he would never give in to the "despotic demands of the USA." "Imagine, Mr. President, what if we were to present to you such an ultimatum as you have presented to us by your actions. How would you react to it? I think you would be outraged."[18]

Kennedy immediately sent Khrushchev a brusque reply, stating, "I regret very much that you still do not appear to understand what it is that has moved us in this matter."

A confrontation was coming within hours. In the warm waters of the Caribbean, a Soviet oil tanker, the *Bucharest*, was approaching the blockade line and nearly all of Kennedy's men were telling the president that the ship had to be stopped and boarded. This was necessary, they said, to demonstrate that the blockade was being enforced.

At about 10:30 p.m. on October 24, Under Secretary of State George Ball told the president by telephone, "I don't think we have any option but to go ahead and test this thing out, in the morning." Forty-five minutes later, Kennedy phoned Ball with an idea. He wanted to give Khrushchev "a way that gives them enough of an out to stop their shipments without looking like they completely crawled down."[19] His idea was for the UN Secretary-General to make a fresh appeal, specifically asking the Soviets to halt all ships so that preliminary talks could be held in New York. The Americans had not yet responded to Thant's first message, but Kennedy was already thinking of asking him to send a second. He wasn't sure that Thant would do it.

The president was essentially turning to Thant to create an opening for diplomacy—which was exactly what Thant wanted.

He was also asleep. It was just past 11 p.m., and Thant had gone straight to bed after a long day. After a few tries, Stevenson managed to get him on the UN phone line that had been installed in the Riverdale house. Thant agreed to send the second message, but not until first thing in the morning as he didn't have the required communications setup at home. It's not clear what communications equipment he needed. More likely, he didn't want to react impulsively to an American request.

The next morning, October 25, the *New York Times* headline read, "Thant Bids US and Russia Desist 2 Weeks." Thant had injected himself and the UN into the very heart of the simmering crisis, capturing global attention. But the next set of messages would remain a closely guarded secret.

As soon as Thant reached his office, Stevenson handed him a piece of paper with the suggested text. Thant wrote up the message as his own, changing almost nothing and telling no one in his office where the text had originated, and sent it to the Soviets.[20] The message implored Khrushchev to keep his ships away from the blockade line so as not to "destroy the possibility of finding a political solution." In a mirror appeal to Kennedy (also drafted by the Americans), he asked that everything possible be done to avoid "direct confrontation" on the high seas.

At the White House that morning, Kennedy and his men were debating whether to stop and search the *Bucharest*. Nothing had been heard from Khrushchev since his initial bellicose remarks; there was no hint of how he might respond to Thant's messages. Many of Kennedy's advisors argued that the US should not waver. The *Bucharest* should be boarded by force if necessary, regardless of the risks. But the president, beginning to sense a way out of the crisis, was clear: "At this point, in view of U Thant's appeal, we let this go." In his own reply to Thant, sent early in the afternoon, the president expressed his "deep appreciation" for "the spirit which promoted your message of yesterday" and assured him of "our desire to reach a satisfactory and peaceful solution of the matter."[21]

Kennedy and Thant were now each using the other to create room for compromise. The president told ExComm, "I'll tell you what . . . let's wait . . . Your point about . . . 'eyeball to eyeball' . . . We could say well, we're waiting for Khrushchev. We're waiting for U Thant . . . We don't want to precipitate an incident."

Bundy tried to cut in, but Kennedy continued, "I would think the only argument would be that, with U Thant and the UN asking us for . . ."

Bundy: "We've given them a letter."

Kennedy: "This is not the appropriate time to blow up a ship."

After a brief flag-raising ceremony for Uganda, the world organization's newest member, Thant sat down in his conference room overlooking First Avenue with Soviet ambassador Zorin and Zorin's deputy, Alexander Morozov. In an aggressive tone, Zorin berated Thant for his appeals, saying that the UN chief should have condemned the American blockade outright. Thant was in no mood to take abuse from Zorin and asked point-blank whether the ambassador was speaking for himself or on instructions from Moscow. This was a veiled threat to bypass the Russian diplomat and take up his unhelpful behavior directly with the Kremlin. Zorin was visibly taken aback and said nothing. Thant added that he might send a telegram to Moscow explaining how hard he was trying to be impartial and ask for clarification on Zorin's stance. Zorin then mumbled something about Thant's statement having been "a bad one," and Thant immediately told Zorin to condemn him publicly at the 3 p.m. Security Council meeting if he felt so strongly. The Acting Secretary-General then stood up and left.[22]

In Moscow, Khrushchev was conferring with other Soviet leaders, including Leonid Brezhnev, Anastas Mikoyan, Alexei Kosygin, Andrei Gromyko, and Vasily Kuznetsov. He had softened his position; instead of another emotional outburst, he suggested that Thant's proposed deal, trading the missiles for a pledge of non-invasion, was "not bad." The Kremlin leaders resolved to respond positively to both of Thant's messages.[23] Media throughout the Soviet bloc that morning emphasized Thant's efforts at the UN to ease tensions and credited the "neutralist" governments with whom he was working.

In Washington, Kennedy continued to leverage Thant's diplomacy to deflect calls for precipitate action. When McGeorge Bundy argued for intercepting an East German ship which was approaching the blockade line, saying it was "not covered" by Thant's message, the president immediately replied, "Well, I think the only argument for not stopping it is this U Thant thing, where we have an incident of a kind tomorrow morning on a ship at a time when supposedly he's asking the Russians to stay out of the area... we should seek to avoid any incident in order not to create a bad effect on U Thant's negotiations."[24] Kennedy also wanted to hedge his bets and blame Thant if necessary: "I'd rather stick the cat on his back.... We can't take the quarantine off until he offers a substitute." Thant was also, the president grumbled again, not doing anything about the missiles already in Cuba.[25]

Though the decision to accept Thant's proposal had been taken in Moscow, word of this had not yet reached Washington or New York. The Americans were therefore preparing for the worst. Stevenson had written a fiery speech to be delivered at that afternoon's Security Council meeting, and blow-ups of the reconnaissance photographs were ready to be displayed. The live television broadcast of the Council meeting was about to begin, and the president was watching.

Just then, Joseph Sisco, a top State Department official, approached Stevenson with the message that Kennedy wanted to speak to him immediately. When Stevenson argued that the meeting was about to begin, Sisco told him that he couldn't refuse a call from the president. Kennedy made clear to Stevenson that he could not deliver his speech until there was word from Thant on Moscow's reply.

Thant was then in his small second office on the ground floor of the UN, about to walk over to the Security Council, when the Soviet diplomat Morozov rushed in holding a little piece of paper and translated the Russian:

> *Dear U Thant,*
>
> *I have received your message and have carefully studied the proposal it contains. I welcome your initiative. I understand your concern over the situation which has arisen in the Caribbean, for the Soviet Government too regards it as highly dangerous and as requiring immediate intervention by the United Nations. I wish to inform you that I agree to your proposal, which is in the interest of peace.*
>
> *With respect,*
N. Khrushchev[26]

Thant immediately informed the Americans, and Stevenson was instructed to "pull out all the stops." With Khrushchev turning his ships back (or so it was hoped), the White House reckoned they could afford to ratchet up the public rhetoric.[27]

The chamber was again filled to capacity with hundreds of men (and a very few women), many smoking cigarettes, a few smoking pipes, and Thant smoking his black Burmese cigar. When it was Stevenson's turn to speak, he laid out his country's case, arguing that "no twisting of logic, no distortion of words can disguise the plain, the obvious, the compelling common-sense conclusion that the installation of nuclear weapons by stealth ... poses a dangerous threat to the peace." He ended his speech by reading out Kennedy's message to Thant from earlier that day, saying that the US was ready for "preliminary talks."

Zorin challenged Stevenson, suggesting that he had no hard evidence on the existence of the missile sites.

"Do you, Ambassador Zorin, deny that the USSR has placed and is placing medium- and intermediate-range missiles and sites in Cuba? Yes, or no? Don't wait for the translation: yes, or no?"

"I am not in an American courtroom, sir, and therefore I do not wish to answer a question that is put to me in the fashion in which a prosecutor does. In due course, sir, you will have your reply. Do not worry."

"I am prepared to wait for my answer until hell freezes over, if that's your decision.... And I'm also prepared to present the evidence in this room."

Stevenson then unveiled the reconnaissance photographs on live television. It was a triumph for Stevenson, who often felt sidelined by the Kennedy White House.

It was a triumph for Thant, too. His gamble had succeeded. Without a mandate, he had mobilized the active support of the non-aligned countries, set out a mediated path, and made himself a neutral point of reference around which both superpowers could begin to back down. He was, however, fed up with Zorin, who had not been helpful in the least. Later that afternoon, Thant sent a confidential message to the Kremlin through his Russian assistant Victor Lessiovski, who he knew was also a member of the KGB. Within forty-eight hours, Khrushchev dispatched his deputy foreign minister, Vasily Kuznetsov, to head up the negotiations at the UN.

Thant understood that the crisis wasn't simply a superpower confrontation; there was a small country caught in the middle. On October 26, the day after his Security Council speech, he reached out to Fidel Castro, informing him that he had received "fairly encouraging" responses from both the US and the USSR and that "Your Excellency can make a significant contribution to the peace of the world" by ending construction of the missile sites. In his response, Castro, while noting his appreciation for Thant's "noble concerns," argued that "Cuba is victimizing no-one; it has violated no international law; on the contrary, it is the victim of the aggressive acts of the United States, such as the naval blockade, and its rights have been outraged." He declared that "unreserved respect" for his country's sovereignty was "a prerequisite for any settlement," and invited Thant to Cuba.[28]

The same day, Kennedy received a rambling, almost stream-of-consciousness letter directly from Khrushchev, in which the Soviet leader accused the US of "piratical measures, which were employed in the Middle Ages" but also portrayed Thant's proposal as "a way out of the situation which has been created, which would give the peoples the possibility of breathing calmly." If Washington gave assurances that there would be no invasion of Cuba, "the question of armaments would disappear." This was, in essence, the framework first articulated by Thant thirty-six hours earlier. The Kremlin also sent a copy of the letter to Thant.

The *New York Times* headline on October 26 read: "Kennedy Agrees to Talks on Thant Plan; Khrushchev Accepts It." American intelligence, however, was reporting that the construction of the missile sites was only accelerating. The crisis was far from over.

In Cuba, both Castro and the Soviet military chief, General Issa Pliyev, believed that an American attack was hours away. Pliyev, who had commanded a tank division against the Nazis in Russia and Hungary, readied his troops as well as the surface-to-air missiles under his direct control. Castro ordered anti-aircraft batteries to shoot down US planes from dawn the next day[29] and cabled Khrushchev appealing for a first strike (meaning a nuclear strike) against the United States: "However difficult and horrifying this decision may be, there is, I believe, no other recourse."[30]

In Moscow, there was growing concern that Pliyev and the Cubans would inadvertently escalate a situation they were now attempting to de-escalate. Three separate telegrams were sent to Pliyev, one telling him to "stop all work on deployment of R-12 and R-14 [the missile sites] ... you are aggravating the United Nations." Thant had created the space for diplomacy, but a clash could still easily spiral into all-out conflict.

In Washington, Kennedy's men, believing that the situation was under control, focused on the talks at the UN and their demand that the construction of missile sites freeze immediately, before they became operational. They did not know that many of the nuclear missiles were ready to launch.

Khrushchev, meanwhile, penned another letter to Kennedy, repeating the offer of withdrawing missiles in return for a pledge of non-invasion. "It is good, Mr. President, that you agreed for our representatives to meet and to start talks, apparently with the participation of the acting United Nations Secretary General Mr. Thant. Consequently, to some extent he assumes the role of intermediary and we believe that he can cope with this responsible mission if, of course, every side that is drawn in this conflict shows good will." But now, he added the caveat that the Americans withdraw their missiles from Turkey as well.

Kennedy replied that he had read the chairman's letter "with great care" and that what was required first was to make all "offensive weapons" in Cuba inoperable. Then, "in co-operation with the Acting Secretary-General," there could be talks on a "permanent solution to the Cuban problem along the lines suggested." He deliberately left out any mention of the missiles in Turkey, and asked Thant to find out urgently if the Soviets were willing to have the UN verify the dismantling of the Cuban missile sites.

Kennedy decided that he would agree not only to Thant's proposal, but also to Khrushchev's additional demand that US missiles be removed from Turkey. That concession would be conveyed in a clandestine conversation between his brother, Attorney-General Robert Kennedy, and the Soviet ambassador in Washington, Anatoly Dobrynin, as Kennedy didn't want to be seen to be caving into Soviet pressure. If Dobrynin refused to go along with this arrangement, the White House planned to use what it termed "the Cordier Maneuver": using Andrew Cordier (the man whom Hammarskjöld had sent to the Congo during Lumumba's overthrow) to ask Thant to publicly propose the withdrawal of the missiles in Turkey. For both Khrushchev and Kennedy, it was far preferable to accept an appeal emanating from the UN Secretary-General than to accept an ultimatum from the other.

That evening, Thant began a series of meetings with American, Soviet, and Cuban representatives to find a way forward.

Though peaceful resolution of the crisis appeared to be in sight, the world was still in danger of events spinning out of control. For days the American military had been preparing for an invasion of Cuba and for a nuclear attack on the USSR. Alert levels for US forces worldwide were raised to DEFCON 2, the level just short of war. The next day, October 27, an American reconnaissance plane flying low over Cuba was shot down. Thousands of miles away, a U-2 spy plane flying at 70,000 feet over the Bering Sea veered into Russian airspace and was pursued by Soviet fighter jets. American jets armed with nuclear warheads scrambled to escort the U-2 back to US territory.[31]

There was a third close call that day. In the waters near Bermuda, US Navy destroyers forced a Soviet submarine to surface. The Soviet officers and men came out on deck, having been low on oxygen for many days. Navy planes swooped over the submarine, strafing the waters nearby. The Soviet commander panicked, thinking war had already broken out, and ordered his nuclear torpedoes to be fired. As the Soviets scrambled back down the hatch, an observant American officer, realizing they had gone too far, quickly signaled an apology. It was only because a Soviet crewman descending back down the shaft was momentarily stuck that another officer still on deck saw the American apology. The torpedoes stayed put. The superpowers had literally come within seconds of a nuclear clash.[32]

That evening, Robert Kennedy met with Ambassador Dobrynin at the Soviet embassy in Washington and the agreement was made. Only a few top people in Washington and Moscow knew the meeting had taken place.

Thant left the UN at 11 p.m. only to get a phone call from General Rikhye minutes after arriving home. Rikhye told him that American nuclear bombers were on full alert and that anything could happen over the coming hours. Anxious, Thant phoned Stevenson at his Waldorf Astoria suite, but the phone was continually busy. When he finally got through, he thought Stevenson sounded exhausted as he said that he had no specific information on what the US Air Force was doing but that the situation was "touch and go."

Thant wanted to meet in person and asked, "Could you see me Sunday morning?"

"Secretary-General, it is already Sunday morning. Can I see you now?"

Thant thought it best that they both get some rest and suggested waiting until 10 a.m. But he didn't sleep at all that night, spending hours consulting with Rikhye and Narasimhan, reviewing what else they could do. He believed that both Khrushchev and Kennedy wanted a peaceful settlement. But he also knew there were hard-liners around the president, including former president Truman's secretary of state, Dean Acheson, whom Kennedy had asked to advise him; Thant thought him "one of the most overrated diplomats of his time."

When Thant met with Stevenson in the morning, the ambassador seemed "weary, almost distraught." Thant realized that his friend had been left out of top-level discussions and was feeling resentful.

With an understanding in hand, President Kennedy and Chairman Khrushchev worked fast to end the crisis before any further confrontations triggered a war neither wanted. On October 28, the Soviets sent a letter to Kennedy agreeing to the framework Thant had proposed at the Security Council four days before: withdrawal of the missiles in return for a pledge of non-invasion. Recognizing that the armed forces of both sides were on a hair trigger, the Soviets broadcast the letter over Moscow Radio so the text could be picked up immediately by the international media.

Kennedy responded just hours later, welcoming Khrushchev's broadcast as "an important contribution to peace" and commending "the distinguished efforts of Acting Secretary-General U Thant" which "greatly facilitated both our tasks." The agreement to withdraw US missiles from Turkey, made through Robert Kennedy and Ambassador Dobrynin, was kept confidential.

Thant informed Moscow and Washington that he would accept Castro's invitation and travel to Cuba within forty-eight hours. Both the Americans and Soviets welcomed this. The Americans wanted the UN to verify that the missiles had indeed been packed up and shipped back to the USSR. For Washington, this was to be the aim of Thant's trip. Khrushchev, meanwhile, had to make sure that Castro would not spoil chances for a diplomatic solution. He and the other members of the presidium had been shocked by the letter from the Cuban premier stating that war was imminent and advocating a nuclear first strike against the United States. In his reply, Khrushchev told Castro he was absolutely wrong in thinking that the Americans were about to invade and that he should calm down. It was "almost inconceivable," said the Soviet leader, that after "the steps taken in connection with the initiative of U Thant," and after Kennedy's most recent response, the Americans would "undertake the adventure of using its military forces" against Cuba. If the US were to do so, it would be seen by the entire world as the aggressor and an enemy of peace."[33] Khrushchev urgently cabled Thant to tell him that he was dismantling the missile sites. He also instructed General Pliyev to invite Thant to visit the sites when he arrived.[34]

Before leaving for Cuba, Thant met with Kuznetsov, the Soviet deputy foreign minister, who brought with him "the heartfelt greetings of Comrade Nikita Sergeyevich Khrushchev." Thant explained that his main objective in Cuba would be to learn firsthand about the dismantling of the missile sites and discuss a possible deployment of UN observers both on the island and in the US and neighboring countries.

Thant and Kuznetsov concurred on the desirability of removing the US blockade straight away, but Thant explained that Washington was still concerned about additional arms coming into Cuba. He had been in touch with the International Red Cross and suggested a role either for them or for "neutral countries" in monitoring ships. Kuznetsov agreed.[35]

Castro, however, had other ideas. When the Cuban leader learned about the Kennedy–Khrushchev deal over the wire services (international news agencies sending news by telegram), he was apoplectic with rage, smashing a mirror in his home and calling Khrushchev a son of a bitch, a bastard, and an asshole.[36] He had been sidelined; he was unable to use the crisis to leverage his position and gain the iron-clad guarantees he wanted against future American interference. He demanded that the US end reconnaissance flights over his territory and withdraw from the base at Guantánamo Bay, a legacy of pre-revolutionary days. Castro saw Thant not just as a possible intermediary but also as a human shield. The Americans were unlikely to invade while the Secretary-General was visiting.[37]

The Acting Secretary-General was deluged by cables and letters from around the world. President Modibo Keita of Mali proposed the eviction from the US of Cuban refugees who were preparing an invasion with American help. Venezuela's president Luis Preto asked Thant to use his "good offices" to "preserve peace in the world." President Tubman of Liberia suggested immediate de-escalation measures and sent his own draft Security Council Resolution banning all "thermo-nuclear weapons" from both Latin America and Africa.[38] Thant's friend the Swedish ambassador Agda Rössel personally handed him a statement from her government condemning the blockade while expressing full support for his efforts.

India's Prime Minister Nehru, stalwart in the fight against colonialism and himself in the middle of a war with China, wrote to Thant to say that "we welcome very warmly the initiative you have taken to ease the crisis. The steps you are taking to find a solution and to ensure peace in the world have our full support." The British philosopher and renowned pacifist Bertrand Russell urged him to go to Cuba "to act as arbitrator," saying that there was "no one else so able to intervene" and "forestall the final folly."[39]

There were also many cables from ordinary people, mainly in the United States. Edith Lorning of New York wrote, "As a private citizen, may I express my admiration and deep gratitude for all you have done to help preserve the peace in a very precarious time." Adele Clarke of Montclair, New Jersey, warned Thant of Castro's and Khrushchev's "underhanded" ways but encouraged him to "continue your work," underlining "we need you" and signing her letter "A loyal American."

A special message came from Ruth Gage-Colby, the international coordinator of the Women's International Strike for Peace. Thant and Gage-Colby knew each other well, having met several times in recent years, when Thant was the Burmese UN ambassador. By coincidence, she was in Russia at the time, and wrote, "You have given the world added faith in the United Nations and a positive hope that the Cuban dilemma can be met and solved peacefully.... On behalf of many women in many countries you have my heartfelt gratitude! For on this Sunday afternoon the world breathes more freely again.... The world is fortunate that a man so above nation and so dedicated to peace fills the Office of the Secretary General at this moment in history."[40]

Not all agreed with Thant. "The only sure way to correct the Cuban situation is for the United States to bomb and blow up all missile bases in Cuba and expel or imprison Castro, and drive out all Russian and foreign soldiers," advised William H. McHenry of White Plains, New York, adding, "I know whereof I speak, having surreptitiously dealt with communists for the past twenty years or so."

From his window on the thirty-eighth floor of UN headquarters, Thant could see thousands of people carrying signs and banners calling for peace. "Negotiations—not war!" read one. "We oppose all bases and all blockades!" said another.[41]

The Acting Secretary-General was heading to Havana.

4 | HAVANA

EARLY IN THE MORNING of October 30, 1962, Thant boarded a chartered Boeing 707 from the flying-saucer shaped Pan Am terminal at New York's Idlewild airport (now known as JFK). Dozens of well-wishers, including Soviet and American diplomats, congregated on the tarmac, together with reporters, photographers, and New York City policemen. The sky was blue, but the weather had turned freezing cold over the past days and many were in overcoats, holding on to their fedoras to keep them from blowing away in the gusty wind. The Acting Secretary-General, briefcase in hand, climbed the steps and turned briefly to smile and wave to the crowd.

He had arrived at the same airport just five years before, straight from Burma, a virtual unknown in the world of international diplomacy. Now he was en route to Cuba to ease tensions between the superpowers. At his request, President Kennedy had suspended American reconnaissance flights over the island.[1] He had forty-eight hours to end the Cold War's biggest crisis.

Thant brought with him a carefully selected team: his political advisor Omar Loutfi, General Indar Jit Rikhye, his press aide Ramses Nassif, and his public information chief Hernane Tavares de Sá, a Brazilian and the most senior Latin American at the UN. Except for Tavares de Sá, all were men from the Afro-Asian bloc at the UN and from non-aligned countries. Also with him was Miguel Marin, a Spanish interpreter, his secretary Hannah Platz, and thirteen others: security men and radio operators. This was Group One. Group Two was comprised of nineteen UN military officers, telex operators, radio engineers, and others who could be at the core of a verification operation. They were to be ready and waiting in New York.

In Havana, Thant was greeted at the airport by Cuba's foreign minister Raul Roa, in similar pinstripes and identical browline glasses. The air was warm and muggy. Armed soldiers waited everywhere; some hurried to surround the plane. Before Thant and Roa stepped into the backseat of a waiting car, an army major in olive fatigues ran up to Roa, whispered in his ear, saluted, and left.

As the convoy sped down Fifth Avenue and across Havana's upscale Miramar district, Thant could see an American navy destroyer. In the near distance were sandbagged anti-aircraft emplacements and a man in tattered clothes waving to the passing car.[2] Roa—a university professor before the revolution, who had been imprisoned for his left-wing views—queried Thant about the twenty-eight big boxes which had been unloaded from the plane. This was the first Thant knew of them, and he told Roa that he had no idea what they contained.

When they reached the villas where the UN delegation would be staying, Thant could see Cuban soldiers storing the boxes in a shed in the garden. Urgently he summoned General Rikhye, who told him that they probably held communications and office equipment. Thant was furious. The Cubans were already suspicious that Thant was coming to do the Americans' bidding, and would certainly have examined the contents. On Loutfi's advice, Thant told the Cubans the truth—that the equipment had been put on the plane without his permission and would be returned to the plane immediately.[3]

Talks began at 3 p.m. in the ornate presidential palace built by the island's pre-revolutionary leaders, with mirrored walls designed by Tiffany's of New York. A solemn-looking Fidel Castro was waiting in military khakis, a pistol strapped to his belt. After a cordial greeting, he and Thant faced each other across a large wooden table with Castro flanked by Roa, President Dorticos, and Cuba's UN ambassador, Mario Garcia Inchaustegui. Thant lit a Burmese cigar. Several of the Cubans were smoking as well.

The Acting Secretary-General started by underlining his neutrality, saying that he enjoyed the strong support of the non-aligned countries in particular "in my quest for peace, not only in the Caribbean, but throughout the world." He also reiterated his respect for Cuba's sovereignty, "as an essential prerequisite to any solution of the problem."

He quickly turned to the specific business at hand: his request to verify the dismantling of the missile sites. He said the Americans had promised to lift the blockade and not to invade Cuba.

But though the Soviets had given Thant their assent, an irate Castro refused.

"Is the demand of the United States for the dismantling of the launching pads in Cuba based on right or a position of might?"

Thant and aides meeting Fidel Castro and other Cuban leaders in Havana in October 1962.

"It is not based on right, but based on apprehension," Thant replied.

Sensing he was going down a dead end, Thant added that he wasn't trying to find a long-term solution, only a short-term measure to end the crisis that had brought the world to the brink of nuclear disaster. He also stressed that no UN action could be taken on Cuban soil without the consent of the government—as was the case at the time in Laos, Egypt, and Lebanon, where a UN presence had been agreed and established.

This seemed to placate Castro slightly. He expressed his government's "great esteem" for Thant and his "noble mission." Even so, he refused to consider any kind of UN operation in Cuba. "Why did the UN attach so much weight to a US pledge of non-invasion but not to a Soviet pledge to withdraw missiles? There are two pledges. Why was it that additional guarantees were required to give effect to one pledge and not to the other?" Any UN operation in Cuba, he believed, was meant to humiliate Cuba.[4]

Unthinkingly, Thant wheeled out the example of Congo, as an independent country that had accepted a UN operation—which only infuriated Castro. "In the Congo the government that made that request is now dead and buried!"[5]

After two hours, Loutfi passed Thant a note saying, "We are not getting anywhere—do you wish to propose to meet Castro alone tomorrow?" Thant took his aide's advice, and Castro consented to the request.

Back at his well-appointed villa, Thant enjoyed a daiquiri, his favorite drink, along with one of the Cuban cigars he had been given. Soon there was a knock on the door, and General Rikhye entered with the Soviet ambassador to Cuba, Alexander Alekseev. Thant thought Alekseev looked very young for an ambassador and seemed nervous. He didn't know that Alekseev was the former KGB chief in Havana and a close confidant of Castro.

Alekseev began their meeting by saying he wanted to "pay his respects" to the Secretary-General and thank him for his efforts toward a peaceful settlement. He said he had received orders from Moscow to dismantle the missile sites. Thant posed two questions: When would the dismantling start? And how long would it take?

Alekseev brought in forty-three-year-old General Igor Statsenko of the Soviet Strategic Missile Forces, who had been waiting outside.[6] Stetsenko commanded the three missile regiments in Cuba, and had been ordered to be entirely open with Thant. He had been told by the Kremlin that his presentation should be comprehensive and include "data on the status of the division and its organization, the number of missile launchers and missiles brought in, and plans for dismantling the missiles and taking them back to the Soviet Union."[7]

In reply to the Secretary-General's query, Stetsenko explained that the dismantling had already begun and would be finished in three days' time, on Friday, November 2. He did not know when the missiles would be shipped back to the Soviet Union, but they were being crated and sent to ports around Cuba. The sites would be bulldozed. "By Friday," he said, "there will be nothing."[8]

Thant understood that his Soviet visitors were under instructions from Moscow to reassure him that Khrushchev's promise to Kennedy would be honored. He thanked them both and then conferred with Loutfi, Rikhye, and Nassif. Loutfi's opinion was that Castro hadn't been told of the visit. Rikhye suggested that the discussion with the Soviets alone had made the trip worthwhile, and Nassif advised a very spare press release, stating only that Thant's discussions with the Cuban government were "fruitful and conducted in a friendly atmosphere."

The next morning, October 31, Thant woke up at 6:30, having slept for about six hours. He sat up in bed, with his eyes still closed, and tried to meditate. Yet his mind kept wandering to images of the American navy destroyer off the coast, the Cuban anti-aircraft gunners, and the nervous Soviet ambassador and the young missile commander.[9] In a few hours, he would try again to convince Castro to accept a UN verification operation. At the very least, he had to calm Castro down and dissuade him from doing anything that might reignite tensions.

This time, he was accompanied only by his interpreter, Manuel Martin. Castro had with him President Osvaldo Dorticos and Foreign Minister Roa. Although information on the previous day's meeting would be made public, today's conversation would be kept confidential.

Thant could see that Castro was still "in a bitter mood," his venom directed as much at Khrushchev as at Kennedy. Khrushchev, he stated, had no right to promise anything without consulting him first. He would go on television that evening to give his version of events.

Thant attempted to appease the revolutionary leader, agreeing that Khrushchev should indeed have consulted the Cubans, but this was now too late to rectify. He mentioned future Security Council meetings where the Cubans could have their say. It was a US election year, Thant explained, and Washington had to show a hard line as the American people were "getting very emotional on such issues." Thant said he understood the Cuban leader's feelings but encouraged him not to be too exercised by what the Americans were saying.

With Castro a little calmer, Thant warned him against making an inflammatory television broadcast. Castro refused to cancel, as the broadcast had already been announced. Certain that a fiery speech would only give ammunition to the hard-liners in Washington and complicate Khrushchev's concession, Thant requested that at a minimum Castro not lash out against Khrushchev, stressing that the situation was still perilous. Finally, Castro agreed to delete the inflammatory paragraphs from his script and promised that the speech would be "a mild one."

Thant then asked if he could leave a couple of aides behind so that there would be a direct link between his office and Havana. No, said Castro; his people would see this as the beginning of the UN operation Washington wanted, and a humiliation for Cuba. He would agree only if the Americans consented to a similar observation force in Florida, since "Everybody knows where the Bay of Pigs invasion was launched from, who trained the invaders, and where the training took place." The Americans would never accept this, Castro said, as it would reveal "their criminal plots."

The meeting had by this point lasted a couple of hours, and as a fresh sea breeze came in through the windows of the presidential palace, the remains of several cigars smoldered in heavy ashtrays on the big wooden table. Thant brought up the subject of Major Rudolf Anderson, the pilot whose reconnaissance plane had been shot down over Cuba a few days before, and asked that he be released on humanitarian grounds. Castro replied the airman had died instantly. Thant could arrange for the body to be returned to the US if he wanted.

As the two men rose to say goodbye, Castro received information over the wire services that the US was still considering an attack on Cuba. He asked Thant to take back "one impression above all—that the Cuban people were determined to protect their national sovereignty by any means necessary."[10]

Castro then asked Thant for a joint photograph. He smiled "a rare smile that day" and told the Acting Secretary-General that the photo would be a historic one if the crisis were solved. "It would mean nothing if not."

On the flight back to New York, Thant concluded that though he had failed to persuade Castro to allow a UN verification operation in Cuba, he had obtained firsthand information on the dismantling of the missile launch pads. This would help him dampen the hysteria sweeping America. As important, he might have convinced Castro not to make an incendiary broadcast and instead begin to see the UN as a useful intermediary.

Back at a wet and blustery Idlewild airport, Thant read out a prepared statement in front of the Pan Am logo, with what seemed like the entire New York press corps, in a sea of trench coats and felt hats, jostling in front of him.

"During my stay in Havana, I was reliably informed that the dismantling of the missiles and their installations was already in progress and that this process should be completed by Friday, that is, the day after tomorrow," he said slowly, to give the reporters time to scribble down his words. Arrangements to ship the missiles back to the USSR were "understood to be already in hand." Thant also told reporters that, at his request, the body of Major Anderson would soon be returned to the US.

There were no questions, only a rush by the reporters to the bank of telephones to dictate their Page One stories.

It was late, but Thant went straight from the airport to his office, where Stevenson and Washington's special negotiator McCloy were waiting for him. He went over what the Soviets had told him, emphasizing General Stetsenko's remarks that he was leaving "at once" and "will be glad to leave." He worried, though, that there could still be "some kind of showdown" between the Soviets and the Cubans, and he asked the Americans to end the blockade so as not to hinder Soviet ships coming to retrieve the missiles. This, he said, would help mollify Castro. Stevenson assured him the US Navy was already allowing Soviet vessels to proceed to Cuba.

The economic situation seemed dire, Thant continued: "They are shut off from the outside world. The people are getting desperate." They have all the military hardware they need, he said, but they are running out of food. He sensed that Castro was "frustrated, intense, psychotic," and infuriated with the United States, believing that they, rather than the UN, would be coming to verify the missile withdrawal. He suggested Washington be satisfied with the Red Cross inspecting the ships as they left.

As the meeting ended, Rikhye stopped Stevenson at the door and whispered, "Please lay off the aerial reconnaissance until Friday. After that they will have bulldozed all of the sites."[11]

Late that same evening, October 31, Thant received a copy of Castro's hour-long speech and was glad to see that the Cuban leader had kept his word. First, he had read out a verbatim transcript of the first day's meeting, at times pausing to add commentary. He was full of praise for Thant, describing him as "sincere and impartial, desirous to find a solution to these problems."

He said that Cuba would not accept inspection because he was not willing to sacrifice the principle of sovereignty and because the United States, in demanding this inspection, was basing it on a position of power and "we will never give in to a power position."

He didn't disclose his confidential discussion with Thant on the second day. He also, as promised, didn't criticize Khrushchev, only saying that while "certain discrepancies had arisen between Cuba and the Soviet government," he didn't want to give Cuba's enemies a chance to "cash in" on these differences. He explained that as the Soviets had sent the missiles; they did not belong to Cuba and therefore Havana did not oppose their withdrawal.

He told his people that the United Nations was trying to carry out its task—to help all countries, especially the smaller countries—and that the Secretary-General was a man of "great experience, competent, who inspires confidence." He concluded: "U Thant respects our ideas and the rights of our country."[12]

The next morning, Thant's friend Ruth Gage-Colby and her Women's International Strike for Peace organized marches of more than 50,000 women in over sixty cities across America under the slogan "End the Arms Race Not the Human Race."

The Soviets were extremely pleased with Thant's visit to Cuba. Ambassador Alekseev sent a top-secret message to Moscow saying that "up until recently Castro was a prisoner of his delusion, and only after his meetings with U Thant . . . he seemed to be assuming the correct realistic positions."[13] Khrushchev dispatched presidium member Anastas Mikoyan to further pacify Castro, and Mikoyan stopped first in New York to be briefed by Thant. It was a critical mission; Mikoyan, an Armenian veteran of the Bolshevik Revolution, left his dying wife to make the journey across the Atlantic, knowing he would never see her again.

Thant intensified his mediation between the Americans and Soviets, now concentrated in his thirty-eighth-floor suite: the Americans, Stevenson and McCloy, in one room, and the Soviets, Kuznetsov and Mikoyan (after his trip to Havana), in another, with Thant and his aides shuttling between them. He was also in contact with the Red Cross and the non-aligned governments that might provide inspectors or observers. As Castro refused to allow UN inspection of the Soviet ships as they left Cuban ports, Thant was searching for a solution that would satisfy Washington.

This anxious period was not improved by a demand from lawyers representing Thant's old landlord, William Wholey, that the Secretary-General appear personally in court to refute the allegations against his cat. At this point, the US government intervened. Requiring the Secretary-General to take any time away from his work would be "shocking and unconscionable," and "a disservice to the United Nations which can ill spare U Thant from his present global duties." The hearing was postponed.[14]

Khrushchev wrote to Mikoyan in support of Thant's idea of a "UN presence" in Cuba as a "guarantor against an invasion."[15] But Castro remained adamantly opposed to this, and even more so to any verification operation. In a letter to Thant, he railed against the continued American blockade as well as military reconnaissance flights, calling them "Hitlerite methods for softening the resistance of peoples."[16]

In an attempt to placate Castro, Thant proposed an inspection regime for the Cuban exile camps in Florida and Nicaragua, and handed Stevenson a "strictly confidential" paper outlining how a group of "eminent personalities" from neutral states could monitor the missile withdrawal and at the same time ensure that there would be no repeat of the Bay of Pigs invasion.[17] This, said Stevenson, was a non-starter for Washington. At last an arrangement was agreed on: verification by air. As the Soviet ships sailed back, they would open the boxes carrying the missiles so that they could be photographed by American planes.

There was one last sticking point. Late in the crisis, the Americans had become aware that Soviet Ilyushin-28 bombers were stationed in Cuba and demanded that they too be withdrawn. Unlike the missiles, Moscow had gifted the bombers to the Cubans, so they were Havana's property. Khrushchev was willing to take them back and requested Castro's agreement, but Castro was far too angry with Khrushchev to accede to any more Russian requests directly. Instead, he told Thant that he didn't want the Soviet planes any more anyway, as they were "antiquated."

On November 20, 1962, President Kennedy announced that the Ilyushin bombers were being shipped back to the Soviet Union as well. The blockade was lifted. The crisis was over.

Over the previous four weeks Thant had proved an invaluable link between Washington, Moscow, and Havana. He had done this directly through his messages to the three heads of government, in his meetings with Castro, and in the many days of discussions with Mikoyan, Kuznetsov, McCloy, and Stevenson, first apart and then together, often over an amiable meal in the Secretary-General's dining room.[18]

On the same day as Kennedy's announcement, *The New York Times* opined that the United Nations and Thant "have emerged from the crisis with greatly strengthened prestige." Some had expected Thant to be more cautious than his predecessor, but "on the contrary, Mr. Thant has acted energetically."[19]

Ten days later, Thant was unanimously appointed to a full five-year term as Secretary-General. Soviet foreign minister Andrei Gromyko was still not entirely convinced that the Burmese diplomat was the best person for the job, but Khrushchev overruled him, believing Thant to be "a man of principle" who wouldn't simply do "the bidding of the Americans" but serve "in the interests of all countries." No one can satisfy everyone, Khrushchev thought. What was needed was "a great deal of flexibility and a very penetrating mind," someone who would not "complicate questions" but know "how to smooth things over, while maintaining a definite position." Thant, he felt, was undeniably the best person to lead the world organization.[20]

On January 7, 1963, Thant received an unprecedented joint letter, signed by Stevenson and Kuznetsov "on behalf of the Governments of the United States of America and the Soviet Union," in "appreciation of his efforts in assisting our governments to avert the serious threat to the peace which recently arose in the Caribbean area." At the Senate Foreign Relations Committee, Stevenson testified, "At a critical moment—when the nuclear powers seemed set on a collision course—the Secretary-General's intervention led to the diversion of the Soviet ships headed for Cuba and interception by our Navy. This was the indispensable first step in the peaceful resolution of the Cuban crisis."[21] President Kennedy said simply, "U Thant has put the world deeply in his debt."[22]

The United Nations had for the first time mediated between the superpowers. This was the work not of the Security Council but of the Secretary-General. It was a demonstration that at the height of the Cold War, with the Council deadlocked, the head of the United Nations, as the world's preeminent diplomat, could de-escalate tensions and prevent a potentially cataclysmic war.

The Afro-Asian countries had embraced the UN and were determined to make it work. A little over a year before, they had helped establish the broader Non-Aligned Movement as a new force for peace in global politics. Thant and his team—Loutfi, Rikhye, and Narasimhan—had acted on their behalf.

The peaceful resolution of the Cuban Missile Crisis could now be a catalyst. President Kennedy himself explicitly linked the successful end to the crisis with future détente—an easing of tensions between the US and USSR.[23] But Thant and the leaders of the Non-Aligned Movement wanted to think bigger.[24] They had for years imagined a new international order grounded in the sovereign equality of nations. They saw no reason why they could not now work together, in a new internationalist spirit, to combat racism and colonialism and turbocharge the economic development of the Third World.

But first, there was unfinished business in the Congo.

5 | GRAND SLAM

THANT GREW UP IN a multicultural world. Every morning as a young child, he stood with his mother, Nan Thaung, outside their teak house in the Irrawaddy delta to offer alms to the passing Buddhist monks. Heads shaven, in tobacco-colored robes, the monks carried lacquer bowls, into which Thant and his mother scooped rice with a big copper spoon. From age six, Thant walked alone, dressed in a cotton *paso* (a kind of sarong), a starched white shirt, and velvet slippers, along a winding road of burned brick, past the banana groves and tamarind trees, to his school, where, alongside mathematics, history, science, and Burmese, English was taught by a Bengali Hindu named K. Bhattacharya. When he returned home, his mother prepared sweet, milky tea with Huntley and Palmer or Peek Freans biscuits.

An early love of English was encouraged by Thant's father, Po Hnit, who had studied in Calcutta and had a small library of Victorian and Edwardian books. Occasionally, after school, Thant entertained his classmates by retelling the stories he'd read: *Lorna Doone*, set in seventeenth-century England, and the adventures of Stanley and Livingstone, speaking mostly in Burmese with excerpts from the original English.

In 1920, he met a European for the first time, an officer of the Glasgow-owned Irrawaddy Flotilla Company who was touring the district. Thant was introduced as the best student in his class and after his brief conversation with the eleven-year-old, the visitor was impressed "at this permeation of English culture into the hinterland."[1]

Burma was then a province of the British Indian Empire, conquered over the nineteenth century through three Anglo-Burmese Wars. It was a frontier, guarding the approaches to China and French Indochina, a land of tigers and elephants, desert kingdoms and snowcapped mountains, teak forests and ruby mines. The British had overthrown the king, created a new capitalist economy, and integrated that economy into their imperial market. Millions of people from the rest of British India, Tamils and Punjabis, Bengalis and Pathans, as well as others from across China and the British Isles, immigrated to Burma in search of a better life. Thant's home region, the Irrawaddy delta, was transformed into the world's biggest exporter of rice. For a while, the economy boomed.

Thant during his student days at Rangoon University.

Thant's family were of mixed Burmese Buddhist and Indian Muslim ancestry. They were affluent landowners and businessmen who had done well under colonial rule. By the time of Thant's childhood, in the 1910s, the patriarch of the family had amassed hundreds of acres of prime paddy land as well as a multimillion-rupee fortune (the equivalent of tens of millions of dollars today). He had no children of his own and Thant's father, who was his nephew and business partner, was seen as his heir. But when the patriarch suddenly died, another branch of the family seized the old man's assets.

Thant's father went to court seeking at least a portion of the estate. But then he too died suddenly and somewhat mysteriously, in the middle of the night. Thant's forty-two-year-old mother was left with only the house in which she lived and four boys to look after. Thant, then fourteen, was the eldest.

For years, Thant's mother tried to win back their inheritance, taking the case all the way to Rangoon's High Court, but failed when the distant relatives bribed the judge. Thant accompanied her on the twenty-four-hour journey by paddle-wheel steamer, taking with them mosquito nets, food, and cooking utensils. It was his first time outside Pantanaw. In Rangoon, they worshipped at the 300-foot-high Shwedagon Pagoda and rode electric trams past the city's many churches, mosques, and Hindu temples. One afternoon, they sat on the grass by the city's lotus-strewn Royal Lake as the Prince of Wales was rowed across in a gilded barge.

Thant had dreamed of a career in the elite Indian Civil Service. But that required a university degree, and he was now too poor to afford one. He decided that he would attend Rangoon University, but for just two years, and then teach at a school in Pantanaw. That would enable him to pay for his younger brothers to go to university, and it would give him time to write.

So, from the late 1920s until 1947, the future UN Secretary-General remained in his ramshackle riverine town, teaching, administering, and raising funds for his perpetually cash-strapped school, through the Great Depression, waves of anti-colonial strikes and demonstrations, the Second World War, and the fight for independence. He became the school's headmaster and one of the town's leading figures. But he tried to be part of a bigger world, too.

The weekly steamship brought new titles from Smart and Mookerdum in Rangoon (also the favorite bookshop of Eric Blair, later known as George Orwell, who was serving as a policeman in Burma at the time), as well as newspapers and magazines from London and Calcutta. At Rangoon University, Thant's mentor was J. S. Furnivall, a civil servant turned scholar who coined the term "plural society" to mean a place, like Burma, where a medley of races and religions mixed but did not combine.

Furnivall set up the Burma Book Club and Thant, a founding member, became an avid consumer of the Fabian socialist ideas circulating at the time. He collected works by H. G. Wells, Bertrand Russell, and Sidney and Beatrice Webb. He also joined London's Left Book Club, the first person in Burma to do so. At a time when many young men in Burma were attracted to the fiery advocates of Fascism and Communism rising on the global stage, the young headmaster was drawn to the Book Club's founder, Sir Stafford Cripps, an earnest Labour Party lawyer and parliamentarian.

Thant also became a prolific writer of letters to the editor, essays, and books, in both Burmese and English. For years, he penned a monthly column, "From My School Window," in which he campaigned for a more liberal approach to education, opposing, for example, the proposal that students wear uniforms. Yes, uniforms could hide inequalities in wealth, but, he argued, the harm done would be greater than the good: "The hardest fight our schools should wage," he wrote, "is the fight against the standardization in human life." Instead, he contended, only when schools are organized as "instruments of expression, self-education, creative-living" would the "meaning of freedom be gradually understood."[2]

He was a liberal, but skeptical of politics and politicians. While at university, he derided the leading political figures in Burma as "England-returned barristers (some of them quite scatter-brained) towering over the scene in their tails and bow ties, striking poses, speaking bad English at political meetings to people who understood no English and therefore liked the speeches very much."[3] He wrote frequently on the need for a tolerant society.

Once keen on an imperial career, he came to detest colonialism and taught his students about Sinn Fein in Ireland, and Mahatma Gandhi, Jawaharlal Nehru, and their nonviolent struggle for home rule in India. More than once he stood up for his fellow teachers when they were accused of plotting against the British. Yet he consistently railed against those in Burma who offered easy solutions, politicians who promised quick fixes for the country's deepening social and economic ills. Thant saw himself as a pragmatist above all.

In early December 1962, just days after the end of the Cuban Missile Crisis and his confirmation as Secretary-General for a full five-year term, Thant gave his first policy speech. He titled it "East-West Relations and the United Nations," and argued that the United Nations, rather than being home to "starry-eyed idealists and moralists," needed to be the center of "hard-headed, enlightened self-interest" and the "pragmatic executive action" essential to address the challenges of this "shrinking planet."

Global cooperation was not only necessary but possible, in part because of the shift in the Soviet Union away from the "ruthless" policies of Joseph Stalin to those of Nikita Khrushchev, whom, he said, "we have very good reasons to believe . . . does not want war."

There was an even more important shift, he told his audience: the emergence of the "third element" in global politics, meaning the Afro-Asian and other non-aligned countries, who now represented a majority in the United Nations. This third element had turned the world body into a "Cold War battleground" and this was a good thing, as the Americans and the Soviets would have to move away from their most extreme positions and nurture relations with the non-aligned. As long as this majority actively supported the UN, the Secretary-General could mediate, even between the superpowers. The Cuban crisis had proven this. While the solution was not perfect, Thant said, the UN had helped craft the best possible outcome "in our not perfect world."

He then turned to the crux of his address. The United States, he said, should be on the side of revolutionary change in Asia, Africa, and Latin America. The spectacular material progress of the US had no equal, and democracy there was not inhibited by either conservative tradition or the threat of social upheaval from below. But two world wars and the intervening Depression had "greatly affected American confidence in the continuity of progress," leading many to fear "political and social changes elsewhere." There was, however, no need to worry. "The revolt of the colonial people, who are in fact the ultimate heirs of 1776" and who wish only to "fashion their own way of life," should not be frightening to the "descendants of those who started it all at Lexington and Concord."

Thant had not been on the side of radicals in Burma—the Fascists who fought alongside the Japanese during the Second World War or the Communists who plotted an armed revolution—but he believed the underlying nationalist impulse was unstoppable and had to be managed.

Washington, he argued, needed to worry less about Khrushchev's USSR and instead focus on building bridges with the nations of Africa and Asia. Together, in a spirit of tolerance, they would enable the United Nations to be as effective as possible.

In an essay published a few weeks later, Professor Hans Morgenthau, a leading advocate of "realism" in international relations, criticized the speech, on the grounds that the new head of the UN had done something Hammarskjöld never did: he had positioned himself as "a kind of superego in the conduct of foreign policy," giving his own thoughts on the international scene and advocating "compromise as a universal principle." He also considered Thant "trivial" in distinguishing between Stalin's and Khrushchev's foreign policies and the opportunities the latter presented.[4]

Another realist scholar, Henry Kissinger, who was then teaching at Harvard, was also critical of Thant's speech. In a confidential note to his patron, New York governor Nelson Rockefeller, he found fault with Thant for not clearly "allocating responsibility for the Cold War"—in other words, for not blaming the Soviet Union. Kissinger dismissed the idea that the Cold War "could be solved on the basis of give-and-take on both sides."[5]

Thant likely believed that *he* was the realist—not the academics caught up in their own geopolitical abstractions. He knew he was building political momentum in his role as Secretary-General and began preparations for a final showdown in the Congo. His goal was to crush the Katanga rebellion and then extricate the UN from the central African nation.[6] Over the past year, he and the Kennedy administration had worked together on the "U Thant Plan" for a federal Congo with Katanga enjoying limited autonomy. They agreed that Moïse Tshombe would only respond to increased pressure. The Americans, like Thant, hoped that economic pressure would suffice, but were willing to help build up the UN's military capacity in case it was needed. They were anxious that Thant not resort to force too quickly.[7] Right-wing newspapers in the US and Europe still portrayed Katanga as an underdog deserving of maximum Western support.

In dealing with the financial crisis, the Congo, Papua New Guinea, and most recently Cuba, Thant had listened to advice and consulted extensively, but tended then to plow ahead without looking back. One aide remarked that Thant "cannot stand people who deliberately mislead, procrastinate, or fake—and he shows it."[8] Another observed that "every now and then you will hear that voice rise just slightly and you recognize what that means." The mild-mannered diplomat was developing a reputation for boldness, and Washington wanted reassurance that on Katanga he would not move too far too fast without their consent.

"When you scrape the patina off this Buddha," said one official, "you find hard metal underneath."[9]

On Sunday, December 16, 1962, Thant met alone in his office with Adlai Stevenson, Stevenson's deputy Charles Yost, and US assistant secretary of state Harlan Cleveland. The Americans asked that the UN accept a US air unit as part of the ONUC force in the Congo. By providing this extra assistance, they could, they said, help ONUC succeed.

The Secretary-General told the Americans that he was fairly confident he could "dispose of the problem" by the end of February. After discussions with President Sukarno, 4,500 Indonesian troops were on their way. The UN air force was being strengthened; eight fighter jets from the Philippines and Ethiopia would soon complement the Swedish planes already there. He intended to immobilize Katanga's army and make any resistance "seem very unwise to Tshombe."

With the Americans taking extensive notes, Thant laid out his specific plan. He would deploy his blue-helmeted troops to key transport hubs, including the railway lines vital for the export of copper and cobalt to Rhodesia. He would then take over the radio station at Elizabethville. And he was in quiet touch with Kenneth Kaunda, the anti-colonial leader of Northern Rhodesia (now Zambia), a British protectorate led by a white supremacist regime. The politics there were changing in no small part due to Kaunda's civil disobedience movement, which was inspired by Martin Luther King Jr. Thant hoped that Kaunda, who would soon become prime minister, could stop his country from being used as a staging ground for white mercenaries heading to Katanga.

Thant told the Americans that there might be a fight, but it would only be to "demonstrate superiority." Tshombe would be compelled to give up. The Secretary-General wanted US help, but he also wanted the optics to be right. He suggested that the Congolese government should ask several countries—the US just one of many—to provide added support for the UN peacekeepers. Instead of unilaterally sending military assistance, the US could respond to the request. Thant asked Stevenson to send details of what Washington wanted to provide as well as their proposed command and control arrangements.

A year before, the British could have overruled him, and the Soviets would have quickly turned against him if he seemed excessively dependent on the Americans. But now, after his handling of the Cuban crisis, he had more room to maneuver, as long as he properly managed his ever-closer relations with Washington.

Thant was not a military man. His instinct was to back his military men to the hilt, including his point man, General Indar Jit Rikhye, who had worked closely with him on Cuba and was back in the Congo as ONUC's commander.

A short, heavy-set man with a broad smile, Rikhye was a Punjabi Hindu Brahmin whose family had in the nineteenth century served at the court of the Sikh maharaja Ranjit Singh. While still a boy, Rikhye had resolved to be a soldier. One day, his father, who did not approve of his ambition, took the young Rikhye to hear a speech by Mahatma Gandhi, undoubtedly hoping that the apostle of nonviolence would have a corrective effect. Afterward, the father and son approached Gandhi for a blessing. Placing his hand on Rikhye's head, Gandhi asked, "What do you plan to do with your life, child?" His father interjected, "The silly boy wants to join the army." Gandhi looked straight into Rikhye's eyes and said, "But that is good. We want good, educated young boys to become officers of the army of free India."[10]

During the Second World War, Rikhye fought with distinction in Iraq and Italy. After Indian independence, he commanded an armored cavalry squadron in Kashmir, against the Pakistani army. In 1956 he was posted to the Sinai to lead India's contingent in the UN's Emergency Force.

Serving under Rikhye was another Indian officer, Major-General Dewan Prem Chand, who was in charge of all UN forces in Katanga. Reporting to Prem Chand, in turn, was an Indian brigade led by Brigadier Reggie Noronha, as well as battalions from Ghana, Sweden, Tunisia, Ireland, and Ethiopia. More than twenty American transport planes, under the agreement just reached, flew in reinforcements along with anti-aircraft guns.[11] It was the first ever international fighting force under the exclusive authority of a United Nations Secretary-General.

In late 1962, ONUC held key positions in Katanga. Other parts of the breakaway province were held by Tshombe's Belgian-trained *gendarmerie* and the white mercenaries who continued to stream in from Northern Rhodesia. Thant's aide Brian Urquhart (a veteran of the British Second Army) thought Tshombe would be foolish to challenge the UN—but this is exactly what he did.

Around Christmas, Tshombe's mercenaries began attacking UN positions. Thant had long passed the point where he had any patience for Tshombe and authorized Operation Grand Slam, with orders to remove the mercenaries and establish full freedom of movement for UN troops. The Secretary-General's chief envoy in Leopoldville, Ghanaian Robert Gardiner, told the press, "We are not going to make the mistake of stopping short this time. This is going to be as decisive as we can make it."[12]

Knowing that the Belgians and the British would panic at the prospect of losing their lucrative concessions, Tshombe threatened to blow up the mines. As they had in the past, London and Brussels piled pressure on Thant. But this time, he held firm. The next morning, ONUC's jet fighters attacked airfields across Katanga, immobilizing Tshombe's planes and cutting off his access to allies in South Africa and the nearby Portuguese-run colonies.[13] The UN's ground forces then went into action, Asians, Africans, Scandinavians, and Irishmen battling against the French Fascist-led white mercenaries and their Katangan soldiers.

In New York, Thant was trying both to back the offensive on the ground and to ensure that pressure from the US and the UK in particular didn't reach a boiling point. He kept his public statements to a minimum, constantly reassuring Washington that he was taking all necessary precautions to avoid unnecessary bloodshed—and unnecessary damage to European investments.

With the fighting dominating global headlines, Thant messaged Rikhye, Prem Chand and Noronha, asking them to pause when it seemed that the mines might be blown up. However, a miraculous "break down in communications" prevented the Secretary-General's cable from reaching his men in time.[14] Indian cavalry units crossed the Lufira River and took the mining town of Jadotville, where a year before a several-thousand-strong Katanga force had overwhelmed an isolated company of Irish peacekeepers.

Secretary of State Dean Rusk phoned Thant to express Washington's "deep concern" that the UN was being excessively harsh on Tshombe. The Katangan leader had been detained to prevent him from blowing up the mines, and Rusk wanted the UN to at least offer Tshombe a role in a political settlement. Thant responded that his officials would speak to Tshombe only if Tshombe stopped making "inflammatory statements." He would have to clearly "renounce his scorched earth policy and grant freedom of movement to the UN."

"Why can't the UN just go and ask Tshombe for the statement it wants?" pleaded Rusk.

"No one wants to see him," Thant replied. It was a reflection of Thant's own irritation as well as the strong feelings of the military men who had been dealing with Tshombe's soldiers for months and who were now on the verge of victory.

He had long tried to reason with Tshombe, but Tshombe had consistently gone back on his word. Everyone at the UN was fed up and Thant told Rusk that he could see no other way. Rusk ended the call by saying he "did not know whether we can follow [Thant] down this trail or not" and "hoped our paths do not diverge." If they did, the secretary of state wanted Thant to know that "there is nothing personal about it."[15]

Thant had staked out his position against the Americans as well as the Europeans. He had to defend his approach against the hard-line Afro-Asian states as well. When Tshombe was released from what was always meant to be a temporary detention, Ghana's prime minister Kwame Nkrumah accused the Secretariat of "vacillation and lack of resolution." Thant replied aggressively, writing that he "took exception" to Nkrumah's charge of vacillation. Political as well as military calculations had to be made before taking any step: "You may have mistaken this for vacillation, but I assure you we would not be as far advanced in the Congo if this principle were not followed." Thant explained that if Tshombe or anyone else incited violence against ONUC, he would certainly be arrested, but the UN was not in the Congo, or anywhere else, to intervene in internal politics and put officials in office or remove them. Doing so, he declared, would be "ruinous" to the UN.[16] An increasingly confident Thant was charting his own course, distinct from both the big powers and the giants of the Afro-Asian world such as Nkrumah.

The Belgians and the French reluctantly fell in line and pressured Tshombe, who fled to Northern Rhodesia. The Americans counseled Thant to allow Tshombe to return to Elisabethville, but he refused, wanting Tshombe to understand that his time was up. In mid-January, Tshombe finally accepted the "U Thant Plan" for a federal Congo. Five days later, with military arrangements secured by ONUC's Brigadier Noronha over tea and peanut butter sandwiches, blue-helmeted Indian troops peacefully entered Kolwezi, the last secessionist stronghold in Katanga.[17]

The *Harvard Crimson*, the university's student paper, saw through Thant's strategy better than most publications. Calling him "a much shrewder fellow than anyone ever expected," the paper reflected on how he had outflanked opponents by "innocently announcing" that his troops were not in the Congo to force a solution, and inviting Belgian and British sympathy by sidestepping away from the anti-colonial rhetoric so infuriating to European conservatives. Brussels was now left to "grasp faintly at U Thant's tactful straws."[18]

Speaking at Harvard not long after, Thant noted that the UN's "most hostile critics and detractors" were among those currently expressing alarm that the world organization might soon leave the Congo.[19] He was trying to find an exit, drawing down troops and reducing expenditure, against robust opposition not only from Washington, who wanted the UN's help in shoring up the pro-American regime ensconced in Leopoldville, but even from Europeans, who were finally reconciled to a future without a white supremacist–run Katanga.

Around this time, Ralph Bunche became the Secretary-General's closest political advisor as well as his default mediator. Omar Loutfi had played this role through the Cuban Missile Crisis, but in May 1963 suddenly dropped dead of heart failure while waiting for the elevator near the Delegates' Lounge. At his memorial the next day, Thant described Loutfi as "a good friend" whose "most important characteristic was his evenness of temper and political realism, which served to guard not

Thant and his Congo military chiefs in April 1963.

only himself but all of us, against excesses of optimism or pessimism... he had those qualities of head and heart which an ideal international civil servant should possess."[20]

Over these months, with the UN's involvement in the Congo winding down, Thant's attention turned to Yemen, the southern Arabian nation along the Red Sea. In 1962, Yemen's theocratic monarchy was overthrown by republican revolutionaries. Neighboring Saudi Arabia was backing the ousted monarch, the Imam, in his attempt to retake power. Egypt's president Gamal Abdel Nasser, who considered the republican government fellow left-wing modernizers, sent troops to support them. The Kennedy administration, hoping to maintain good relations with both Saudi Arabia and Egypt, wanted the fighting to stop—and wanted the UN to stop it.

Washington tried to foist the American diplomat Ellsworth Bunker on Thant as UN envoy, but Thant, wary of appearing too intimate with the Americans, said no. He had already aided the US by preventing a Dutch–Indonesian war. Despite tactical differences, he had steered the Congo crisis toward an outcome satisfactory to Washington. On Cuba, he had even secretly accepted the very specific request to send Khrushchev a second message to turn back all Soviet ships. He was now growing increasingly annoyed that the Americans were taking him for granted. Understanding this, Adlai Stevenson warned Rusk that Thant will "shy away from future US assignments for him no matter how sensible and desirable they may be" if he appeared to be simply following Washington's lead.[21] A National Security Council staffer wrote to McGeorge Bundy that "our effort to sell Bunker to Secretary-General as mediator has struck rock of U Thant's reluctance to seem a US stooge."[22]

Thant chose Bunche as his envoy to Yemen instead. A Harvard-educated Democrat who had served in US intelligence during the war and later in the State Department, Bunche was an old friend of many in the Kennedy administration, including Dean Rusk and Adlai Stevenson. At the same time, Thant trusted Bunche as someone whose loyalty to the UN was beyond reproach.

In Yemen, Bunche met with the republican government and Egyptian army leaders and even traveled to the Iman's stronghold of Marab, the legendary capital of the Queen of Sheba. Back in New York, he and Thant cobbled together a peace plan that involved future non-interference in Yemen by any foreign power and a package of UN assistance.[23] The Americans, however, pressed for a peacekeeping mission, something neither Thant nor Bunche thought a good idea given the desert and mountain terrain, lack of clear front lines, and uncertain political commitments by the different sides.[24] As the Congo imbroglio had demonstrated, the UN was not good at intervening in civil wars.

But Thant relented in the face of unyielding pressure, and rushed two hundred Yugoslav soldiers and a Canadian air unit to Yemen from the Sinai to police a hastily arranged ceasefire.

The mission quickly ran into trouble, as Thant and Bunche had predicted. The small force was withdrawn, and the war sputtered on. Yet Thant had managed, with difficulty, to retain his balance, satisfying the

Americans without seeming to take orders from them. Importantly, he and Bunche were nurturing a closer relationship. Bunche would become Thant's meditator not only in trouble spots around the world but with an often intemperate Washington as well.

In June 1963, President Kennedy spoke at American University on what he said was "the most important topic on earth: world peace." He criticized those who thought peace somehow unattainable and war inevitable, mankind "doomed" and "gripped by forces we cannot control." He called instead for a focus on "a more practical, more attainable peace—based not on a sudden revolution in human nature but on a gradual evolution in human institutions." Central to this was a stronger United Nations which would "develop into a genuine world security system . . . creating conditions under which arms can finally be abolished."[25] In Moscow, Kennedy's words were broadcast in full, without censorship.

Thant sent a letter to the president straight away, praising the speech. "We must work harder than ever to move toward peace and justice," Kennedy wrote back. "You have been in the forefront of this effort. We must now get beyond rhetoric and create conditions which will make possible concrete steps toward concrete goals. I need hardly say that I share your conviction that a stronger United Nations is the key to keeping the peace and creating a genuine world security system."[26] The United Nations, barely twenty years old, was for the first time on stable footing, with both superpowers pleased with its efforts and a membership that reflected the majority of the world.

In August, Thant was invited by both superpowers to attend the signing of the first nuclear test ban treaty. In the Kremlin's vaulted St. Catherine Hall, under weighty chandeliers and white lights set up for the myriad photographers and cameramen, with Adlai Stevenson, Senators William Fulbright and Hubert Humphrey, and nearly the entire Kremlin leadership present, Soviet foreign minister Andrei Gromyko, US secretary of state Dean Rusk, and UK foreign secretary Alec Douglas-Home together signed an accord that would end the explosion of atomic bombs in the atmosphere. There was no reduction in existing nuclear arsenals, but the treaty nonetheless represented a breakthrough in Cold War relations. Thant found himself at the very center of the ceremony, standing behind the three signatories and alongside a beaming Nikita Khrushchev. Afterward, in a glittering ballroom, nearly seventy American, Soviet, and British leaders, together with the Secretary-General, exchanged warm handshakes over caviar and champagne as a band played George Gershwin's "Love Walked In."[27]

Khrushchev assumed the role of host with gusto and kept Thant constantly by his side. He told Humphrey that anyone who opposed the treaty needed "psychiatric treatment"; the Chinese had refused to have anything to do with the treaty, as had the French. In his speech to seventy leaders from the atomic powers, Thant called for talks on the reduction of atomic weapons and the creation of "de-nuclearized zones" in Asia and Africa.

Thant believed that the non-aligned countries had helped set the stage for this event by "year after year" calling for disarmament to be the priority. The actual moves toward the treaty had been made by Washington and Moscow; however, he contended, the Afro-Asians and other neutral countries had made "a moral impact, a psychological impact" via the United Nations.[28] At the airport in Moscow on his way home, Thant said the atmosphere had been "charged with optimism."[29]

A few weeks later, in New York, Thant hosted a dinner in his thirty-eighth-floor suite for Dean Rusk, Andrei Gromyko, Alec Douglas-Home, and their UN ambassadors. All concurred with Thant's suggestion to begin with efforts to ban nuclear weapons in outer space.[30]

Fifteen years earlier, Thant and his young family had been living in a little Burmese town, a paddle steamer his only connection to the outside world. Now, from his office on top of the United Nations headquarters in midtown Manhattan, the schoolteacher-turned-diplomat could see the Sunshine Biscuit factory across the East River and the beacons on its roof which lit up after dark to guide the planes flying into the airports on Long Island. He had kept Hammarskjöld's Scandinavian furniture, but replaced his predecessor's Picassos, borrowed from the Metropolitan Museum, with Impressionist landscapes and Japanese paintings more to his liking, together with a stone head of a Mayan maize god from Mexico. On the wall near his desk was *The Chariot of Apollo* by the French artist Odilon Redon, which portrayed the boy who foolishly dared to steer the horses of the sun and whom Zeus had killed to save the world.[31]

6 | TURN! TURN! TURN!

THANT LIKED TO ENTERTAIN. Over just a couple of weeks in April 1962, for example, he hosted separate luncheons for President Joao Goulert of Brazil, New York governor Nelson Rockefeller, newspaper magnate William Randolph Hearst, Hollywood producer Robert Benjamin, and British prime minister Harold MacMillan, all in the dining room of his thirty-eighth-floor suite with its picture windows overlooking the Manhattan skyline, the jagged spires of the Chrysler Building and Empire State Building gleaming in the near distance. Grand white-tie dinners, including one around the same time for the Shah and Empress of Iran, were held downstairs in the Delegates' Dining Room, where the floor-to-ceiling windows offered sweeping views of a darkened East River. There were many luncheons as well with senior aides and assortments of ambassadors.

At the end of that month, Thant hosted the Duke and Duchess of Windsor at a luncheon of "filet de boeuf" and "soufflé Alaska." The social columnist Elsa Maxwell, also a guest, headlined her weekly piece "Thant Proves a Charming Host at Lunch."[1] "Young, gentle, with a fine sense of humor," Thant was, Maxwell told her considerable readership, "down to earth in discussing the various world problems with ease and authority . . . and though from the East, a good mixer."

Given the UN's financial straits, Thant paid for some of the lunches from his personal entertainment allowance, which he could spend or pocket as he pleased. He also chose the menus from options provided by the catering department, favoring what he thought his Western guests would prefer, such as steak with soup and salad, and avoiding the Asian cuisine that was sometimes suggested. For dessert he usually went with cheese, though in the instructions he would scribble "cake for me."[2]

Meals on the thirty-eighth floor were well lubricated with cocktails, champagne, and brandy. Daiquiris quickly became Thant's favorite aperitif, always enjoyed with a cigar, more recently Partagas from Cuba rather than his Burmese imports. A humidor given to him by Fidel Castro enjoyed pride of place near his desk. As he was not a wine aficionado, he ordered his *chef de cabinet*, C. V. Narasimhan, to study the wine list in the Secretariat's commissariat and scout around the city for good deals.

Narasimhan's other special assignment was to provide at lunch every day a mango pickle called *avakaya*, a potent mix of green mangos, red chilis, garlic and other spices, which was a specialty of his native Andhra Pradesh. The pickle became a favorite of British ambassador Sir Patrick Dean as well as the Soviet under secretary, Nikolai Federenko, both of whom would ask for the "C. V. Special" immediately they sat down. Ralph Bunche avoided the pickle, and was happiest when Thant included him in cake and ice cream.

These gatherings were almost always lighthearted affairs, as Thant's main vehicle for bringing people together and fostering a relaxed and jovial mood. He might wheel out well-worn jokes while veteran UN hands recounted their most amusing anecdotes. Visiting presidents and prime ministers mixed with ambassadors from countries on the other side of the Cold War divide. The luncheons were also a way of helping recently arrived Afro-Asian ambassadors familiarize themselves with the UN world. Afterward, in private, over coffee in his office, Thant answered questions from the novice ambassadors and gave them tips on living in New York.[3]

A regular at the Secretary-General's table was Alex Quaison-Sackey, the Ghanaian ambassador. Like Thant, he was portrayed in the American media as "the soul of compromise," his "steely" nature belied by the "moderation" he exuded in public.[4] Other regulars included Bunche and Thant's two closest ambassadorial friends, Adlai Stevenson and Sweden's Agda Rössel, the sole woman ambassador at the UN, whose dark, carefully coiffed hair was dramatically accented by a shock of white. All helped Thant set a friendly tone.

Delegates from Africa sometimes wore national dress, and Alex Quaison-Sackey occasionally matched his richly colored robes with a carved walking stick. Thant, however, never wore Burmese dress at the UN. Perhaps he didn't want to risk appearing outlandish; more likely, he preferred suits, which he had tailored at Brooks Brothers on Fifth Avenue. His fashionably cut navy and charcoal herringbones and pinstripes, complemented by Egyptian poplin shirts and striped ties, even caught the attention of *Tailor and Cutter*, the official magazine of the British tailoring trade, which reckoned the Secretary-General "a more elegant figure than any other world leader." In a world of ill-fitting machine-stitched suits, Thant was, they opined, the "man to lead a sartorial revolt among diplomats and statesmen."[5]

The UN was a society with its own social hierarchy and protocol. It was more racially mixed than it had been a decade before, but its top ranks remained almost exclusively male. The organization's first Secretary-General, the Norwegian Trygve Lie, had to make do for much of his tenure with the temporary UN headquarters, first in the Bronx and later on Long Island, and occasionally treated ambassadors to hot dogs at Yankee Stadium baseball games. Dag Hammarskjöld spent much of his spare time perfecting the UN's new headquarters, adding a new library as well as a dark and austere meditation room; his tenure involved few social events. Now, the Burmese Secretary-General was adding a ceremonial element to his diplomatic role, with his own chief of protocol, the Belgian count Pierre de Meulemeester, carefully stage-managing the ascent of visiting dignitaries from the Secretariat's First Avenue entrance to the thirty-eighth floor.[6]

Even Staff Day, the annual gathering of UN civil servants, became a glamorous event. In September 1963, the festivity included black-tie drinks followed by music in the General Assembly Hall. Frank Sinatra was the emcee as well as the star entertainer. There was tumultuous applause as Thant entered the domed chamber and "in his mellifluous dry monotone" introduced the singer as "one of humanity's great lifters of spirits." A smiling Sinatra, then under scrutiny for his alleged ties to Chicago mobster Sam Giancana, lit a cigarette, thanked Thant, and said it was important to take some time to relax, with all the "hot spots around the world, in the Congo, Vietnam, and Lake Tahoe. Anybody want to buy a used casino?"[7]

Sinatra brought with him the actress Jill St. John, who wore an emerald satin evening gown. She approached Phillip Lambro, who was organizing the event, and asked, "Would you do me a great favor? I'm just so impressed with Mr. Thant. Could you arrange for me to have my picture taken with him?" After Sinatra sang "They Can't Take That Away from Me," "I Get a Kick Out of You," and a few other hits, St. John again pressed Lambro for the photograph, which she insisted should be of just the two of them. Thant readily agreed. Sinatra too made a request: "You know, in all my years in show business, I've never asked for anyone's autograph, but it would be a privilege to have U Thant autograph one of the photos we took together."[8]

Two weeks later, on September 20, 1963, Thant welcomed President Kennedy to the UN. The two had not met in person since before the Cuban crisis.[9] As the president was escorted to the thirty-eighth floor, Ralph Bunche noticed that Kennedy was in considerable pain, walking with difficulty and clenching his fists. He asked to lie down and was taken to the private bedroom, where Timmy's paintings hung on the wall. The White House physician was called, probably, Bunche thought, to "give him an injection." The president also asked for a Bloody Mary.[10]

Before long, Kennedy was well enough to give a rousing address in the General Assembly. He reminded political heads from around the world that just two years before, "some men wondered aloud whether this organization could survive," but today "the clouds have lifted a little so that new rays of hope can break through." He declared that "the conquest of space" should be an international project. And he called for the United Nations to be at the very center of efforts toward world peace, disarmament, an end to discrimination, and global economic development.[11]

Afterward, Thant hosted a luncheon featuring "Le Coq de Cornouaille Roti" and "Le Turban Glacé aux Fruits," with Kennedy, Canadian prime minister Lester Pearson, Soviet foreign minister Andrei Gromyko, and sixty other ministers and ambassadors.

The world seemed to be going Thant's way. He wanted to be a bridge between the West and the new nations of Asia and Africa, and this was what he seemed to have become. He also wanted the UN to be a practical instrument for peace. The day of Kennedy's visit, *The New York Times* portrayed him as "blunt-spoken and tough-acting," a "deceptively placid man," and the first Secretary-General who was able to remain "persona grata on both sides of the Iron Curtain" without "sacrificing his principles."[12] American–Soviet relations were better than at any time since the start of the Cold War, and Thant imagined that progress could soon be made across a range of issues, including the exploration of space. On October 16, the Soviet cosmonauts Yuri Gagarin and Valentina Tereshkova, the first man and the first woman to go to outer space, visited UN headquarters as Thant's guests.

Later that autumn, on November 22, Thant was at a lunch at the Waldorf Astoria with former president Dwight Eisenhower and a group of leading American businessmen supportive of the UN when, just before two o'clock, he received the news that President Kennedy had been shot.[13] Thant rushed back to his office, where he was told that the president was dead.

At a special meeting of the General Assembly convened the following day, a stunned Thant, his voice cracking with emotion, was effusive in his praise, saying that "President Kennedy was a mortal, like the rest of us . . . [but] not so his place in history, where he will live as a great leader who sought peace at home and abroad, and gave his life as a true martyr, in the service of his country, and of all mankind."[14]

Thant and Ralph Bunche, in rented morning coats and striped trousers, flew to Washington for the funeral.[15] At an event at the State

Department that same day, the new president, Lyndon Johnson, told the assembled staff that he intended to continue Kennedy's policies "in the field of international cooperation." Adlai Stevenson suggested to Johnson that he reaffirm American's continuing support in an upcoming speech at the UN. Fine, replied Johnson, "but make it strong."

The next day, Thant met Johnson at a reception. With a vigorous handshake, the tall Texan proclaimed, "It would be hard to be a more vigorous and effective supporter of the UN than President Kennedy was, but if I can manage it, that's what I will be."[16]

Thant realized that Kennedy's death was a blow to the world organization, but he had little reason to suspect any major shifts in US foreign policy. The new president had retained Kennedy's entire foreign policy team, including Stevenson as UN ambassador. In any case, Thant was keen to press ahead with two of the agendas that preoccupied him and others from the ex-colonial world: economic development and the fight against racism. These were not separate agendas; they were linked in a single vision of global equality.

A year earlier, at the University of São Paolo, Thant had argued that the "widening gap between the industrialized nations and the developing countries in Asia, Africa, and Latin America" was even "more dangerous, more explosive" than "ideological differences" between East and West.[17] He was building on ideas that went back to the first Afro-Asian conference at Bandung in 1955. Average per capita income in developing countries was then just over $150 a year, compared to more than ten times that amount in the industrialized world.[18] Western capitalist economies were powering ahead. The planned economies of the Soviet bloc were growing even faster.

In speeches and interviews, Thant underlined his conviction that development for the Third World had to mean industrialization. And central to industrialization, he said, was the transfer of scientific and technological know-how, access to capital, and access to the markets of the rich countries.[19] Thant often gave the example of solar power as a new technology that could remake less developed economies.

At the same time, he warned of the "disruptions which may be caused by a superimposition of modern knowledge and techniques on a society whose habits and thinking, methods of work and way of life are entirely unprepared for them." The former school headmaster's answer was a "vigorous" parallel effort to improve education.[20]

Over the late 1950s and early 1960s, the Afro-Asians allied with the Latin Americans at the UN to drive a sweeping new economic agenda. The Afro-Asians imagined that independence would quickly lead to economic transformation, but the Latin Americans knew that industrialization would remain elusive without changes in a global trading system skewed in favor of the rich capitalist world. The Argentine economist Raul Prebisch was then pioneering "dependency theory," the idea that the current system benefited a few rich countries at the expense of poor countries locked into the export of raw materials.[21] Thant met with Prebisch and was impressed by his ideas.

In the spring of 1964, the United Nations Conference on Trade and Development (UNCTAD) was convened in Geneva at the site of the old League of Nations. With 119 governments in attendance, including Che Guevara leading the Cuban delegation, and with Prebisch by his side, Thant spoke of the division of the world into a rich "North" and a poor "South." He pointed to the fabulous new advances taking place in the North in science and technology and the "continued economic bondage" of the South. The choice, he said, was between a fairer economic system for all or "a series of convulsions" that would threaten global peace.[22]

UNCTAD was made a permanent UN body and Thant appointed Prebisch as its head, against strident American opposition.[23] For the Third World, UNCTAD embodied their greatest hope—that national independence would be followed by the remaking of the global economy.

Over those same months, Thant traveled to Africa for the first time. He went first to Morocco, where King Hassan II hosted a black-tie reception, and then to neighboring Algeria, which had finally won its war of independence against the French but was entangled in a border dispute with Morocco. The Algerians had not forgotten the work Thant had done, as Burmese UN ambassador, in support of their Front de Libération Nationale.

At the airport in Algiers, tall, slim President Ahmed Ben Bella, who had led the fight for independence, was at the airport to greet the Secretary-General, together with the entire cabinet and the entire diplomatic corps. Thant was given the reception of a head of state, the first time for any UN chief, with a full military honor guard and a twenty-four-gun salute.

In his several discussions with the socialist revolutionary Ben Bella, Thant attempted to mediate the border conflict, and discussed economic development and future Afro-Asian and Non-Aligned Movement conferences. But the issue that exercised them most was racism.[24] Algeria was at the time energetically backing armed revolutionary movements against white supremacist regimes in southern Africa.

In an address to the National Assembly, Thant branded racial discrimination "an odious human aberration" and said he understood "all too well the emotional, even the furious reaction which racial discrimination, supported by physical force, can engender," as well as the "deep scars" left on its victims. Racism was nowhere near to being eradicated, Thant warned; rather, "in its most virulent form" it was seeking to expand, in parts of Africa especially. Combating "this sickening anomaly" was one of the United Nations' principal tasks.[25] Yet racism should be seen as a kind of "sickness," Thant argued, that arises from "a sense of fear and insecurity rather than from a superior pride"; racists ought to be viewed as "mentally ill" human beings who need to be "rescued and cured from an affliction they sometimes do not even recognize." Otherwise, the Secretary-General said, "hate will only breed hate in a disastrous and vicious circle."[26]

Most Algerians publicly lauded the speech, while in private some wondered how realistic a peaceful approach would be against regimes like those in South Africa and Portuguese-ruled Angola.[27]

Thant was attempting to amplify and at the same time moderate a pivotal issue for his fellow leaders in the Third World. Some in the UK took note. Sam Falle, head of the Foreign Office's UN Department, thought Thant's words in Algeria should be widely circulated in Whitehall. "The United Nations is *not* necessarily a malevolent institution out to interfere with us and do us down," Falle opined in an internal memo, and "U Thant *is* a man of great wisdom. He is in fact astonishingly well-disposed to us and very well balanced on the colonial issues facing the United Nations."[28]

Elsewhere in Africa, the UN had recently wrapped up its operation in the Congo, despite intense pressure, including from Washington, to keep what had dwindled to a 3,000-man force in place. The Indian generals had told Thant that a minimum of 6,000 troops was needed for the operation to be viable, and Thant saw little possibility of financing even half that. Moreover, the same Western countries that had heavily criticized him for his actions in Katanga were the ones most eager for the UN to stay—not, Thant believed, as a proper peacekeeping operation, "but to perform the function of boy scouts or Sunday school teachers."[29] The Congo was still in disarray, with armed factions fighting one another, but as long as foreign intervention was kept at bay, it wasn't, Thant contended, the UN's problem to solve.

Even with the Congo operation concluded, the Secretariat was running four peacekeeping or observer missions: in Kashmir, an operation established in 1949 after the first India–Pakistan war; in Lebanon; in Gaza and the Sinai, between Egyptian and Israeli forces; and in Yemen. Ralph Bunche headed up the Office of Special Political Affairs and his small team, never numbering more than a dozen professionals, had to mobilize and manage thousands of blue-helmeted troops from a multitude of national armies on a shoestring budget.

In 1964, a new peacekeeping challenge was added to the mix, on the eastern Mediterranean island of Cyprus. Tensions between Greek Cypriots and Turkish Cypriots had been brewing for some time, and after independence from Britain was achieved in 1960, the island had quickly veered toward civil war. Many Greek Cypriots wanted to merge with Greece, while Turkish Cypriots demanded the island be partitioned. Violence threatened to draw in both the Greek and the Turkish militaries. This was a serious problem for the Americans, as both were NATO members bordering the Soviet bloc.

As with Yemen, Thant tried to find the right balance with Washington. The Johnson administration wanted to appoint Cold War veteran Dean Acheson as the UN mediator and hold talks at Camp David, but Thant rejected this categorically.[30] Months of less than successful mediation by the UN chief and his envoys ensued. While Thant was in Africa, the Security Council, prodded by Washington, established a peacekeeping operation in Cyprus.

Thant was now responsible for its success even though few governments were interested in funding it and ever fewer in providing troops. Thant was left to go around "like a Buddhist monk with a begging bowl" before Canada, Denmark, Ireland, and Finland stepped into the breach and supplied the troops needed to patrol the new Green Line across the island.[31] The conflict was far from resolved, but at least civil war and a broader regional conflict were avoided.

Financial pressures notwithstanding, the United Nations in 1964 was at the very height of its global standing and influence. The Secretary-General enjoyed good relations with both superpowers as well as with his many allies in the Third World. His Bandung-spirited Afro-Asian beliefs, genial disposition, an instinctive friendliness to the West, fused with a coolly calculated, compromise-seeking pragmatism, was defusing one set of international tensions after another—for now.

The ground would soon shift. But in 1964, even relations with Paris were warming. French journalists were writing positive portraits of the Secretary-General, with the influential *Réalités* magazine reporting that "an era of smiles has replaced a period of acrimony in the relations between the UN and France." In part this was because Algerian independence had removed a principal irritant between the Fifth Republic and New York. But *Réalités* also contrasted Thant's style favorably with Hammarskjöld's, saying that the Swede "viewed his task as a crusade of

Thant and his mother, Nan Thaung, at a Buddhist ceremony in Rangoon in July 1964.

good against evil," while Thant sought compromise. "This moderation," the writer concluded, "explains his growing prestige."[32]

The United Nations was also becoming an ever more frenetic beehive of social activity. Thant's luncheons were exclusive affairs of no more than twenty at most, usually just ten to twelve. The parties given by the 130-plus ambassadors were much bigger affairs. In the early autumn, when the General Assembly was in session and the top dignitaries were in town, there was fierce competition to throw the most popular or extravagant events, all happening against the backdrop of fast-changing fashion and popular music (the Beatles had just played at Shea Stadium). In September, the Greek ambassador hosted five parties in just one week, including two big receptions. Not to be outdone, the Pakistani ambassador hosted a dozen parties over thirteen days. In October, Adlai Stevenson and the Norwegians co-hosted one of the biggest receptions, in honor of the year's Nobel Peace Prize laureate, Dr. Martin Luther King Jr. American diplomats organized no fewer than ten smaller events for the same occasion.

These gatherings were the lubricants needed for a growing United Nations machine. An average diplomat might attend three or four parties a night. There were dinners as well, conservatively arranged, with guests seated by precedence and men and women still parting company after dessert, the women going into one room for coffee while the men retired to another to chat over brandy and cigars. Parties at the suburban Westchester homes of Ghanaian ambassador Alex Quaison-Sackey and Nigerian ambassador Chief S. O. Adebo were especially popular.[33]

Soon Marietta Tree and other New York society hostesses began inviting some from the diplomatic crowd to mix with professors, playwrights, and politicians. "It is now chic to have an ambassador at one's table," Tree told *The New York Times*.[34]

Still, it wasn't the same world for everyone. African diplomats were celebrated at society dinners, but many were denied basic rights beyond the UN's carpeted corridors. Chad's ambassador, Adam Malick Sow, was accredited both to the UN and to the US government and so needed to drive regularly from New York to Washington. On one occasion he stopped en route for coffee but was refused service; the diner owner's wife explained later that she had no idea he was an ambassador, saying, "He looked like just an ordinary run-of-the-mill nigger to me."[35]

There was violence, too. Youssouf Gueye, a young diplomat from newly independent Mauritania, was assaulted by a gang of "white youths" in Manhattan's Yorkville neighborhood and had to be hospitalized. The police denied that the incident was racially motivated, saying that Gueye had probably been mistaken for a member of a rival "Puerto Rican gang." Incensed African ambassadors, along with their Asian colleagues, called on Thant to raise their concerns with New York's authorities. Several declared that they had been victims of "intolerable incidents" over the years.[36]

For many, housing remained a challenge, as it was for Thant in his early years in New York. One of the Secretary-General's top aides was the Cambridge-educated Godfrey Amachree, a Nigerian who had been the organization's civilian chief in the Congo. Amachree had a large family and wanted to rent a house in Riverdale, near Thant, but when the owner found out that Amachree was "non-Caucasian" he refused to allow a viewing. A complaint filed with the City Commission on Human Rights was dismissed.[37]

There was also discrimination within the bureaucracy. The UN Secretariat was then comprised of approximately 3,500 men and women in New York and another 14,500 elsewhere in the world (not including peacekeepers). The overwhelming majority were from North America and Western Europe. When Thant first became Acting Secretary-General, he received a letter from a Chinese staff member, Wen-Yu Yen, who worked in the library, asserting that many in the Secretariat were only in their jobs "because of their race and color, not by qualifications."

Thant and Soviet premier Nikita Khrushchev in Moscow in July 1964.

Yen had thirty-six years of library experience and had been chief librarian at Peking University before the Communist revolution, yet he was now in a position junior to the library's director, deputy director, and six section heads, all white Americans or Europeans, none of whom had any library education or experience whatsoever.[38]

Most of the top-ranking officials in the Secretariat had never before served under someone who was not white and would have rarely socialized, at least before they came to the UN, with people from Africa or Asia. Hernane Tavares de Sá, a white Brazilian who had been appointed under secretary for public information by Hammarskjöld and was kept on by Thant, had little but scorn for the wives of African diplomats, sneering that "some of them literally cannot communicate, since they speak no civilized language . . . and know only an obscure African dialect."[39] Thant fired him—not for racism but for "certain financial and administrative problems" after he was found to have been passing bad checks in Geneva.[40]

In July 1964, Thant returned to Burma for the first time since he and his family had left in 1957. It was a brief stay, only a few days, hastily arranged and oddly sandwiched between official visits to London, Paris, and Moscow. So he went alone, without Thein Tin. The country had changed dramatically in seven years, and not for the better. A Revolutionary Council headed by General Ne Win had overthrown the elected government, locked up political opponents, cut nearly all external economic ties, and expelled hundreds of thousands of people of Indian descent. The economy was in a tailspin.

As head of the UN, Thant could not become involved in his country's domestic politics. His relationship with the general had always been cordial and Thant wanted to keep it that way. Ne Win, in turn, was wary of antagonizing Burma's most well-known citizen and instead fêted his compatriot at a grand reception and dinner.

Thant spent the little time he had in Burma with friends and family, including his octogenarian mother, over a steady stream of pungent dishes, including curries of giant tiger prawns fresh from the Andaman Sea. His daughter and son-in-law had been in Burma for many weeks; missing them and worried that they might stay longer, he gently tried to persuade them to return with him via Moscow (promising they could meet Khrushchev, too). Together they laid flowers at Timmy's tomb. and Thant gave alms to fifty-five Buddhist monks in the hope of creating good karma for his son in whatever incarnation he was now in. Thant was thinking of his family and of his homeland. But he also thinking more and more of the war brewing nearby, in Vietnam.

7 | VIETNAM

AT A PRESS CONFERENCE in Ottawa in late May 1964, Thant told reporters in a calm and measured voice, "I am against the use of atomic weapons anywhere, under any circumstances. Anybody who proposes the use of atomic weapons is, in my view, out of his mind." He had been asked what he thought of a suggestion by Republican presidential candidate Barry Goldwater that "low-grade" nuclear bombs could be exploded over the Vietnamese jungle to destroy Communist supply lines.

Canada's foreign minister, Paul Martin, who was sitting next to Thant, pounded the table and shouted "Hear! Hear!" Emboldened, the Secretary-General pressed on. "In 1945, when atomic weapons were dropped over Hiroshima and Nagasaki, there was a widespread feeling in many parts of Asia that these deadly weapons were dropped on Japanese cities because the Japanese were non-whites and that they would never have been dropped over cities in Nazi Germany. So, there is a racial element which I could commend to the attention of those who are thinking of launching such atomic blasts."[1]

Thant was in the Canadian capital to meet prime minister Lester Pearson and address a special joint session of Parliament, a rare honor previously bestowed on Winston Churchill, Jawaharlal Nehru, and most recently John F. Kennedy. In the three years since he first took office, Thant had traveled over 120,000 miles across the Americas, Asia, Europe, and Africa, explaining what the UN was doing and why. As importantly, he was feeling the pulse of world opinion and, in private, gaining understanding of the attitudes of world leaders on the big issues of the day.

Over the summer of 1964, his pace quickened. As well as his trip home to Burma, he went to Cairo to attend the first summit of African heads of government, to London to hold talks with prime minister Alec Douglas-Home, to Moscow for three days with Nikita Khrushchev, and to Paris to meet with President Charles de Gaulle. A central topic in all these discussions was the rapidly deteriorating situation in Vietnam.

The monsoon-soaked nation along the Pacific's western shore had been part of French Indochina for much of the nineteenth and early twentieth centuries. At the end of the Second World War, nationalists led by Ho Chi Minh opposed the reimposition of French rule and declared an independent Democratic Republic of Vietnam. As a young man, Ho Chi Minh had spent years in the US, including as a baker in Boston, as well as in France, and had collaborated with the Americans against the Japanese. But he was also a Communist, and as the Cold War heated up, the US turned against its erstwhile ally. From 1945 to 1954, Ho Chi Minh's forces fought a fierce war against the French, whose colonial legions received growing US support. The French lost.

At a conference in Geneva in 1954, the French and the Vietnamese, as well as the UK, Soviet, and Chinese governments, agreed to temporarily partition Vietnam at the 17th parallel, with Vietnamese forces withdrawing to the north and the French to the south. Reunification and elections were to follow a year later. The United States, which took an active part in the peace conference, didn't sign the agreement but "took note" of the ceasefire arrangements and pledged to "refrain from the threat or use of force to disturb them."

Few doubted that Ho Chi Minh would win a clear victory if an election was held. Therefore, Washington opposed elections and instead looked to consolidate a rival Vietnamese state in the south. A new war began between this American-backed, Saigon-based administration and Communist insurgents, assisted by Ho Chi Minh's government in the north. The defense of "South Vietnam" became an American Cold War goal. By the time Lyndon Johnson became president in late 1963, the US had 13,000 military "advisors" reinforcing Saigon's new army.

Thant had been saying for months that the problem in Vietnam was "not essentially military, it is political, and therefore political and diplomatic means alone, in my view, can solve it."[2] In private, he told Adlai Stevenson that the Americans should aim for a broad-based government in Saigon, which would include left-leaning exiles then in Paris.[3]

In July 1964, he called for the Geneva Conference to be reconvened. "Whenever I read of the death of an American or the death of a Vietnamese my heart bleeds," he declared. "It makes no difference whether the man killed is an American or a Vietnamese." The 1954 conference had not been organized by the UN as it involved two governments—the Chinese and Vietnamese—that were not United Nations members. Thant therefore rejected the idea that the world organization should be involved this time, but opened the door to a possible peacekeeping role if any agreement was reached.[4]

His remarks made the front pages of newspapers around the world. The Soviets and the French, as well as the non-aligned countries, urged him to help find a solution.[5] The French, having quit Indochina and more recently Algeria, now wanted a speedy American exit as well. Charles de Gaulle, in his tête-à-tête with Thant over a glass of 1954 cognac, expressed Paris's preference for the "neutralization" of South Vietnam. Thant, who desired all of Southeast Asia to be neutral in the Cold War, as Burma was, enthusiastically concurred.

"Neutralization" was the last thing the Americans wanted. In South Vietnam, the tide was turning in favor of the Communists, known as the Viet Cong. They dominated the countryside, and public support for Saigon's corrupt and incompetent military-run regime was ebbing fast. Ordinary people were tired of the fighting, which had been going on almost nonstop since the 1940s, and even the generals who ruled South Vietnam were inching toward a compromise with the North.

What was needed in this situation, Washington's foreign policy chiefs thought, was not diplomacy but military escalation, including the bombing of North Vietnam. Negotiations leading to neutralization, as advocated by Thant and the French, would only play into the hands of Hanoi and ultimately Red China, who they believed would dominate any Vietnam that didn't include a strong pro-American regime in the south.[6]

In early August, the Johnson administration blamed North Vietnam for attacks on US Navy ships in the Gulf of Tonkin. The ships had been spying and supporting South Vietnamese raids along the coast, and Thant, like several members of Congress, believed that the attacks had been deliberately provoked to justify direct US intervention. On August 5, Lyndon Johnson submitted a resolution to Congress that would authorize him to "take all necessary measures" in response to the attacks. It was a request to go to war.

Thant flew to Washington the next day.

Thant had arrived back in New York only a few days earlier. Before leaving, he read a long letter from his friend Ruth Gage-Colby, the leftist peace activist, pointing out that he would be seeing the president on the anniversary of the bombing of Hiroshima. The meeting, she wrote, "may well be one of your most important in your career for peace." The world was entering an "explosive situation," where not only Barry Goldwater (Johnson's opponent in the upcoming presidential election) but his own closest advisors were advocating a deeper military involvement. She recalled the non-aligned countries which had worked with Thant to defuse the Cuban Missile Crisis: "The world can be blown up any day in an atomic holocaust.... Surely, dear U Thant, there must be enough Asian and African members to call for a ceasefire in Southeast Asia."[7]

Accompanied by Ralph Bunche and Adlai Stevenson, Thant was transported in a US military plane from La Guardia Airport's Marine Terminal to Andrews Air Force Base. There, he was received by White House chief of protocol Angier Biddle Duke and helicoptered directly to the South Lawn of the White House, where over a hundred officials had been assembled to greet the Secretary-General, headed by the president himself.

Johnson had started his day a few hours before, meeting in his bedroom with Chicago's mayor, Richard Daley—Johnson's gangly frame stretched out on the bed, Daley next to him in a rocking chair, the president's wife, Lady Bird Johnson, sitting nearby, all drinking coffee and talking about the ongoing "race riots." Johnson had recently signed into law historic civil rights legislation, which he hoped would form part of a bigger domestic agenda aimed at ending poverty and racial injustice.

Now, standing in the hot D.C. sun, Johnson's thoughts were fixed on Vietnam. A masterful politician, he knew he needed to win over the Burmese statesman—or at least prevent him from being a nuisance. A few weeks before, Senator William Fulbright, chair of the Senate's Foreign Relations Committee, had told Johnson that he liked the idea of negotiating with Hanoi, using Thant as broker. But nearly all the president's advisors were telling him that military action alone could win the day. For Johnson, the most important thing was to make sure he won reelection in November.

The president and his Burmese guest shared a strangely similar life trajectory. Both were fifty-five years old, born within a few months of each other. They had attended university at the same time, left after two years for financial reasons, then taught school in a small backwater town, Johnson in rural South Texas, Thant in the Irrawaddy delta. They were married on the same day, November 17, 1934. Both achieved their high offices in tragic circumstances, after the killing of their illustrious predecessors. Parallel lives—but in many ways the two men couldn't have been more different. In contrast to the soft-spoken and cosmopolitan Thant, Johnson was domineering and foul-mouthed, with only a limited interest in international affairs.

The welcoming formalities took place in the Rose Garden. No UN head had ever been received at the White House in this way. There were warm words, hearty handshakes, and smiles for the cameras, the six-foot-five-inch Johnson, in a light gray suit, towering over the Secretary-General. A band played under the big magnolia tree, but there was no military pomp on display. "A very delicate touch," thought Lady Bird Johnson, "for a United Nations ceremony."[8]

National Security Advisor McGeorge Bundy had warned his chief that in addition to Cyprus, Cuba, and the UN's financial woes, the Secretary-General would want to discuss Vietnam and his recent visits to Paris and Moscow. Bundy had graduated at the top of his class at Yale before becoming Dean of Faculty at Harvard in his early thirties. He was seen as a brilliant Cold War strategist and was a strong proponent of American military intervention in Vietnam. Thant, in Bundy's opinion, tended to "speak as a Burmese, rather than a UN official, and has been critical of our present military effort in the area, expressing strong views in favor of an early Geneva Conference . . . He thinks much like de Gaulle on this." Bundy, like many in Washington, was acutely suspicious of the French, believing that their stance on Vietnam was motivated less by an interest in Asian peace and more by a desire to hem in the US's global position.[9] France was staking out its own big-power role in the world, independent of the Americans, NATO—and, indeed, the UN.

Johnson and Thant met alone for about twenty minutes in the Oval Office before being joined by Secretary of State Dean Rusk, Bundy, Stevenson, Bunche, and Assistant Secretary of State Harlan Cleveland.[10] The conversation was almost entirely about Vietnam, and Thant wanted to give Johnson a feeling for the politics in the part of the world he knew best.

He had met Ho Chi Minh in Hanoi ten years previously and described him as a nationalist first and foremost, "deeply influenced by French culture and traditions," and far more amicable toward Moscow than Peking. The two Communist giants were then careening toward open conflict; the US saw China as the more implacable foe. Thus, Thant was hinting that engagement with Ho Chi Minh might prevent Hanoi sliding in Peking's direction. There should be a "private probe," he offered, with Burma as a possible interlocutor.

Johnson was listening, but Bundy interjected, "It doesn't look to us as though the North Vietnamese are ready for political discussion." The bespectacled, sandy-haired scion of Boston's most prominent intellectual families wasn't inclined to give much weight to the views of the Burmese schoolteacher-turned-diplomat.

Undeterred, Thant pointed out that the Rangoon government had managed to "break the back" of its own Communist insurgency without military assistance from the United States or anyone else. China had declared that they would not intervene on the side of the insurgents as long as Rangoon refrained from accepting any "Western bases."

Bundy replied, somewhat disingenuously, that if what the Chinese wanted was to see America out of the region, "on this at least we could agree." There was nothing clearer "than our desire to leave Southeast Asia under the proper conditions."

"We are ready to get out tomorrow if they will behave," Johnson piped in.

The Americans regarded South Vietnam as an independent country requiring protection against Communist aggression, and Communist North Vietnam as an extension of the Communist regime in China. Johnson believed that with the right dose of American power, the security of South Vietnam, like South Korea, could be maintained indefinitely. It was impossible to imagine, in the summer of 1964, that US military might would not be able to bring a Third World country to heel.

Thant's perspective was entirely different. He saw Vietnam as a single country which would eventually be unified. He was anti-Communist, but he believed that whether Vietnam became Communist or not was unimportant in international terms. Foreign intervention would only strengthen radicals and hard-liners.

After an hour, Lady Bird Johnson came in, stood and listened for a few minutes, and then took the Secretary-General for a tour of the White House gardens. The private briefing note had (erroneously) mentioned the Secretary-General's "interest in flowers." Trailed by Johnson and Stevenson a few paces behind Thant, the First Lady pointed out the gaillardia, which she told her guest "grows in masses wild in Texas when it rains" and the "lovely lavenders which, I understand, grows in [your] native Burma."[11]

In an afternoon talk with senior State Department officials, Thant again floated the possibility of an outreach to Hanoi, this time explicitly offering himself as mediator. Rusk, he thought, "seemed receptive." Averell Harriman, a foreign policy advisor to every Democratic president since Franklin Roosevelt, "was enthusiastic." Bundy said nothing.[12]

That evening, Johnson presided over a grand dinner for Thant, by his account the biggest he had yet given at the White House. All of Johnson's senior officials were there, as were more than two dozen leading senators, as many congressmen, and four state governors including Pat Brown from California, nearly all with their wives. Renowned scientists, artists, musicians, and Hollywood celebrities like Gregory Peck had been invited, as well as journalists including David Brinkley and Walter Cronkite. The hawkish Henry Cabot Lodge, former senator, UN ambassador, vice-presidential candidate, and more recently ambassador to South Vietnam, was brought all the way from Saigon. *The Washington Post* called the dinner "a historic assemblage."[13] No UN Secretary-General had ever been honored in this way.

In the state dining room, redecorated three years before by Jacqueline Kennedy in French Empire style, the president and his guests enjoyed a menu of "crabmeat surprise," "chateaubriand White House," and "coppela U Thant," served with California wines. The women wore ball gowns, the men dinner jackets: Thant and Bunche in black, Johnson, Rusk, and many others in summer white.

In giving his toast, Johnson described Thant as "the man who is the public servant of the world." He remarked on their similar life stories, and then declared in a stentorian voice: "We here in the United States take great satisfaction from the success of the United Nations. It is the embodiment and fulfilment of an old American vision." He concluded, "We are so proud, Mr. Secretary-General, to have the United Nations on these shores."

"I am suddenly overwhelmed by the very gracious words of you, Mr. President, not only about the United Nations but also about me," Thant replied, visibly moved. In his prepared remarks, he talked about the UN's pivotal role in preventing war and the importance of practicing tolerance, not only among people but also among states. There was a need for pragmatism and compromise, but also, he said, for a new outlook and a new education.

"It seems to me that pure intellectual development unaccompanied by corresponding moral and spiritual development," he added, "is sure to lead humanity from one crisis to another."[14]

Lady Bird Johnson was delighted with Thant's gift of silverware, "the most magnificent tea and coffee service from Burma that I expect ever to see ... with little animals and flowers." The Johnsons, in return, gave the Secretary-General framed photos taken by astronauts and a letter signed by President Andrew Jackson.

After the meal, the nearly 150 guests were treated to a performance by the popular folk group Peter, Paul, and Mary. There was a sing-along to "Puff the Magic Dragon," with the president and Thant both joining in. As midnight approached, the folk music trio, with Thant, Johnson, and the entire Washington foreign policy establishment arrayed in front of them, including all the architects of the war in Vietnam—Dean Rusk, McGeorge Bundy, Henry Cabot Lodge, Defense Secretary Robert McNamara, and the very members of Congress who would the next morning pass the Gulf of Tonkin Resolution and effectively begin the Vietnam War—sang Bob Dylan's "Blowin' in the Wind":

Yes, and how many deaths will it take 'til he knows
That too many people have died?

Thant spent the night at Blair House, the presidential guest house across Pennsylvania Avenue, before returning to New York the next morning. He felt that Johnson, who had "relished talking about our personal lives [and his] well-researched revelations about me," was "one of the warmest, most informal, and most congenial men to talk to"—but at the same time "juvenile" on international affairs. He had told Thant that "if South Vietnam fell to the Communists, then the next target will be Hawaii."[15] Nevertheless, Thant came away from his day in Washington upbeat, under the impression that he had a green light to try his hand.

Thant had no mandate to work on Vietnam. Neither the Security Council nor the General Assembly—the two bodies of the UN that could authorize his diplomacy—had even debated the conflict, much less asked him to do anything about it. Communist China, North Vietnam, and South Vietnam were not members of the world organization. But Thant was convinced that US military involvement was a recipe for disaster, not just for Vietnam and the United States but for the peaceful global future he and many of his Afro-Asian colleagues had thought was within reach.

The Secretary-General resolved to reach out to Ho Chi Minh discreetly, so as not to alert Peking. Taiwan occupied China's seat at the UN, and Mao Tse-Tung's Communist government saw the UN as little more than an appendage of the White House. Thant had no contact with Peking whatsoever. But he noted that in Rangoon just a few weeks back, the Chinese ambassador had attended a reception in his honor. Thant thought the ambassador's attendance was a good sign. Perhaps the Chinese were sending him a signal.

Thant was in uncharted territory. As the UN had no formal ties with North Vietnam, he decided to send an oral message through his Russian aide Vladimir Suslov without telling the new Soviet ambassador, Nikolai Federenko, with whom he had a frosty relationship.[16] With no official mandate, everything he did had to be kept closely guarded. Suslov was an under secretary, and so a top international civil servant on a level with Ralph Bunche—but, as Thant knew, he was reporting everything he did directly to Moscow through Soviet intelligence. In July, when they met, Khrushchev had encouraged Thant to take the initiative on Vietnam. Thant hoped Moscow would now prove quietly helpful.

Within a fortnight, he received a positive reply from Hanoi via the Soviets. He was elated. He told Adlai Stevenson the good news immediately and a "favorably surprised" Stevenson promised to inform Washington at once.

Over the coming weeks, however, nothing happened. Thant queried Stevenson every few days about a response from either the White House or the State Department. There was none.

Around this time, the Secretary-General visited the World's Fair across the river in Queens, accompanied by Robert Moses, New York's legendary power broker, urban planner, and now president of the fair.

It was a warm, late-summer afternoon, and he rode around in a "glide-a-ride," stopping at the Burmese, Japanese, Spanish, African, Vatican, and American pavilions, all showcasing their varied cultures and achievements. Before he left, he told reporters, "The more you witness this panorama of human creation, the more you feel these things must be preserved—the more averse you are to bitterness and hysteria and war, which could destroy everything. This is the great lesson you learn here."[17]

Thant was growing irritated. He believed that Hanoi was willing to talk, and Washington was missing a genuine opportunity for peace.

In Hanoi, the leadership of the ruling Workers' Party was indeed interested in sitting down with the Americans—if only to further its objective of US withdrawal and the reunification of Vietnam. Over the past years they had consolidated their power through ruthless repression and were now single-minded in their desire to see an end to all foreign intervention. Ho Chi Minh was in his mid-seventies, and a younger, harder-line generation within the Workers' Party was gaining the upper hand. Some were also more willing to side with China at a time of mounting Sino-Soviet competition. For the Vietnamese Communists, the objective of complete victory was not up for negotiation. But "complex forms and methods" could be employed to reach that objective.[18]

On October 5, the prime minister, Pham Van Dong, traveled to Peking to see Chairman Mao and Premier Chou En-lai. The Chinese were playing their own game. They had no wish to start another war with the Americans—a little over a decade previously half a million Chinese soldiers had been killed or wounded in Korea. They were indifferent on the subject of Vietnamese reunification. But they wanted the Hanoi government closer to them than to the Russians.

Mao advised Pham not to send North Vietnamese troops south. The Americans are making "all kinds of scary statements," Mao boasted, but they do not want to fight China in a "big war." Pham agreed that provoking the Americans at this time was unnecessary.

Mao asked, "Is it true that you are invited to attend the Security Council meetings?"

Chou: "That is still a secret. The invitation was made through U Thant."

Mao: "And U Thant made it through whom?"

Chou: "The Soviets."

Mao: "So, the Soviet Union is the middleman."

Pham: "According to the Soviet ambassador to Vietnam, they met with U Thant on the one hand and with Rusk on the other."

Mao: "It is not completely a bad thing to negotiate. You have already earned the qualification to negotiate. It is another matter whether or not the negotiation will succeed..."[19]

The two Asian Communists may have mixed up Thant's outreach via the Soviets and an American suggestion that both North and South Vietnam be included in a future Security Council discussion. In any case, what seems clear is that the Chinese were not adamantly opposed to talks. Neither were the Vietnamese.

In early October 1964, a frustrated Thant again asked Stevenson what was happening in Washington, and Stevenson counseled patience, explaining that Johnson was preoccupied with the upcoming election. In addition, he claimed Washington had "checked" to see if Hanoi was "serious" and concluded they were not. Thant asked how this checking had taken place and was told it had been done by a Canadian diplomat, J. Blair Seaborn, who was stationed in Hanoi as part of the International Control Commission. The ICC was a body set up after the 1954 Geneva Conference but was now inactive.

Thant was impatient because he knew Hanoi was waiting for an answer and also because his own credibility was on the line. He was nervous especially about his relationship with the Soviets. On October 14, Khrushchev was overthrown in a Kremlin power struggle. As the news broke in New York, Thant felt he had to say something and told an electrified press briefing at the UN that Khrushchev, who was being held incommunicado, should be allowed to make a statement "on the circumstances leading to his exit." As UN chief, it was not his business to comment on political change in any country, but he had developed a genuine regard for Khrushchev, whom, he believed, had moved the USSR away from the dark days of Stalinist rule. He praised the ex-Kremlin boss as a man of peace.[20]

Thant worried that his relationship with the Kremlin's new rulers, Alexei Kosygin and Leonid Brezhnev, was a precarious one. The Soviets were still dragging their feet on UN funding and refusing to pay their peacekeeping dues. Washington, in turn, was threatening to activate a provision in the UN Charter which decreed that non-payment would lead to a suspension of voting rights. Thant feared that if this happened, the Soviets and their allies might then walk out of the world body. He also realized that the Soviets had gambled on his Vietnam initiative. Moscow's ties with Peking were growing more acrimonious by the day and the USSR couldn't afford to lose North Vietnam in any future struggle with Mao over leadership of the Communist world. The Soviets had agreed to be a conduit for the UN chief but were adamant that their role be kept under wraps (it's unclear whether they knew the Chinese were already aware of their assistance to the Secretary-General). They didn't want to give Peking any opportunity to claim Moscow was in cahoots with New York and Washington in trying to dampen Vietnam's drive for independence and reunification.

It was Khrushchev who had encouraged Thant. If Washington didn't respond, the new Kremlin leadership might see Thant as a spent force who couldn't even bring the Americans to preliminary talks.

A few weeks later, an increasingly despondent Thant met Canada's foreign minister, Paul Martin, and asked about Seaborn, the person Stevenson had mentioned. Martin said that Seaborn had no access to top Vietnamese leaders. Thant thought it equally unlikely that the Vietnamese would tell Seaborn about his initiative.[21]

Unknown to Thant, however, Seaborn *had* been secretly delivering messages from Johnson. In June, the Canadian diplomat had even met with Prime Minister Pham and informed him that Johnson would provide billions of dollars in aid if North Vietnam would give up on reunification. He also passed on threats from Johnson that American bombing could turn his country into a "wasteland." By the time Thant met with Martin, the Vietnamese had no further desire to hear from Seaborn.

Thant's proposal may not have been different in form from what had been tried through the Canadians—secret communication directly between Washington and Hanoi—but it was entirely different in outlook and strategy. Thant wanted the US to leave Vietnam and to see Vietnam reunified, as the Communists in the North did. But he wanted this to happen over time, with a broad-based government in Saigon that would include the Viet Cong, thus providing the Americans a "face-saving exit" and hopefully moderating Communist rule.[22] He knew that the North Vietnamese would respond differently to an Asian UN Secretary-General than they would to a Canadian delivering an ultimatum from Washington. More than anything, he wanted all of Southeast Asia neutral, so that it would not become a giant Cold War battlefield. Millions of lives were otherwise at risk.

But no one in Washington thought America's military prowess couldn't eventually dictate outcomes, even halfway around the world.

Around this time Thant attended a lunch organized by "UN We Believe," which brought together the organization's biggest supporters in the American business community, including the heads of Pepsi, Proctor and Gamble, Macy's, New York Life Insurance, and dozens of other companies.

The guest of honor was Thant's friend Sol Linowitz, the chairman of Xerox, who had donated $4 million for the production of six television dramas about the work of the UN, including "A Carol for Another Christmas," an updated version of Dickens's tale in which an American industrialist finally understands the importance of global cooperation. Rod Serling, Ian Fleming, Peter Sellers, Yul Brynner, Omar Sharif, Rita Hayworth, and Princess Grace of Monaco had all taken part. The well-intentioned series received mixed critical reviews.[23] But the project demonstrated an impressively broad base of American support.

This public support, however, would mean little if his relationship with the president soured. On November 3, 1964, Johnson won a landslide victory over Republican Barry Goldwater. But his administration was still not responding to Thant's most important peace initiative since the Cuban Missile Crisis.

At the beginning of December, Thant met with Soviet foreign minister Andrei Gromyko, and noticed at the meeting that Suslov and Federenko were no longer on speaking terms. He mentioned to Gromyko that he had used Suslov to pass messages to Hanoi, at which the steely Cold Warrior simply nodded. There were no assurances on Soviet funding for the UN.

To top things off, the crisis in the Congo reignited with a vengeance. After Thant pulled UN troops out of the Congo the previous summer, African states had tried to coordinate plans to aid the hapless nation. But the US and other Western powers had schemed to install Moïse Tshombe, the erstwhile Katangan secessionist leader and white supremacist puppet—whom Tanzania's president, Julius Nyerere, had called a "pawn of colonial, financial and racist interests who regard Africa as their property and Africans as less than human"[24]—as prime minister of the *entire* Congo. African leaders were dismayed.

A left-wing rebellion centered in Stanleyville, a onetime Lumumba stronghold in the northeast of the country, quickly gained ground with Soviet and Chinese support. The Belgians responded by mobilizing a new mercenary army under the command of the British soldier of fortune Michael "Mad Mike" Hoare. As Hoare's forces advanced on Stanleyville, the rebels seized and threated to kill several hundred hostages, mostly Americans and Belgians. A Belgian brigade was then parachuted into the area from US Air Force planes. Unlike Kennedy, Johnson had no qualms about working closely with the British and the Belgians to promote Western interests in the Congo. The West called the action a "humanitarian intervention." The mercenary army soon butchered as many as 20,000 Congolese believed to have sided with the rebellion.[25]

Thant was feeling increasingly unwell. On December 3, he canceled a meeting with the prime minister of Malta and left for his house in Riverdale. His spokesman said the cancelation was due to a cold and overwork. At home, looking pale and weary, he asked his wife for a ginger salad and went to bed.

The next morning, he returned to work so as not to miss a meeting with Martin Luther King Jr., who was on his way to Oslo to receive the Nobel Peace Prize. As an admirer of Mahatma Gandhi's nonviolent protests in India, Thant was impressed by King's fight for racial equality. In his thirty-eighth-floor suite, he hosted a luncheon for King and his wife, Coretta Scott King, attended by Ralph Bunche and the ambassadors from Ghana, Nigeria, India, France, the US, the USSR, and the UK. Bunche, a leading figure in the civil rights movement, had attended the June 1963 funeral of the slain activist Medgar Evers in Jackson, Mississippi, and in August 1964, together with 250,000 Americans, had marched in Washington and heard King deliver his "I have a dream" speech.[26]

King felt that the "the spirit of the United Nations" as well as the "facts shared" by those at the meal were "extremely valuable in broadening my perspective and deepening my insight into our world dilemmas of peace, poverty, and racism."[27] In a private chat afterward, Thant shared his thinking on Vietnam.

A few hours later, Thant collapsed.

He was rushed by ambulance to the Le Roy Hospital on 61st Street, where he was diagnosed with a bleeding ulcer. He had been eating lots of steak and cake and putting on weight, chain-smoking cigars, and taking over-the-counter antihistamines for recurrent headaches. The doctors told him he needed a vacation. Since becoming Secretary-General three years before, he had traveled to thirty-two countries.[28] Other than Sundays, he had not taken a single day off.

While Thant was in hospital, an emergency meeting of the Security Council was convened to discuss events in the Congo. After the American- and British-backed Belgian operation, a wave of fury had swept across Africa. In New York, the foreign minister of Congo-Brazzaville (a former French possession just west of the Congo) called the Western military intervention "the most ruthless and scandalous aggression of our era." The Guinea foreign minister accused "self-styled civilized countries of caring no more about Africans killed in the Congo than about

US ambassador Adlai Stevenson, former French premier Edgar Jean Faure, Jacqueline Kennedy, Ambassador Alex Quaison-Sackey of Ghana, and other guests at one of Thant's luncheons on the thirty-eighth floor in February 1965.

American citizens with black skins murdered in Mississippi." The Czech foreign minister compared the appeal by whites in Stanleyville to the appeal by Sudetenland Germans to Adolf Hitler in 1938.[29] It was a racially charged debate. There were heated calls for UN action.

In an unrelated development, early in the morning of the same day, American intelligence informed Thant's *chef de cabinet* C. V. Narasimhan that two Cuban émigrés were plotting to kill Che Guevara—an Argentinian Marxist and a top figure in the Cuban revolution—that day in the General Assembly.

Narasimhan, "in guarded language," briefed Thant over the phone and Thant instructed him to take "any steps you deem necessary . . . and you can be sure that I will support any action that you take."[30] Narasimhan consulted with Alex Quaison-Sackey, Ghana's ambassador, who was serving as the year's president of the General Assembly, and they decided that no one should be allowed into the hall except the diplomats of their respective missions. They soon discovered that the Nicaraguan mission had applied for fifty guest passes. The Nicaraguans were sworn enemies of Castro. The guest passes were canceled.

Sitting on the General Assembly rostrum, behind the podium where Che Guevara was about to speak, a nervous Quaison-Sackey asked Narasimhan, "C. V., what happens if the assassin misses Guevara and hits me?" Unknown to both men, the émigré Cuban marksmen had been unable to get into the building and so had crossed to the other side of the East River. From there, they fired two bazooka shells at the UN. Because of a faulty sighting mechanism, the shells fell into the river just yards short of a packed Security Council chamber where an impassioned Congo debate was in full flow.

The two men were apprehended but then released by US authorities, ostensibly for lack of evidence. Che Guevara was able to deliver his multi-hour tirade against American imperialism unhindered.[31]

A week later, Thant was informed by Adlai Stevenson that there was still no news from Washington on his proposal for secret talks with Hanoi. He was discharged from the hospital and spent a few days at home, where he was forced to confine himself to meals from a "bland" menu including white toast, Rice Krispies, and Jell-O.[32] After Christmas, with two trusted security aides, a pair of swim trunks, and a few books and magazines, the fifty-five-year-old Secretary-General flew to the US Virgin Islands for his first quiet break.

In Washington, Lyndon Johnson, his reelection secured, was getting ready to send the first American combat troops to Vietnam.

8 | ROLLING THUNDER

ON NEW YEAR'S DAY 1965, the UN chief sent home a postcard showing little sailboats and the white sands of St. John's in the Virgin Islands. "Am feeling very well," he wrote, "Thoughts of home, affectionately, Thant." There were no phone calls from New York, and for a few days he was spared the goings-on at the UN and around the world. However, he may well have been assessing his changing fortunes.

Over the past three years, since first becoming Acting Secretary-General, Thant had managed to find the right blend of language and policies to keep his Afro-Asian and non-aligned colleagues pleased, the United States invested, and the Soviets satisfied enough in his leadership that they were at least not seeking to undermine him.

The UN had not only survived but appeared more stable than ever, incorporating scores of newly independent states, all of which welcomed their first chance ever to have a voice at a global table. And he could point to a string of successes, from crushing the Katanga secession in the Congo to the de-escalation of the Cuban Missile Crisis.

But the ground beneath his thirty-eighth-floor perch was beginning to sway. Lyndon Johnson had few of his predecessor's internationalist instincts. With the immediate shine of independence wearing thin, several Afro-Asian states were facing internal turmoil or veering in less than savory directions, Burma included. And the Secretary-General's most prominent backers in the Third World, such as Jawaharlal Nehru, were dead or about to be pushed out in (primarily US-encouraged) military coups. To top things off, the Soviets were still dragging their feet on paying their dues, despite Thant's constant pleas.

All these challenges seemed manageable. The UN could still climb new heights. But now a ferocious war was gaining pace in Southeast Asia.

Thant was aware that he came from a poor Asian country and that no one who looked like him had ever negotiated between the big powers. In their meetings with him, the leaders of the US, UK, and France would never have thought of accommodating his Burmese background and culture. The Anglo-American elites and other Western statesmen and diplomats, alumni of the world's top universities, could be themselves around him. But Thant had to manage a special version of himself, keeping up an image that those who had grown up in a white-only world could respect. He knew that whatever prestige he had garnered was fragile.

Over the coming months, the one-time Burmese schoolmaster would have to determine how far he was willing to go in confronting the world's biggest power on what was fast becoming the pivotal international question of the day: Vietnam.

On his return to a freezing New York, under half a foot of powdery snow, a freshly tanned Secretary-General asked to see Charles Yost, the US deputy ambassador, as Adlai Stevenson was away on holiday. Thant was hopeful that, after four months, there might finally be word from Washington about his Hanoi initiative. Yost replied politely that he had no idea what the Secretary-General was talking about. Thant, shocked, informed Ralph Bunche, who was shocked as well. Both remembered Stevenson taking copious notes at all their meetings. Yost phoned Harlan Cleveland at the State Department, who said he had no idea either.

Back in August, Thant thought that he had a green light from Washington to try his hand at exploratory talks. He was wrong. In September, when Thant first informed Stevenson about North Vietnam's positive response to his proposal of secret communications, Stevenson had apparently only told Secretary of State Dean Rusk, by phone, with no written record. Rusk, it now appeared, did not mention the proposal to anyone, and all of President Johnson's advisors were instead readying to escalate the war. The Gulf of Tonkin Resolution had been quickly approved by Congress on August 7, and the internal debates about what action should be taken had effectively closed. While Stevenson may have queried Rusk a few more times over the following months, Rusk never took the proposal seriously.

On January 13, 1965, Stevenson, back from vacation, asked Thant where talks with the Hanoi leadership might take place, "just in case." He had been questioned by both Yost and Cleveland, and probably felt he needed to bring the issue to a head. Thant said there were five places where both Washington and Hanoi had diplomats—Pakistan, Switzerland, France, Cambodia, and Burma—and suggested Burma as the best choice. He had already checked with General Ne Win, who agreed to host a meeting in Rangoon and keep it secret.

Stevenson understood that negotiations with North Vietnam ranked nowhere on the Johnson administration's list of priorities. At this point, the US had over 20,000 military advisors supporting about 500,000 South Vietnamese soldiers and police. But the South Vietnamese forces were being routed by upwards of 40,000 Viet Cong guerrillas, whose large-scale operations were coming perilously close to Saigon. General Maxwell Taylor, Johnson's ambassador in South Vietnam, warned of a "seriously deteriorating situation" which could lead to "the installation of a hostile govt which will ask us to leave while it seeks accommodation with the National Liberation Front and Hanoi."[1]

Defense Secretary Robert McNamara and National Security Advisor McGeorge Bundy jointly advised the president that the US had two options: negotiations to "salvage what little can be preserved," or the use of military might to defeat the Communists. They left him in no doubt about their preference for the latter.

Some in Washington, including Senate Majority Leader Mike Mansfield, were publicly suggesting negotiations leading to American withdrawal and the neutralization of South Vietnam—exactly what Thant was advocating. But Bundy labeled negotiations "surrender on the instalment plan."² Johnson messaged Taylor that "the US will spare no effort and no sacrifice in doing its full part to turn back the Communists in Vietnam."³

On January 30, Stevenson told Thant that Washington's answer was no. The Johnson administration was worried that news of the talks would become public and "demoralize" Saigon, leading to the fall of its government. Thant replied that the Saigon government (then a military junta about to be replaced with another military junta) was falling all the time. What was vital was "bringing peace to a land that's been at war for a quarter century." Stevenson, who seemed genuinely disheartened, said he didn't disagree.⁴

Thant informed his Soviet contacts, who in turn conveyed the negative message to the North Vietnamese. The Soviet premier Kosygin was then visiting Hanoi. By an unfortunate coincidence, US Navy fighter-bombers, on the same day, struck targets across North Vietnam. The Kremlin was furious.

Johnson had received from his top aides a memo stating a "general agreement" on increasing military pressure. What was necessary on the political side, argued his aides, was "to make clear to the world that our objectives are peace and freedom" and "pre-empt a possible peace offensive by the Communists."⁵ From then on, Hanoi's unrelenting position would be to reject any talks until the bombing stopped. The window for negotiations closed.

Over a meal, Thant confided the story of his initiative to the political commentator Walter Lippmann, whose writings he had admired since his days in Burma. Lippmann, who was sympathetic, explained that Johnson and his people would only negotiate once they believed they enjoyed "convincing military superiority."

———

The Secretary-General had to consider his next steps carefully. There was no resolution to the UN's financial crisis in sight, with the Americans now advocating a suspension of the USSR's voting rights. The Soviets, who gave Thant no indication that they would pay their arrears anytime soon, seemed to be gearing up for a fight.[6] Meanwhile, the Indonesian government, which had been a solid backer of Thant, pulled out of the UN altogether. Jakarta was then in a confrontation over Borneo with the new state of Malaysia and were incensed that Malaysia had just been elected to the Security Council for a two-year term.

At the beginning of February, Thant held a luncheon in his suite for the former French premier Edgar Jean Faure, together with Alex Quaison-Sackey and several other ambassadors. President Kennedy's widow, Jacqueline Kennedy, came as well. She wrote to Thant the next day about her conversation with the French politician. "It made me think how complicated your life is—always situations where the situation is never black nor white—but always gray—I do admire you—You never let the attrition show—That lunch—high in your beautiful tower—was very good for me. Thank you for thinking of me."[7]

Perhaps encouraged by the friendship of Jacqueline Kennedy and the ambassadors like Alex Quaison-Sackey who had been by his side all these years, Thant forged ahead. He must have been aware of what was at stake. Challenging the Johnson administration on Vietnam risked undermining, perhaps critically, American support for the world organization.

Stevenson was unhappy over the turn of events. Rusk told him bluntly the US could not possibly meet secretly with Hanoi behind "the back of its ally," so Thant's proposal was "never seriously considered." For months, Stevenson had kept Thant on tenterhooks when he could have pushed for a definitive reply perhaps as early as September. But with no close ties to Lyndon Johnson, Stevenson had to balance his advocacy of the UN with making sure he wasn't shut out completely from policy-making discussions in Washington.

Stevenson asked Thant if there was any reaction from Hanoi to the US rejection of talks. Thant said no, but suggested that if a bilateral meeting was not possible, perhaps he could convene an "exploratory" seven-government discussion involving both Hanoi and Saigon, together with China, the US, USSR, the UK, and France. He warned Stevenson that the Chinese and the Russians were drawing closer again after a period of frosty relations, and explained that the Afro-Asians were extremely displeased with America's air attacks on North Vietnam. If Washington was "afraid of showing weakness, afraid of the Congressional reaction," he could make the proposal and let the administration respond.[8]

The next day, Stevenson sent a memo to the president outlining Thant's idea. This time, he bypassed Rusk and transmitted the note through Bill Moyers, who had recently started working in the White House as Johnson's press secretary.

On February 19, the *Chicago Sun-Times* published a piece by William R. Frye, a longtime UN correspondent, detailing aspects of the Secretary-General's Vietnam initiative. Thant had no contact with Frye, and neither did Bunche or Narasimhan, the only two people on the UN side whom Thant had kept in the loop. The source of the information was a mystery.

At a lengthy press conference a few days later, Thant was unable to hold back. To the dozens of international reporters, he first explained how the Burmese government had dealt with its own Communist insurrection "by its own means, without asking for any outside military assistance or outside military advisors." "Not one American life has been lost in Burma," he declared. "Not one American dollar has been spent in Burma in the form of military assistance over the last seventeen years."

He then stated publicly what he had been saying privately for some time: the US's aim should be a face-saving exit from Vietnam. The journalists were stunned. In response to questions, a vexed Secretary-General then confirmed that he had made a specific proposal to Washington:

> *I am sure that the great American people, if they only knew the true facts ... will agree with me that further bloodshed is unnecessary. The political and diplomatic method of discussion and negotiation alone can create conditions which will enable the United States to withdraw gracefully from that part of the world. As you know, in times of war and hostilities, the first casualty is truth.*[9]

Though he understood his remarks were provocative, he may not have fully foreseen the consequences. With these words, he fundamentally and irrevocably transformed his standing in Washington, especially with Lyndon Johnson and his top advisors.

That same afternoon, all the major papers and wire services queried the White House about Thant's proposal. The White House, without checking with the State Department, answered that there had been no proposal. As the story broke, Assistant Secretary of State Harlan Cleveland urgently phoned the White House to explain that the State Department considered Thant's "suggestion" to be "procedural" and not a "proposal." A mess was getting messier.

The president was livid. Dean Rusk knew he would be blamed for not handling Thant effectively at the exact moment the administration was trying to exert maximum pressure on Hanoi. Over nearly two decades in the State Department, Rusk had been closely associated with the founding and development of the United Nations; he believed in the US's commitment to the UN. He had played a critical role in backing Thant's diplomacy during the Cuban Missile Crisis, and the two men had until now kept up an amiable if not particularly close relationship. But Rusk was also adamant that the world organization had a moral duty to stop Communist aggression, including against South Vietnam.

At 10 p.m. that night, an agitated Rusk phoned Thant at home. They argued first over whether there had been an actual proposal, Rusk insisting that the Secretary-General had only made a "procedural" suggestion. In ever more strident tones, Rusk said there had been "quite a reaction in Washington to the Secretary-General's implication that the truth was being withheld from the American people." Thant recounted the story of the past months from his perspective and kept repeating that for months he had received no response. Rusk also insisted that Burma was receiving "disguised" military assistance from the United States, "in considerable volume."[10] The US had actually been providing over $70 million in covert military aid, including ships and helicopters. The conversation grew heated. As Thant continued to press his views, the secretary of state barked, "Who do you think you are, a country?"

Stevenson was instructed to read Thant the riot act. The American ambassador had been in Jamaica on another holiday when he was summoned to the White House, where, he later told Thant, he spent much of the day with an intemperate Lyndon Johnson discussing "the press conference, the Secretary-General, and the United Nations." The next day, he and his deputy, Charles Yost, met with Thant and Bunche. Stevenson expressed regret at "having to request this meeting," but, he said, he was "in the dog house."[11]

Reading from points given to him by Rusk, Stevenson underlined how irked Washington was, in particular by Thant's comments about US assistance to Burma. Referring to the secret Canadian outreach the past summer, Stevenson also said that "a third party, whose identity he was not permitted to disclose," "had recently approached Hanoi" and reported that the North Vietnamese "were unreceptive to the suggestion of negotiations." The situation, admittedly, was not good for Saigon and Washington, but the US had yet to really "turn up the military heat." Stevenson knew that he had to be tough on his friend. He told Thant that the UN's standing in Washington was now "the lowest he had ever seen" and there was talk of ending any future confidential discussions with the Secretary-General. Congressional funding for the UN might even be in jeopardy.

Thant defended his approach, and also denied, based everything he knew about his government's policies, that Burma had ever received American military help. He regretted any embarrassment he had caused, especially to the president, but after the leak in the *Chicago Sun-Times*, he felt he had to say something. He was now so upset that he was considering never holding a press conference again.

Just after the meeting, Stevenson confided in Bunche that feelings in the administration were even more heated than what he had conveyed. Johnson was incandescent. "I'm not accepting any more proposals from U Thant!" the president had barked. Stevenson said he himself "was through" and would likely have to resign. A thoroughly dejected Thant told Bunche that he would cancel the UN twenty-fifth anniversary celebrations he had planned for June in San Francisco. Meanwhile, Thant's Russian aide, Vladimir Suslov, reported that the Soviets were upset that the Secretary-General had not insisted on an immediate withdrawal of

American forces from Vietnam. An exasperated Thant simply replied that he "couldn't make everyone happy."

The pressure on Thant grew white hot. Congressman Edward Derwinski of Illinois labeled the Secretary-General a "Red addict" and a "Marxist whose philosophic addiction to Communism shows itself repeatedly," who had now reached a "new low." In the *Washington Evening Star*, columnist William S. White asserted that Thant, "With a rarely matched twisting of the truth, but at least with a certain insolent candor ... has now openly become an apologist and propagandist for Communist aggression in South East Asia."

Other newspapers were equally critical. The editor-in-chief of the *Syracuse Herald-Journal* opined that Thant, "Head Eunuch of the new sterile UN," was doing more to "kill the United Nations as a peace-making and peace-keeping force than any single individual in its history."

Ordinary Americans also sent letters asking why the Secretary-General was not supporting the US in Vietnam. Elizabeth Anderson of Fort Worth, Texas, asked: "just why do you think Americans—I mean real Americans—want to 'retreat gracefully'—you sold us out to Castro + Khrushchev—how much are you getting now to get us out of Vietnam? I will be glad to see U. Nations fall." Likely referring to articles reporting the allegations made by Thant's old landlord, she added, "You deserve to get chucked out of your plush hotel suite—which reporters say looks like a pigsty!"

Hundreds more sent letters and telegrams to express their sympathy. Samuel Cohen, a construction engineer in New York, wrote that "your statement about the necessity of a negotiated settlement, now, of the Vietnam War, is courageous, admirable and history making. It may be the one opening wedge toward the prevention of a third World War." Lucy Haessler in Detroit said, "We appreciate with all our hearts the tremendous efforts you are making, not only on the horrible situation in Vietnam, but in other areas of world tension, to achieve and maintain world peace. There is no other way for us to survive."[12]

Thant was also attracting support from leading American voices. Martin Luther King Jr., speaking at Howard University, said that the military escalation was "accomplishing nothing" and called for a negotiated settlement.[13] Norman Cousins, a fervent UN advocate and editor of the influential *Saturday Review*, began a steady drumbeat of editorials in favor of peace talks. Thant and Cousins had become friends, with Thant even making an appearance at Cousins's surprise birthday party, at which he said how pleased he was to celebrate "one of the greatest minds of our time" and "an unfailing source of inspiration to me." Cousins wrote later to say he was "moved beyond concealment."[14]

On March 8, 1965, two battalions of US Marines landed on the sandy white beaches near Da Nang, the first of 60,000 American combat troops authorized by Lyndon Johnson. Already in the country were 25,000 military advisors. At the same time, the air campaign, Operation Rolling Thunder, was expanded to include North Vietnam's civilian infrastructure, with US Navy and Air Force planes attacking road and rail junctions, bridges, and supply depots. To the surprise of Johnson's inner circle, Hanoi did not cave in to the US's display of muscle.

Johnson remained upset with Thant, and was now equally angry at allied leaders offering unsolicited advice. He told British prime minister Harold Wilson that he had no interest in hearing other views on Vietnam. The only alternative to his present course, the president reflected, was "retreat to Hawaii" or "bomb the hell out of China."[15]

The Secretary-General, meanwhile, was in constant contact with the Afro-Asians and other non-aligned ambassadors in New York, as well as heads of government around the world. All were pressing him to do more. On March 15, seventeen non-aligned leaders including Ben Bella of Algeria, Kwame Nkrumah of Ghana, Gamal Abdel Nasser of Egypt, Jomo Kenyatta of Kenya, Emperor Haile Selassie of Ethiopia, and India's new prime minister, Lal Bahadur Shastri, signed an urgent appeal for negotiations, saying they were convinced that the spiraling violence was "the consequence of foreign intervention." To get something moving, Thant tried to persuade the Soviets that the South Vietnamese government—not just Hanoi and the Viet Cong—had to be involved in any future discussions. He also tried to reach out to Peking, via Ben Bella.

In April, the Johnson administration, disappointed that the escalation so far had not produced results, doubled down on military involvement, while at the same time looking for a new diplomatic move. They wanted some sign that Hanoi was willing to talk about a ceasefire that would include a halt in men and supplies coming to the Viet Cong from North Vietnam through eastern Laos. The president's press secretary, Bill Moyers, came to New York and told Stevenson the anger at Thant had dissipated and he should "forget it."

A few days later, Thant made a secret proposal through Stevenson: he would publicly call for a three-month ceasefire along the 17th parallel, including a stop to Communist infiltration through Laos. Looking for a way back into some kind of working relationship with the Johnson administration, he even offered to edit the proposal to match exactly what Washington wanted.[16] Often, though not always, Thant relied on Ralph Bunche for political advice. Bunche—a former State Department official and a member of the Office of Strategic Services, a forerunner of the CIA, during the Second World War—kept up his own ties to the Johnson administration, including to Dean Rusk. He had tried, over many private meals and drinks, to explain Thant to Rusk and vice versa. On this proposal, there was no real response, only a message from Rusk to Stevenson: "We want to preserve the Secretary-General as a useful channel for quiet diplomacy as this situation develops."[17]

On April 6, in a speech at Johns Hopkins University, Johnson offered "unconditional" talks as well as a new "development initiative" for Southeast Asia. At the president's instruction, the speech included mention of Thant: "the prestige of his great office, and his deep knowledge of Asia."[18]

Thant didn't lose the opportunity to soothe the president, welcoming the speech publicly and in private writing that he hoped the speech "will mark a turning point in the long-standing Vietnam conflict." Johnson reciprocated the same day, his letter stating that he was "greatly encouraged" by Thant's words and that it was "good to know that we think alike." He added that he had instructed Stevenson to "keep in closest possible touch with you" so that "no opportunity for forward progress is missed."[19]

The relentless bombing, however, had only made Hanoi more, not less, determined to win on its own terms. They distilled those terms into what they called their Four Points: the withdrawal of all US forces, the neutralization of Vietnam, the adoption of the Viet Cong's program for the South, and reunification "without foreign interference."

Stevenson relayed Johnson's disappointment that Hanoi had not responded to the president's call for unconditional talks; Thant explained that a halt to the bombing campaign had to come first. Hanoi was also insisting on the Viet Cong being the sole representatives of South Vietnam. Thant had advised them via the Algerian government that this second demand was unrealistic.[20] In public, Thant grumbled that the UN risked becoming "merely a debating forum and nothing else."[21]

On April 14, Prime Minister Harold Wilson visited Thant at the UN. Wilson's Labour government had been in power for several months and was keen to show its commitment to the world organization. After a rocky start over the Congo, the Secretary-General's relationship with the UK was good, in large part due to Thant's Anglophile tendencies: his passion since childhood for English literature, his fondness for most things English, and his declaration that London was his favorite city in the world. It was also due to the hard work of the UK's ambassador in New York, Lord Caradon (Hugh Foot).[22]

There was genuine affection between Caradon and Thant, as well as shared political views. Caradon, a former colonial official, had left an earlier posting with the UK's delegation to the UN when he felt unable to defend the prior Conservative government's tacit support for white-minority rule in Rhodesia.[23] In a recent statement to Parliament, Caradon said of Thant: "We believe in no man's infallibility, but it is restful to be sure of one man's integrity. My Lords, here is a man trusted by every group and every nation."[24] Caradon was assisted by Sir Leslie Glass, who had worked in Burma for decades as a civil servant and was fluent in Burmese. His Burmese name was U Hman (Mr. Glass). Even in official meetings, his discussions with Thant might slip into Burmese for five or ten minutes at a time—which made the Soviets suspect a plot.[25]

With flattery and friendship having paved the way, Wilson was able to enjoy a convivial meeting with the Secretary-General, discussing the situation in southern Africa as well as Cyprus and Southeast Asia. The UK had fought its own war in the region, suppressing a Communist insurrection in what became Malaysia. It was now deploying a sizable part of its armed forces in northern Borneo, part of the new Malaysia state, against threats from Indonesia, which also claimed the territory. A UN team dispatched by the Secretary-General had come down on Malaysia's side in the dispute, but Thant was wary of further involvement.[26]

There was, instead, on that early spring day, the sunlight reflecting off the skyscrapers to the west, a bibulous luncheon of jellied eggs, veal, and ice cream, the twenty men present consuming between them most of a bottle of scotch, a bottle of gin, nine bottles of Château Laville Haut-Brion, and five bottles of Veuve Clicquot champagne, finished off with French liqueurs and brandy. This was not an unusual quantity of spirits for a UN (or New York) lunch at the time.[27] The Labour leader puffed on his pipe, in preference to the Cuban cigar offered by Thant. Wilson would see President Johnson the next day and was anxious about his reception. He was resisting sending British troops to Vietnam, as the Americans were aggressively demanding, but he had to make sure he didn't alienate Washington. Exactly how the Burmese statesman fit into this equation, Wilson wasn't yet sure.

On June 25, the UN chief flew to San Francisco to preside over celebrations marking the twentieth anniversary of the world organization—which, in a fit of despondency, he had thought to cancel. At the last minute, Lyndon Johnson decided he would join in. It would be their first in-person encounter since the White House dinner the previous summer.

The event was at the Opera House, where the forty-five nations that had declared war on Germany and Japan had adopted the United Nations Charter in 1945. After lofty speeches by both the Secretary-

General and the president, Johnson asked Thant for a private word in one of the dressing rooms. Stevenson and California governor Pat Brown tried to follow, but they were told to stay outside. A "red-faced" Stevenson told Bunche that Johnson "does not want me present." Bunche said he was not going in either. The only other person in the room was Lynda Bird Johnson, the president's twenty-one-year-old daughter, who sat in the corner reading a novel. Johnson seemed to Thant to be in a "serious, even sour mood."

The conversation started with the crisis in the Dominican Republic, where Washington was aiding a military regime against supporters of an overthrown left-wing elected government. Several weeks earlier, Johnson had dispatched the 82nd Airborne Division, ostensibly to protect Americans but in fact to prop up the generals and prevent the country becoming "another Cuba." The Soviets demanded the Security Council take action; the US used its veto. So the Council asked Thant to take the lead, a thankless task that only complicated his already fraught standing in Washington.[28]

After an exchange of blunt words—Johnson criticized Thant's mediator, a Venezuelan diplomat, as anti-American, and Thant defended him—the president moved swiftly to his main concern.

Because of his "esteem, even affection" for Thant, said the Texan, as well as his dedication to the United Nations, the August dinner was the biggest he had ever held at the White House. He wanted "the whole world" to know that he regarded Thant as a "man of peace" and that the United Nations was the "only hope for peace." But he was, he said, distressed at the criticism of his Vietnam policies and the "general attitude of the UN" toward Vietnam. He didn't criticize Thant directly.

Thant explained what he had tried to do with his outreach to Hanoi. Johnson's face didn't betray surprise, but Thant sensed that the president hadn't received the full story. Rather than responding directly, Johnson tore into Stevenson, saying the ambassador was "twice a loser" and had "no sense of correct judgment of public opinion." He was "an idealist with his head in the clouds," while the president had to take public opinion into account. But now, Johnson said, Averell Harriman was "ready to go anywhere and would talk to anybody" on Vietnam. Harriman was a veteran diplomat who had been Roosevelt's envoy to Stalin during the war. A plane was at his disposal. He could leave at twenty-four hours' notice.

It was "too late," said Thant; Hanoi insisted that the Viet Cong be involved. Johnson was silent for a little while, before continuing,

"I have always wanted a peaceful solution. Curtis Lemay [until recently the US Air Force chief] wanted to bomb China but I would never agree with his outdated attitudes and so retired him." The president then said that he had earmarked $1 billion for the rehabilitation of both North and South Vietnam and was sending Eugene Black, the former president of the World Bank, "to pave the way."

"I just saw Black last week," replied Thant. "It will come to nothing as long as the bombing continues."

"I have confined the bombing to military targets," said Johnson.

Thant decided to shift gears. "I know public opinion is in favor of bombing."

Johnson seemed to ease up and, in his slow Southern drawl, emphasized: "Public opinion is important." He had thought of not coming to the celebration because "the UN" was critical of his policies on Vietnam and some had told him to stay away.

Thant had lightened the mood. The Secretary-General and the president went over the Dominican crisis again, as well as civil rights in America, Johnson's legislative agenda, and US aid to India and Pakistan. By now, Johnson was "relaxed and all smiles." Lynda was still reading her novel in the corner.

It had been more than an hour. When the two men reappeared, Governor Brown, Stevenson, and Bunche were waiting, along with a gaggle of photographers and newsmen. Johnson called the photographers around and encouraged them to take pictures. Thant and Johnson jostled in a jovial way to stand on each other's right-hand side (in diplomatic protocol, the host stands to the right of the dignitary). Johnson was now "in an extremely good mood." Stevenson, however, looked perplexed and ill at ease.[29]

Two weeks later, Stevenson dropped dead from a heart attack outside the US embassy in London. Over the past months, Stevenson had put on weight, drinking and partying into the morning hours and worrying his doctor. In Paris, he complained to his colleague Averell Harriman about having to defend Washington's intervention in the Dominican Republic, "an enormous blunder from the beginning to the end."[30] The night before his death, he had met with the journalist Eric Sevareid, expressing his vexations over drinks and relating in detail Thant's efforts to broker direct talks with Hanoi.

Thant was "grievously shocked" at the loss of a man he described as his "good friend."[31] He was now at a crossroads. While the president was mollified, for now, his chief ally in the administration was dead. He had no direction on Vietnam from either the Security Council or the General Assembly, but could see no choice but to struggle on.

A few days after Stevenson's death, in late July, Thant met secretly for the first time with North Vietnam's covert representative in Paris, Mai Van Bo. The French, who shared Thant's analysis of the Vietnam situation, facilitated the encounter. The UN chief and the Communist envoy agreed that the meeting would be "strictly personal," Thant emphasizing from the start that he was acting not as Secretary-General but as an "individual." He had no one with him, not even a note-taker. It was a strange role: the head of the United Nations attempting peace talks as a private citizen.

Thant expressed his hope that some kind of international conference might be possible, with South Vietnam represented by both the Saigon government and the Viet Cong. After the meeting with Johnson in San Francisco, he felt the president might agree. He told Mai that the key was selling the idea to Congress and winning over public opinion. Yet Mai insisted that an American withdrawal from Vietnam had to be the starting point for any talks, or at least the acceptance of this "in principle." The US was free to stop its "criminal bombings" of North Vietnam, but this could not be traded for any concessions by his government.[32] Before concluding, Thant asked Mai to use only the French government as intermediaries in the future, including in the passing of oral messages.

Back in New York, Thant and Rusk had a difficult meeting. They argued over almost everything, over recent history and whether Hanoi's infiltration of South Vietnam or the "American presence" had "started it all." After a while, Thant cut off the back-and-forth: "We must have a further discussion of the facts in the Vietnam case."

They then argued again over whether Burma had ever been given US military assistance. On this, Thant conceded. Since their last conversation, he had questioned the regime in Rangoon, which first denied the arrangement but then, when pressed, told Thant they had indeed received military hardware. Thant told Rusk that as the assistance was not visible to the public eye, it was beside the point. A disagreement over Laos came next, with the Secretary-General alleging and the secretary of state denying that the CIA was trying to undermine the neutralist government in Vientiane.

Thant underlined the main point he wanted to make: there had been real opportunity up till last September to reconvene the Geneva Conference and establish a neutral, independent Vietnam. The idea that a neutral Vietnam had ever been possible, Rusk replied, was "news to him."[33]

The Johnson administration wanted negotiations that would lead to an independent South Vietnam. The North Vietnamese would only consider talks aimed at reunification. Both sides were willing to escalate the fighting. Both wanted the other out of South Vietnam.

Thant remained convinced that through direct talks, a peaceful resolution could be found. He understood that for the Americans much was about image and prestige. He didn't know, but might have guessed, what a top-secret Pentagon memo to the White House stated clearly: that 20 percent of America's war aim was to deny Vietnam to the Chinese and only 10 percent to allow the people of South Vietnam "to enjoy a better, freer way of life." The remaining 70 percent was to avoid "a humiliating US defeat."[34]

In late July, fifty-six-year-old Arthur Goldberg, a white-haired former Supreme Court justice, arrived in New York to take over as US ambassador to the UN. The son of Russian immigrants, with long experience of clever bargaining as a labor lawyer, he had resigned from a lifetime tenure on America's highest court after Lyndon Johnson convinced him that a UN position meant a pivotal role in finding peace in Vietnam.[35]

Through Goldberg, the French, and new back channels, in private and in public, Thant tried to craft fresh ideas to end the war. As Thant had predicted, Peking was massively increasing its aid to Hanoi. Late that summer, he renewed his call for negotiations. At the same time, he strongly and publicly protested the expansion of American bombing in North Vietnam to infrastructure such as irrigation systems and hydroelectric plants. His stock in Washington fell to a new low.[36]

Henry Cabot Lodge, a hard-liner and Johnson's man in Saigon, wrote to the president on his "innermost preoccupations," saying he worried that there was now too much stress on "negotiations" and not enough on the right "outcome." "It is surely possible," he ended the letter, "to handle U Thant carefully without over-praising him."[37]

Thant was planning his next moves, including a new outreach to Hanoi.[38] But then came reports of another war in Asia.

9 | KASHMIR

IN EARLY AUGUST 1965, high in the Himalayan foothills, United Nations military observers spotted convoys of buses from Pakistan crossing the ceasefire line in Kashmir, known as the Line of Control. The observers had been anxious for months; there had been a sharp increase in armed violence and now their worst fears were coming true. Over the following week, thousands of Pakistani soldiers, disguised in the long loose gowns of local civilians, attacked Indian positions in four different parts of Kashmir. "We could be busy for a while," the UN commander, the Australian general Robert Nimmo, reported to New York.[1]

Like many of the conflicts that ended up in the lap of the UN, the Kashmir situation was a legacy of colonial rule. In 1947, the British partitioned its Indian Empire into two independent states, India and Pakistan, based on the religious majority, Hindu or Muslim, in various regions. Both claimed Kashmir, a principality about the size of the United Kingdom or California, which was strategically located along the borders of both China and the Soviet Union. Kashmir had a Muslim majority, but in late 1947 the ruling prince had opted to join India. War quickly ensued (with British generals commanding both armies), and when it ended, the newly formed UN was tasked with "observing" the ceasefire. Over the years and on countless occasions, the observers had helped to end skirmishes and dampen tensions.

Attempts at talks to resolve the dispute went nowhere. Both governments believed that Kashmir belonged to them by right, and few on either side wanted to budge. India accelerated plans to integrate Kashmir into its territory. The government in Pakistan, led by President Mohammed Ayub Khan, saw military action as their only possible response. After being routed by the Chinese in a short, sharp war in 1962, India had drawn closer to Moscow, and was determined to boost its strength with new Soviet hardware. The Pakistanis, in turn, were buying the latest military equipment from a Johnson administration eager to sell arms and forge closer ties.

President Khan had recently opened a new front hundreds of miles to the southwest of Kashmir, in the desolate salt marshes known as the Rann of Kutch. Harold Wilson mediated a temporary agreement. Khan took this as a sign of weakness on the part of Indian prime minister Lal Bahadur Shastri and began infiltrating his men across the Line of Control in Kashmir. By late August 1965, uniformed Pakistani troops were added to the mix and a full-scale invasion of Indian Kashmir was underway. India scrambled at first to defend its positions and then counterattacked.

Thant summoned Nimmo to New York. The Australian general had been sending a stream of battlefield assessments, but the Secretary-General wanted a better sense of the thinking on both sides as well as Nimmo's views on the options for diplomacy. Muslim countries sympathized with Pakistan's claim to Muslim-majority Kashmir, but few if any governments wanted a war, and certainly not a prolonged one that might trigger big-power confrontation. There was also the specter of a new wave of bloody communal violence among Hindus, Sikhs, and Muslims across the subcontinent; partition in 1947 had led to between one and two million deaths. Thant first floated the idea of sending Bunche as a mediator, but after discussion with Nimmo and Bunche, he decided to go himself.

On September 1, the Secretary-General issued a public appeal to both

President Khan and Prime Minister Shastri to end the fighting "in the interest of the world," and withdraw troops to their respective sides of the Line of Control. He understood, he said, "the complexities of the issues involved," but trusted they could be solved without violence. The next day he released a report to the Security Council based on Nimmo's assessments, confirming India's account that Pakistani infiltration had started the present round of conflict.[2] For some time, he had been pestering the Council to meet, and he now pressed harder, as he wanted a clear mandate before heading to the subcontinent.

Harold Wilson, who had been fishing for another mediation role, threw his government's support behind Thant and mobilized backing from other Commonwealth countries. As important, the non-aligned states, led by Egypt's Nasser, Ghana's Nkrumah, and Yugoslavia's Tito, offered any help that Thant might request. The Americans, irritated by Thant's continued musings and maneuvers on Vietnam, agreed that he was the man for what they suspected might be a thankless job.

On September 2, President Johnson assembled his most senior advisors and military chiefs. Both India and Pakistan were recipients of substantial American assistance, including food aid. Pakistan was a Cold War ally, but for the Americans to intervene on the side of Pakistan would destroy relations with India and accelerate India's embrace of Moscow. On the other hand, not helping Pakistan would bring China and Pakistan closer together. And other allies, such as Turkey and Iran, might start to question Washington's commitment to their defense.

Dean Rusk painted an apocalyptic scenario in which the war touched off intercommunal riots, leaving millions dead and destabilizing the entire "Western position" in Asia. The Secretary-General, Rusk told the president, had issued an appeal and the US had made known its strong support.[3]

Johnson wasn't much moved. "We should get behind a log and sleep a bit," the president told his assembled aides. He had discovered, he said, over recent months, "how little influence he had with both the Paks and the Indians." He didn't want to intervene and would like to "sit it out."

Rusk tried again for a more dynamic American role, bringing up Washington's unique position of having armed both sides. "Let U Thant do it," Johnson instructed. "Let's hide behind that log."[4]

On September 4, the Security Council finally convened and agreed in rapid succession on two resolutions calling for a ceasefire between India and Pakistan. Both the US and the USSR lined up behind Thant. With relations between Moscow and Peking at an all-time low, the Soviets wanted to see the war halted before China intervened on the side of Pakistan. This, they feared, would not only prove a political win for China but might compel the Americans to up their support for India, leaving the Soviets without the strong relationship with Delhi that they had been cultivating for years. At Thant's urging, the Council called on him to "extend every possible effort" to stop the fighting.[5] It was the mandate he desired.

Rusk advised Johnson that the Secretary-General's mission gave "a chance for the two countries to pull back from the abyss."[6] The president offered Thant the use of *Air Force One*, but Thant demurred. He couldn't appear to be an American agent. In his reply, he said only that he would feel "awkward" in such a big plane with just a few people.[7]

On the eve of his departure, *The New York Times* ran a portrait of Thant titled "Fighter for Peace," declaring that hopes for a halt to the war now were carried on the shoulders of a "short, neat, round-faced man" who had over the past four years "demonstrated his ability to deal coolly and quietly with crises." Westerners might be critical of him on issues like "Red China's seat at the UN," but that was precisely his value, the paper of record assessed, as he could not be accused by Asians of holding "colonialist views."[8]

That week, with battle raging in Kashmir, Prime Minister Shastri ordered a massive armored thrust, not in Kashmir but in the densely populated plains further south, right into the heart of Pakistan.

On September 7, Thant boarded a BOAC flight to London. With him were Bunche's deputy, Brian Urquhart, his press assistant Ramses Nassif, and a security aide. It wasn't entirely clear how Thant and his team would reach the Pakistani government in Rawalpindi, much less cross the front lines and get to Delhi. The Pakistani and Indian air forces were engaged in fierce combat, flying dozens of sorties daily. There were reports too of Pakistani commandos being parachuted behind Indian positions and attacking airfields. Urquhart frantically coordinated logistics with United Nations staff and governments around the world. Speed was important—but they had to arrive in one piece.

For Thant, traveling to the subcontinent was almost like going home. When he was a young man, Burma was a province of the British Indian Empire, like Bengal or the Punjab. Rangoon under the British was an Indian city, with hundreds of thousands of immigrants from across the Bay of Bengal and dozens of mosques and Hindu temples. Most restaurants were Indian restaurants; the police were mainly Sikhs and Pathans; the businessmen were Gujaratis, Marwaris, and Tamils. Thant himself was of partial Indian descent, his great-great-grandfather having come to Burma from India in the 1820s in search of a better life. And Thant's very first trip overseas, in 1951, was to India as part of an official delegation. In Kashmir the delegation had been hosted by the state's leader, Sheikh Abdullah, the Lion of Kashmir.[9]

At London's Heathrow airport, Thant was met by the foreign secretary, Michael Stewart, in a show of support. He also encountered a small crowd of angry Pakistani students outside the airport hotel, carrying signs saying "We Want War" and shouting "Down with U Thant!" From London he flew to Tehran, where the Iranian prime minister personally greeted him on arrival despite the late-night hour, and ordered that the Shah's luxurious airport lounge be made available so Thant could rest.[10] From Tehran he flew on to Karachi and finally to Rawalpindi, only about sixty miles from the nearest battlefield.

Thant's principal advisor for this mission was Brian Urquhart. The two men spent most of the twenty-four-hour trip mulling over possible strategies, preparing draft statements, and fine-tuning their agenda. Then in his early forties, the slightly built Scot was already one of the UN's longest-serving officials, having joined the world body at its inception.

An undergraduate at Oxford when the Second World War broke out, Urquhart joined the army (he had intended to join the navy but filled out the wrong form) and soon volunteered for the airborne forces.

Urquhart was nearly killed during an exercise in 1942 when his parachute didn't fully open and he crashed into a reviewing stand, feet away from generals Eisenhower and Montgomery. As an intelligence officer in the 1st Airborne Corps, he tried unsuccessfully to warn his superiors against the disastrous Operation Market Garden, dramatized in the film *A Bridge Too Far*. Later in the war he was part of the T-Force, an elite Anglo-American unit whose mission was to secure Nazi secrets and scientists. He was also the first Allied officer at Belsen concentration camp. With a razor-sharp wit and a wicked sense of humor, Urquhart was utterly loyal to the organization he had served for nearly two decades.

Rawalpindi was the interim seat of the Pakistani government as well as the army's headquarters. Set along the foothills of the Himalayas, the sprawling town was adjacent to the planned new capital, Islamabad. With its mix of Victorian, Gothic, and Saracen-styled buildings, porticoed bungalows, and Raj-era gardens, there was little to distinguish hot, humid Rawalpindi from Rangoon. Both had been frontier towns not long before, at opposite edges of British India.

Thant's first meeting was with Pakistani foreign minister Zulfiqar Ali Bhutto, at the government guest house where he was staying. The Oxford-educated Bhutto reminded Urquhart of "those stylish, slightly raffish sons of Whig noblemen" whom he had admired at university. Pakistan sought close alliances with both the United States and China as a way of strengthening its hand vis-à-vis India," and Bhutto made a strong case for his country's position, arguing that Pakistan was the aggrieved party and that no conclusion to the conflict was possible without addressing the future of Kashmir. While they were talking, an aide entered and passed Bhutto a message. "Massive tank battles are ranging on all fronts!" exclaimed the foreign minister.

Next was a working lunch with President Ayub Khan, a six-foot-two-inch, mustachioed, Sandhurst-trained field marshal, who greeted Thant as if welcoming a long-lost friend. Khan's bearing and imperiousness reminded Thant of Charles de Gaulle. Urquhart thought Khan's shoes the most expensive-looking he had ever seen.

The war was reaching a climax. India's First Armored Division, supported by cavalry and infantry regiments, had penetrated deep into the Punjab's northern reaches only to be halted by Pakistani tank formations, while Pakistan's First Armored Division, pushing toward Amritsar, the holy city of the Sikh faith, was being fiercely resisted by an Indian armored brigade. The fighting had also spread into the deserts of Rajasthan. But with thousands now dead, a stalemate was looming.

The UN chief knew that neither side could expect a military victory and both were reportedly low on fuel, ammunition, and spare parts. His strategy was to develop a respectful relationship with both sides while constructing the framework through which they could be nudged toward a ceasefire.

Khan outlined his nation's case. Kashmir had always been intended to be part of Pakistan, and its Muslim-majority population would in any free plebiscite vote to join. Thant wouldn't be drawn into any discussion of Kashmir's future; instead, he argued that any escalation of the war would be economically disastrous for Pakistan and would constitute a threat to world peace—an even greater threat than what was then unfolding in Vietnam, due to the risk of drawing in both Peking and Moscow and igniting a broader regional conflict.[12] His intention was to propose a specific time and date for a ceasefire as soon as he had spoken to Indian leaders in Delhi. Khan and Bhutto insisted that a ceasefire had to be linked to a plebiscite on the future of Kashmir. Thant gently disagreed.

That night, Thant and Urquhart drafted a ceasefire proposal and sent it to Bunche for his advice. "May I again warmly congratulate you on your wisdom and courage," Bunche cabled back, with a few suggested changes. "I hope you are getting some rest and watching your eating habits."[13] Bunche and Thant were increasingly apprehensive about each other's health.

The next day, during another working lunch, Thant mentioned his lifelong ambition to see the ruins of Taxila, about twenty-five miles northwest of Rawalpindi along the Grand Trunk Road to Afghanistan.

Bhutto immediately offered to drive him. Two thousand years earlier, during the age of the Indo-Greek kings, the heirs of Alexander the Great had made Taxila into an extraordinary seat of Buddhist learning. From Taxila, the Buddha's Four Noble Truths were exported to Tibet, China, and Japan.

Early Buddhism was centered on the individual. It was a prescription for coping with the anxieties and discontents of life, in part through the acceptance of the impermanence of all things. A solitary life was held up as an ideal.[14] In Taxila, however, there was an additional focus on kindness and compassion toward all living things. A new ideal developed around the Bodhisattva: a person who can reach *nirvana*, or enlightenment, but chooses instead to remain and help others on their path to salvation. Thant's own brand of Buddhism was closer to this more socially engaged creed.

Looking out across the ruins of Taxila, the Secretary-General was, he later remembered, "speechless with awe and veneration." He was as well deeply moved by the sandstone statues of Buddhas and Bodhisattvas housed in the local museum, some modeled after the Greek god Apollo.

On the drive back, Thant saw uniformed soldiers handing rifles to busloads of young men in civilian clothes, doubtless, he thought, heading to Kashmir. Bhutto mentioned to Thant that Saravepalli Radhakrishnan, now president of India, had been his professor of comparative religion at Oxford many years back. He asked the Secretary-General to convey his respects to his old teacher.

The two may have discussed Buddhism too. What they almost certainly didn't discuss was Thant's own Muslim heritage, something the Secretary-General had chosen to keep hidden. Thant's paternal line stretched back to Calcutta, and his ancestors there considered themselves Mughals, meaning they claimed descent from central Asian and Persian Muslim immigrants to Delhi. When Thant's father died, his mother raised him as a Buddhist and his Muslim identity was submerged aside from an aversion to pork, something Thant had never eaten before coming to New York.

That afternoon, Thant and Ayub Khan met alone on the expansive green lawn of the president's house, sitting on teak chairs and drinking tea. A small transistor radio sat on a table next to Khan, so that he could hear news of the aerial combats and tank battles underway. Khan reiterated Pakistan's position and suggested increased diplomatic involvement by all the big powers. He also showed the Secretary-General a Burmese silver bowl in his possession. He had commanded a British Indian battalion in Burma during the Second World War and reminisced with Thant about his days there.

As darkness settled the lights went out, a precaution in case of air strikes. Thant said he had noticed the housekeeper putting heavy shades on his bedroom lights the night before. "So long as the Secretary-General is in Rawalpindi, a blackout is certainly not necessary!" asserted Khan. Both laughed. Thant had not yet produced a miraculous ceasefire, but he was establishing the personal bonds necessary for when the tide against war began to turn.

Meanwhile, in Washington, Lyndon Johnson, while taking a walk along Pennsylvania Avenue, had a chance meeting with an Indian and two Pakistani students from Fort Wayne, Indiana. They were good friends, they told the inquisitive president, and expressed hope that the Secretary-General's efforts would succeed. "Well, I'm glad to see you boys together," exclaimed Johnson before inviting the bewildered young men back to the White House, where he showed them around, handed out souvenirs, and asked, "Do you think your leaders would listen to U Thant?"[15]

The challenge for the UN team was now to get from Rawalpindi to Delhi in the middle of a war, with fighter jets blowing each other up along the entire front line. Urquhart found his boss entirely uninterested in the frantic discussions about his safety.[16] With no other options in sight, Thant accepted the offer of the American air attaché in Tehran's propeller plane, which flew at around 200 miles an hour.

A direct flight might have taken around two hours. Thant's journey lasted nearly two days, as the plane (which both sides assumed was packed with American intelligence equipment and crew) was routed over a thousand miles off course over the Arabian Sea and then east to Bombay and northeast to Delhi. On board was a small statue of the Buddha from Taxila, a gift from Bhutto. Also on board was a box of Burmese mango jams, specially delivered by the Burmese ambassador in Pakistan for Thant's wife.[17]

Delhi was on a war footing. Thant and his colleagues were lodged in the President's House, a 340-room Edwardian Baroque residence built at the zenith of the British Empire for the Viceroy of India. He noticed antiaircraft guns everywhere as well as pools and fountains drained of water so as not to be seen easily from the sky. There, Thant met with General Nimmo, who briefed him on the latest military developments. Together with Urquhart, they began discussing how the UN might best police a ceasefire. They wanted no delays once an agreement was reached.

The Secretary-General passed on to his host, the slim and turbaned President Radhakrishnan, the message from Bhutto, his former student at Oxford. The president was deeply touched.[18] They then spent over an hour discussing the *Dhammapada*, a collection of ancient Buddhist texts which Radhakrishnan had translated from Sanskrit into English, with a scholarly introduction. Thant viewed Radhakrishnan not just as the president of the world's biggest democracy but also as a distinguished philosopher.[19] The president handed Thant a text of the speech he had delivered the previous evening over All India Radio, "to read at your leisure." It called on the Indian people to avoid "any form of hatred of the people of Pakistan, who are our kith and kin," but also stressed the need for an Indian victory and blamed Pakistan for "taking the law into its own hands." Thant judged it more the speech of the political leader than the philosopher.

That evening, he had dinner at the modest home of the prime minister, the diminutive and austere Lal Bahadur Shastri. The scene reminded Urquhart of a Bedouin encampment, with "wise old men, gurus, fires and lamplight everywhere." Thant was struck by Shastri's humble manner, "quite unlike the formidable Field Marshal" Ayub Khan. Shastri suggested "His Ferocity the Field Marshal" as an honorific for his Pakistani counterpart. Thant thought "His Simplicity the Prime Minister" a fitting one for Shastri.[20]

Simple, but forceful. The prime minister condemned Pakistan's actions as well as the Security Council's failure to act promptly to stop "thousands of armed infiltrators equipped with Pakistani arms" who had launched a "massive attack on India." Thant explained that the purpose of his mission was to establish a ceasefire; he would be sending identical appeals to both governments specifying a time and date. The Indian leader understood what Thant couldn't say explicitly: that he was not attempting to insert a broader discussion of Kashmir's future (as Pakistan wanted) into the picture.

At a cabinet meeting the next day, Shastri argued for an acceptance of Thant's ceasefire proposal, saying that Pakistan was unlikely to agree. This would give India a diplomatic win. A divided cabinet eventually agreed, with qualifications. Shastri immediately messaged Thant to say that India would cease fighting in forty-eight hours but that military operations would continue against "Pakistani infiltrators." The UN, he asserted, needed to distinguish between Pakistan as the aggressor and India as the victim of aggression.

When they met again, Thant pointed out that these were in effect preconditions. Shastri agreed to go back to his ministers and send "a more agreeable" reply. There would still, however, need to be a positive Pakistani reply.[21] Wanting to give Shastri more room to maneuver, Thant cabled Bunche that night that the "Indian desire to make reasonable reply is affected by tricky parliamentary and political situation and time is needed to consult and forestall criticism of Government."[22] Both Rawalpindi and Delhi were inching toward a ceasefire but were still not quite there. The only alternative, as Thant continually stressed, was a war of attrition and an explosive international crisis.

The Secretary-General had managed to cultivate amiable relationships with both Khan and Shastri and calculated that more pressure, together with a little more time, might do the trick.[23] Thant was also quietly urging both leaders to meet in "neutral" territory. Bunche suggested Tehran or Kuwait, and advised Thant to make the idea public before his return to New York.[24] Thant then issued another public ceasefire appeal—"both as Secretary-General of the United Nations and as a citizen of a sister Asian country"—and proposed a summit at which Khan and Shastri could discuss a settlement directly.[25] He was already in contact with the Soviets about hosting this summit in Tashkent.

Before he left, Thant enjoyed a meal at the home of the Burmese ambassador in Delhi, Khin Kyi, and her teenage daughter (the future Nobel laureate) Aung San Suu Kyi. He also made a final call on President Radhakrishnan to explain his strategy. India's philosopher-president concluded their conversation with some thoughts on the dual nature of man: infused with elements of the diabolic as well as of the divine.

On September 16, Thant arrived back in New York. It was a warm, late-summer day. In an unprecedented gesture, the entire Security Council was waiting for him on the tarmac at JFK airport as a demonstration of their united support. Even the belligerents went out of their way to express their backing for the Secretary-General's efforts, the Indian ambassador stating that Thant was "the greatest international servant in the world" and "would always be welcome in India" and his Pakistani counterpart adding that whatever disagreement there might be, "the people of Pakistan have the warmest regard for the Secretary-General."[26] There were positive messages from around the world, including from the last Viceroy of India, Lord Mountbatten, who had presided over the creation of Pakistan. His handwritten note conveyed "how much I admire your efforts to settle this deplorable fratricidal, indeed suicidal war in India which I find quite heart-breaking."[27]

Thant reported at once to the Security Council and advised that this body responsible for international peace, whose resolutions carried the weight of law, *order* India and Pakistan to stop fighting. Previous resolutions had only *called* on the countries to stop. Under the enforcement provisions of the UN Charter, said Thant, any side to a conflict that refused an order could be subject to sanctions. These provisions had been used only once before: in 1948, when the Council successfully ordered a halt to the Arab–Israeli war. Thant also repeated his suggestion of a summit between Khan and Shastri and recommended ways in which the UN could monitor a ceasefire and a withdrawal of forces across the Line of Control. Working around the clock, Nimmo, Bunche, and Urquhart had already drawn up detailed plans.[28]

Over these hours, the fighting intensified, with the Pakistanis on the defensive. The Chinese then accused India of violating their border near the Himalayan kingdom of Sikkim and demanded a withdrawal as well as the return of fifty-nine allegedly stolen yaks.[29] This was, of course, a thinly disguised threat to intervene militarily on the side of Pakistan. At one point in the Security Council's deliberations, the Indian ambassador interrupted with a dramatic announcement that the Chinese were "massing" on his country's northern frontier and were "poised for an invasion." There was talk in the papers of World War Three.

US ambassador Goldberg also received a phone call that day from President Johnson, who wanted Thant to understand that Washington was, in a way, on his side.

"So, the President of the United States, the most powerful country in the world, is standing there and getting down on its knees, and not standing ten feet tall, but even standing lower than U Thant of Burma, to support him all the way on this thing," Johnson said. "Now, I think you ought to use this with U Thant. I think you ought to just say ... that the President and the Secretary of State have said that where he leads us, we will follow. We will support this man. They turn him down and kick him in the ass, but we're going to put our arm around him, and you just tell us which way you'd go, and we'd support you as best we can."[30]

Just after midnight on September 20, the Security Council passed the resolution as advised by Thant, ordering a ceasefire within forty-eight hours. The US and the UK supported the order by cutting off arms supplies to both countries. India immediately agreed to the ceasefire; Bhutto was on his way to New York with Pakistan's reply. With the deadline hours away, news came that Bhutto's plane had been diverted to Montreal because of fog. It was the middle of the night, but every seat in the Council chamber was taken and the adjacent rooms were crammed with diplomats and reporters. There was speculation that Bhutto might have to take a car from Canada, but at the last minute the fog lifted and he flew into New York just in time. After an emotional denunciation of India and only minutes to the deadline, he pulled a piece of paper from his pocket and read out his president's message to a hushed chamber. Pakistan too agreed to a ceasefire.

Yet clashes continued. Two of the world's biggest armies were standing face-to-face along a thousand-mile front. There was no decision to deploy peacekeepers, as in the Sinai, and renewed fighting could easily kick off at any time. Thant, Bunche, Nimmo, and Urquhart worked feverishly to pull together as many observers as possible for deployment not only in Kashmir but also along the Punjab, Rajasthan, and Sind borders. Soviet ambassador Federenko criticized Thant for exceeding his authority, but Thant stood his ground and other Council members rallied to his support.

The fighting soon petered out. Khan and Shastri met in Tashkent, as Thant had suggested, to iron out a formal agreement, mediated with deft precision by the USSR's premier, Alexei Kosygin.

On this rare occasion, the United Nations had functioned as intended. The big powers collaborated at the Security Council and the Secretary-General, through objective reporting, public appeals, private diplomacy, and advice on when to increase pressure, crafted the necessary pathway for peace.

A week after the Council's ceasefire resolution, Pope Paul VI arrived in New York. The sixty-seven-year-old head of the Roman Catholic Church was there as a guest not of the US government but of the Secretary-General. President Johnson would make a special trip from Washington to see him. No pope had ever before set foot in the New World.

Thant had met the Pope once before, in the Vatican, and thought it would be a good idea to invite the pontiff, who had a keen interest in international affairs, to address the General Assembly.[31] He increasingly recognized the need for influential allies. He also wanted to demonstrate his commitment to tolerance and diversity and brushed aside advice that he had no mandate to invite the Pope, saying, "No impartial observer could accuse a Buddhist Secretary-General of prejudice in inviting the head of the Roman Catholic Church to the UN."[32]

It was a sunny early October morning when the chartered flight carrying the Pope landed in New York.[33] Thant, who had been eagerly awaiting this moment, ascended the stairs of the Alitalia plane alone and then, after a few minutes, descended behind a waving, red-robed Paul VI. There was a service at St. Patrick's Cathedral, followed by a brief meeting with Lyndon Johnson at US ambassador Goldberg's official apartment in the Waldorf Towers. A little later, the Pope entered the domed General Assembly chamber to thunderous applause. His appeal to the governments of the world "for a peaceful battle against the sufferings of their less fortunate brothers" had moved him deeply, the Secretary-General stated. "It is the cause of peace which brings His Holiness into our midst. It was for the cause of peace—for all men on earth, without distinction as to race, religion, nationality or political belief which led me to invite him to this General Assembly."

With Jacqueline Kennedy, who had been invited by Thant, sitting to the side, the Pope took the podium and spoke in French.

"Our profound gratitude to Mr. Thant, your Secretary-General," he said. "The peoples turn to the United Nations as to the ultimate hope for harmony and peace.... You are not satisfied with making co-existence between nations easier; you are organizing brotherly co-operation between peoples.... This is what is most beautiful in the United Nations; this is its most truly human face."

When he completed his prepared speech, he cried, "*Jamais plus la guerre, jamais plus la guerre!*" No more war, no more war! The audience, many visibly moved, rose to their feet in an ovation that lasted more than ten minutes.

Later there was a reception, a meeting with the Soviet, American, British, and French foreign ministers, and a smaller gathering on the thirty-eighth floor before a midnight mass at Yankee Stadium before the papal flight back to Rome—all in less than twenty-four hours.

In his office, Thant gave the Pope a Burmese silver tray engraved with a Burmese maxim he had chosen himself: "The greatest conquest is the conquest of oneself."

That week, Norway's ambassador to the UN, Sievert Nielsen, showed Thant a letter from the Nobel committee stating their intention to award the Secretary-General the 1965 Nobel Peace Prize. Thant had turned down Burma's highest title a few years earlier, as there was a tradition for Secretaries-General not to accept titles from any government. He consulted his *chef de cabinet* Narasimhan, who said that this was different—a private endowment conferred by neither the Norwegian nor the Swedish governments. Thant replied to Nielsen that he would be honored to receive the prize.

However, in a mysterious last-minute turnaround, the committee chairman, Gunnar Jahn, blocked the decision, and the prize was awarded instead to UNICEF. Narasimhan, who had been in discussion with Nielsen, believed that though the Nobel committee was not "normally" influenced by political considerations, "it was obvious that there were forces at work which would not like the Peace Prize of 1965 to go to U Thant in view of his continued and open criticisms of the involvement of the United States in Viet-Nam."[34] Bunche, a Nobel Peace Prize laureate himself, considered it a "gross injustice to U Thant."[35]

In less than a year, Thant's term as Secretary-General would come to an end. Neither of his two predecessors had survived two terms: the first Secretary-General, Trygve Lie, felt forced to resign after the Soviets, angry at what Moscow saw as his pro-American stance on the Korean War, broke off relations; Hammarskjöld had been killed. For Thant, attempting a second term would be testing fate.

He could look back on several peacemaking successes. But as important as these was his role in keeping the United Nations going—not as the tool of any big power but as the catalyst for a new world order. In recent months, Zambia, Malawi, the Gambia, the Maldives, and Singapore had joined the world organization, bringing membership to 117.

Their admission, like the admission of dozens of former colonial possessions before them, wasn't just about states joining an institution. It was about the Afro-Asian nations, after centuries of European domination, asserting an equal place in the world. They would have a seat at the same table as the UK, France, and Belgium. India and Pakistan did not need to turn to a British or American mediator; they could turn to one of their own as Secretary-General of the United Nations. For the Afro-Asians, this new world order needed to be defended and enlarged.

For Thant, the clock was ticking. If he wanted to stay on in his role, he needed more than the support of the Third World. He had to get his relationship with both Washington and Moscow exactly right. The world's attention, which had turned for a few weeks to the war in the Indian subcontinent, was riveted once again by the carnage in Vietnam. Thant knew he had to act.

10 | THE SOUND OF SILENCE

IN LATE 1965, FIGHTING was raging across South Vietnam, with "search and destroy" operations by the American and South Vietnamese militaries uprooting tens of thousands of civilians. Communist soldiers streamed in from the North to fight alongside the Viet Cong. In the Ia Drang Valley in the central highlands, Hanoi's infantry regiments held off the 1st Cavalry Division, one of the US Army's most decorated formations, despite coming under four days of relentless air and artillery bombardment. It was the first direct combat between the two foes.

American casualties were mounting. In the last week of November 1965, the US lost more than 250 soldiers, more than in all of 1964. That same week, 35,000 people demonstrated near the White House in a March on Washington for Peace in Vietnam, the biggest antiwar protest yet. Three days later, after a trip to Saigon, Secretary of Defense Robert McNamara recommended to President Johnson that troop levels should be increased to 400,000 over the following year with possibly 200,000 more in 1967. Even with this, he stressed, there was no guarantee of success.[1]

In its November issue, the popular biweekly magazine *Look* published a lengthy article by Eric Sevareid entitled "The Final Troubled Hours of

Adlai Stevenson."[2] It was based almost entirely on Sevareid's long late-night chat with Stevenson in London hours before the ambassador's death. Sevareid had also spoken with Thant at his Riverdale home. The article made plain that an opportunity for peace in Vietnam had been missed.

When the issue hit the newsstands, Secretary of State Dean Rusk, who was on holiday, panicked and sent a meandering "Eyes-Only" cable to Johnson.[3] Rusk suggested that the veteran correspondent had "probably received a very substantial fee" and was likely to have embellished the facts for "dramatic effect." He also charged Stevenson with having had "a touch of Hamlet."

Rusk prevaricated on his role in dismissing Thant's proposal for talks: On "the Hanoi matter, my recollection is there was some discussion of some such contact... but I would have to check my own calendar." He admitted to a "brief exchange" with Thant and Stevenson but claimed that "there's a difference between rejecting a proposal and not accepting one." He added, "This distinction was made to U Thant but was apparently lost on him."

He concluded, "I would have to say that neither U Thant nor Stevenson would lose the chance to believe that peace was about to break out and that they themselves had played an important part in it."

The article may have boosted Thant's standing with those opposed to the war, who at the time were still a minority in America, but it doubtless cemented Rusk's ill feeling toward him. The critical relationship between the UN Secretary-General and the US secretary of state was now in tatters.

In Thant's view, improved superpower relations after the Cuban Missile Crisis should have opened the door to international cooperation on everything from economic development to space exploration. The obstacle was Vietnam. The war was making everything else impossible, draining American energy and optimism, and setting the Secretary-General on a collision course with the world's biggest power.

He was under no illusion about who would win a sustained confrontation between himself and the United States government. But he felt more certain than ever that a graceful American exit from Southeast Asia was in the interests of everyone, except perhaps the Chinese, who benefited from Hanoi's dependence on their largesse.

Thant was even more certain of his analysis of global politics generally, which echoed the views of other Afro-Asians: there was no need to think in Cold War terms. The Cold War was a European phenomenon which didn't apply globally. A win-win approach was possible. "The war we have to wage today has only one goal, and that is to make the world safe for diversity," he often stated. This was not idealism, he felt, but clear-eyed realism. Only the "peaceful co-existence" of different political systems could avert a new slide toward nuclear war.[4] With peaceful co-existence, governments could work together in concrete and practical ways, most urgently to raise living standards around the world.

The UN chief kept an eagle eye on relations between the Chinese and the Soviets, who were jostling to be the world's preeminent Communist power and vied to be Hanoi's top backer. Thant was in regular contact with several different Warsaw Pact governments and understood from them that Moscow might soon break formally with Peking.[5] The Soviet ambassador at the UN, Nikolai Federenko, was a Sinologist who knew Chairman Mao well. At a dinner, Federenko told Thant that the Chinese leader was "deranged."[6] Meanwhile, the French were telling him that the Vietnamese were receiving "massive aid" from the Soviets and also that the Chinese had "massed" along the Vietnamese border, ready for action against the Americans.[7]

The North Vietnamese, for their part, were playing a complicated balancing game between the two Communist giants, colored by their historical antagonism toward the Chinese (which few Americans appreciated). Over recent months, as Sino-Soviet relations worsened, North Vietnam had tilted decisively toward the USSR.[8] Under Khrushchev, Moscow had encouraged the Secretary-General to broker talks between Hanoi and Washington. Now, under Brezhnev and Kosygin, the Kremlin's overriding aim was a military victory for North Vietnam.

None of this was good news for Lyndon Johnson. At the president's ranch in Texas, Rusk, Defense Secretary McNamara, and National Security Advisor Bundy gathered to deliberate what was clearly a deepening quagmire of their own making. The intense bombing campaign, both against the North and within South Vietnam, had done little, if anything, to blunt enemy resolve, and there were now 185,000 US troops in Vietnam.

"Any evidence they are getting ready for a peace offer?" asked Johnson.

Rusk: "Not yet received."

McNamara: "The evidence points to the opposite view: a decision to escalate."

Johnson, who had read Sevareid's article on Stevenson, asked, "Is there any reality in the notion that there were real peace feelers?"

No, they insisted. Rusk then reviewed the "U Thant case," concluding for the president that Hanoi was only "ready to give us a face-saving exit."[9]

A "face-saving exit" was exactly what Thant had always had in mind, but it was what neither Rusk nor Johnson was willing to contemplate.

UK prime minister Harold Wilson returned to New York in December. Though he was still refusing to send British troops to Vietnam, he was now hewing close to the American line that unconditional talks should be held while the bombing continued. When he told Thant that there was a risk of South Vietnam becoming Communist if the fighting simply stopped, Thant replied that if Vietnam became neutral, the county's internal political system should matter little to the rest of the world. "The longer the war goes on," said Thant, the more likely "the end result will be a South Vietnam completely in the hands of the Communists." If there had been a real peace process the year before, he insisted, the situation could have been saved. Wilson had no response.[10]

Thant had no interest in a military solution, which he believed from the start was nonsensical. With thousands of atomic weapons positioned around the world, his principal concern was the potential that the conflict could explode into a wider confrontation.

In mid-December 1965, Thant received a secret message from Ho Chi Minh via the left-wing British journalist Felix Greene, who had just returned to London from Hanoi. The North Vietnamese leader said he wanted to send his "personal appreciation" of the Secretary-General's efforts to secure a just settlement of the war."[11] It was the signal Thant wanted, but with the prospects for diplomacy negligible, he decided to turn first to public opinion. In a statement released on December 22, he characterized the war in Vietnam as "a war more violent, more cruel, more damaging to human life and property, more harmful to relations among the great powers, and more perilous to the whole world, than at any other time during the generation of conflict that country has known."

Two days later, Johnson announced a pause in the bombing of North Vietnam. This had been decided over the previous weeks, on the recommendation of McNamara and others who thought a suspension of a few weeks—when, in any case, the cloudy winter weather made bombing more difficult—would show that the administration was open to negotiations. There was little faith that the diplomatic track would actually work, via Thant or anyone else, only a desire to demonstrate that it was being tried before the US set off on a new round of military escalation.

Thant wrote to Johnson to say that he welcomed the pause and Johnson immediately replied that he hoped "you will do whatever you can to help bring an end to the tragic conflict in Vietnam."[12]

Johnson was keen for the appearance of a "peace offensive." He sent a navy plane to fetch Arthur Goldberg, who was on holiday in the Caribbean, and told the ambassador that he would be leaving the next morning for the Vatican. The president wanted to keep the pontiff onside during the pause, especially given South Vietnam's mixed Roman Catholic and Buddhist population, and he took particular pleasure in the idea of sending "a Jew" to see the Pope.[13] Rusk called Bunche to threaten "harsh developments" if the peace offensive led to nothing.[14]

At the same time, veteran negotiator Averell Harriman circled the globe, stopping in Warsaw, Belgrade, Cairo, Delhi, Tehran, Vientiane, and Tokyo to expound Washington's policy and underline the president's interest in a settlement. There were also secret attempts to sit down with North Vietnamese representatives at embassies in third countries, including Burma. McGeorge Bundy reported that the British were assisting by telling everyone the Americans were sincere. The French, however, only "sneered at our efforts," Bundy wrote.[15]

Hanoi quickly concluded Washington wasn't really interested in peace, at least not one meant to lead to an American withdrawal. Ho Chi Minh labeled the overture a "sham peace trick."[16]

On January 27, 1966, Johnson met with his top Vietnam team, including McNamara, Rusk, Bundy, and Chairman of the Joint Chiefs of Staff General Earle Wheeler. Nearly all favored a resumption of bombing. Johnson, however, seemed hesitant.

"Did we make a mistake in starting to bomb in the North?" he asked.

McNamara: "No."

President: "Doesn't it worry you that Russia might heat up the world somewhere else?"

McNamara: "No. I think Russians are less a risk than China. And we are strong enough to handle other commitments."

Johnson: "What will U Thant say?"

Rusk: "U Thant will say 'too bad.' 'Some negotiations were in progress and they could have worked.'"

Johnson: "We don't have anyone defending us.... We have to be sure. We must be sure."

McNamara: "I am sure we need to resume bombing."[17]

Over the previous week, Thant's friend Norman Cousins, the editor of the *Saturday Review*, had been working with the Polish government to see if some kind of back channel could be set up with Hanoi. The White House had asked for his assistance as part of the "peace offensive" and a flattered Cousins was eager to help. On January 30, the Poles told Cousins that they had received a message from the North Vietnamese offering to see Cousins in Warsaw. Cousins thought a Warsaw meeting could be the start of something significant and was desperate for Johnson to keep the bombing pause in place.

That evening, Cousins telephoned the United Nations operator and was told that the Secretary-General was at home hosting a dinner party.

He drove up to Riverdale, parked his car by the gate, and trudged up the driveway blanketed with snow to the ivy-covered house, where he could see Thant through the window, in a brightly lit room with a dozen or so people "who seemed in a rather gay mood."[18] Thant's birthday was a few days earlier, and his wife, Thein Tin, would have her birthday a few days later; it was their habit to celebrate together with close Burmese friends over a meal and cake. They had another reason to celebrate, too: their daughter, Aye Aye Thant, had just left for Presbyterian Hospital in Manhattan to give birth to their first grandchild.

Cousins pleaded with Thant to phone Johnson right away. Thant demurred; he had never presumed to phone the president directly. Instead, he promised Cousins that he would get hold of Goldberg, see what was happening, and take it from there. He also suspected, like Ho Chi Minh himself, that the president's "peace offensive" was little more than a propaganda exercise. A few hours later, a dejected Goldberg informed Thant that the bombing was indeed resuming the next day and there was no way that the president would change his mind.

During the early months of 1966, the war in Vietnam soared to new levels of horror. By May, there were nearly 250,000 American soldiers in country, the vast majority inexperienced conscripts whose average age was twenty-two. Fighting alongside them were 500,000 South Vietnamese troops loyal to the military government of General Nguyen Cao Ky. Arrayed against them were 50,000 North Vietnamese regulars and an estimated 280,000 Viet Cong guerrillas. Tens of thousands of civilians had so far been killed (no one knew the exact numbers) and millions of gallons of chemical defoliants were being sprayed over forest and jungle. The Secretary-General had called for a broad-based government in South Vietnam. Instead, that spring, the Saigon military regime, with US support, crushed a Buddhist uprising demanding civilian rule.

In the US, there was simmering discontent. Senate Foreign Relations Committee chairman William Fulbright convened televised hearings in which eminent Cold War figures like George Kennan argued for an end to American involvement. In May 1966, protests against the war spread to nearly a hundred cities across the country.

Thant had to carefully calibrate his next move. The Americans wanted a Security Council discussion, for show as much as anything else. As three of the principal players—China, North Vietnam, and South Vietnam—were not members of the UN, Thant was adamant that the Council was the wrong forum in which to try to resolve the war. There would be no practical outcome, only the trading of insults between American and Soviet representatives, which would worsen global tensions.

He searched instead for a quiet diplomatic mechanism, perhaps a group of non-aligned states working with him informally. He discussed options with the Yugoslavs and several African governments including Mali, Uganda, and Nigeria. He was also in contact with Ghana's president, Kwame Nkrumah. Nkrumah, an early stalwart of Afro-Asian solidarity, was anxious to play a role and was preparing to travel to Hanoi and then Peking. Thant explained to the African leader his belief that only a new Geneva Conference leading to an American withdrawal and the reunification and neutralization of Vietnam could end the war. With the Americans gone, Thant was certain that the Vietnamese themselves would ensure that they remained free from either Soviet or Chinese domination.

How, though, to create the politics that would make such a conference possible? For Thant, the essential ingredient was an indefinite end to US bombing and then steps toward de-escalation by both sides. The Americans had to be convinced to move in this direction. At the same time, it would be good, the Secretary-General explained, if Nkrumah could encourage the Vietnamese to drop their "unrealistic" insistence that the Viet Cong, known officially as the National Liberation Front, should alone represent the South.[19]

Two weeks later, Nkrumah, after talks in Hanoi and en route to Peking, was overthrown in a military coup backed by the US and the UK.[20] He had devoted his life to freedom from colonialism and the emergence of a united and powerful Africa. Like so many other Afro-Asian figures, he had tried to find the right balance between East and West. Washington and London supported his overthrow ostensibly because he wasn't balancing sufficiently in their direction; they worried about Ghana moving too close to their Soviet adversaries.

The same thing occurred in Indonesia, where just a few months before, another leading light of the Non-Aligned Movement, Sukarno, had been ousted in a military coup supported by the United States. Up to a million people were killed in the carnage that followed.[21]

As in Vietnam, the idea of a Cold War extended from Europe to the rest of the world provided the West with the rationale to meddle in the ex-colonial world at will. Some of this meddling may have been motivated by a desire to promote or protect commercial interests. But at its heart, it was something far more basic: a feeling that the West knew best.

In an interview with the BBC in London, Thant described the Secretary-Generalship of the United Nations as "the loneliest job in the world."[22] On Vietnam, he was not only working without a mandate (something even his activist predecessor, Dag Hammarskjöld, never did), he was often working entirely alone.

Thant with his daughter and grandson at their home in Riverdale in the summer of 1966.

Omar Loutfi, who had been his political advisor during the Cuban Missile Crisis, was dead. As Burmese ambassador, Thant had developed warm friendships with many other delegates, like Sweden's Agda Rössel, but they were now in ambassadorial posts elsewhere. He had an amicable relationship with Arthur Goldberg, but it was nothing like the rapport he had enjoyed with Adlai Stevenson.

Thant became dependent on just two men: C. V. Narasimhan, his *chef de cabinet*, and Ralph Bunche. He trusted both and confided in them about most things—but not everything. Over early 1966, he set up other links, through journalist contacts and through the French, with whom he found himself seeing eye to eye.

In early 1966, the Secretary-General used secret communications from Ho Chi Minh, received via British journalist Felix Greene, to finetune his own thinking.[23] He was also receiving information from another British journalist, Simon Malley, who had long worked with anti-colonial movements. At Thant's request, Malley met in Algiers with National Liberation Front (Viet Cong) representative Tran Hoai Nam, who asked that the Secretary-General refrain from speaking of "negotiations" as this, to the Vietnamese, meant negotiating under the pressure of American aggression. He should instead deploy harsher language in demanding an end to the bombing and a return to the agreement reached at the 1955 Geneva Conference. Tran said that "the Burmese statesman was the object of all our admiration and of our confidence.... He has our deepest respect and we have always refrained from attacking him." But, he continued, Thant was "wrong advised," surrounding himself with "Indians" whose government, by also calling for negotiations, was playing into the hands of the Americans. "Even the French have told us that." If Thant did speak out as he should, the Viet Cong official added not very helpfully, the Secretary-General would likely fall foul of American machinations and be forced to resign.[24]

In March, as Washington announced yet another increase in troops, Thant put forward a "Three Point Proposal" for ending the war: one, an unconditional halt to the bombing of North Vietnam; two, the scaling down by all sides of all military action in South Vietnam, leading to a ceasefire; and three, discussions involving all those who were actually fighting, including the Viet Cong. These steps would be followed by the reconvening of the Geneva Conference where, said Thant, there could be a renewed agreement on the reunification and neutralization of Vietnam. The US would withdraw over a period of time, its prestige repaired. Thant had been meeting almost daily on Vietnam with ambassadors and ministers from around the world, and based on those discussions he believed this was the only path forward. The points were inseparable and had to be followed in order.

Peking immediately lashed out at Thant, asserting that he was equating victim and aggressor. Hanoi was milder in its rebuke, saying that Thant should simply have called for the withdrawal of the Americans. Washington said it liked the point about scaling down the fighting but not the rest.

The French, however, were delighted. In early May, Thant was in Paris, where President Charles de Gaulle was keen to embrace a United Nations Secretary-General with whom he shared a near identical position on Southeast Asia. France was leaving NATO and enjoyed being a thorn in Washington's side. De Gaulle was not displeased that Thant was becoming a thorn as well.

Over a luncheon in the baroque splendor of the Élysée Palace with prime minister George Pompidou, the writer and government minister André Malraux, and other French luminaries, de Gaulle declared, "As Secretary-General of the United Nations, you are in a position to see the world situation as a whole, and it so happens that you see it lucidly and impartially . . . we appreciate this contact because of your personality. It is a fact that, after [your] four years in office, no enlightened person in the world is reluctant to pay a fair tribute to you." Thant replied that "without vision, man perishes" and at that moment "all man's creations" were in danger of being annihilated "by the atom bomb."[25]

In Washington, estimations of the Secretary-General were less lofty. Dean Rusk was particularly irritated and at the annual Gridiron Dinner asked Ralph Bunche, "Can't you keep U Thant quiet?" Rusk disliked most Thant's repeated calls for a broad-based government in Saigon:

"Why doesn't he come out for a coalition government in Burma?" A Marine general sitting next to Bunche at the same dinner offered an extra thought: "Even if we killed all the North Vietnamese in South Vietnam we couldn't win unless we killed all the Viet Cong guerrillas."[26]

Looming over Thant's deepening discord with the Johnson administration was the question of a second term. Discussions both at the State Department and the White House led to a feeling that despite his irksome statements, the Burmese diplomat was likely better than the alternatives. A UN Secretary-General couldn't be anyone from the West or an "Asian ally," and, according to White House officials, Thant was better than "a weak African acceptable to Moscow."[27] More positively, *The New York Times*, in an April editorial, had called reports of his possible departure "bad news." "Perhaps no man is indispensable. But U Thant's retirement at this time would be a critical loss for the cause of peace."[28]

With protests and student teach-ins attracting tens of thousands in Berkeley and across America, Thant doubled down on his rhetoric. Speaking before the Amalgamated Clothing Workers in Atlantic City on May 24, he asserted: "In Vietnam, there is growing evidence that the so-called 'fight for democracy' is no longer relevant to the realities of the situation ... what is really at stake is the independence, the identity, and the survival of the country itself."[29]

No Secretary-General had ever done this before: challenge the world's most powerful country on its most important national security issue.

On May 26, in a piece entitled "Mr. Rusk vs. Mr. Thant," *The New York Times* opined that the world was being given "two contrasting views of the meaning of the war in Vietnam," with Rusk representing the Johnson administration and Thant representing a "large segment of world opinion." For Rusk the problem is "moral, almost religious and Wilsonian," a struggle of "democracy against communism." For Thant, it is "illusory" to look at the conflict in those terms, as it is essentially about the "independence and identity" of the country. Saying that neither was necessarily right or wrong, the *Times* concluded that "it must not be forgotten that

Mr. Thant is himself an Asian, and one who certainly reflects the feelings of millions of non-Communists throughout the uncommitted world."[30]

In late July, Thant flew to Moscow for talks with Party General Secretary Leonid Brezhnev at the Kremlin. The bushy-eyebrowed party chief had cut short a holiday on the Black Sea and, in "a bitter mood," warned Thant that thousands of Soviet volunteers were ready to fight in Vietnam if Hanoi called for them. Brezhnev believed that President Johnson, who had recently escalated the bombing campaign to include North Vietnamese cities, was getting "bad advice." He brushed aside any suggestion of new negotiations; any initiative, he insisted, had to come from Hanoi. Thant assumed that the Soviet stance was based, at least in part, on fear of Chinese criticism, but his Russian host wouldn't be drawn into a discussion about Soviet relations with Mao Tse-tung.[31] Just that morning, a million people had crowded into Peking's Tiananmen Square to hear China's revolutionary radicals warn America "not to misjudge your opponents."

In all their meetings, Brezhnev, Kosygin, and other Soviet leaders made plain their desire for Thant to stay on for a second term. "Even if you decide to leave your post, we will demand that you stay on," Brezhnev said half-jokingly.[32] Thant's primary worry was that the Kremlin would insist that he include a Soviet in his inner circle, to balance Bunche. Until now, he had kept his steady stream of Soviet Under Secretaries at arm's length. He maintained cordial relations with these men, who proved useful on occasion, but knew full well where their real loyalties lay.

After a brief sojourn in Leningrad, where he toured the Hermitage Museum, Thant returned to scorching weather in New York, with temperatures soaring to 110 degrees Fahrenheit. He conferred individually with important senators including William Fulbright, Mike Mansfield, Edward Kennedy, and George McGovern. All requested the Secretary-General to do more on Vietnam. "It seems to me that we are in the midst of one of those periods when the fate of mankind is in the balance," concluded McGovern.

A few days later, Arthur Goldberg went to the hospital to see Bunche, who was recuperating from a foot injury. Goldberg was early and caught Bunche naked, emerging from the bath. "Good morning, Ralph," said a smiling Goldberg as Bunche hopped into his pajamas. There was a large basket of fruits and nuts on the table next to the bed, a gift from Duke Ellington. They chatted about Yemen and the Middle East before Goldberg relayed an invitation from President Johnson to Thant to come to the White House. Johnson wanted to charm the Secretary-General and ensure that he would make himself available for a second term.

Bunche urgently passed this on to Thant, who, however, was not keen to go. He had nothing new to say to Johnson, he told Bunche, and "doubted very much" that Johnson had anything new to say to him. Thant was the first Secretary-General to receive an invitation to the White House (from Kennedy in 1962); he was now only the second to decline an invitation. Goldberg then met directly with Thant, who repeated his misgivings. As a result of "this attitude of U Thant towards an invitation from the President," Johnson told Rusk to go to New York and fix the situation.[33]

It's unlikely that Dean Rusk looked forward to the task. The Secretary-General and the secretary of state had been doing little to hide their dislike of each other; their words were measured but their body language showed the stress they felt when meeting. Thant tapped his foot, and Rusk doodled furiously.[34] But Johnson's top diplomat was now on his best behavior.

Rusk began the conversation by saying that he didn't understand why Hanoi was "consistently negative," and Thant by arguing for his "Three Points" as the only way forward. They had paused the bombing six months earlier for thirty-seven days, Rusk reminded him, to which Thant replied that pausing wasn't the same as stopping. Remembering his task, Rusk then probed Thant for advice on possible diplomatic approaches and his ideas on Hanoi's thinking. They even discussed the future neutralization of Vietnam.[35] Afterward, Thant told Bunche that it was "the best meeting" he had ever had with Rusk.

Before accepting a second term, Thant wanted to be assured of two things: a prospect of helping to end the war in Vietnam, and unqualified backing from the entire UN membership, including the US and the USSR. He wasn't interested in being Secretary-General as the organization became impotent and the world slipped into a new global war. Over the past couple of years, Afro-Asian solidarity had dissipated from its heyday around 1960: Nehru, Nkrumah, and other leading lights had departed the scene, economic challenges had mounted, and the push and pull of Washington, Moscow, and Peking had exacerbated tensions between several of the newly independent states. For Third World governments, this was all the more reason to have an experienced Afro-Asian diplomat remain at the helm of the United Nations. Nearly all the Afro-Asian ambassadors privately urged him to stay. But Thant had to make sure the big powers asked him to stay as well, and not the other way around. Being the supplicant would undermine his position. He had to maneuver carefully over the coming weeks.

A US intelligence assessment reported that Thant's wife, Thein Tin, was "violently opposed" to him continuing in his job: "She dislikes New York and life in the United States and exerts every pressure she can on her husband."[36] On this, the intelligence was profoundly flawed. It was true that Thein Tin never attended functions at the UN; if she was invited to an event as the Secretary-General's spouse, Narasimhan declined on her behalf, explaining that she spoke no English and that her health was "indifferent." She was indeed suffering from high blood pressure. But in all other ways, she and her husband were very happy with their life in New York. The Secretary-General's only lament was that his schedule left him precious little time to enjoy it.

Their Riverdale home was a lively, eclectic haven, shared with their daughter, son-in-law, new grandson, Burmese maids, multinational security guards, an Italian American gardener, and a Scottish nanny, along with a cat and a German shepherd puppy. For the Secretary-General, a grueling day at the office was usually followed by a Burmese meal and some television: the Smothers Brothers or perhaps Danny Kaye. Thein Tin relished trips into town with Burmese friends to Macy's and then to her favorite grocers on Mott Street and the butchers on McDougall. On weekends, Thant liked to catch up on reading, mainly books on history and politics, and enjoy a swim in the heated pool (recently covered so that he could swim year-round). When the weather was warm enough, Thant and Thein Tin might read or just take a nap in the canvas hammocks they had set up next to a little vegetable garden, with a sweeping view of the Hudson River and the sheer cliffs of the New Jersey Palisades just beyond. Sunday evenings were always reserved for *The Ed Sullivan Show.*

Thein Tin didn't like attending events in the city but was glad to host gatherings at home—usually animated Burmese affairs, with old friends who had left their military-run and increasingly isolated country and were building a new life in America. Once or twice a year, there were bigger events under a white tent in the garden, with Burmese musicians and dance performances and a mix of home-cooked food, Indian samosas, and catered dishes from a favorite Chinese restaurant. Ambassadors and senior aides, including Bunche and Narasimhan, together with their wives, came to Riverdale for these gatherings, as did other friends from the Secretary-General's UN life, such as Norman Cousins and John D. Rockefeller. These were the rare occasions when Thant's two worlds came together.

If there was no second term, the couple had already decided that they would try to stay on in New York. Their daughter and son-in-law began exploring options in the leafy Fieldstone neighborhood a couple of miles away, and on one occasion Thant joined them to look at a particularly promising house. But the UN chief knew that the impression his wife was badgering him to return to Burma might be useful as he charted his way through the coming months.

By late summer, pressure to accept a second term was coming from many quarters. Over a thousand letters and telegrams flooded in from private individuals and organizations. Thirty-six African member states of the UN appealed jointly to Thant to stay in office. Toward the end of August, 177 members of Congress, including Gerald Ford and other Republican Party leaders, also urged the Secretary-General stay on.[37]

So, too, did the UK Parliament. Earlier in the year, Thant had addressed a combined session of the House of Lords and the House of Commons. He was one of a handful of people to have had this honor, the previous two being Charles de Gaulle and Queen Elizabeth herself. A cross-party motion led by the Nobel laureate (and Olympic medalist)

Philip Noel-Baker called on him to continue his "courageous leadership" of the world organization.[38]

NBC's star reporter, Pauline Frederick, sent a private note, not as a journalist "but as an admirer," asking Thant to remember "all of us who believe so completely that you alone are the real spokesman for an anguished humanity."[39]

On August 31, after a three-day trip to South America, Thant returned to what was becoming frenzied speculation about his future. The next morning, he issued a statement that he had written during his flight home from Santiago. Citing a "lack of new ideas and fresh initiatives and a weakening of the will," he outlined the ways in which the "high hopes" of earlier years, including hopes for the economic development of poorer nations, had "fallen short." But his focus was on the "cruelty" of the conflict in Vietnam and the suffering it was causing. He warned that "the pressure of events" could soon lead to a "major war." Choosing his words with extreme care, he ended the statement by saying, "I have decided not to offer myself for a second term ... and to leave the Security Council unfettered" in finding an alternative.[40]

Thant then went into hiding for a week and refused all calls.[41] He wanted a very specific choreography to be followed, and relayed this covertly to Washington via the CIA. In a memo dated September 12, the CIA reported that "a source who is intimately familiar with the subject matter" conveyed information to "a representative of this Agency, whom he knew as such, with the hope and expectation that it would reach the highest United States Government officials." The source stated that the Secretary-General was prepared to continue but "it was vital to him" that his acceptance of a second term should come as the result of "appropriate representations" by both the Security Council and the General Assembly. In other words, Thant wanted to be drafted. He also wanted a sequence in which the Council and the Assembly would first separately commit to their future responsibilities in areas including peacekeeping and UN finances. He wanted, in particular, to play hard-to-get with the Soviets, so as to deny them an opportunity to impose conditions.[42]

Thant was not confiding fully in Bunche, only Narasimhan, who may have been the "source" used to pass on the message to the CIA.

Over these same weeks, Thant was again nominated for the Nobel Peace Prize by a group of Swedish parliamentarians led by Alva Myrdal, a prominent campaigner for global disarmament. As in the previous year, the chairman of the prize committee, Gunnar Jahn, opposed the Secretary-General's selection for unstated reasons. There was no question that awarding Thant the prize would strengthen his hand in pushing for peace in Vietnam. Whether Washington had a hand in influencing Jahn is unknown, but because of the continuing deadlock no one received the 1966 Nobel Peace Prize.

On October 7, Johnson made a surprise visit to the man who had twice in the past few months turned down a White House invitation. That week, *Newsweek* ran a closeup photograph of a pensive looking Secretary-General on its cover with the words "The Troubled UN."[43]

Initially, the president was jovial and seemed very relaxed. He said he was attending an event at the Carnegie Endowment and "could not be just across the street from the UN and not come to pay his respects to the Secretary-General as evidence of his confidence in both the United Nations and the Secretary-General."

He was, however, in "total disagreement" with Thant about his not staying on. Then, "looking extremely serious and disturbed," the president said there were those "telling him that he was talking too much and too often about peace and that this was being interpreted as a sign of weakness." Staring straight across the conference table at Thant he asked, "What would you say about that?"

Thant's response was studied: "I would not agree at all with those who advised not to keep reiterating the president's desire for peace . . . it is very necessary to continue to do so and this should never be interpreted as a sign of weakness." He told Johnson of a new effort, about which he had "not even told Ralph": a letter to Ho Chi Minh which he had dispatched while in Moscow. About six weeks before, he had received word "from one of the Ambassadors" that Ho wished him "to continue his peace efforts," though this was coupled with a "polite rejection" of his three-point proposal.

Thant also went over his efforts with Adlai Stevenson in 1964, which he described as like a Greek tragedy. Johnson replied that he was "unaware of most of this" and that "it was like a new book to me." He then looked at Rusk, who "interjected rather weakly" that there had a been a "misunderstanding" between Stevenson and himself over the telephone and that Stevenson had never been authorized to reject the initiative. "Stevenson was told to keep the door open." Thant and Bunche were "stunned into disbelief." Johnson said, "I very much regret the failure of your previous efforts.... I was totally unaware of any desire on the part of the other side to talk with us."[44]

Thant was adamant that if he stayed on, Bunche must stay on as well. On this, he and the Johnson administration were in complete agreement. At a reception at the White House, Goldberg told Johnson that Thant and Bunche were the two "indispensable men" at the UN.

Thant relied on Bunche's political advice more than anyone else's. Over the years, the two had also become good friends, sometimes watching baseball together on television when they had free time in the evenings. In August, Bunche had told the Secretary-General that he would leave the UN at the end of Thant's term. The now silver-haired sixty-two-year-old had been working tirelessly for decades, spending little time with his family and often feeling the guilt of an absentee parent. That month, his daughter, Jane, committed suicide by jumping from the roof of her apartment building in the Bronx.

"One could never hope for a better chief... [and] to serve under your leadership has been both an honor and a pleasure," Bunche wrote. But he was determined to spend more time with his wife, Ruth. His health was also taking a turn for the worse, with diabetes affecting his eyesight and causing him extreme fatigue.[45]

By early November, Thant was seen as the only candidate, but he still had not agreed to continue. He wanted enough momentum to ensure that his reappointment would come without constraint from any government. He wanted a free hand. He also told Bunche point-blank that he wouldn't accept a second term unless Bunche stayed as well.

In a personal note, Bunche reflected, "U Thant has been a real puzzle to me in these recent days, an enigma. Although I have been convinced for months that he was determined not to stay, in the last few days he has given the impression to me that he wants very much to stay and wishes to avoid doing or saying anything which might jeopardize the opportunity."[46]

A few more weeks of haggling followed, until the Security Council, "in view of his proven qualities and sense of duty," formally nominated Thant for a second term. Thant accepted. That afternoon, the General Assembly—with all 122 member countries of the UN represented—unanimously, and by secret ballot, reappointed him Secretary-General until the end of December 1971.

Over the past half decade, Thant had stood up to both superpowers and survived. And his survival meant the survival of an Afro-Asian vision of the world at the very apex of global diplomacy. The USSR had not only buried its "troika" formula but had even backed down from insisting on a Soviet advisor in the Secretary-General's inner circle. "The office of the Secretary-General which was close to destruction in 1961 was very much alive in 1966," Thant later reflected. "A former small-town school teacher in faraway Burma receiving such universal trust and confidence was indeed a miracle."[47]

The British writer and publisher Nigel Nicolson saw Thant just after his reappointment and found him "rather gay ... his conversation discreet but full of life." "He seems to divide the world not into East and West, white and colored, but into the different categories of temperament and behavior that can be matched in every nation on earth," Nicolson noted soon afterward. "He told me that when he was confronted by some particularly troublesome problem he would stand at the window and look down upon the little red and green light of the passing ships, deriving comfort from the 'decent traffic of mankind.'"[48]

11 | EVE OF DESTRUCTION

THANT BEGAN HIS SECOND term with a renewed ambition to end the bloodshed in Vietnam, which was then careering toward ever bigger battles and human suffering on a scale unsurpassed since the Second World War. Day and night, from sprawling new air bases in Thailand and across the western Pacific, supersonic F-105 Thunderchiefs destroyed bridges, power stations, and factories, B-52 bombers pulverized little wooden villages and bamboo hamlets, and squadrons of Douglas A-1 Skyraiders dropped tons of napalm, engulfing entire communities in fire.[1] The wealthiest and most technologically advanced nation ever known was unleashing its awesome military might on one of the planet's poorest societies.

The freshly reappointed Secretary-General was at the height of his popularity in the US. A Gallup poll asked, "What man that you have heard or read about living today in any part of the world, do you admire the most?" Thant came in sixth, behind Lyndon Johnson, Dwight Eisenhower, Robert Kennedy, the Pope, and Billy Graham, and ahead of Richard Nixon and Ronald Reagan.[2] A similar poll in Italy placed him as the "Man of the Year," followed by Mao Tse-tung and Charles de Gaulle.[3]

However, his support was far from universal, especially on Vietnam. Most Americans still backed the war and the bombing of the North.

Another Gallup poll found Americans evenly divided on Thant's Three Point Proposal.[4]

In early January 1967, the UN chief publicly appealed for a halt to the bombing and launched a full-frontal attack on the basic premise of Washington's involvement in Southeast Asia. "I do not subscribe to the generally held view that if South Vietnam falls, then country X, country Y, and country Z will follow," he stated. "I do not agree with this so-called domino theory. In my view, the destiny of every country is shaped by its own peculiar circumstances, its national characteristics, its historical background."

In a charged press conference that lasted over an hour, the Secretary-General, facing rows of correspondents from across the world—all men except NBC's Pauline Frederick—and with Bunche and Narasimhan listening pensively behind him, Thant insisted that the leaders of Vietnam were "very independent" and would resist any foreign domination, including from the Communist powers.

Congressman Mendel Rivers, a Democrat from South Carolina and an ardent segregationist who advocated using atomic weapons against North Vietnam, immediately responded with an attack on "the so-called Secretary-General of the so-called United Nations, really the modern Tower of Babel, who has thrown whatever weight he has against this country in our bombing of North Vietnam ... it is disgraceful, it is regrettable, and it is deplorable."[5]

On the other side of the Atlantic, Harold Wilson's Labour government kept a studied distance. He had turned down Johnson's request to send troops and was perhaps hoping to avoid further antagonizing the Texan president. But Wilson and his foreign secretary, Michael Stewart, also differed from Thant on the need to stand tough against Communist aggression, in Asia and elsewhere. Fresh from a meeting in Washington with Dean Rusk (who made a face when Thant's latest appeal for a halt to the bombing was mentioned), Stewart wrote to his prime minister that the Secretary-General's views "as an uncommitted Asian" must carry weight around the world and that the Americans valued his "perhaps unique contribution" in keeping the UN going, but they are "understandably disappointed in his inability to grasp the real elements of the problem." Stewart gathered that Johnson would like to "force an unrealistic Asian to take another look and see the world as it really is."[6]

Soon afterward, Wilson messaged Johnson to complain that for the first time he was facing a hostile vote in Parliament from members of his own party, who demanded that his government support Thant's appeal.[7] Both London and Washington were eager for the Secretary-General to tone down his rhetoric.

Thant, however, was proving stubborn, including in his determination to keep Ralph Bunche by his side. In January, Bunche reminded Thant of his desire to resign, but Thant was anxious not to lose a trusted advisor and refused to listen to suggestions of a possible replacement. He also understood that if Bunche left, the Johnson administration would try to coerce him to accept a Washington-selected successor. Bunche finally gave in, sacrificing the "plans and dreams" he had made with his wife to his loyalty to the UN and to Thant personally.[8]

With a unanimous reappointment and with Bunche by his side, the Secretary-General was in the position he wanted to make another, desperate bid for peace in Vietnam. He understood that both the White House and Hanoi's Communist leaders needed some political incentive if a diplomatic move were to gain even the slightest traction. Lyndon Johnson believed that he couldn't stop the bombing of the North without first extracting concessions from Hanoi. Hanoi, in turn, could not agree to talks without an unconditional end to the bombing. The Chinese, in the midst of their ultra-left-wing Cultural Revolution (which Thant labeled a "collective nervous breakdown"), were relentless in insisting that the Vietnamese think only of military victory. And the Soviets, wary of China's burgeoning influence among radical movements internationally, felt compelled to do the same, at least in public. With both sides in the grip of those determined to triumph on the battlefield, any peace process would almost certainly be doomed from the start. Even so, with thousands, perhaps tens of thousands, dying every month and a real danger of direct confrontation between the Soviets, China, and the US, Thant believed that diplomacy had to be given another chance.

Thant reckoned that the answer to the puzzle lay in Vietnam's fierce desire to be free of all foreign control. Ho Chi Minh's influence was fading, and hard-liners were on the rise. But no Vietnamese wanted the Chinese or anyone else to decide their future. The Polish foreign minister, Adam Rapacki, came to Thant's home in Riverdale one weekend to tell him that his Chinese counterpart, Chen Yi, had "violently brushed aside talk of negotiation." When Rapacki reported this to Pham Van Dong, the North Vietnamese prime minister, Pham was angry. The Chinese had "no business" saying this, he stated bluntly.[9]

In 1964, when Nikita Khrushchev still ruled the Kremlin, Thant had used Soviet intermediaries to communicate with Hanoi. Now he collaborated with the French and in particular with their UN ambassador, Roger Seydoux. A near contemporary of Thant's, the aristocratic Seydoux was a former professor and was descended from a long line of diplomats and industrialists.

Over the past four years, the two men had developed a warm relationship, with Seydoux praising the Secretary-General for his "very clear idea of what the United Nations can and cannot do." One example, he told French journalists, was Thant's "courageous" decision to end the Congo operation in the face of fierce and powerful opposition. As importantly, said Seydoux, by carefully maintaining constant contact with a broad range of the UN's members, especially the big powers, Thant was often able to "identify the path to a compromise better than most." He kept little offices next to both the Security Council and the General Assembly and "sometimes disappears into that office for a few minutes" with one delegate or another. "In a few minutes one can sometimes hold a very important conversation; the shortest talks are not necessarily the least profitable."[10]

Seydoux's praise may have reflected his genuine estimation of the Burmese statesman. It certainly reflected the French foreign ministry's satisfaction with Thant's views on Vietnam. Speaking recently to a crowd of over 100,000 people in Cambodia, President Charles de Gaulle had denounced the war and called for a quick US withdrawal. De Gaulle promised Thant his "full cooperation," and a young French diplomat, Alain Dangeard, was placed in the Secretary-General's office, primarily to assist him on Vietnam.[11] Over early 1967, Thant and Seydoux conspired over next steps. "There were no secrets between us," noted Thant.

Toward the end of February, the Secretary-General and his wife departed for Burma. The weather was well below freezing when they left New York; Rangoon was a sunny 80 degrees Fahrenheit. It was Thein Tin's first trip home since the family, including Timmy, had moved to New York nearly a decade before. Thant's only visit, in 1964, had lasted just a couple of days. This would be a proper ten-day vacation. They would spend time with Thant's eighty-four-year-old mother, who was still slim and elegant, his three younger brothers, and a legion of friends and relatives. Thein Tin valued especially the opportunity to make offerings and attend ceremonies at Buddhist pagodas and monasteries, which she believed were vital for the good karma of loved ones past and present.

Early one morning, about midway through his holiday, Thant was collected in an unmarked car by a senior military officer, who drove him from the state guest house to the North Vietnamese consulate by a roundabout route, so as to avoid being followed by the press. Seydoux had arranged for the Secretary-General to meet with a special delegation from Hanoi.

At the consulate, Thant was welcomed by the head of the delegation, deputy foreign minister Ha Van Lau, and treated to a spread of Vietnamese delicacies, which reminded him of the food he had enjoyed at Ho Chi Minh's table in 1954. The atmosphere was amiable, and the conversation quickly turned to the business at hand.

"The Vietnam War is first and foremost the struggle of the people of Vietnam against United States aggression," the trim, smooth-faced Ha stressed. "It is very wrong for the Americans to overestimate their military strength and scientific superiority. They will never conquer the Vietnamese people." He asked for an end to the bombing of the North and an American withdrawal from the South, so as to allow "our people [to] settle our own problems."

Thant, speaking not as the head of the UN but as "an Asian" and a "private citizen," reassured his Vietnamese interlocutors that he fully appreciated their views, in particular their desire to be free of outside interference. He also disabused Ha and the others of any wishful thinking around Johnson's position, explaining that the protests spreading across American campuses wouldn't stop the military escalation underway. Many Americans were in favor of tougher action, he warned. There could well be a long and far bloodier war—and this was what he was trying to avoid. Since the White House would not agree to an unconditional halt in its bombing of North Vietnam, he suggested instead a "standing down by all parties of all military activities," what he termed a "standstill truce." This would be followed by direct talks between the US and North Vietnam and a reconvening of the Geneva Conference, with the participants to be determined by Washington and Hanoi.[12]

The Vietnamese expressed appreciation for the Secretary-General's many efforts over the past three years, but reiterated that he must not equate the aggressor and the victim of aggression. They promised nonetheless to report his new proposal to the leadership in Hanoi.

Thant then spent a couple of days on a white sandy beach on the Bay of Bengal before returning to New York. The Vietnamese had reacted "somewhat negatively" to his ideas, he felt. But in fact, unknown to him, they had liked what they heard.[13]

Immediately after the Rangoon meeting, the Vietnamese delegation had flown to Peking to confer with the Chinese leadership on possible next steps, telling prime minister Chou En-lai of their wish to cooperate with the Secretary-General.[14] They were even thinking of inviting him to Hanoi.

The Chinese said no. Chou En-lai, revolutionary leader, statesman, and survivor of the Maoist purges mushrooming all around him, told Ha Van Lau and his colleagues in no uncertain terms to stay away from Thant. He had nothing against Thant personally, Chou said, but thought he was under the "mistaken belief" that once he had the support of the US and the USSR he could act as pleased. He had become a "tool" of the two big powers "at the expense of the Afro-Asians." Thant's proposal would lead only to a spiral of demands for more Vietnamese concessions. "This is a dialectic of those who fear the victory of the NLF [the Viet Cong]—basically the USSR."[15] Sino-Soviet tensions were then at a near boiling point, with the Chinese wishing to demonstrate that Peking, not Moscow, was the center of global Communist revolution.

The most the Vietnamese could extract from Chou was a promise that the Chinese "would ease up on their attacks" against Thant.[16]

Back at UN headquarters, a rested Secretary-General was suddenly finding himself on the defensive. He had acted entirely on his own, meeting the Vietnamese without even a note-taker, but intelligence reports quickly reached Washington. Ambassador Goldberg, tasked with getting a text of Thant's new "proposals" to the North Vietnamese, asked Bunche about his boss's thinking. Bunche knew nothing about the meeting, and was flabbergasted when told by Thant that he had indeed put forward a new formula.

What Thant had done was essentially collapse two of his earlier points—a bombing halt and then a de-escalation—into a single "standstill" proposal. By dropping the bombing halt as an explicit initial step, he was gravitating toward Johnson's position. He hoped he could use any understanding he had nurtured with Ha Van Lau to compensate for this. He had never meant to put anything in writing until he heard back from Hanoi. But Bunche and the Americans were insistent, so Thant spent the weekend putting his proposal in writing.

In Bunche's opinion, Thant was completely wrong in dropping the demand that the bombing stop first and was "unaware of how far he had gone."[17] He tried to impress on his boss that an end to the bombing had become—in no small measure because of the Secretary-General—the rallying cry of people against the war across America and internationally.

It was a key demand of Robert Kennedy and William Fulbright. Furthermore, Hanoi would never accept a proposal without it, Bunche asserted. He thought Thant was being naive and urged him to reinsert the appeal.

Within days, everyone at the UN had learned of the Secretary-General's new proposal. Thant defended his apparent shift by saying that of course he wanted an end to the bombing but saw little use in "saying the same thing over and over again" when it was clear that the White House wouldn't accept it.[18] With the cat out of the bag, he met with Seydoux and other ambassadors and then circulated a formal aide-mémoire outlining his position to the US, North Vietnam, South Vietnam, and the NLF (Viet Cong). Hanoi responded with a broadcast on state radio warning that the Americans were "using the UN" to interfere.

Feeling that his effort was now on life support, Thant, following Bunche's advice, tried a different tack. In a carefully worded statement, he called on the United States, a nation "with power and wealth unprecedented in human history," to break the impasse by taking unilateral action toward the "standstill truce" and "stop the horrible slaughter" in Vietnam. This echoed a recent call by American senator Joseph Clark. Thant was essentially back-pedaling, and again asking Washington to make the first move.

The statement made headlines around the world and won the backing of *The New York Times*. Peking, unsurprisingly, condemned what it called America's "peace talk swindle," grouping Thant in a "gang of monsters" that also included the UK, India, and the Pope.

Secretary of State Rusk advised Johnson to accept Thant's proposal—not the call for a unilateral American ceasefire, but the "standstill" proposal he had formally outlined on his return from Rangoon.

"Well, I just have this thought," mused the president in a phone call with Rusk. "I proceed from one negotiation to the other constantly waiting for something that never comes and usually find myself in worse shape at the end of the proposal than I do at the beginning."

Johnson was growing wary of playing ball with the Secretary-General.

"I don't think that U Thant is our friend. I don't think he'll do much for us except embarrass us. I think the whole outfit up there is potentially a very embarrassing thing." Then he got to his main point: "But I know this: that when U Thant makes a proposal or Bobby Kennedy makes one or somebody else makes one, although we are ready to do our part, it just costs us five or ten points [in the public opinion polls] next week."[19]

A persistent Rusk, however, managed to convince the president to accept Thant's proposal, not because he valued Thant's diplomacy but because he saw an opportunity to score a propaganda victory.

What had begun as an effort by the Secretary-General to cultivate a quiet relationship with Hanoi was now a tangle of official UN memos and public pronouncements. Hanoi hurried away. On March 20, Ha Van Lau sent a formal letter rejecting Thant's proposal, stating that it was not meant to be shared until the North Vietnamese government had had time to consider it and reply:

"We are sorry you have made public your considerations though in Rangoon you confirmed that you would do it only when they were accepted by the Government of the DRV [North Vietnam]." Thant took solace in the fact that the reply was a polite one which concluded, "You wish to help the Vietnamese people . . . we welcome your good will."

Thant immediately wrote directly to Ho Chi Minh, saying that there had been a misunderstanding and that he had always intended, once back in New York, to share his proposal in strict confidence with the Americans. He stated as well his "steadfast" belief that the bombing had to stop.[20] In a meeting that month with Felix Greene, the British journalist in contact with Thant, Ha Van Lau confessed he couldn't understand why Thant had to make his ideas public when there was a need for total secrecy.

Hanoi's hard-line Communist Party Secretary Le Duan speculated that it was "U Thant who tricked himself and the Vietnamese."

A few days later, Thant hosted a dozen members of the Senate Foreign Relations Committee at a luncheon on the thirty-eighth floor, among them the chairman, William Fulbright, and senators Albert Gore, Frank Church, and Eugene McCarthy. The Secretary-General was going for broke and diving head-first into the maelstrom of US politics.

With many of America's leading politicians around his dining table, Thant stressed how important it was to appreciate the power of nationalism in the former colonial countries. Burma was far better off for having dealt with its own Communist insurgency alone. Accepting American military assistance would have "given our people the idea that we are bringing back the whites," which would have led to a backlash. The Vietnamese, he argued, were of a similar mindset.

Thant then gave a forensic account of his abortive peace effort in 1964. He recalled that when he had said all this to President Johnson "sitting in that very chair"—he pointed to Senator Fulbright—the president said he had "never heard of it." He attempted to draw a clear distinction between the kind of conditional pause to the bombing that had already been tried and an actual ending of the bombing campaign, and said that he was certain that if the bombing stopped there could be meaningful talks after just a few weeks. An animated discussion followed, about Hanoi's thinking, future ceasefires, and Sino-Soviet relations. It was, Bunche noted, "one of the frankest exchanges he had seen take place between a Secretary-General and any group."[21]

One of the senators later told the press: "We had more candor from U Thant on the Vietnam question than we have had from the President and the Secretary of Defense combined over the past several years."[22]

Thant's aide Alain Dangeard analyzed his chief's recent moves and concluded that his increasingly convoluted attempts to find a ceasefire formula were getting nowhere. Perhaps Thant's real strength, the Frenchman counseled wisely, was in framing the ways in which people thought about the war. The Secretary-General's forte was in leading public opinion. Perhaps taking the advice to heart, an exasperated Thant, at a press conference in late March, lamented that the continued war was bringing only "more death, destruction, devastation, and consequent misery." The "growing fury of the war," he warned, might soon spill beyond Vietnam's borders and engulf "larger areas of Asia."

Thant then left for a two-week tour of South Asia, visiting India, Pakistan, Ceylon, Nepal, and Afghanistan. Across much of the subcontinent, April was the muggiest time of the year, just as the monsoon winds began to reverse direction, adding humidity to the sky-high temperatures, and before the first torrential downpours offered relief. Everywhere, fans whirled overhead as men in starched white outfits offered tea, lime soda, and the sweet ripe mangos that were in season. Everywhere, the conversations focused on Vietnam.

In Delhi, at an impressive and colorful ceremony, Thant accepted the first Jawaharlal Nehru Award for International Understanding, as a recognition for his role in ending the 1965 Kashmir war. In fact, the ties went much deeper. Handsome tributes were paid by an array of distinguished speakers. Prime minister Indira Gandhi, Nehru's daughter, then fifty and a little more than a year into her job, described Thant as "a dedicated champion of a united and peaceful world" who had "brought together the Buddhist's compassion" with the teacher's "infinite patience." President Radhakrishnan, who had hosted the Secretary-General during the 1965 war, said that all Indians were aware of Thant's "ceaseless efforts" to end the "senseless slaughter of innocent men, women, and children" in Vietnam. "As a true Buddhist U Thant aims at peace, without victory or defeat for either side, but with reconciliation."[23]

For Thant, the trip also included a pilgrimage. In Nepal, he rode on an elephant to Lumbini, the Buddha's birthplace, where he was awed but also deeply saddened to see the forlorn remnants of brick buildings lying neglected in nearly empty scrubland. He told the Nepali officials with him that it was "the most important day of my life." He resolved that day to declare Lumbini a UNESCO World Heritage Site.

Two thousand miles to the south, at Kandy in Ceylon, Thant paid his respects to the *mahanayaka*, or chief monk, of the local Buddhist chapter, who lauded his efforts to bring peace to Vietnam. "The teachings of the Buddha will always guide my efforts," the Secretary-General replied. The blessing fortified him.[24]

Half a world away, Martin Luther King Jr. was leading 400,000 marchers from Central Park to the United Nations in support of peace in Vietnam. In Thant's absence, Ralph Bunche received King, the renowned pediatrician Benjamin Spock, and other organizers of the march. Antiwar sentiment was growing exponentially, and millions were looking to the UN Secretary-General for direction.

The New York Times, in an editorial, underlined its support for Thant's view that an unconditional halt to the bombing of North Vietnam would lead to talks. "There is probably no person in the world outside North Vietnam with a better right to hold an opinion on this subject than U Thant," the editors argued. "He has been in contact with North Vietnamese, Russians, and all Asians. As a Burmese, he understands the psychology of the Vietnamese in a way no Westerner can. He now has had years of experience in statesmanship covering every nation on the globe."[25]

On his return, Thant felt more determined than ever to forge ahead, risking Washington's ire as necessary. Over his first five years as head of the world organization, he had found the right strategies to connect his Afro-Asian and non-aligned views with Washington's interests and tacit patronage. Then, he had been able to imagine himself the "harmonizer" he wanted to be—but not anymore. But if he backed down now, he would make a mockery of the UN he and his fellow Afro-Asians had for years been struggling to create.

His thoughts also turned back to his early life as a teacher. In a speech at the University of Michigan at Ann Arbor, where there had been sustained student protests against the war, the Secretary-General asserted that "in our interdependent, crowded, dangerous but also challenging world, tolerance, understanding and fresh thinking on national and international problems are the key to nothing less than human survival."

Only education, he told the assembled students and scholars, could begin "the urgent task of transferring men's thoughts from their conflicts to their common interests" and from "the obsession with sterile and outmoded political and military competition to the far more challenging and fascinating problems of peace, justice, and co-existence and co-operation."[26]

Thant was also worried that another conflict, largely ignored, might soon erupt into full-scale war. On May 8, 1967, he informed the Security Council that attacks into Israel by Palestinian guerrillas based in Syria were a serious breach of the 1949 Armistice Agreements which had ended the first Arab–Israeli war.

He was right to be worried. He couldn't have imagined, though, that what came next would change his life and the United Nations forever.

12 | GAZA AND THE SINAI

WHEN THE TELEPHONE RANG on May 15, 1967, Indar Jit Rikhye was thinking about playing golf. He had spent the day inspecting a newly arrived Swedish battalion but was now back in his hilltop villa in Gaza, concrete with red shutters, overlooking the silvery blue waters of the eastern Mediterranean. The airfield was not far away; that was where the Canadian Royal Air Force had set up a golf course, between hulking Caribou transport planes and wandering herds of goats and sheep.

The forty-seven-year-old Rikhye was still the Secretary-General's chief military advisor. For the past eighteen months, he was also in command of the global organization's biggest and most successful peacekeeping operation, the UN Emergency Force (UNEF), which policed the armistice line between Egypt and Israel and was headquartered in the Egyptian-administered Gaza Strip.

On the phone was Brigadier-General Ibrahim Sharkaway, the Egyptian army's bespectacled liaison officer to UNEF, relaying news that a special courier was on his way from Cairo with an urgent message. Golf plans postponed, Rikhye drove to the Egyptian army liaison office a few miles away and an hour or so later was handed a letter from General Muhammad Fawzy, the chief of staff of the United Arab Republic's armed forces.[1] (Egypt was then known officially as the United Arab Republic or UAR.) Rikhye read the letter at once:

I gave my instructions to all UAR Armed Forces to be ready for action against Israel the moment it might carry out any aggressive action against any Arab country ... our troops are already concentrated in Sinai on our eastern borders. For the sake of complete security of all UN Troops which install OPs [observation posts] along our borders, I request that you issue your order to withdraw all these troops immediately.

This letter was the death knell for UNEF, thought Rikhye.[2] The general could not, however, take any action on his own. Only the Secretary-General could decide how to respond.

Eleven years earlier, the British, French, and Israeli militaries had together invaded Egypt, taking the Sinai and Gaza in an effort to seize control of the Suez Canal. They might have succeeded had it not been for a furious United States government, which compelled the invaders to withdraw from Arab territory. UNEF was the first peacekeeping operation of its kind, its lightly armed soldiers remarkably successful in heading off potential clashes between the Egyptians and the Israelis. The operation was so successful that it had been practically ignored. Until now.

The courier, General Eiz-El-Din Mokhtar, asked for Rikhye's response, saying that he had to communicate it immediately to General Fawzy. "Do you know what you are doing, do you know this will lead to war?" was what Rikhye wanted to say. Instead, he answered simply that he "noted" the contents of the letter. "I will immediately report to the Secretary-General for instructions."

The Egyptian frowned. "General, you are requested to order the immediate withdrawal of UNEF troops from El-Sabha and Sharm El-Sheikh tonight. Our Supreme Commander anticipates that when Israel learns of our request to you, they will react immediately. In anticipation of any action they may take, our army must establish control over El-Sabah and Sharm El-Sheikh tonight!"

El-Sabah was a strategic post along the front line. Sharm El-Sheikh, at the southernmost end of the Sinai desert, bordered the Red Sea and overlooked the Straits of Tiran, just three miles wide at its narrowest point. Whoever controlled Sharm El-Sheikh could block ships heading through the Red Sea to Israel's port at Eilat. Since 1956, a company of Yugoslav soldiers, part of UNEF, had been stationed there.

Rikhye reread the letter. There was no mention of El-Sabah or Sharm El-Sheikh. When he mentioned this, the Egyptian officer repeated what he had said, adding that he feared a clash with the peacekeepers as Egypt's military units moved forward. He advised that the Yugoslavs not establish their normal positions the next morning, but stay in their camp nearby. The UN general responded politely but firmly that as "long as the UAR did not attempt to use force against UNEF personnel, there would be no clash."

He asked if they were prepared for what might follow. "Oh yes sir!" replied a beaming Brigadier-General Sharkaway. "If there is a war, we shall next meet in Tel Aviv!"

It was now nearly midnight. Rikhye excused himself and rushed a highest-priority cable to the Secretary-General. He also assembled his chief officers and instructed the Yugoslavs at Sharm El-Sheikh to "carry on as usual," but under no circumstances to use force against approaching Egyptian troops. Everyone now waited for Thant's response.

UNEF had kept the Egyptian–Israeli front line calm for more than a decade. But there were no international peacekeepers along Israel's borders with Syria and Jordan. In the mid-1960s, Fatah, a militant Palestinian organization, began launching guerrilla raids into Israel from Syria and the West Bank of the river Jordan, which prompted an Israeli incursion into Jordan in 1966. In early 1967, Israel's prime minister, the avuncular Levi Eshkol, warned publicly that his government would take decisive action if the cross-border raids continued.

To frighten the Syrians, the Israelis relayed disinformation to Moscow using a double agent working for Shin Bet, the Israeli intelligence agency.[3] The Politburo soon received a report from someone they mistakenly believed was a KGB spy confirming that the Jewish state was readying for an invasion of Syria. The Soviets alerted the Syrians, just as Tel Aviv wanted, knowing that Damascus would take seriously intelligence emanating from Moscow. The Syrians could have looked from the Golan Heights (which they controlled) down into Israel and seen that there were no troop concentrations, as alleged, but they were happy to pass on to Cairo the misinformation as it confirmed their longstanding claim of an imminent threat. They even added speculation the attack might take place in five to ten days. Egypt's vice president, Anwar Sadat, who was visiting Moscow, was given the news by his Russian hosts. An alarmed Sadat immediately cabled Cairo.

The next day, the first Egyptian infantry divisions rolled into the Sinai and toward the front line.

General Rikhye's cable was received at UN headquarters late in the afternoon of May 16 New York time. Brian Urquhart was in his thirty-eighth-floor office, meeting with press aide Ramses Nassif, when a secretary entered with a folder. Urquhart jumped to his feet: "I must go and see Ralph!" Within minutes, Bunche and Urquhart were hurrying down the long corridor to see the Secretary-General.[4]

Thant immediately messaged Rikhye to await further instructions and in the meantime "to be firm in maintaining UNEF positions, while being as understanding and diplomatic as possible" with the Egyptian authorities. He then called in the Egyptian ambassador, Mohammed El-Kony, who had no idea what was going on, but said he would check with Cairo and report back.

Thant huddled with Bunche and Urquhart. Both men had been intimately involved in setting up and managing UNEF over the years, along the way crafting new international norms and methods of working. They knew exactly what UNEF could and couldn't do. The force was made up of 3,400 lightly armed men from ten countries, primarily India, Yugoslavia, and Canada, whose principal task was to maintain a buffer between the antagonists. The Israelis refused to have UN troops on its side of the line. The Egyptians, however, consented and kept their own troops 2,000 yards back from most of the line. Once the Egyptian military entered the buffer zone—which was all within its territory—and moved up to the line and into Sharm El-Sheikh, as it did over these few hours, UNEF was effectively put out of action.[5]

On anything related to the Arab–Israeli conflict, Thant relied almost entirely on Bunche, who considered UNEF his life's work. Despite all his globetrotting, Thant had not once been to the Middle East as Secretary-General, except for a brief visit to Cairo to attend an African summit. He had, instead, a long history of friendship with Israel, having visited with his prime minister in 1955, and maintained amicable relations with many Arab diplomats. But he did not have a firsthand feel for the passions surrounding the conflict.

Bunche advised Thant that Egypt's President Nasser was bluffing. With much of his army bogged down in Yemen (where Egyptian troops were boosting republican forces fighting the Saudi-backed Imam), the Egyptian leader couldn't be planning war and so wouldn't want to see UNEF entirely disbanded. Bunche knew that the removal of UNEF could only lead to hostilities. Meanwhile, Thant's legal counsel, Constantin Stavropoulos, advised that the Secretary-General had no legal basis on which to reject an Egyptian request for the withdrawal of UNEF.

Thant gave Egyptian ambassador El-Kony an official note saying that Cairo had proceeded wrongly. Any request to withdraw UNEF had to come directly to the UN Secretary-General from the government of Egypt, not from the Egyptian army to General Rikhye. If Egypt were to request a complete withdrawal of UNEF troops, the Secretary-General could not refuse; however, a temporary withdrawal from the line was unacceptable. The purpose of the force was "to prevent a recurrence of fighting, and it cannot be asked to stand aside in order to enable the two sides to resume fighting." The peacekeepers couldn't redeploy— remaining in Gaza, for example, and protecting Egypt's flank—while Egypt undertook aggressive action elsewhere.

Thant thought he was calling Nasser's bluff.

In a separate meeting, the Israeli representative, Gideon Raphael, warned Bunche that the reply would back Nasser into a corner, but Bunche disagreed.

That afternoon, the Secretary-General, Bunche, and Urquhart met informally with ambassadors from all the countries supplying troops to UNEF. The Indian, Pakistani, and Yugoslav representatives said they would respect Cairo's call. If Egypt was reacting to a perceived Israeli threat to its Syrian ally and wanted UNEF to leave, the peacekeepers had to leave. International law was clear. Canada, Sweden, and Denmark all expressed their extreme unhappiness with the situation but, when pressed, couldn't suggest an alternative.[6]

Thant searched for space for maneuver. He accepted that Egypt as a sovereign country had the right to ask for a withdrawal. The Afro-Asian states had fought hard to win their sovereignty, and the protection of this sovereignty was a critical task of the world organization. In practical terms, Thant said, it was impossible for UN peacekeepers to stay without Cairo's permission. But he also had to consider the UN's overarching task: preventing war. He told the ambassadors that if he received an official request from the Egyptian government either to withdraw or redeploy UNEF he would, before taking any action, appeal it. The head of the UN military office in Jerusalem, the Norwegian general Odd Bull, had reported that the Syrian–Israeli border was calm. There was no Israeli troop buildup. It should be possible, the Secretary-General reckoned, to de-escalate tensions.

Canada's ambassador, George Ignatieff, suggested that the matter be put to the General Assembly. It was the Assembly, rather than the Security Council, which had mandated the setting up of UNEF during the Suez Crisis, in order to circumvent British and French vetoes in the Council. But this would require a two-thirds vote, which was impossible, given that the new Afro-Asian majority would side with Egypt and refuse even to discuss the matter.

Bunche provided some history: UNEF's peacekeepers were first mustered in nearby Cyprus and sent to Gaza and the Sinai only after an agreement on their deployment was reached between then Secretary-General Hammarskjöld and Egypt's President Nasser. There was never any doubt that the Egyptians could rescind their consent in the same way that the Israelis had refused to have the troops on their side of the line. Thant and Bunche both stressed that any hint of the peacekeepers attempting to remain without the host country's permission would imperil operations elsewhere, in Cyprus and Kashmir.[7]

The Americans were not in the room, but they were briefed soon enough. Rusk sent Johnson a memo reporting that Thant seemed to be "playing for time," but that neither he nor the governments with troops in UNEF "would be eager for a test of will."[8]

The next morning, the pressure on UNEF grew. The Egyptians were limiting flights across the Sinai, thereby cutting food supplies to the peacekeepers' far-flung outposts. In several locations, the UN troops arrived at their regular positions to find Egyptian soldiers, some with armored vehicles, already there. In places where UNEF soldiers tried to remain, the Egyptians exploded artillery shells nearby. At Sharm El-Sheikh, Egyptian officers flew in by helicopter and gave the Yugoslavs there fifteen minutes to leave. General Rikhye tried to see for himself what was happening, but his plane was intercepted and forced down by two Israel military jets, presumably in an attempt to warn the UN against infringing on Israeli territory or airspace.

The UN chief conferred with Israeli ambassador Gideon Rafael.[9] The two men had enjoyed an affable relationship since Thant's days as Burma's ambassador. In a "long and lively discussion," the Berlin-born Rafael strongly advised his friend to refuse any request from Nasser to remove the peacekeepers. At the very least, he should send the Egyptian leader a personal communication asking him to reconsider. Thant agreed. Next came a discussion with Goldberg, who said that Washington hoped Nasser could be persuaded to change his mind.[10]

The Egyptian ambassador El-Kony was waiting in Thant's outer office for Goldberg to leave. He told Ramses Nassif, Thant's Egyptian press aide, that he was delivering a formal request for a full withdrawal. President Nasser had interpreted Bunche's comments the day before as an attempt to cut off any discussion of redeployment and force Cairo to choose between the status quo and a complete termination of the peacekeeping operation. Nasser, aware that Bunche had advised this response, had concluded that Bunche was part of an American–Israeli plot to embarrass him.[11]

El-Kony told Nassif that he had just spoken by phone to his foreign minister, who reported that the atmosphere in Cairo was "very tense." There was speculation that the Secretary-General was being bullied by some Western countries to disrespect their country's sovereign rights.

"If worse comes to worst," El-Kony suggested, "UNEF will be disarmed and shipped in trucks out of Egypt!"

"I'm sure you are not going to tell U Thant all that!" Nassif cautioned.[12]

The letter to Thant, signed by Egyptian foreign minister Mahmoud Riad, stated Cairo's decision to "terminate the presence" of the United Nations Emergency Force from the territory of the United Arab Republic (Egypt) and Gaza and asked that "the necessary steps be taken for the withdrawal of the force as soon as possible."

Bunche had been mistaken. Nasser wasn't bluffing.

El-Kony repeated to the Secretary-General what he had said to Nassif about the "great indignation" felt against the US, UK, and Canada for suggesting that UNEF remain against Egypt's will. If the peacekeeping force tried to stay, he argued, it would become an "occupation army." Thant, fearing the worst, said he would appeal to Nasser. That evening, after checking with his foreign minister, El-Kony returned to say that the decision was "final" and pleaded with the Secretary-General not to appeal, telling him he would be "rebuffed."

"Then I will travel myself to Cairo," replied Thant. El-Kony agreed that this was a good idea and phoned Cairo again. He was told the Secretary-General would be very welcome, "The sooner the better." It was Thursday, May 18. Thant said he would be there by Monday. Why he couldn't leave right away is unclear.

An apprehensive Nassif, who had been a journalist in Egypt, told Thant privately that he should send the appeal anyway. Perhaps Nasser had backed himself into a corner and the appeal could help him find a face-saving way out, as had occurred during the Cuban Missile Crisis. In 1962, the Secretary-General had acted without consulting either the Soviets or the Americans, and he had been proven correct. Thant listened to Nassif, but told his press aide that Bunche had a different view.[13]

A couple of hours later, Thant convened a meeting of the ambassadors in UNEF's Advisory Committee and those representing the countries providing troops.[14] He told them that he had no choice but to formally agree to Cairo's request for a withdrawal of UNEF.

Angry exchanges followed, setting the Indian and Yugoslav ambassadors—whose countries represented the largest contingents in UNEF—against several Western countries. Canada's Ignatieff was particularly assertive, declaring that he could not accept the view that Egypt "is in a position to demand immediate compliance with the withdrawal of UNEF."

Bunche intervened to give "some hard facts." UNEF was there on the basis of consent. No government had given troops for anything other than peacekeeping, and certainly not to go to war with Egypt; these troops weren't equipped or configured to fight. However, he was aware that politicians and journalists in the US, the UK, and Canada were already criticizing what they saw as a hasty decision to withdraw.

Under Thant's orders, Bunche and Urquhart prepared for an orderly withdrawal that would take the maximum time possible so that if Cairo changed its mind, the troops would still be in theater. Unknown to them, the Egyptian foreign ministry had told the Yugoslav and Indian governments that morning, via their embassies in Cairo, that their UNEF contingents should leave. Without consulting the Secretary-General, the Yugoslav and Indian governments agreed to do this immediately.

Later the same day, Thant submitted a report to both the Security Council and the General Assembly warning about an "extremely menacing" situation that could soon lead to "disaster." Canada and Denmark requested an urgent session of the Security Council and a resolution in support of any diplomatic effort by Thant. The Soviets said there was no point; Egypt was only taking measures to safeguard its own security and the security of other Arab states against a belligerent Israel.

Goldberg, who had been on a cruise, phoned Bunche to let him know that he was returning to speak urgently with both President Johnson and Thant. There was "great disturbance" in Washington over the withdrawal of UNEF, he warned. Bunche explained what had happened so far and said that "the story wasn't over."[15] Johnson, pleased that the Secretary-

General had decided to go to Cairo, again offered *Air Force One*. Thant, again, politely declined.

Early the next day, it was Gideon Rafael's turn to come up to the thirty-eighth floor. He handed Thant an official letter from Israeli prime minister Eshkol imploring the Secretary-General to avoid "any change to the status quo" before the "broadest international consultation." Thant mentioned a Canadian suggestion that UNEF could redeploy to the Israeli side of the border. "Ridiculous!" Rafael shot back. "Israel is not the Salvation Army and would not be willing to accept UN discards from Egypt."[16]

Eshkol didn't want war. Like Nasser, he was facing economic ills at home and had little desire for a regional conflagration. This caution, however, was not shared by hawkish commanders in the Israel Defense Forces, or IDF, or its former commanders, including Moshe Dayan. They had long planned for a war that would conquer the Sinai, Gaza, the West Bank, and the Golan Heights. Some were beginning to see an opportunity in the unfolding crisis. Israel, they argued, should certainly not wait for an Arab attack.

For now, Eshkol pushed back. He ordered heightened patrols along the Syrian border to rebuff any new Palestinian raids that could set off hostilities. He also dialed back his own rhetoric. Having relied in the past on British and French arms, he wanted assurances of American support. Eshkol thought this was the way to square the circle: if the US could give guarantees, there would be no need to take military action.[17]

That afternoon, Thant told Canadian foreign minister Paul Martin that he had only two real choices: comply or delay.[18] He was dragging his feet as much as possible and exploring diplomatic avenues that might reduce tensions. The Canadians had been particularly critical of the decision to withdraw UNEF and there was much speculation of a growing rift between the Secretary-General and Ottawa, but Martin reassured Thant that the Secretary-General enjoyed his government's full confidence. Thant explained that over the seventy-two hours that had elapsed since the initial notification to General Rikhye, resentment in Egypt was reaching fever pitch, with local media speculating that UNEF might transform into an Anglo-American-directed "army of occupation." Egyptian forces were now at the front line, and UNEF had neither the authority nor the resources to do anything about it. The situation was deteriorating by the hour and Thant had to take responsibility for the safety of his men. If, because of prevarication on Thant's part, the Egyptians turned on the lightly armed Canadian peacekeepers, what would his critics say then?

There was a bigger picture, too. In all the capitals most involved—Washington, Moscow, Tel Aviv, Cairo, and certainly Damascus—there were influential voices favoring war. Neither superpower had much interest in de-escalating tensions, as each believed escalation could further its own strategic ambitions. Johnson was a fervent supporter of Israel, having authorized in recent years a delivery of the latest A-4 Skyhawk and F-4 Phantom fighter planes. He had also looked the other way when confronted with intelligence on the Jewish state's nuclear ambitions. With the Vietnam War in full swing, Johnson did not want a new military commitment in the Middle East, but he had developed a loathing for Nasser and had nothing against a swift Israeli victory over its Arab foe.

Thant had come into office five years before with support from a united Afro-Asian bloc. Nearly all the leaders of that bloc were no more: India's Nehru was dead; Indonesia's Sukarno and Ghana's Kwame Nkrumah had been overthrown in US-backed military coups. Nasser was one of the only ones left standing. As important, Thant's standing in Washington had deteriorated sharply because of his opposition to the war in Vietnam. Dean Rusk, who had championed Thant's efforts during the Cuban Missile Crisis, should have been a key ally in the present crisis. But relations between the two men were strained, to say the least.

At a personal level, the Secretary-General had a way out. He could invoke Article 99 of the United Nations Charter, which gave him the right to summon a meeting of the Security Council on any issue which he believed was a "threat to international peace and security." He could give his best analysis of the blow-up about to take place in the Middle East, then wash his hands of the matter and walk away. He knew that a Security Council debate would, however, only lead to an "undignified brawl" between East and West, and he felt it would be irresponsible to call a meeting that would only raise the temperature further. Thant concluded he had to take responsibility and act "on the basis of his own conscience."[19]

On Sunday, May 21, Gideon Rafael told Thant that the Egyptians should be in no doubt of Israel's reaction if they attempted to block the Straits of Tiran. He gave Thant a "Secret and Personal" message from foreign minister Abba Eban. Freedom of passage for Israel-bound ships was, Eban stated, a "supreme national interest" which Israel will "assert and defend" "whatever the cost." In other words, closing the Straits of Tiran would be seen as an act of war.[20]

The message also noted that "at one stage the Egyptian authorities requested an alignment of UNEF which did not require the total removal of all United Nations forces. This opportunity was not taken." Thant pointed out that this was not correct; the only communication officially received categorically requested a total withdrawal of UNEF. This was disingenuous: he could have responded differently after seeing the initial message to General Rikhye.

Both Thant and the Israelis were now posturing: Thant trying to defend his actions of the past five days, the Israelis laying the grounds for future censure.

Goldberg, like Rafael and El-Kony, was seeing Thant in his office almost every day. The former Supreme Court judge told the Secretary-General that the Egyptians were preparing for "offensive operations" and affirmed Washington's commitment to the defense of "all states in the Near East."[21] Just before Thant left for Cairo, Goldberg argued for a new UN mechanism that would ensure the freedom of Israeli shipping.

The Americans wanted the Secretary-General to take Bunche with him to Cairo. Thant felt the same but was dissuaded by El-Kony. "Ralph Bunche was held in very high esteem" in Egypt, the ambassador said, "from President Nasser down to the man in the street," but because he was an American, his presence "would be resented at least by a section of the Egyptian people."[22] So, Thant decided to travel to Cairo without his top Middle East expert and advisor. He took with him only junior staff: Ramses Nassif, his Canadian assistant Lucien Lemieux, and a security aide. His aim was to extract from Nasser a promise not to start hostilities as well as an agreement to some kind of de-escalation process. There was now a deluge of criticism, in many Western capitals, of Thant's handling of the crisis so far.

In Gaza, General Rikhye was, as instructed, dragging his feet. Sharm El-Sheikh should have been evacuated already, but Rikhye, wanting to give Thant maximum flexibility, had told the Egyptians that they were "encountering some problems" and asked for an extra three days. The Egyptians refused; the peacekeepers overlooking the Straits of Tiran had to be gone before the Secretary-General arrived.[23]

Barely five months into his second term, which he'd intended to devote to bringing peace to Vietnam, Thant was fighting for his political life. He had a final shot at getting this right.

13 | THE SIX-DAY WAR

THANT'S PLANE LANDED AT Paris's Orly airport early in the morning of May 23, 1967. He had traveled on an overnight Air France flight and was scheduled to be in transit for only a couple of hours before heading on to Rome, then Cairo. Waiting for him were glum-faced officials from the French foreign ministry, who passed on an urgent cable from Brian Urquhart. While the Secretary-General was in the air, Nasser, accompanied by Egypt's armed forces chief Field Marshal Abdel Hakim Amer, had announced the closure of the Straits of Tiran. An Egyptian parachute battalion was in Sharm El-Sheikh, and naval units including submarines were heading from the Suez Canal to the Gulf of Aqaba.

Thant was horrified. He told Nassif and Lemieux that war was now inevitable. He felt he should turn back. A miserable-looking Nassif recommended he continue. If the Secretary-General turned around, it would look like he was giving up and "inviting both sides to fight it out." By carrying on, however, Thant knew he would shoulder even more of the blame for whatever happened next. He thought of phoning Bunche, but as it was 3 a.m. in New York, he didn't want to wake him up, out of concern for his friend's health.[1] Instead, he asked to be left alone. After a few minutes, he called in his colleagues and told them he was going on to Cairo.

In Rome, the Italian foreign minister, Antonio Fanfani, came to the airport and read aloud for Thant extracts from a statement Nasser had just made. Israeli troops were massing on the Syrian border, said the Egyptian leader, and if Syria was attacked, Egypt would respond. Egypt had believed the initial Israeli disinformation, which had been planted to warn off the Syrians; the Israelis had likely not expected Egypt to respond by demanding the withdrawal of UNEF. When this occurred, some in Israel came to the conclusion that a war against Egypt might be advantageous after all—and, conveniently, Thant could be blamed for starting it.

In his statement, Nasser condemned "the big world-wide campaign" led by the US, the UK, and Canada to turn UNEF into a tool of "neo-imperialism." If UNEF had tried to stay, he would have "forcefully disarmed it." He also noted "the campaign against U Thant" who had "made an honest decision" and refused to "surrender to the pressure brought to bear." Thant told Fanfani that his aim was to extract a pledge from the Egyptians not to strike first.[2] Little did he know that the Israeli military were preparing for their own first strike. At the same time, warships belonging to both the US Sixth Fleet and the Royal Navy were streaming toward the eastern Mediterranean and the Red Sea.

In Cairo, Foreign Minister Riad, together with UN generals Rikhye and Odd Bull, welcomed a serenely smiling Thant as he descended the ramp of his Pan American jet. Nearby, policemen in white uniforms held back dozens of journalists and photographers scrambling for position. From the balcony of the terminal, enthusiastic crowds waved and shouted, "Welcome U Thant!" and "Long Live Nasser!" As the Egyptians saw it, Thant had stood up for their rights as a sovereign Third World nation and refused to be part of a conspiracy in which his peacekeepers would protect Tel Aviv's southern flank while the Israeli army invaded Syria to the north. As the motorcade made its way to the Nile Hilton, past the towering statue of the pharaoh Ramses II, ordinary people in cars and buses or on foot "cheered him lustily."

Thant had been traveling for almost twenty-four hours and Nassif was surprised that he showed no signs of fatigue. Upon arriving at the hotel, Thant called all senior UN officials to a working dinner to discuss options. They could hear the sound of demonstrators in the distance crying "Glory to Egypt!" and "We Want War!"

The next morning, Thant, accompanied by a uniformed Rikhye, drove past the city's graceful Ottoman-era palaces and across the Nile for talks with Foreign Minister Riad, a veteran of the 1948 Arab–Israeli war. Thant and the mustachioed Riad knew each other well from their days together as ambassadors in New York and enjoyed a good-humored rapport.

Lighting a Partagas cigar, the Secretary-General asked why the Straits of Tiran had been closed while he was on his way to Cairo. Riad said President Nasser would explain. Thant then briefed his former colleague on the politics in New York, the widely divergent opinions of the various governments, and the real dangers ahead. Riad defended the withdrawal of UNEF and said Israel was to blame for threatening Jordan and Syria. Egypt had to demonstrate that it was prepared to assist. Abba Eban and Israeli army chief Yitzak Rabin wanted to become "the masters of Damascus," Riad claimed. "The government knows the Israeli plan to invade Syria and, with the help of dissident elements, to attempt a coup d'état to establish a less aggressive government in Damascus." Israeli troops, he said, were massing along the Syrian front. "The Israelis want the Golan Heights," he continued. "Egypt had to move into Sinai as a defensive measure and removing UNEF enabled Egypt to retake positions at Sharm El-Sheikh."

Thant urged Riad to look at the entire picture. The closing of the Straits of Tiran meant that Israel would go to war.

Riad wanted to show some flexibility. His government would "stand firm," but was open to discussing the future legal status of the Straits. Thant suggested a "freeze" for two to three weeks: Egypt suspending its closure in return for a pause in certain ships passing through. He mentioned Cuba and the reciprocal pause of both the American blockade and Soviet shipping. He also suggested the appointment of an envoy to mediate between the two sides and the reactivation of UN observers, as agreed under the original 1949 Armistice, on both sides of the line. Riad was encouraging but noncommittal.[3]

The main test came in the evening, over a working dinner at the president's residence. Nasser had been an army officer and still lived in a military cantonment, in the same modest house he had first occupied as an instructor in the staff college, with an annex recently added for official functions. Nasser and Thant had met several times before, in Rangoon, Bandung, New York, Belgrade, and Cairo, and they greeted each other warmly. The Secretary-General was accompanied by General Rikhye. Riad was there too, as well as General Muhammad Fawzy, the Egyptian army's chief of staff.[4]

Nasser, a chain-smoker of Kent cigarettes, offered one to Thant. "It's an American one—difficult to find now in Cairo." Thant took out a cigar for the president: "A Cuban one." Nasser smiled and shook his head. "I have plenty of those, as Señor Castro keeps me well supplied!" Both lightheartedly agreed to smoke their preferences.[5]

Thant viewed Nasser, who was six feet tall with closely cropped hair and a ready smile, as a man of considerable charisma, a leader of his people. He was also extremely polite and in private somewhat shy. The Secretary-General must be tired from all the travel, the president said deferentially, and then showed him some highly polished teak furniture, "a gift from U Nu [the former Burmese prime minister] to my daughter for her wedding!"

Over a spread of Egyptian dishes in the family dining room, Thant brought up the proposal he had set out to Riad earlier in the day. The dynamics were now explosive, he emphasized, and the blockade was at the center of the crisis. A diplomatic way out had to be found.

Nasser replied that he wasn't doing anything other than moving troops within his own country. All his forces were entirely on his soil. "Why were the Israelis raising such a fuss over the Straits?" he asked. Almost no Israel-flagged ships sailed through the Straits; nearly all Israel's trade went via the country's Mediterranean ports. The only exceptions were ships carrying oil from Iran, which would otherwise be forced to travel around the Cape of Good Hope.

"The Israelis are always exaggerating threats and are now planning on changing regimes in Syria," argued Nasser. He had to honor his defense pact with Syria; that was why UNEF had to be withdrawn. His military chiefs had told him they were ready in case of war. "But if we lose, then we deserve to be the losers and will accept Israel is better than us," they had told him. He himself, however, did not want to fight.

A "meandering exposition" of his relations with the United States followed. The Egyptian president wanted his guest to see the escalating crisis as the fault of the Anglo-Americans and the Israelis, all bent on crushing him and asserting their dominance over the region.

Thant cut in to ask why Egypt had announced its blockade during his flight. The president explained that the decision had been taken long before, but they had to finesse the timing.[6] If they had announced the closure of the Straits before Thant departed New York, they would seem to be deliberately torpedoing his mission. If they waited until he left Cairo, the president explained, "it would appear a snub." Also, Nasser explained, "If we waited until you were here and you asked us not to blockade the Gulf, it would have been impossible for us to refuse a request from the Secretary-General of the United Nations." After much back and forth with his advisors, he said, they had settled on making the announcement while the UN chief was in the air!

Nasser assured Thant that he didn't want to create problems and certainly didn't want to provide the Israelis a ready excuse to invade. Already, after searching just a couple of ships, he was relaxing the blockade. He welcomed Thant's idea of a moratorium. He could announce a suspension of the blockade for, say, two weeks, as long as the Israelis undertook not to send any ships or strategic materials through the Straits. He would also accept a mediator, as the Secretary-General suggested, as well as the deployment of military observers under the 1949 Armistice Agreement. Again, the Israelis would have to do the same, and allow observers on their side of the line. Egypt would no longer accept an arrangement in which foreign soldiers were stationed on its territory alone.[7]

Before leaving, Thant asked his host for a pledge that Egypt would not strike first.

"Mr. President, the Israelis fear that you might carry out a military attack on them. Will you give me your word that this is not going to take place?"

"We have never at any time intimated that we will attack Israel," replied Nasser. "It was Israel who has formally threatened to invade Syria. What we are attempting now is a defensive measure to prevent such a threat from materializing." He looked directly at the Secretary-General: "You have my word. We will not attack first."[8]

Nasser was open to the Secretary-General's diplomacy because Thant had shown him, through his actions as well as his words, the respect to which he believed his country was entitled. Rikhye believed that Thant's day in Cairo had been "a great personal triumph for his negotiation skills, his persuasiveness, and personal diplomacy," and that he enjoyed "immense popularity throughout the Arab world."[9]

After Thant left, Nasser asked Damascus to halt all activity by Palestinian Fatah guerrillas operating out of Syria. And he instructed Field Marshal Amer to stop preparing for even a limited attack on Israel.

Back at the Hilton, Thant sent a coded message to Bunche in New York, asking him to see if Tel Aviv might also agree to a moratorium.

———

Meanwhile, in New York, the Security Council was at last creaking to life and holding its first meeting of the year. The bow-tied Soviet ambassador Nikolai Federenko dismissed any need for action, saying the crisis in the Middle East was being "over-dramatized." The onetime professor of philology intimated that dark "Anglo-American" designs were in the works. He also enjoyed wheeling out proverbs such as "He points at the moon but sees his own finger." The simultaneous interpreters translated this, but no one understood what he meant. "His motives are as transparent as his proverbs are obscure," suggested the UK's Lord Caradon, to which the Soviet replied, somewhat more lucidly, "When the lion bares its fangs, it is unreasonable to suppose that he is smiling."[10] As Thant had predicted, the debate achieved little. Even a mild resolution drafted by the Danish and Canadian ambassadors expressing support for the Secretary-General's efforts went nowhere.

Thant left Cairo on May 25—Egypt Air bumped four first-class passengers to make room for him—and reached New York that night. He had been meant to stay an extra day in Egypt, but he felt he'd achieved everything he could and it was more important that he was back at the UN. The Israelis had made the closure of the Straits a *casus belli* and there was no way the Egyptians would simply reopen them. The most Thant could hope for was what he termed "a breathing spell," where both sides agreed to a moratorium and gave diplomacy a little more time.

Thant had a pledge from Nasser that the Egyptians would not strike first, but he was under no illusions that war might still be just around the corner. The Danish and Canadian governments had suggested that the Secretary-General travel on to Tel Aviv, where he might be able to assuage Israeli concerns or at least hear firsthand Prime Minister Eshkol's thoughts on whether any diplomatic moves might avert war. At the very least, he could show his equidistance from the main protagonists. But Thant didn't go. On the flight back, Nassif found his usually cheerful boss in a gloomy mood.

As Thant may have suspected, Tel Aviv was in the middle of its own turbulent debate about whether or not to invade Egypt. The populace was gripped by fear of an Arab attack. Yitzhak Rabin and other army generals put forward different options for the timing and extent of offensive operations. At the same time, Prime Minister Eshkol and foreign minister Abba Eban tried to discern exactly where the US might stand if Israel attacked first.

In Washington, there had been talk of forcefully reopening the Straits, using an international "armada" to guarantee free shipping. But few, if any, other countries were interested in participating. Both Rusk and McNamara counseled Johnson that any attempt would need approval from both Congress and the UN. This was unlikely to happen. Instead, the White House, the Pentagon, and the CIA all began gently signaling to the Israelis that Tel Aviv might want to sort out the situation for themselves.

When Thant arrived at UN headquarters, the Israeli ambassador Gideon Rafael informed him that as "Nasser wanted war," his government would not accept a moratorium or a UN mediator. Nor would it entertain the idea of military observers on its side of the line. He would shortly have to brief the Security Council, and he planned to say exactly what he knew: Egypt had agreed to his proposals and Israel had not. But both Bunche and his Soviet aide Alexei Nesterenko advised him strongly against this, since it would shut any doors left for negotiations with Israel. Reluctantly, Thant dropped the passage from his speech.

The next day, at the Council, the Secretary-General described a crisis growing "more menacing than any time since 1956." He wanted robust action and suggested that the Council remind Egypt and Israel of their binding obligations under the 1949 Armistice Agreements and warn them that any violations would be punished. He told the Council of his desire to see military observers deployed immediately on both sides of the line. He didn't mention the moratorium, but did say that Nasser had pledged not to attack first. There was no easy path to peace, he concluded, but "I feel my main concern must be to gain more time" and defuse the crisis.

In Washington, President Johnson was presiding over a meeting of cabinet members and other top advisors.[11] Chairman of the Joint Chiefs of Staff Earle Wheeler reported that 50,000 Egyptian troops were now in the Sinai, as well as some fighter aircraft. They were, however, organized in defensive lines and "do not look as if they are preparatory to an invasion of Israel." Israel, on the other hand, had marshaled 160,000 army personnel. Its navy and air force were fully mobilized. Should there be a conflict, the general concluded, "Israel would prevail." Dean Rusk advocated diplomacy, arguing that US intelligence didn't support the view that Israel was threatened with an imminent attack and that everything Thant had heard in Cairo suggested the same. There should be an attempt at de-escalation, using the UN if needed.

One of his assistant secretaries, Joe Sisco, took a different view. Israel had no faith in the UN, he said. The Security Council had done nothing to deal with Palestinian attacks across the Syrian border, and the General Assembly, with its Third World majority, was now very different than what it had been in 1956. Any UN action was likely to be "anti-Israeli." The Israelis also now believed that "U Thant is biased against them," as he had hastened to pull out UNEF and then went to Cairo and not Tel

Aviv. "They feel he will not come up with anything more than some 'gimmick proposals' to rationalize the status quo."[12]

Both the Soviets and the Americans were officially encouraging restraint. By May 26, however, Johnson was using his own channels to Tel Aviv to work around a State Department which the Israelis believed was sympathetic to their Arab enemies.[13] "Israel would not be alone unless it decided to go alone" was the somewhat cryptic message from the president.

Arthur Goldberg was one of those secretly passing messages from the president to the Jewish state. At his office across the street from the UN, Goldberg disappointed Abba Eban by dismissing any need for joint planning between their two militaries. (Eban and Eshkol were fishing for a definite sign of American commitment.) The reason, said Goldberg, was that no Egyptian attack was likely any time soon, and if there was an attack "you would knock them out." The United States didn't want to take the measures needed to reassure Israel, but at the same time Johnson didn't want to hold them back. The president's feeling was that "Israel alone can judge what it should do."[14]

Fierce attacks on the Secretary-General were now coming thick and fast, primarily in the American and British press. His actions were labeled "poltroonery" by the leading columnist Joseph Alsop, while Cyrus Sulzberger, writing in *The New York Times*, said that the Secretary-General had "used his international prestige with the objectivity of a spurned lover and the dynamism of a noodle."[15] Alec Douglas-Home, former prime minister of the UK, called Thant's mission to Cairo a "dreadful mistake," while Senator Dirksen accused him of acting like "a thief in the night." All this, despite Bunche and Urquhart having spent an inordinate amount of time sending journalists as well as governments information detailing every step the Secretariat was taking and its justifications. *The Telegraph* suggested that Thant should have "read the riot act" to Nasser. On May 26, *The Spectator* ran a cover story entitled "U Thant's War."[16]

It was not lost on Thant that many of those attacking him had vociferously opposed his stands on the Congo and Vietnam. He may have thought about what he himself had written five years before: "One of the most important roles of the United Nations is that of the old English institution, Aunt Sally—the large and conspicuous figure at which things can be thrown both with impunity and with almost complete certainty of hitting the target."[17]

That weekend in New York, thousands of people demonstrated in support of Israel. Thant was made a special target. During his time as Burma's ambassador, he had spent years working alongside Israeli diplomats, speaking at their events when no other Afro-Asian ambassador would show his face—partly because it was Rangoon's policy, but also because of his genuine conviction that Israel had a right to exist and that its Arab neighbors should accept this and agree to peace. He had a friendly relationship with Eshkol, Eban, and Rafael. All this was unknown or forgotten by the crowds, who labeled him Israel's nemesis. In one impassioned speech, Barbara Tuchman, author of the *Guns of August* and so "something of a specialist in eve-of-war situations," told cheering demonstrators that Washington had to act firmly to assist the Jewish state and not wait for "futile fiddling in the United Nations." She then denounced "Thant's collapse" to a chorus of "hoots and boos."[18]

Hundreds of letters and telegrams poured into the Secretary-General's office, the vast majority blaming him for leaving Israel exposed to an impending Arab war of annihilation. He was being blamed in Israel, too, for the unfolding crisis. He had neither the time nor anything like the press team he would have required to fight back effectively. He also had no training for television (now far more influential than when he first became Secretary-General) and little inclination to proactively shape media perceptions. Few members of the general public understood how the UN worked or the limits of his office.

Thant was facing the biggest challenge of his Secretary-Generalship. Unlike in the 1965 India–Pakistan War, the superpowers had no overriding interest in supporting his diplomacy. Egypt may not have wanted war but Nasser was willing to play with fire, likely thinking that any war would be short and sharp, with the UN quickly intervening and ordering a ceasefire. He was dialing up his rhetoric, declaring that an Arab victory would mean the end of Israel. The Soviets, for their part, were pleased for the opportunity to fish in troubled waters. War could only make the Arabs more dependent on Moscow.

———

UNEF wouldn't have made any difference one way or another; in fact, the bulk of the force was still in place.[19] Since the beginning of the crisis ten days before, the Canadians had been the most vocal critic of Thant's decision to accept Nasser's request to withdraw the force. Yet on May 27, when the Canadians received a direct request from Cairo to remove their troops, they were gone within two days.[20] Bunche and Urquhart had been working toward an orderly, delayed withdrawal over many weeks. But as the Canadians supplied the logistics component, the rest of UNEF found itself stranded without transport teams or aircraft.[21]

That same day, Thant prepared "private, personal, and confidential" letters to Nasser and Eshkol.[22] He appealed to the Egyptian president to avoid, for two weeks, stopping any non-Israeli ship passing through the Straits of Tiran. He made clear that he was not asking for a public commitment or even a formal reply. In his letter to Eshkol, he stated his understanding that "in the normal course of things, in the next fortnight, no flagship of Israel will be seeking passage through the Straits of Tiran." This phrasing, too, did not ask for a commitment, and Thant promised that his letter would not be made public in any way. He wanted a two-week period in which "to do everything possible to avert war."[23]

Thant liked Eshkol, whom he had first met during his trip to Israel in 1955. At a lunch in the Israel leader's honor in 1964, Eshkol recalled the two men "driving together through the Galilee and along the shores of the Jordan as children lined the roadside waving flags to welcome him and the Prime Minister of Burma at the time." The United Nations, Eshkol said then, was "fortunate in having as its Chief Executive a man as wise and selfless as U Thant."[24]

But the letters never left New York.[25] On the morning of Sunday, May 28, a frantic Egyptian ambassador El-Kony phoned Bunche. Both he and Rafael had copies of their respective messages, which they would relay to Cairo and Tel Aviv. But El-Kony complained that the message was not in line with what the Secretary-General had said to Nasser, which was that the moratorium would include a ban on third countries sending any "strategic" material, meaning oil, through the Straits of Tiran.

Bunche telephoned Thant, who was swimming in his pool at home. Thant confirmed to a surprised Bunche that this was indeed what he had proposed to Nasser. For Bunche, this was another example of his boss not being clear on the details of his mediation—as with the North Vietnamese. Bunche asked both the Egyptian and Israeli missions to halt transmission. The next morning, he and Thant argued over what to do. Bunche believed that Thant's suggestion of no third-party shipping of oil would in effect endorse the blockade.

Thant's idea was that all non-Israeli ships, except oil tankers, would continue to sail past the Straits and Nasser would look the other way.[26] This was what he took away from his dinner with the Egyptian president: while Nasser wanted to look tough, he didn't want war. The tankers could surely wait a couple of weeks. Israel had a four-month supply. A "breathing spell" was not impossible.

Thant, Bunche felt, "did not realize at all the enormity of the mistake he was about to make." Under pressure from his under secretary, Thant agreed to cancel the letters altogether.[27]

Twelve days into the crisis, the Secretary-General had no real options left. At the same time, the Security Council was deadlocked. Some governments declared that Egypt had every right to close the Straits, while US and UK diplomats talked about ways to force them open. The Soviets simply tried to score as many political points as they could. Few were interested in finding a constructive way forward. During these often round-the-clock meetings, Thant urged the Council to step up to its responsibilities and take decisive steps toward "reasonable, peaceful, and just solutions" to the problems in the Middle East.[28]

By the end of May, there were nearly 100,000 Egyptian soldiers in the Sinai. Syria had massed six brigades, with approximately 30,000 troops, opposite the Golan Heights. The 55,000-man Royal Jordanian Army was now mainly deployed in the West Bank. Facing them, with 265,000 troops and 800 tanks, were the Israel Defense Forces, now at full strength and ready for combat. On May 30, Jordan's King Hussein arrived in Cairo and with much fanfare signed a military pact with Egypt. Syria and Iraq signed similar agreements. The public mood in all the Arab countries was for war.

The next day, El-Kony came up to Thant's office and reported that Nasser would accept his two-week moratorium. El-Kony was adamant that nothing could be agreed which infringed on Egypt's sovereignty, but Nasser wanted to keep the door open to possible diplomacy.[29]

It was too late. Israel was set to invade Egypt. All that Tel Aviv needed was to make sure the Americans would not object.

On June 1, General Meir Amit, head of Shin Bet, Israel's intelligence service, flew to Washington and told Defense Secretary McNamara and CIA director Richard Helms that Israel would go to war soon and would win. There was no response; everyone in the room knew this meant acquiescence. Amit predicted that the war would last seven days. He was assured by his counterparts that the conversation would be reported to Lyndon Johnson.[30]

That same afternoon, as Thant came under yet another barrage of harsh criticism in the American and British press for withdrawing UNEF, he received a sympathetic telegram from Martin Luther King Jr., Linus Pauling (the only person to have won two Nobel Prizes), and sixty other distinguished participants then at a peace conference in Geneva, affirming their "unqualified support for your untiring efforts to bring peace and stability to the Middle East."[31] It was a welcome message at a time of almost unrelenting stress and despair on the thirty-eighth floor.

On June 3, the UN chief spent over three hours in his office with UK prime minister Harold Wilson. With Thant smoking a cigar and Wilson his pipe, both men acknowledged that time was running out. The Secretary-General argued for practical steps at de-escalation, focusing on the Straits of Tiran.[32] "The Israelis were not wholly blameless," acknowledged the British leader in his memoirs. "Indeed, many people thought that the present troubles derived largely from the fact that President Nasser had had reasonable grounds for apprehending an Israeli attack on Syria." Wilson said he feared an "Abyssinia moment" for the UN, alluding to the League of Nations' failure to halt Italian aggression against Abyssinia in 1936, which began its slide toward irrelevance in international affairs.

Thant defended his decision to withdraw UNEF: within the first twenty-four hours of the crisis, Yugoslavia, India, and Sweden had said they would comply with Nasser's request to withdraw their peacekeepers. Egyptian forces were already at the line. Had the remaining Canadian and other troops tried to stand firm, fighting would have broken out between Egypt and what would have been primarily NATO troops. Bunche interjected and explained to Wilson that they had been managing an orderly withdrawal and that even now only the Canadians had actually left. Wilson, surprised, said this was very different from the impression he had been given in Ottawa.[33]

As war approached, even the Egyptians tried to shift the blame onto Thant. In Cairo, officials told James Reston, reporting for *The New York Times*, that they had not intended to eject UNEF at Sharm El-Sheikh, implying that this was the Secretary-General's decision. Reston did not ask how this squared with Nasser's decision to blockade the Straits.[34]

While Thant and Bunche racked their brains trying to find some way prevent hostilities, they had no idea that Israel, with Washington's top-secret and highest-level approval, had already decided on war. They were thinking only in terms of de-escalation measures and their next discussions with governments. They were not thinking much, if at all, about how to position the UN in the eyes of the public, in Israel, in the Arab countries, or in the rest of the world. They planned to see the Israeli and Egyptian ambassadors again the next morning to fish around for ideas. Before leaving the office at 6:30 p.m., they cabled General Rikhye in Gaza, requesting him to keep them informed.

A few hours later, early in the morning of June 5, local time, Rikhye was at UNEF headquarters penning a short update to Thant when he heard loud explosions from the beach and gunfire from near Gaza City. Israeli jets had just attacked Egyptian positions. Within minutes, reports of fighting were coming in from every UNEF peacekeeping battalion along the line and near the refugee camp at Rafah, at the southern end of the Gaza Strip. UNEF, which the press portrayed as having simply disappeared at Nasser's request, was now caught in the middle of a war.

At 2:40 a.m. in New York, 9:40 a.m. in Gaza, the UN received an urgent cable from Rikhye. Bunche was immediately informed and at 3 a.m. telephoned Thant: "U Thant, war has broken out!" An Indian convoy was strafed by Israeli planes, leaving three UN peacekeepers dead. Thant messaged Rikhye with orders to safeguard his personnel while sending as much detailed information as possible. He knew there would be conflicting accounts from governments and in the media. He dressed and raced to the UN.

At his desk, Thant read messages from Rikhye saying that he was trying his best to move his battalions to safer locations as fighting was now raging all around them. The radio connecting Gaza and New York was still working, but other UNEF communications were beginning to break down.

Over the past few hours, nearly two hundred Israeli jets, mainly French-made Dassault fighters and fighter-bombers including the supersonic Super Mystère, had pounded Egyptian bases and destroyed almost the entire Egyptian air force of five hundred planes. When Jordan and Syria attacked in retaliation, another wave of Israeli strikes destroyed their air forces as well. At the same time, IDF tank formations pushed into the Gaza Strip.

That evening and over the following day, Rikhye's headquarters came under direct assault. Israeli artillery fire first knocked out the antenna, temporarily severing links with New York. One shell fell within several feet of Rikhye while he was in his car.[35] As the fighting drew closer, the UN commander ordered all his staff to protect themselves against the sturdier wall of their office building, with only a few blue-helmeted Indian sentries remaining in trenches outside. Several UN personnel were killed and the wounded brought into the conference room. Just as Rikhye was dictating an urgent message to Thant, asking him to appeal to the Israelis at the highest level to halt their attacks on the UN, a shell exploded right outside the window, shattering the glass and forcing everyone to the floor. Rikhye decided to evacuate. With whatever cars they could muster, he led his staff to a UN police camp further down the coast, where the general enjoyed more than one gin and tonic.

The picture being painted in the American and British press was of Israel acting heroically against an imminent Arab threat of total destruction. A deluge of denunciation continued to be directed at Thant as the man who had mishandled the crisis and forced Israel into a fight for survival. Likely in reaction to nearly daily articles denouncing the Secretary-General, Jacqueline Kennedy, the late president's widow, sent a note to Thant, handwritten on light blue stationery:

> *All the work which you do to keep this world from going up in flames must take its terrible toll on you. I can imagine how desperately tired you must be now. I hope the fatigue and discouragement which must always be yours, will not keep you from realizing the light and hope you are to everyone. How lucky we are that you are there, with your rare quality of spirit. I just wanted to tell you that . . . With my deepest admiration and friendship always.*[36]

Thant wrote back immediately, saying that he was "at a loss for words to describe my feelings of gratitude . . . Among the many letters I received during the most difficult and most misunderstood phase of my public career, your kind note gave me the greatest comfort and encouragement. I know it came from someone whom I greatly esteem and respect and that the kind sentiments did indeed flow from the heart."[37]

By June 7, three days after the start of the attacks, the Israel Defense Forces had overwhelmed the Egyptian army everywhere in the Gaza Strip and across the Sinai, including at Sharm El-Sheikh. Eshkol messaged Jordan's King Hussein not to get involved but the king, who had placed his army under Cairo's command, replied that "the die was cast." In the clashes that followed, Israel emerged easily victorious, with two paratroop battalions fighting their way into the old city of Jerusalem (which was under Jordanian rule). By June 8, Israeli forces were in control of the entire West Bank. That same day, after strenuous debate, the Security Council finally adopted a ceasefire resolution, followed by a second resolution the next day. Egypt, with its forces in tatters, relented. Israeli armored and infantry brigades then seized the Golan Heights from Syria, leading the panicked Syrian government to warn that the Israelis would soon advance on Damascus.

Thant was in constant contact not only with General Rikhye but also with the chief of the UN military observers in Jerusalem, the Norwegian general Odd Bull, and relayed their reports to the Security Council. On June 10, Odd Bull contacted both the Syrians and the Israelis to make ceasefire arrangements. Both Tel Aviv and Damascus accepted. By the time the fighting ended on June 11, fifteen peacekeepers had been killed (fourteen Indian and one Brazilian), and seventeen others wounded.

The war was a disaster for the Arab states, as it left Israel in possession not only of the Gaza Strip and the Sinai but the West Bank and Golan Heights as well. Pro-Israeli sentiment on both sides of the Atlantic rocketed to sky-high levels. The six-day campaign was seen as an amazing demonstration of military effectiveness at a time when a half million-strong American force had been unable, after three years, to vanquish the Viet Cong.

In the aftermath of the fighting, the story that Thant was to blame, because of his spineless submission to Nasser, only gathered pace. On June 14, Rusk told a NATO ministerial meeting in Luxembourg that Thant's rapid acceptance of Nasser's demand had surprised Nasser.[38] An anonymous Western diplomat described Thant to *The Wall Street Journal* as "a tower of jelly." Another said that he was at fault for the war because he had not applied a "white heat of diplomatic pressure" on Cairo. An unnamed American remarked that Thant's predecessor, Hammarskjöld, was a "man of great courage" who would have flown immediately to Cairo and not left until there was an agreement. Only one defender of Thant was quoted in the piece: a former associate of Hammarskjöld, who alleged a racist bias: "if only this blue-eyed genius of a Scandinavian were around to go over there, everything would be all right. Well, the hell with that!"[39]

A few American journalists took the Secretary-General's side. James Wechsler, a leading columnist at the *New York Post*, argued that the attacks on Thant were primarily the work of "pro-administration journalists whose real quarrel is with his refusal to accept our simplistic version of events in Vietnam." He asked the obvious question: If Israel had been defeated, the search for a scapegoat would be understandable, but given what had happened, should it not be the Soviets and Arab countries who were most vociferous in their condemnation of Thant? Yet they were not. Wechsler believed that "the anti-Thant onslaught" was "nourished by American sources ... traceable to the highest official levels in Washington." The "campaign against Thant" could only be fully understood, Wechsler wrote, in the context of his stand against US policy in Vietnam and more particularly his profound disagreement with Dean Rusk.[40] He described Thant as "a bigger man than many of those in our government—and others—who select him as whipping boy when their own inadequacies and ineptitude are exposed."[41]

In mid-June, a Special Emergency Session of the General Assembly was convened at the request of crestfallen Arab states. A slew of world leaders attended, including Jordan's King Hussein and the heads of most Eastern European countries. Western governments sent foreign ministers. Soviet premier Alexei Kosygin flew over and Johnson, in a signal of displeasure with the world organization, met with his Soviet counterpart not at the UN but in Glassboro, New Jersey.

During the General Assembly debate, the eloquent Israeli foreign minister Abba Eban, in a blistering soliloquy, asked, "What is the use of the fire brigade which vanishes from the scene as soon as the first smoke and flames appear? Is it surprising that we are firmly resolved never again to allow a vital Israeli interest and our very security to rest on such a fragile foundation?"

Thant was livid. He had seen Eban just days before and they had talked at length about the reasons for UNEF's withdrawal. Secretaries-General rarely speak in the middle of General Assembly debates, but now, having run out of patience, Thant took the floor and told his side of the story. "Israel always and firmly refused to accept [UNEF] on Israeli territory on the valid grounds of national sovereignty. There was, of course, national sovereignty on the other side of the line as well." He received a long ovation.

With these remarks, he entrenched perceptions of himself as an adversary of Israel—something he had never intended. Wechsler was probably correct that journalists close to the administration were eager to undermine the Secretary-General. But there were many others, supporters of his stance on Vietnam, who genuinely believed that Thant's actions in recent weeks had endangered the very existence of the Jewish state.

A few days later, *The New York Times* ran a headline piece reporting on a "secret" memorandum written by Hammarskjöld nearly a decade earlier.[42] According to this alleged private agreement, Nasser would limit his sovereign right and not order the withdrawal of UNEF until both he and the Secretary-General agreed on it. Hammarskjöld had supposedly given a copy of this text to his friend Ernest Gross, a lawyer who had worked for the UN.[43]

Thant phoned Bunche early that morning to ask about this. Bunche replied that Gross had informed him about it the day the Secretary-General left for Cairo and that he, Bunche, had mentioned it to Thant at the airport. Thant had no recollection of this. Bunche also told Thant that he had never heard of the document until Gross contacted him. At the office, Thant called in Bunche and Urquhart, both of whom had worked closely with Hammarskjöld on UNEF. They scoured all his files. Urquhart was then writing a biography of Hammarskjöld and had been through all his private papers as well. Bunche also checked with El-Kony, who sent an inquiry to Cairo. No one had seen or heard of anything of the kind.

El-Kony said Nasser would never have agreed to UNEF if he had been aware of a note like the one alleged. Gross said he was planning on writing about the memo in a scholarly journal and had not given the document to the *Times*. But then, who had? Over lunch, Thant, Bunche, Urquhart, and Narasimhan wondered about the motives and the timing of the report. The memorandum was, after all, only a private note—not in any official file, with no signature, and never seen by the Egyptians or Hammarskjöld's closest aides.[44] If it was genuine, it was probably only an expression of Hammarskjöld's "hope" of what an understanding with Nasser might be.

But the damage was done. Thant had been portrayed, yet again, as having acted rashly and without justification.

Within weeks of the ceasefire, the Israel Defense Forces, now at the westernmost edge of the Sinai, clashed with Egyptian army divisions positioned along the Suez Canal. Thant appealed for the stationing of UN observers, and the Security Council agreed. Thirty-two military officers were quickly dispatched, from Sweden, France, Finland, and Burma—the few countries acceptable to both sides.[45]

At this point, the Soviets intervened, claiming that only the Security Council could authorize the exact number and national makeup of such a team. Moscow was always looking for ways to limit the role of the Secretary-General and boost the role of the Council, over whose decisions the USSR enjoyed a veto. The Secretary-General, evidently now in a combative mood, stood firm and Soviet ambassador Federenko felt compelled to withdraw his objections.[46] For a while, the observers managed to dampen hostilities. Thant consulted widely, including with the leaders of the non-aligned states like Yugoslavia's Josip Broz Tito, with whom he was in regular contact.[47] He also sent a personal representative to Jerusalem in response to Arab apprehension over the holy city's incorporation into Israel. The future of the land conquered by Israel—Gaza, the Sinai, the West Bank and East Jerusalem, and the Golan Heights—climbed at the top of the UN's agenda.[48]

Thant's own ability to broker a way forward was, however, heavily compromised. By summer, even the Egyptians were lambasting Thant for the war, with Nasser telling American diplomats he had been "surprised" by the speed with which the Secretary-General had responded to his request to withdraw UNEF. If the Secretary-General had not acted "so precipitously," the defeated leader claimed, the crisis over the Straits might have never happened.[49]

One of the few who did stick up for Thant was his old friend Gideon Rafael, the Israeli ambassador. In an interview with the Israeli paper *Maariv*, he said, "The Secretary-General tried to control the situation and failed but he cannot be blamed for it.... U Thant is not responsible for the crisis in the Middle East."[50]

Brian Urquhart believed that Thant and Bunche, both of whom had been working round the clock for weeks, had "suffered irreparable psychological damage" from the nonstop and exceptionally unfair public attacks.[51] There was a physical toll, too. Bunche developed a debilitating infection on his neck and his eyesight deteriorated to near blindness.[52] Thant was taking several antihistamine tablets a day for what he complained were intense headaches. He was also seeking distraction, perhaps inspiration, in less worldly directions. Like many of his countrymen he was a believer in astrology, and Bunche once found him at his desk "diligently working over a chart on his grandson's 'house' or place in the star system."

Josephine Blacklock, an Australian who had been Thant's assistant when he was Burma's UN ambassador, was a fellow astrology buff. At the very start of his time as Acting Secretary-General, Thant had appointed her a press assistant, and the two had met regularly in the Secretary-General's office to talk about their mutual interest.[53]

Perhaps through Blacklock, Thant had begun to nurture a fascination with UFOs. "He reads all the books and articles about 'flying saucers,'" Bunche noted. In early 1967, Thant wanted the UN's Department of Political and Security Council Affairs to undertake a proper study of UFOs, only to be dissuaded by a rare joint intercession of his top American and Soviet advisors, Bunche and Alexei Nesterenko.[54]

The Secretary-General's passion, however, did not dissipate. On June 7, at the height of the Six-Day War, Thant had University of Arizona physicist James E. McDonald, with whom he had been corresponding for some time, brief the UN's Outer Space Affairs Committee on UFOs. It was, he noted, a matter of growing concern to delegates from the smaller states, especially in Africa. He had looked forward to attending himself, but the ongoing fighting in the Middle East forced him to cancel at the last minute.[55] McDonald told the UN committee of the "quite astonishing number... of machine-like objects" which he thought were "some form of extra-terrestrial probe."

Scarcely six months into his second term, the Secretary-General may well have looked forward to alien intervention. His standing on both sides of the Atlantic had been severely damaged. The dynamics that had propelled him into office in 1961—in particular, the desire of Washington and a network of visionary Afro-Asian leaders to build bridges at the UN—no longer existed. With the withdrawal of UNEF, his detractors were able to depict him in the worst possible light, not just as a UN chief who made a mistake but as a Third World bureaucrat who flinched under pressure.

At this precarious juncture, Thant seems not to have considered any changes to his staff or his management style, or ways to bolster, for example, his ability to mold public opinion via television. He was loyal to his colleagues and never wavered in his conviction that being right on the issues would be enough.

British journalist Nigel Nicolson considered Thant an "easy person" with an "effortlessness about him, a lack of self-importance, which is most engaging." But in public, there was often, Nicolson felt, "a stiffness about his phrases" which gave "quite a false view of his personality."[56] One British diplomat speculated, "You know, the trouble with us is that, because we're Westerners, we always assume that we speak directly and that because U Thant is Burmese, he is playing some clever, devious game. The truth is that too often we're playing the games and he's speaking directly and so we miss the point."[57]

Years before, when he was ambassador and had more free time, Thant sometimes played cards at home with family and friends; he was easy to beat at poker because he was unable to conceal his feelings.[58] By 1967, he was becoming well known in Western media for his poker face. That unreadable countenance may have served him well during tense Security Council debates and delicate diplomatic negotiations, but it meant that only those who actually met him had a sense of Thant as a person. His enemies could paint whatever picture they chose.

Thant's primary recourse was to reinforce his Buddhist practice. This included the cultivation of *upekkha*, or equanimity, a mental state which sought to elude both apathy and anger. It meant doing your best while not getting angry. Perhaps as a result, the unfair criticism of his handling of the events leading up to Six-Day War, far from debilitating him as Urquhart surmised, seemed to steel him.

New challenges were now coming thick and fast. The Arab–Israeli conflict was simmering, ready to explode again and draw in the superpowers as never before. And the war in Vietnam was on the verge of a devastating turn.

14 | REVOLUTION

FOR YEARS, COMMUNIST LEADERS in Hanoi had been divided between a dovish "North-first" faction, which saw reunification as a staggered process, involving negotiation as well as fighting, and a militant "South-first" faction which prioritized what they maintained was a winnable war against the United States. By early July 1967, the militants had gained the upper hand. In an underground conference room, its lime-green walls covered in maps, the militants argued successfully that the Americans could be defeated through a surprise operation. Saigon and other cities would be attacked, triggering a popular revolt. At the very least, Washington would be forced into negotiations on Hanoi's terms. Planning for the "General Offensive and General Uprising" was to begin immediately. The target date was the lunar new year, or Tet, on January 30, 1968.

In the United States, Vietnam had divided society as no other issue since the Civil War. Over the previous three years, Lyndon Johnson had hoped at every turn that heightened military action would somehow lead to political success. But success was nowhere in sight. Instead, the president's unmatched record of domestic legislation, aimed at combating poverty and racial discrimination, was increasingly overshadowed by the war as well as by escalating racial and social divisions across society. The president's poll numbers plummeted.

The president's men, however, continued to counsel against diplomacy. Failure, the CIA advised, would come not from an American "military and political collapse" but from a "peace settlement" that could only work to the advantage of the Communists, and which would inflict "permanent damage" on the United States internationally.[1]

Thant's nightmare was coming true: an escalating war, immense human suffering, a more radical regime in Hanoi, and the United Nations unable even to kick-start a path to peace. His fraught relationship with Dean Rusk was central to his problems. As the war soured, the secretary of state became progressively more defensive.[2] The question of who had been right three years before, Thant or Rusk, had not gone away, and it had embittered each man against the other. In a meeting with American educators, Rusk mocked Thant's accent and said that the Secretary-General's so-called initiative only involved some "junior" Russians in the UN Secretariat: "You have heard about the end of '64 beginning of '65 business when peace was about to break out in Rangoon," he remarked, as the audience laughed. "There are an awful lot of candidates for the Nobel Peace Prize running around the world these days."[3]

Rusk told the British that the Soviet ambassador in Washington could find no record of any message from Thant being passed to Hanoi from Moscow and suggested Thant had "misread something... which was no more than cocktail party gossip." The Foreign Office in London noted that "the most painful part of this whole affair was that somebody was not telling the truth and it could, of course, be U Thant."[4] Rusk was clearly intent on undermining Thant, not only in Washington but overseas as well.

The Secretary-General only amplified his rhetoric. In August 1967, speaking to a conference of over three thousand Quakers in Greensboro, North Carolina, Thant tore into what he called "a savage war" in Vietnam. "I am convinced," he said, "that the war cannot be brought to an end until the United States and her allies recognize that it is being fought by the Vietnamese not as a war of Communist aggression, but as a war of national independence." He had never stated his thesis as plainly.

To the suggestion that those fighting against the foreigners were a small minority, he pointed out that history was replete with examples where "freedom fighters often constituted a minority." "Is it not a fact," he asked, "that during the American revolution, the colony of New York recruited more troops for the British than for the revolution... that thousands of rich Americans fled for their lives to Canada?"[5]

There was a danger in imagining that the only alternatives were escalation or immediate withdrawal. An "honorable peace" was achievable. The continuation of the war was unnecessary. He was, he said, absolutely convinced of this. There was a standing ovation. The next day, newspapers around the world featured the Secretary-General comparing Hanoi's fight to the American War of Independence.

Vietnam was always on Thant's mind. Morning radio and evening television brought harrowing news of a war the Secretary-General felt he had a personal and moral responsibility to try to stop. He was still in good standing with Hanoi. In a meeting with Norwegian diplomats, North Vietnamese representatives "made it very clear" that they did not share China's negative views of the UN chief. They had rejected his proposal, but they valued his efforts and judged him an Asian statesman "with full understanding of what the war in Vietnam involved."[6]

At the same time, there was no letup in other work. The conflict in Cyprus flared up again, threatening the collapse of the four-year-old peacekeeping operation.[7] The Americans had forestalled a Turkish invasion of the island but couldn't secure a new peace deal, requiring Thant to intervene with his own appeals to the Cypriot, Greek, and Turkish governments, which successfully eased tensions.[8] There were also a constant stream of deliberations and decisions to be made on the Middle East, in particular related to escalating skirmishes across the Suez Canal.

Far more enjoyable were the near-daily luncheons at Thant's table on the thirty-eighth floor, which still featured Narasimhan's Avakaya mango pickle. Guests in late 1967 included the kings and queens of Thailand, Greece, and Nepal, the prime minister of Japan, and the leader of newly independent Singapore, Lee Kuan Yew. Thant made a point of including in these functions representatives not only of the big states but of the smaller ones too. He sometimes slipped out of the building with one or two Afro-Asian ambassadors and their aides to try a new restaurant on Second Avenue and make sure he kept in close touch with their thinking.

There was also a special gift from Jacqueline Kennedy. The former First Lady had been on a trip to Cambodia to see the ancient temples of Angkor Wat. On the way back, her plane stopped briefly in Rangoon, where she collected some wild grass from the side of the runway to bring to New York as a gift for her Burmese friend. Thant loved the gesture and for a long time kept the grass in a vase by his desk.[9]

Meanwhile, he hatched a new initiative on Vietnam.

———

In late September 1967, in San Antonio, Texas, Lyndon Johnson declared that the United States was "willing to stop all aerial and naval bombardment of North Vietnam when this will lead promptly to productive discussions. We, of course, assume that while discussions proceed, North Vietnam would not take advantage of the bombing cessation or limitation."[10] Thant was not involved, there was no other mediator, and there was no response.

A few weeks later, in the biggest antiwar demonstration yet, as many as 100,000 people—writers Norman Mailer, Allen Ginsberg and Noam Chomsky among them—rallied near the Lincoln Memorial in Washington. Approximately half of the marchers, including Young International Party (Yippie) leaders Jerry Rubin and Abbie Hoffman, then walked across the Potomac River to the Pentagon, where they were confronted by soldiers of the 82nd Airborne Division.

With the US's involvement in Vietnam at an inflection point, Johnson convened a meeting of the country's preeminent Cold War thinkers, including Dean Acheson, Clark Clifford, and Henry Cabot Lodge. They urged him to stay the course. The US was set for victory, they advised, and what was needed most was for the president to give the American people a more optimistic assessment."[11] Not everyone agreed. On November 29, Defense Secretary Robert McNamara resigned. He had been the war's principal architect, and he could no longer pretend it was anything other than unwinnable.

The following January, at a luncheon in his office for leading journalists and film producers, Thant confided that the Johnson White House was not involving him in its latest outreach to Hanoi. Talks would need to take place while fighting continued, and he speculated that this might be impossible for Johnson to accept during an election year. An essential element of any process should be the establishment of a broad-based government in Saigon, but there was no interest in this in Washington. "I guess we are missing another opportunity," he told his guests. James Wechsler of the *New York Post* believed that the Secretary-General was "injured and pained by Washington's attitude towards him, but characteristically philosophical about it."[12]

Thant still had allies on Vietnam, but he also had a growing legion of influential enemies not shy of making their feelings known. Congressman John Rooney, a staunch backer of Franco's Fascist regime in Spain, was a vocal critic. "He annoys me every time he gets on television," the congressman said during a televised Capitol Hill hearing. "He sticks his nose into areas of our foreign policy he does not belong in. It occurs to me he is so hungry to get some personal publicity for himself that he is behaving like a fellow that never amounted to very much until he got the job in the United Nations."[13]

The preceding months had seasoned Thant to this kind of attack, but still he looked for spiritual fortification. In January, he met for over an hour with the Maharishi Yogi, an Indian mystic who promoted Transcendental Meditation and had recently become spiritual advisor to the Beatles. The Yogi's teachings were distinct from Thant's Burmese Buddhism, but the Secretary-General was increasingly curious about religious ideas of all kinds, particularly from within the Hindu–Buddhist tradition. Proclaiming afterward that his discussions with Thant had "made the field fertile for permanent world peace," the Yogi underlined the need to focus not on the symptoms of conflicts, but on the heart of the problem: "the stress which is the cause of strife."[14]

At the end of January 1968, the fighting in Vietnam reached a climax. After months of meticulous planning, tens of thousands of Communist forces, both North Vietnamese regulars and the Viet Cong, propelled themselves against cities and towns across the South. Saigon came under heavy attack, stunning the entirely unprepared American and South Vietnamese militaries. Nineteen Viet Cong guerrillas breached the walls of the US embassy compound before being killed or captured. Days of ferocious fighting followed, but the popular uprising anticipated by Hanoi never materialized. Instead, the Communists were decimated, having lost as many as 50,000 soldiers without achieving a single tactical objective.

It was a military defeat for the North, but it soon proved a political victory. Millions of Americans watched the battles on the evening news and were shocked by scenes so at odds with the positive stories emanating from the White House. General Westmoreland asked for 200,000 more men, and even die-hard supporters of the war began to doubt its winnability.

Thant embarked on an urgent diplomatic push, and within days of the Tet offensive was on a lightning trip across Asia and Europe. He was eager to end the bloodletting in Vietnam, but was even more anxious to prevent the conflict from spiraling into a direct confrontation between China and the United States, perhaps involving nuclear weapons. And for what? He was convinced there was still a route to a negotiated settlement that would do no damage to the US's position in the world.

One of his first stops was Brussels, where he explained to foreign minister Pierre Harmel that Peking was unlikely to become "a respectable member of the international community in the foreseeable future." More than ever, Thant saw China as a malevolent force in Asian politics. He mentioned as well his "anxiety about Chinese pressure on Burma."[15] Chinese-backed Communist forces had recently crossed the border into

Burma and seized the eastern uplands. He reckoned that the Vietnamese, like the Burmese, had little desire to fall under the domination of their northern neighbor. Both countries had faced repeated invasions from China over past millennia.

In India, Thant called on prime minister Indira Gandhi and then met with Hanoi's representative in Delhi, Nguyen Hoa. The Secretary-General was searching for a blueprint that might finally bring the US and North Vietnam to the negotiating table. Stressing his government's respect for Thant's efforts, Hoa stated that talks could only take place after an unconditional halt to the bombing. He rejected Johnson's "San Antonio formula" as falling short of what Hanoi could accept. Thant asked for clarification on exactly what Hanoi required for talks to begin, and Nguyen promised to pass on the Secretary-General's question to the North Vietnamese leadership.[16]

Next was Moscow. Thant and Soviet premier Alexei Kosygin enjoyed a performance of *Carmen* at the Bolshoi Theater before a late-night dinner discussion of Vietnam. The following day, they were joined by party leader Leonid Brezhnev, who cut short his Black Sea holiday to impress on the Secretary-General Moscow's determination to support its Vietnamese ally no matter the cost. Brezhnev's vulgar and bellicose language shocked Thant. Worse was the realization that the Kremlin was no longer interested in UN mediation. Thant now worried that the Soviets as well as the Chinese would further escalate the war.

The next morning, in London's palatial Foreign Office, in a room just a stone's throw away from the office from which Britain had ruled Burma for over a century, Thant sat down over tea and biscuits with George Brown and other high-ranking officials. The owl-faced, sharp-tongued Brown was the Labour government's foreign secretary and a former trade unionist. Thant, who was alone, having traveled with just his security aide, told his hosts that only an unconditional halt to the bombing would lead to talks and that the San Antonio formula was unacceptable because it was conditional.

Brown, unconvinced, said that "this was getting us no further towards negotiations."[17] They argued for hours. Brown didn't share Thant's anxiety about the Russians; he felt that the real threat would come from Hanoi bolstering its forces in the South. Warning that Vietnam would soon become "a vast refugee camp," Thant countered that the bombing had no military value. Why not just stop and talk?

During a particularly testy moment, Thant told Brown that it was "hard to argue with the North Vietnamese, who claimed that the whole country was rising against the Americans." He was intimately familiar, he said, with Burma's civil war and the way villagers had been mobilized by different armed factions. It was impossible, he argued, for the Americans to win this kind of war.

At midday, Brown took Thant to 10 Downing Street for a working lunch with the prime minister. When they arrived, Brown said to Harold Wilson: "This man is wet, repeat wet." Wilson felt the same. The Labour leader immediately sent a note to Johnson saying that he and Brown "were thoroughly disturbed" by Thant's "pathetically weak-kneed and biased posture."

Despite "his evident desire to help, Thant is again ruling himself out as an interlocutor by the total one-sidedness of his approach," Wilson cabled Johnson. "We had a long theological exposition from him at lunch of Hanoi's view that, because the North Vietnamese were not bombing the United States, it was perfectly reasonable that they should expect you to stop the bombing unconditionally."[18]

Likely hoping to please his American counterpart, Wilson reported to Johnson that after a "reasonably controlled burst of temper" he advised Thant that peace would not come from "one-sided appeals" and that the Secretary-General's "double standards" were "destroying his credibility either as a mediator or as a world statesman."[19]

Just then, Thant received word from the French government that Hanoi's representative in Paris, Mai Van Bo, wanted urgently to see him. Johnson, who was briefed on this by the British, complained in a telephone call to Clark Clifford, who was about to take over from Robert McNamara as secretary of defense, "Now U Thant is screwing the thing up and just as much as he can. And he's their agent almost. And he's gone to Moscow and he didn't see anybody but some clerk. Then he dashed over and tried to put it to Wilson, and Wilson's no good, but he did at least tell us what's happening. Now he's going to run over and try to see de Gaulle. Then they're going to come in and demand that we stop bombing tomorrow."[20]

Hours later, in France, Thant was whisked off in a black Citroën, the UN's blue and white flag fluttering in front, to the Élysée Palace, where President Charles de Gaulle told him that the Americans had been "wrong from the beginning." He too worried that the United States might resort to using battlefield nuclear weapons.[21]

Later that day, at the North Vietnamese mission, Mai Van Bo, a moon-faced self-styled connoisseur of French literature, provided answers to the questions Thant had posed to his colleague in Delhi. Mai was, he said, "authorized to declare that talks with Washington could begin as soon as the cessation of bombing became a reality"—meaning, once enough time had passed to see that it was actually taking place. If the Americans announced an end to the bombing publicly, talks could begin immediately.[22]

As soon as he got back to New York, Thant passed on the message to Arthur Goldberg, who quickly arranged for the Secretary-General to see President Johnson. The Americans had received a similar signal via the Italians and their own State Department channels. Both Thant and Goldberg hoped that a formula for the start of direct talks could finally be agreed on.

On February 21, as Thant, Bunche, Goldberg, and the Secretary-General's two security men were flown by military jet to Washington, Robert McNamara, days from leaving his position as secretary of defense and taking a new job as head of the World Bank, remarked contemptuously to Johnson, "I'd get it off my calendar as fast as I could, and just be pleasant, and leave no bad taste if you can."[23] When the cars carrying Thant and his party arrived at the White House, they were inspected thoroughly by a battery of guards. Bunche couldn't remember ever having experienced such a thorough check. They then proceeded along the driveway, which was lined, in the Secretary-General's honor, by uniformed men from every branch of the armed forces.

A smiling Johnson, in a brown suit, came out to greet both Thant and Bunche warmly, before shepherding Thant alone into the Cabinet Room, where they sat across the table from each other in black leather and mahogany chairs. Thant's mission was to convince Johnson of the opportunity at hand. "Hanoi wants to be independent of Peking," he explained. They could, he said, be "weaned away" from Peking's embrace—and added that the Chinese were attacking him personally as the US's "messenger boy." It was the Vietnamese who had met with him and suggested this proposal, despite what must have been severe misgivings in Peking. This was all true. Playing up Chinese hostility was also Thant's tactic to gain whatever he could of Johnson's confidence.

"Why not end the bombing for X number of days, then begin talks on a de-escalation in the South?" asked Thant. Johnson said he couldn't really see much difference between what the Secretary-General was saying and his own San Antonio formula. "Now, we yearn for peace. We want self-determination in that area. We have no desire to stay there as a colonizer and occupier."[24]

Afterward, there was a working lunch with Rusk and other senior officials. Like the president and the British, Rusk couldn't understand why Hanoi rejected the San Antonio formula so categorically. Thant set out, for the umpteenth time, the importance to the North Vietnamese of an unconditional halt to the bombing. It had to be portrayed in this way. At the same time, the North Vietnamese understood that if the United States sensed they were "taking advantage" of the halt, the bombing might resume.

"The basic difference between the United States and the North Vietnamese positions is that the US wants the North Vietnamese out of South Vietnam and the North Vietnamese want the United States out of South Vietnam," the onetime Burmese schoolmaster instructed the president's men. "The only alternative to negotiations is war for years to come.... I wonder if anything would be left of Vietnam." He stated that none of the Asian governments he was in touch with wanted to see the US defeated. There was an honorable way out.

When Rusk warned Thant that saying anything publicly at this point might disqualify him as a mediator, the Secretary-General responded, "I never wanted to be a mediator. Better for governments to do this. I just wanted to set things on the right path."

On February 24, Thant issued a statement about his trip and stressed, as he had for nearly four years, that Vietnam required a political and not a military solution. The first step had to be an unconditional end to the bombing of the North: "The world is anguished and sickened by the continued intensity and savagery of the war. It is heart-rending to witness the agony of innocent civilians ... the ugliness of the war is matched only by its futility."

With an end to the bombing, he emphasized, talks could begin within weeks, perhaps even days. Nor did the problem end at the borders of Vietnam. The war was already having a deleterious impact on international relations, he cautioned, and was impairing the "effective functioning" of the United Nations.[25]

The French had been indispensable in facilitating the Secretary-General's recent discussions with the North Vietnamese and were, as usual, delighted with his public pronouncements. President de Gaulle even convened a special meeting of the Council of Ministers and read out a translation of Thant's statement. He declared that his views and Thant's were "entirely identical," on both the dangers of escalation and the opportunity for negotiation. The Secretary-General, said de Gaulle, enjoyed the Fifth Republic's "full support."[26]

Meanwhile, within the Johnson administration, the gloom was deepening. CBS evening news anchor Walter Cronkite, "the most trusted man in America," told viewers after a two-week trip to Vietnam that victory was nowhere in sight and negotiations were the only realistic way forward. In early March 1968, Secretary of Defense Clark Clifford told Johnson that there was no guarantee that another 200,000 troops or the continued bombing of the North would turn the tide. There was, he said, "no plan for victory."

On March 26, the president assembled his most senior officials, together with past and present military chiefs. The majority of them, reported longtime hawk Dean Acheson, no longer believed that the US could "do the job we set out to do ... and we must begin to disengage." The "people of the country are dissatisfied," observed America's first Chairman of the Joint Chiefs of Staff, General Omar Bradley. A halt to the bombing was necessary, but they added a caveat: "only if we can get the suggestion to come from the Pope or U Thant... Let's not show them we are in any way weakening."[27]

That Sunday, Johnson shocked the nation and the world. In an evening television broadcast, a grim-faced president, speaking from his desk in the Oval Office, announced an end to all bombing of North Vietnam except in the area just beyond the demilitarized zone where, he said, "the continuing enemy build-up" directly imperiled American troops. He was now prepared for "peace through negotiations." He would also, he said, not seek or accept "the nomination of my party for another term as your President."[28] Elections were then seven months away.

A few days later, Johnson was at New York's St. Patrick's Cathedral for the installation of Terence Cook as archbishop. After the ceremony and a few minutes with Jacqueline Kennedy and Governor Nelson Rockefeller, the president, with his daughter Luci, crossed Fifth Avenue and boarded *Marine One* in Central Park. With the helicopter blades whirring overhead, he suddenly turned to his aides and said he'd like to go and see Thant. Within minutes, the presidential motorcade was dashing across town, with scores of policemen and Secret Service agents clearing the way, correspondents Helen Thomas of UPI and Hugh Sidney of *Time* magazine in tow.[29] Ralph Bunche was given barely five minutes to rush downstairs to be on hand to welcome the president of the United States.

On the thirty-eighth floor, Thant enthusiastically congratulated his surprise visitor on his statesmanship. The two men sat across from one another in the Secretary-General's conference room, with Bunche and Goldberg at their sides, Thant's amber glass ashtray in between.

Johnson opened by saying that he couldn't go further than the partial bombing halt and "be responsible for the massacre of his own fighting men." Thant was positive. He had been in constant touch with the North Vietnamese since the surprise television broadcast and strongly encouraged them not to reject the president's proposal, regardless of pressure from the Chinese.

For nearly an hour, the Secretary-General and the president chatted amiably about Burma's experience of civil war and Vietnam's possible

Thant and Ralph Bunche with President Lyndon B. Johnson and US ambassador Arthur Goldberg during Johnson's surprise visit to Thant in April 1968.

future as a non-aligned state. Johnson said, somewhat disingenuously, that the solution in South Vietnam was elections: "one man, one vote." As soon as that happens, "we will pick up and pull out everything we have in six months." He pondered on the war and the problems he had faced as result. "I do not think they understand us as Americans," he said. "Maybe you could help us there ... we want no real estate, we do not want our hand held up in victory. With the $30 billion we are spending this year on the war in Vietnam, we could make the whole area bloom."

"I am a poor communicator," he continued in his Texan drawl, "but I can communicate with you because I like you. I respect you." Thant, perhaps more immune to Johnson's charms than he had been a few years before, replied simply that he was heading to Geneva and might stop in Paris to see Mai Van Bo.[30]

That evening, Thursday, April 4, 1968, Martin Luther King Jr. was killed in Memphis, Tennessee, by a lone white gunman, James Earl Ray. As news spread, arson and looting tore through more than a hundred American cities, including Washington, D.C., where more than 11,000 troops confronted rioters over several days. The Secretary-General was already in Europe when he heard the news and asked Bunche to represent the UN at the slain civil rights leader's funeral. Thant himself led an outdoor commemoration at the Peace Palace in the Hague, site of the International Court of Justice. Under a darkening sky, he told a crowd of thousands that the world had "lost one of its most earnest, respected and commanding voices in the allied causes of peace, freedom, and the dignity of man."[31]

Shaken by King's assassination, Thant fretted that the nature of the world was turning ever more violent.

―――

The next few weeks were focused on helping the North Vietnamese and the Americans to find a mutually agreeable venue for talks. In Paris, Mai Van Bo confided his skepticism about Johnson's sincerity and complained that US bombing was only intensifying in the area north of the DMZ. Back in New York, Thant relayed this to Goldberg, who said that the American military feared another all-out offensive.[32] They also discussed possible negotiation sites, with the Americans preferring Rangoon and the North Vietnamese suggesting Warsaw. Thant thought Paris might work best.[33]

Johnson appointed veteran diplomat Averell Harriman, wartime ambassador to Moscow and onetime governor of New York, to lead the discussions. Goldberg resigned. For years, the former Supreme Court justice had been laboring to bring about direct talks between Washington and Hanoi, and now that they were about to start the president, who had convinced him to leave his lifetime appointment to the Supreme Court, had selected someone else. There was a chilly exchange of letters between Johnson and Goldberg, who in public said little except to express his "affection" for Thant, "a great world statesman."[34]

Thant respected Harriman, but the feeling was not mutual. In a conversation with columnist Drew Pearson, one of America's leading political commentators at the time, the patrician Harriman mused on the possible location of talks: "I don't think much of U Thant. But the American people do, so it might be a good idea to have him pick the site."[35]

Paris was chosen.

On May 13, 1968, delegations from Washington and Hanoi, each more than two dozen strong, sat down in the chandeliered conference room of the Majestic Hotel to try to find a road to peace. This was the small first step Thant had hoped they would take place in the autumn of 1964. In New York, Thant described himself as a "professional optimist," but cautioned reporters that a "solid wall of mistrust, fear, and suspicion" now existed between the two sides.[36]

A few weeks later, Robert Kennedy was shot in California. With Lyndon Johnson out of the race, the assassinated president's younger brother had become a favorite to win the Democratic Party nomination and with it the presidency. Over the past two years, he had come to the UN to see Thant on several occasions and echoed in public the Secretary-General's three-point plan to end the war.

Thant immediately messaged the senator's wife, Ethel, to express his "horror and dismay at this incomprehensible attack." It was a "tragedy for the world," he wrote, that "in the great nation of the United States violence should continually jeopardize the lives of society's finest men."[37]

After Kennedy's death was announced, a visibly distraught Secretary-General reminded journalists of a comment he had made just a couple of weeks earlier: that the "climate" created by the Vietnam War was "bound to have repercussions elsewhere."[38] A few days later, at a special memorial service at the UN, Thant warned there was "too much hatred" in the world. Speaking of his feelings after the killings of John F. Kennedy and Martin Luther King Jr., he cautioned the assembled diplomats and officials of the need to "fight complacency," so that when the "emotions fade," everything doesn't simply "go on much the same as before while mankind moves ever closer to the ultimate catastrophe."[39]

Thant had a little book made comprising all the statements at the service, and sent it to Ethel Kennedy. She replied that they "made me ever more poignantly aware of the fundamental spirit of kinship which unites all men and all nations" and said she would "always remember the pleasure Bobby derived from those occasions when you and he were together in New York. They always refreshed his hope and confidence in the future."[40]

The world seemed to be on fire. Over the spring and summer of 1968, protests swept campuses across the US, including in New York, where students occupied administrative buildings at Columbia University before being violently ejected by police. In Italy, nearly all universities were taken over by protesters calling for fundamental social and political change. In Paris, weeks of unrest brought the country to the brink of revolution.

Also in 1968, *2001: A Space Odyssey* was released. Thant's fascination for all things related to aliens and outer space was undiminished, and he arranged for a special screening at the UN. In the film, an alien monolith appears to speed up human evolution, leading eventually to sentient supercomputers and interplanetary travel. Arthur C. Clarke, who wrote the short story on which the film was based, was sitting behind Thant, Bunche, and director Stanley Kubrick when he was suddenly "struck by the by the astonishing parallel between the shape of the monolith and the UN Headquarters itself; there seemed something quite uncanny about the coincidence." Perhaps, the famed science fiction writer thought, it wasn't a coincidence after all.[41]

Thant told the political commentator Drew Pearson that he believed UFOs were the biggest challenge facing mankind, next to the war in Vietnam.[42] In July 1968, he met with the astronomer J. Allen Hynek, scientific advisor to Project Blue Book, the US Air Force's secret study of UFOs. Thant wanted to know whether extraterrestrials might indeed be visiting Earth. Hynek, a skeptic at the time, explained that the distances involved would make it extremely unlikely. "You know, I am a Buddhist," replied Thant, arching his eyebrows, "and we believe in life elsewhere ... what may seem like years to us, may be just a day or two to others."[43]

At a press conference that summer, Thant ruminated that humanity had come to a crossroads in history where it was faced with two alternatives: to work together for a "planned and prosperous future for all—the rich and the poor ... or for rich and poor countries to march separately, to go their own ways ... towards an unplanned and chaotic future."[44] He was increasingly thinking in planetary terms. He spoke of a possible apocalyptic turn, a world war triggered by the war in Vietnam, as well as the opposite possibility, the promise of a shared future, uniting science with his interest in spirituality.

That summer, at another special UN screening, Thant watched Milos Forman's romantic comedy *Loves of a Blonde*. The Czech ambassador, who had arranged the screening, was at that time calling on Thant almost daily to make sure that he was kept abreast of the political and economic reforms taking place in his Eastern European nation—later known as the Prague Spring. While some in the Communist bloc were supportive of the reforms, others, including the Kremlin, were wary. Thant accepted an invitation from Alexander Dubček, Prague's reformist leader and First Secretary of the Communist Party, to speak at Charles University in Prague. He was eager to see what was happening firsthand.

On August 20, the evening before he was meant to leave, Thant heard on the radio that Moscow-directed Warsaw Pact forces had invaded Czechoslovakia and seized the capital. Dubček called on his people not to resist. Thant couldn't sleep that night as he ruminated on how best to respond. This was, without a doubt, a clear violation of the United Nations Charter. He was already challenging one superpower; could he afford to challenge the other too? Moscow had always been friendly to him, if not always helpful. At the office the next morning, he asked not to be disturbed for thirty minutes as he wrote a statement.

When the Soviet ambassador arrived to excuse the USSR's action as an intervention "requested" by Prague, Thant responded firmly. The invasion not only flew in the face of the UN's most fundamental principles, he explained, it was also a serious blow to détente and would only help Richard Nixon, who had just been nominated by the Republican Party, win the presidential election in November. American opinion of the UN was already at a low ebb because of the situation in the Middle East. The inability of the Security Council to do anything about this crisis would only entrench the view that the world organization was impotent. In such a situation, Thant told the "weary, uneasy, and embarrassed"–looking Russian diplomat, it would be "very difficult even for me to work."[45]

A little later, the Secretary-General's spokesman, Ramses Nassif, read out Thant's statement to the assembled press corps, condemning the invasion of Czechoslovakia as a "serious blow" to everything the UN had been striving to achieve since its founding. Urquhart thought it was the strongest statement ever made by any UN chief.[46] Thant was keeping in close contact with the Czech government, and canceled his trip on their advice. He urged the Czech ambassador to speak out at the Security Council.

But none of this changed what was actually happening in Czechoslovakia itself, where resistance was crushed by the nearly 500,000 invading troops, backed by 2,000 tanks. As Thant feared, the UN, at least to the American public, looked hopelessly ineffectual.

A few days later, outside a deeply divided Democratic Party convention in Chicago, massed antiwar protesters clashed with nearly 20,000 police and National Guardsmen. In Paris, the talks between the US and North Vietnam had stalled. Johnson's partial bombing halt had brought Hanoi's envoys to Paris, but they refused to negotiate seriously unless the bombing halt became total and unconditional. In South Vietnam, a new Communist offensive left tens of thousands dead.

At a press conference in September, Thant, in a dour mood, said that he had been trying to "reflect the conscience of humanity" in stressing the need for an end to the bombing as the essential step needed to move the conflict from the battlefield to the conference table. He suggested that a resolution saying exactly this would receive the backing of the majority of countries at the UN.[47]

The Johnson administration was apoplectic. A "rather tense" George Ball, Goldberg's replacement as UN ambassador, told the Secretary-General that he was "disturbed" by his comments. They might jeopardize the talks in Paris, he said brusquely. Thant, in his own brusque response, told Ball that he was only repeating what he had been saying for years.

The next day, Ball publicly called Thant "naive." Then he resigned.[48] "I never claimed that once the bombing stops there would be heaven on earth," was Thant's reply to journalists asking for a comment.[49]

Drew Pearson wrote of his admiration for Thant's grit. Playing "to the hilt his role as international gadfly," the Secretary-General, in his opinion, had given a "bravura performance" over recent weeks: he "smote the mighty, he succored the weak, he called for diplomatic initiative." There was, Pearson thought, "an element of tragedy in this situation which pits a brave, determined man, operating through no fault of his own without any real power except the prestige that he derives from his position, against great states intended on national not international goals."[50]

There was soon another tetchy meeting with Dean Rusk. When Thant inquired about Ball's resignation, the secretary of state retorted that it was Ball's own decision: "This is a free country, there is no slave labor." When, after a brief exchange on the Middle East and other issues, Rusk turned to "the Southeast Asia question," the conversation deteriorated further.

Rusk was surprised, he said, by Thant's call to the "conscience of humanity" to end the bombing. Thant countered that the US, as the far stronger power, should take bolder action: "It's absolutely clear that's what most countries want." Rusk disagreed, and asked why Thant always took Hanoi's view and not Washington's. Thant said the war was a civil war. "I'm just as anti-Communist as anyone, but the United States is using the wrong method of fighting Communism in Vietnam."

Eventually the conversation turned back to the Middle East, the brewing civil war in Nigeria, and then to Thant's idea of a meeting of the "Big Four" foreign ministers. "Would the foreign ministers see a draft of Thant's letter of invitation before it was sent?" asked Rusk. Thant said they would not, as each would ask for changes and then it would become impossible for him to send the letter.

"Well, Mr. Secretary-General, we are not children to be written to by the teacher," countered Rusk.

The meeting abruptly ended.[51]

That evening, Rusk told Bunche at a reception that he feared "he had gone a little too far" and was "a little too blunt at one point or two" with Thant. Bunche asked if he was referring to the "schoolchildren" comment, and Rusk admitted that was what he meant.

Thant was not very happy about it, explained Bunche, but showed "no anger or resentment."

"What's wrong with the man? He ought to get angry and even hysterical sometimes!" Rusk replied.[52] Bunche may have agreed.

In October, the Paris talks finally showed signs of progress. Johnson, desperately wanting to end his time in the White House with a peace deal, announced that Operation Rolling Thunder—the bombing of North Vietnam—was coming to an end. Both sides hoped that a new round of negotiations would soon commence, with participation from the Saigon government as well as the Viet Cong. The Soviets informed Thant that they were quietly applying pressure on Hanoi. The prospects seemed good.

What the White House didn't know was that Henry Kissinger, a Harvard historian who was a consultant to the Johnson administration on Vietnam, was also covertly aiding the Nixon campaign. Alerted by the professor that a breakthrough might be around the corner, the Republican presidential candidate quickly schemed to "monkey-wrench" the process underway. A peace deal would only boost the chances of Nixon's rival in the election, Johnson's vice president Hubert Humphrey.[53] At Nixon's secret urging, the Saigon government pulled out of the talks at the last minute. As the outlook for peace again dimmed, Johnson's and Humphrey's poll numbers dived.

Nixon won the election.

Three weeks later, on November 26, the president-elect, accompanied by his soon-to-be National Security Advisor, Henry Kissinger, came to the UN to see the Secretary-General. The two men had first met in Burma in 1955 when Thant, then secretary to the prime minister, guided the visiting US vice president around sites in Rangoon. Thant's friend, the *New York Post* columnist James Wechsler, privately predicted that the new administration, wanting to "escape a repetition of the Johnson debacle," would seek a speedy end to the war. The Secretary-General replied somberly that he had no such illusions; he had discussed Vietnam with Henry Kissinger and found him as uncompromising as Dean Rusk. Ahead, Thant could only see more death and destruction.[54]

15 | BAD MOON RISING

THERE WAS A FUNDAMENTAL contradiction at the heart of Thant's role. The Secretary-General of the United Nations had no real power; the status attached to his office was what allowed him to intervene and defuse crises when possible. But this meant that expectations were always very high. When he could not or would not intervene, there was little to protect him from charges of inaction.

The Afro-Asians wanted a global institution that could safeguard their new states against the return of empire. The Americans wanted the UN to be a core component of a Washington-centered liberal world. From his first day on the job, Thant wanted to reconcile the West and the Third World. This was, however, proving a Herculean challenge.

On January 20, 1969, Richard Nixon succeeded Lyndon Johnson as president of the United States. William Rogers, Nixon's longtime friend and confidant, was named secretary of state, though he had little experience in foreign affairs. From the start, however, Nixon allowed Henry Kissinger, operating from a room near the Oval Office, to be his lieutenant on all things related to Vietnam. The baritone, German-accented Kissinger was a specialist in European history but knew next to nothing about Southeast Asia.

In response to overwhelming domestic political pressure, the new president began drawing down American troops in South Vietnam.

Nixon and Kissinger assumed, inexplicably, that South Vietnamese forces would somehow be able to hold their ground against the Communists, though Saigon's soldiers had for years been unable to manage the same when half a million Americans were fighting alongside them. In Paris, Kissinger talked tough with Hanoi's representatives, absurdly believing that he could convince the North Vietnamese to draw down their troops as well. The talks stalled, and Nixon and Kissinger began secretly carpet-bombing eastern Cambodia, for no reason other than to demonstrate American strength. Thant was purposely sidelined.

In September 1969, Thant and Nixon met just after the president's first address to the UN General Assembly. In his speech, the president had mentioned his desire for elections in South Vietnam, but in their private conversation Thant warned that elections were unrealistic in a war-torn and heavily armed society. The focus should instead be on stitching together a broad coalition in Saigon—a point he had first made to Adlai Stevenson six years earlier. The Secretary-General thought that Cambodia's Prince Norodom Sihanouk, with whom he had been in touch, might be able to play a helpful role. Nixon complained that despite the reduction of troops, Hanoi was still not willing to compromise. "The United States would not suffer a defeat or humiliation in Vietnam," Nixon declared. There would be no "unilateral withdrawal" and no settlement that was not "fair."[1]

The White House Chief of Staff, H. R. Haldeman, noted that the president had given "a very good speech" but that the reaction was "pretty lukewarm," with no applause during the speech and no standing ovation at the end. "Really a useless bunch," he reflected, presumably referring to Thant and his aides. Kissinger grumbled about Thant's idea of a more representative South Vietnamese government: "Some gall!"[2]

Others in Washington were more encouraging. In February 1970, a bipartisan group of over two dozen political leaders including senators Alan Cranston, Mark Hatfield, Jacob Jarvis, George McGovern, Walter Mondale, Edmund Muskie, and Claiborne Pell called on Nixon to invite Thant on a state visit to Washington, during which he could address a joint session of Congress, something never done before by a United

Nations Secretary-General. They hoped to organize a dinner in Thant's honor, to which all members of the House and Senate would be invited.[3] Nixon and Kissinger were uninterested.

Though the war in Vietnam preoccupied Thant, over these same few years, from around mid-1967 through early 1971, he was compelled to focus equally on the festering violence in the Middle East. There were two overarching questions: would Israel withdraw from any or all of the occupied territories, and was Egypt prepared to make peace? If the answer to either question was no, the region could easily slip back into war. Thant's credibility, at least in Western capitals, had waned considerably, but in the eyes of much of the world, his responsibility to prevent war was undiminished.

Unlike Vietnam, where the UN was officially uninvolved, the world organization had been part of the Middle East conflict from the start. The UN had partitioned Palestine, effectively creating the Jewish state; it had negotiated the 1949 Armistice and deployed peacekeepers after the Suez Crisis. And it was a decision by the Secretary-General which withdrew those peacekeepers on the eve of war. While Vietnam was never once discussed in the Security Council, the Middle East was at the top of its agenda.

The Middle East conflict had also become a global one. The United States now stood unambiguously on the side of Israel, and the USSR on the side of Egypt and Syria. Back in June 1967, a few days after the end of the Six-Day War, when Lyndon Johnson was president, the Israeli cabinet had voted by a slim margin in favor of a future deal which included a return to pre-1967 borders with both Egypt and Syria—but not Jordan.[4] Goldberg told Thant that Israel had little interest in keeping the Sinai but would probably want to annex East Jerusalem and the West Bank. For the Israeli government, relinquishing all the territories conquered was not on the cards. At a September summit in Khartoum, Arab leaders vowed "no peace with Israel, no recognition of Israel, and no negotiations with it," as well as an insistence on "the rights of the Palestinians."

In New York, a tortured round of negotiations followed, which led finally, in November 1967, to Security Council Resolution 242. Authored primarily by UK ambassador Lord Caradon, the resolution emphasized "the inadmissibility of the acquisition of territory by war" and called on the "withdrawal of Israel armed forces from territories occupied in the recent conflict." In other words, Israel should withdraw to its prewar borders in exchange for peace.[5]

The unanimously approved resolution also requested the Secretary-General to appoint a Special Representative tasked with making this happen. Thant chose Sweden's ambassador to Moscow, Gunnar Jarring, a formidable linguist fluent in a dozen languages including Persian, Turkish, Arabic, and Hindi, a scholar of central Asian history, and a diplomat of the old school. Once, when he was reported to have replied "No comment" to the press, Thant observed, "I'm sure Jarring would never have gone as far as that." Journalists referred to him "the silent Swede" or "the clam."[6]

The tall, balding sixty-year-old was also a methodical worker, which meant that he sometimes slowed things down. After each meeting, he set aside an hour to write down his account of what had occurred. Bunche and Urquhart suggested waiting until the end of the day, but the Swede replied that after just a few hours "your mind began to adjust your recollections in your own favor—*esprit d'escalier*—and the record would thereby be falsified." What about dictating?, they asked. No good, he explained, "as there would be a 'natural temptation to impress your secretary' and the record would be further distorted."[7] As with all his close aides, Thant admired Jarring for his unimpeachable integrity and calm-headedness.

Jarring immediately went to work, shuttling between Tel Aviv and the neighboring Arab capitals. Egypt and Jordan accepted Resolution 242 as the basis for a peace settlement, and in February 1968, Israel accepted the resolution as a "framework." Thant and Jarring judged this sufficient to begin indirect talks in Nicosia, Cyprus.

In early 1968, Jarring crafted a possible solution. Israel would vacate the Sinai, which would then be demilitarized. Sharm El-Sheikh and the

Golan Heights would be garrisoned by a new UN peacekeeping force, this time under a strong Security Council mandate—meaning that Egypt could not order the force to be withdrawn. Gaza would be placed under UN administration. The future of the West Bank would be decided by direct talks between the Israelis and the Jordanians, with some adjustments mutually agreed. The Palestinian refugees would be absorbed into Jordan, with the added incentive of substantial international financial assistance.[8]

However, the talks in Cyprus never got off the ground. The Israelis insisted on direct talks, with Jarring in the room. They also wanted to discuss "secure boundaries," whereby they would keep Gaza, parts of the Sinai, East Jerusalem, the Golan Heights, and parts of the West Bank, perhaps in a trade for land elsewhere. The Egyptians responded that Resolution 242 had to be implemented first, meaning that Israel had to withdraw from all occupied territories before other issues could be discussed. Egypt was also opposed to a formal treaty with the Jewish state.[9] Frenzied diplomacy was accompanied by little progress.

At the same time, the brittle ceasefire began to crumble, with repeated clashes along all of Israel's borders. In March, Egyptian and Israeli forces fought their biggest battle since the Six-Day War, with air strikes and artillery fire across the Suez Canal. The Secretary-General was in constant contact with his general, Odd Bull, whose small team of military observers—mainly Swedes, Finns, Irish, and Burmese—were doing all they could, under nearly continuous fire, to dampen hostilities.

The conflict took on far-reaching dimensions. In July 1968, the UN chief spoke out forcefully against the hijacking of an El Al plane by Palestinian militants—the start of a wave. (El Al was Israel's national airline.) Describing it as a "criminal" action, the Secretary-General demanded the unconditional release of the Israeli hostages and refused to broker, even secretly, any negotiations.[10] After another hijacking, this time at Zurich, Thant again issued a strong condemnation and convened an emergency meeting with international civil aviation authorities. Abba Eban messaged from Tel Aviv to say there was "deep interest" in the Secretary-

General's actions and asked what more could be done. Thant outlined some measures for international police cooperation, but stressed that what was really needed was a just resolution of the conflict.

He believed peace was possible, but only if the big powers were willing to work together. The outlines of a settlement, he reckoned, were there. The new American president also wished for a speedy resolution, as the Arab–Israeli standoff imperiled Washington's relations with the Arab world and might undermine prospects for a US–Soviet détente. Nixon didn't share Johnson's instinctive sympathy for Israel and instructed his secretary of state, William Rogers, to collaborate with Moscow in finding a settlement.

In early 1969, American, British, French, and Soviet representatives met formally at the UN as the "Big Four." Their objective, they said, was to back Jarring's diplomacy and find a blueprint for Middle East peace. In April, Secretary of State Rogers said the Big Four were "prepared to use the force of public opinion" to compel the two sides to agree.

Thant was pleasantly surprised when Nixon's new representative at the UN, fifty-three-year-old veteran diplomat Charles Yost, who had been Adlai Stevenson's deputy, told him that Washington was in favor of "concerted action" by the Security Council to implement Resolution 242. The Soviets had recently proposed a "compromise" formula, similar to what Jarring had earlier suggested, and Yost thought this was "a step in the right direction." The Israelis, however, condemned the Soviet compromise as "a Moscow plan for a Middle East Munich." The Palestinian organization Fatah declared that "armed struggle was the only way towards the liberation of Palestine."[11]

Discussions so far had been about states and borders: the conflict between Israel and its neighboring Arab countries. But Thant began to argue that other issues, in particular the "question of the Palestine refugees," which he increasingly felt was "the crux of the problem," needed to take center stage. "Without trying to tackle this very tragic problem in earnest," he told Yost, "I am afraid the move towards a just and peaceful settlement will be very slow."[12]

On a visit to Washington in April 1969, King Hussein of Jordan told Nixon that he and President Nasser were willing to add free navigation by Israeli ships through the Suez Canal and the Straits of Tiran as part of a future settlement. They would acknowledge Israel's right to live in peace. In return, there would have to be a "just settlement" for Palestinian refugees and the return by Israel of all territories taken in June 1967. In New York, King Hussein informed Thant there could even be some "adjustments" to the West Bank border.[13]

Tel Aviv, however, quickly dismissed the negotiation process as "propaganda." The tough and matronly Golda Meir, formerly Israel's foreign minister, had recently become prime minister. She opposed Big Four involvement and specifically rejected the idea of a strong UN force in the area. Israel, she said, could only accept direct talks with the Arabs. In a private meeting, Abba Eban told Thant the same.

For Meir, a withdrawal to the 1967 borders would only place Israel under renewed threat. Israel could never rely on international guarantees, she believed, and certainly not a new UN peacekeeping operation.

The seventy-one-year-old Zionist leader had been no fan of Thant's predecessor, Dag Hammarskjöld, whom she felt had been partial to the Arab side. "I know that today a small cult has grown up around the personality of Mr. Hammarskjöld," she said, "but I am not a party to it." She was, however, flummoxed by the Burmese diplomat at the head of the UN. "Despite all the years of Burmese–Israeli friendship and his own really warm personal relationship with the country, and with us, the moment that U Thant became Secretary-General we were in for a very hard time. He... found it absolutely impossible, apparently, to be firm either with the Russians or with the Arabs, though he had no trouble at all being exceedingly firm with Israel."[14] It was a sentiment that would only grow, in Israel and in the US.

Fighting intensified across the Suez Canal. Some UN observers were injured, mainly by Egyptian fire. The Secretary-General warned the Security Council that his men were "like defenseless targets in a shooting gallery." Palestinian guerrillas raided into Israel from Jordan, and in response, Israeli commandos blew up Jordan's main irrigation canal. Israeli commandos also cut the critical power line connecting the Aswan Dam to Cairo.

In a speech to US Navy veterans at Manhattan's Waldorf Astoria Hotel, a glum Secretary-General predicted that the Middle East was in something like "the early stages of a new Hundred Years' War." More ominously, he felt that the UN's inability to stop the fighting—the first time since the UN's founding that a Security Council order had been so openly disregarded—represented "a very dangerous step backwards toward anarchy."[15]

In late September, Golda Meir, in sturdy black shoes and a colorful checked suit, came to see Thant, accompanied by Abba Eban.[16] They greeted one another amiably, as did Bunche, who had known Meir since his days as the armistice negotiator twenty years before. They then quickly got down to business. "There is only one question," insisted the silver-haired Israeli prime minister, "namely, whether the Arab states are prepared to have a real peace with Israel." Thant replied that in his opinion, "the Arab governments were prepared for peace and would recognize Israel."

But Meir doubted this. Though the 1949 Armistice had implied recognition, she argued that the Arabs did not want to live peacefully alongside Israel. After the Six-Day War, they accepted a ceasefire but had not kept it. "Israel is not prepared to go through a similar situation again for in the last resort there was no one upon whom Israel can depend." Tel Aviv wanted to negotiate with its neighbors "as between sovereign states" and could not agree to the big powers preparing a ready-made package.

"I fully understand Israel's desire for peace and secure boundaries," Thant replied. Peace in return for a withdrawal from the newly conquered territories and a "realistic solution to the refugee problem" was at long last possible. Meir wouldn't accept this. There had been many promises in the past, but in 1967 Israel had been "left alone again." "The objective," she said, was "peace, no violence, no UN observers and no gimmicks... the Arabs must get rid of the mental and psychological block that they are unable to sit in the same room with the Israelis."

Thant concluded by saying that he feared the situation would become "even more intractable in the years to come."[17] A few days later, in the General Assembly, he cautioned that unless there was progress soon, "this great and historical region, the cradle of civilization and of three world religions, will recede steadily into a new dark age of violence, disruption, and destruction."[18]

Several months later, American and Soviet diplomats again tried to identify a common position that could lead to a deal, which they would share with the British and the French for their approval. Thant would then have Jarring negotiate an agreement based on this outline with Cairo, Amman, and Tel Aviv, with whatever modifications were needed to get everyone on board.

Thant studied a plan which had been unveiled by Secretary of State Rogers, as well as earlier ideas submitted by the USSR and France, and saw little difference between them. At the heart of each was the idea that Israel would withdraw from the territories taken in 1967 in return for peace. There were differences, for example on whether or not there should be a "binding contractual agreement" at the end of the process, but these, he felt, could be ironed out.

Israel, unsurprisingly, rejected this approach entirely. When Rogers unveiled his plan, Meir characterized it as a "disaster for Israel." Meanwhile, unknown to Thant, Henry Kissinger was advising Nixon not to pressure the Israelis. Kissinger had little time for UN diplomacy and viewed Rogers as a bitter rival. Though he had initially been focused on Vietnam, the German-born academic's attention was increasingly turned toward the Israeli–Arab conflict.

The violence escalated. With clashes raging along the Suez Canal, Israel launched air attacks deep into Egyptian territory, including a raid near Cairo which killed over seventy people.[19] Egypt turned to the Soviets for help, and they responded by sending surface-to-air missile batteries, fighter planes, and over 12,000 military personnel. In February, Palestinian militants opened fire and threw grenades at a bus on the tarmac at Munich airport carrying passengers to a London-bound El Al plane. Ten days later, an explosion ripped through an El Al flight from Zurich to Tel Aviv, killing everyone on board. A new factor adding to the complexity was the beginning of Jewish settlement in the West Bank—territory seized from Jordan—despite strong opposition from within Israel's own Labour Party.

By early 1970, it was clear that the Big Four discussions were going nowhere. The Secretary-General thought of reviving Jarring's mission, in the hope that the superpowers would work together at the UN toward a settlement rather than backing rival sides. Unless this happened, he believed, another "calamity" was inevitable.[20]

Thant was at a crossroads. His early career had been meteoric: from the backwaters of Burma to New York as an Afro-Asian ambassador at a time of Afro-Asian unity and growing weight in global affairs. In 1961, when the world needed a mild-mannered Third World diplomat who could calm tensions between the superpowers, he had appeared straight out of central casting. His multicultural background, conviviality, propensity for hard work, and principled approach to his job had served him well. Until now. Vietnam and the Arab–Israeli conflict were straining his ties with Washington to near breaking point. He could influence public opinion but, in the end, there was little he could do to alter US foreign policy, however ill-conceived.

Thant enjoyed, however, the unwavering support of the newly independent nations of Asia and Africa. By the end of the 1960s, these nations, still overwhelmingly poor, riven by internal strife, and undermined by superpower intervention, were a weakened force. But their foundational desire, for the age of empires to be replaced by the sovereign equality of states, remained as fierce as ever. What this really meant in an increasingly messy world was, however, a work in progress. The vast majority sided squarely with the Arab states in the aftermath of the 1967 war, further souring relations at the UN between the West and the Third World.

Over these same years, Thant became mired in another crisis: the war between Nigeria's government and the breakaway region of Biafra, which had caused a humanitarian catastrophe of epic proportions. The conflict over Biafra brought his increasingly vexed relations with American and

Western European media to a head. And it shone a spotlight on his core beliefs about the future of the postcolonial world.

Africa's battle for freedom had fashioned Thant's Secretary-Generalship from the very beginning. That battle was ongoing, with the dictatorship in Portugal brutally repressing liberation movements in Angola and Mozambique, and white supremacists locking up opponents—including Nelson Mandela—and tightening their grip over South Africa, Namibia, and Rhodesia. Thant came to office at the height of the Congo imbroglio; his earliest test was the fight against white supremacists in Katanga. Over the years, he nurtured close bonds with the leaders of the continent's newly minted states, including Ahmed Ben Bella of Algeria, Kenneth Kaunda of Zambia, Jomo Kenyatta of Kenya, and Julius Nyerere of Tanzania. Emperor Haile Selassie of Ethiopia was one of Thant's first guests in New York, and the two had met frequently over the years. Together, they shared a vision of an Africa—and a world—free from white domination, and made the elimination of the colonial and white supremacist regimes entrenched across southern Africa a priority at the UN.

The West African nation of Nigeria—about twice the size of California and with a population of over 50 million—had been a British colony until its independence in 1960. Like many former British possessions, it had been cobbled together from several precolonial communities. A military coup in 1966 was followed by a countercoup, vicious inter-ethnic bloodshed, and, in May 1967, a declaration of independence by Biafra, an oil-rich region home to the largely Christian Ibo minority.

Civil war was quickly accompanied by a famine which killed hundreds of thousands of people.[21]

The Soviets and the Americans both backed the federal government, as did the UK, which was keen to protect the flow of oil from Nigeria's enormous Shell-BP–operated fields and refineries. France, which was scheming to gain its own foothold in the petroleum-rich Niger Delta, provided arms to the Biafran secessionist state. The same white mercenaries who had been involved in Katanga, and before Katanga in Algeria, were now fighting for Biafra, men like German-born Rolf Steiner, who commanded Biafra's Fourth Commando Brigade and was reputed to be fond of "beer, Benson & Hedges cigarettes, violence and very little else."[22]

Some African nations, notably Tanzania and Zambia, opposed keeping Nigeria together by force. But at two Organization of African Unity summits, a clear majority of the continent's leaders resolved that the war was a Nigerian "internal affair" and asked that the UN refrain from any action likely to damage "the peace, unity and territorial integrity" of Nigeria. Attempts at a negotiated compromise led by Haile Selassie gained little traction with Biafra's commander, the Oxford-educated Colonel Chukwuemeka Ojukwu, who insisted on complete independence.[23]

Thant refused to mediate and didn't want the UN to be politically involved. In 1963, African heads of government had set up the Organization of African Unity as a regional body that could look after the continent's affairs. Thant wholeheartedly championed the body's aim of a strong and independent Africa, and made a point of attending all of their summits even when there was a possible threat to his life. In September 1967, a strange voice on his private line at home warned, "If you go to Kinshasa, you will land in Bukavu."[24] Kinshasa, formerly Leopoldville, the capital of the Congo, was hosting an OAU summit; Bukavu was then under the control of white mercenaries linked to erstwhile Katanga leader Moïse Tshombe (then in exile). Very few people knew the Secretary-General's private number. Was it a threat or a warning? The killing of his predecessor, Dag Hammarskjöld, still a mystery, might well have resulted from an attempted diversion of his plane by white mercenaries in the Congo. Thant's aides believed that a similar plot could be underway, perhaps to hold the Secretary-General hostage until Tshombe was allowed to return to the Congo. But Thant felt strongly that his presence at the summit was vital as a demonstration of solidarity, so, after rearranging his travel at the cost of missing the first session, he flew to the Congo. There was no incident, and the enigma of the phone call was never solved. Thant's commitment to his African colleagues remained intact.

These same African leaders, through their regional organization, were now explicitly asking Thant to leave the Nigerian crisis to them. For Thant, there was no question of doing anything else.

As importantly, he was dead set against secession and the breakup of states (or territories not yet states) emerging from colonial rule. In Burma, he had served a government that battled secessionist movements. More recently, in western Papua New Guinea, he had allowed the UN to ignore local sentiment and pave the way for the consolidation of Indonesian state control.

In press conferences, he did not mention Burma or Papua but did link Nigeria to the Congo, where, he said, the UN had spent over half a billion dollars "and many precious lives" in part to prevent the secession of Katanga. That was the "right attitude" for the UN to take, Thant argued. "There are secessionist movements in many parts of the world . . . if the UN were to give endorsement to the principle of secession, there would be no end to the problems besetting many Member States."[25] The idea of self-determination had to be realistically applied. A Third World of ever smaller states would only benefit the big powers and their big corporations. Along with most African governments, he

Thant with Ethiopia's Emperor Haile Selassie at a summit of African leaders in Addis Ababa in February 1969.

called for a peaceful end to the Biafra secession and "national reconciliation" for Nigeria.[26]

There would be no political role for the UN, but Thant determined that there should be a humanitarian one, through UNICEF and the recently established World Food Programme. As the crisis worsened, Thant pleaded with both sides to allow aid to reach civilians by road and by air. At times, he interceded directly with governments; he appealed personally to Equatorial Guinea to allow the Red Cross to fly life-saving assistance from the airport there directly to Biafra.[27]

Photographs of severely malnourished children were everywhere on the front pages of newspapers and the covers of magazines. By 1969, Biafra was the recipient of the largest relief operation since the Second World War. It was the first international "humanitarian crisis," where pressure to alleviate suffering took precedence over peace efforts. In the West, the war also generated the first solidarity campaign, especially by Christian charities, for a threatened people in the Third World.[28]

Over the early weeks of 1970, Thant toured eleven West African countries, including Nigeria.[29] At the same time, UNICEF's executive director, the American Henry Labouisse, traveled extensively through the conflict areas, sending the Secretary-General detailed accounts of the heartbreaking scenes he witnessed, including of little children starving to death.[30] Federal forces had just won a decisive military victory. Humanitarian need, however, remained acute.

In Lagos, Thant urged Nigeria's thirty-six-year-old leader, General Yakubu Gowan, to allow the Red Cross immediate access to the formerly rebel-held areas of Biafra. Gowan replied that only Asian doctors, not doctors from "white countries," would be allowed. When Thant asked about observers from the UK, Canada, Sweden, and Poland coming to investigate possible war crimes, Gowan said that he did not want white observers "as if the black man could not do observation properly."[31] For Gowan and many other Africans and Asians, the rising chorus in the West calling for humanitarian intervention could not be detached from the continent's colonial past and present.

Many Western journalists, outraged by the plight of civilians, especially children, in Biafra, turned on the Secretary-General for not "doing more." Following Thant's visit to Lagos, Anthony Lewis, in *The New York Times*, composed a blistering attack: "There are times to be angry. One of them is when an international civil servant uses his position to suggest that there is nothing to worry us in a situation actually stinking of human misery."[32] Building on Thant's actions in the run-up to the Six-Day War, a new image of the Secretary-General began to form. Writing in *The Washington Post*, Robert Estabrook suggested that the Burmese diplomat was "nice" but "passive" and often acted "as an Asian."[33]

At a press conference in February, Thant lost his patience. He had just come back from another African trip, this time to a summit hosted by Haile Selassie in Addis Ababa, where, he explained, "the attitude and approach" of the many African heads of government was entirely different from what was being written by "a substantial section of the European press." The African leaders, he said, were determined to safeguard and consolidate their hard-won independence. Of course, African leaders "wanted to end the agony and misery and starvation and death and destruction" they saw in Nigeria. But Haile Selassie and others had outlined "very concrete steps . . . and were amazed to find that . . . the mass media blamed the side which accepted these proposals and praised the side which rejected them"—by which he meant Biafra.

"Colonel Ojukwu," Thant contended, "had gambled with hundreds of thousands of African lives to serve his political ends." He was repeating, he said, what he had heard in Addis Ababa, but he no doubt felt similarly himself.

As the assembled correspondents continued their heated questioning, Thant shifted to the nub of what he really wanted to say: what African leaders "resent most is . . . the patronizing or paternalistic attitude from those from the outside" who look upon them "as children who do not know how to run their affairs." The Secretary-General recalled "the volume of criticism leveled at the United Nations and the then Secretary-General" during the Congo crisis. He pointed out that the same public relations firm which had worked for Moïse Tshombe and his white supremacist regime in Katanga, the shadowy Geneva-based Markpress, was also working for Biafra and Colonel Ojukwu. "A very substantial section" of the media that was "solidly with Tshombe" was now solidly with Ojukwu. "It is a very interesting phenomenon."[34]

In increasingly strident tones, he pointed out that from "Oslo to Vienna," the press had come out against him, in sync and "in full blast," saying that "a European would not have done this or a European would not have said that." Thant asserted that the commentators criticizing him now were the same people who had condemned him for his decision to withdraw peacekeepers from the Egyptian–Israeli border in 1967 and who blasted his "mistake" of not going to Prague after the Soviet invasion.

"I have been at pains to answer those charges for the past two and a half years," he stated, the exasperation clear in his voice. Anyone who thought he should have flown to Prague after the Czech government itself had told him not to come "should have their heads examined." There were no more questions.

Over the following days, a few journalists wrote that Thant was a victim of racial prejudice. The *Boston Globe*'s diplomatic correspondent, India-born Darius S. Jhabvala, suggested that it was not unusual at the UN to hear Western diplomats say "he is brown" or "he is only Burmese" and so we shouldn't "expect much." These were, Jhabvala wrote, "lines fed to like-minded cohorts in the home capitals where they are spouted indiscriminately." On everything from the allegations that he had given Nasser a "free hand" to invade Israel or failed to protect Czechoslovakia from the Russians or refused to help Biafra, Thant had become the West's "select whipping boy."

During the Biafra war, the *Boston Globe* reporter went on, "a well-functioning public relations machine greased with oil interests" had settled on Thant as their principal target, using much the same "poisonous language" that was first brewed at the behest of Moïse Tshombe's regime in Katanga.[35] A week later, the African American writer and activist Winston Berry warned that "a full-scale campaign of vilification" was being orchestrated against Thant, by "circles that are hostile to his positions on the Middle East, Nigeria, Vietnam ... [it] harks back to the crisis around the secession of Katanga." "Colonialists, imperialists, and racists of all stripes have seemed to band together against this modest but courageous man," he wrote, and noted Thant's own censure of the racism leveled against him.[36]

Thant's image in the West was shifting, and his own views were evolving as well. Lionel Landry, then the director of the Asia Society in New York, had first met Thant in the early 1950s, when Landry was with the American embassy and Thant inhabited the mildewed offices of the Victorian redbrick Secretariat in Rangoon. Now, he found the Secretary-General in a room of sleek Scandinavian furnishings and spotless glass windows overlooking an overcast Manhattan skyline. But he was "the same U Thant," smoking a cigar, his graying hair the only change. "He was far from Burma, but one could sense in the quiet room," thought Landry, "the presence of J. S. Furnivall, Alfred Lord Tennyson, and the Indian Civil Service—and perhaps, some sainted abbot of the *sangha*, quietly preaching detachment."[37]

Landry was mistaken. A decade before, Thant had believed he could help craft positive ties between the West, the US in particular, and the new nations of Asia and Africa. In the aftermath of the Cuban Missile Crisis, he had hoped the UN could be a catalyst for global peace and unleash economic development. If he was still optimistic, it was an optimism scarred by years of dealing with a Washington at war. The conflicts in Africa, Vietnam, and the Middle East had made him far more suspicious of Western states. He also had fewer illusions about Soviet goodwill toward the world organization.

He was, however, as committed as ever to the Afro-Asian agenda of his ambassadorial days, with the fight against colonialism and racism at its heart. At a personal level, he was happy living and working in New York. His closest colleagues, like Norman Cousins and Ralph Bunche, were American. But when push came to shove, his political instincts were Afro-Asian.

He was not, however, trapped in a time warp. He didn't believe that the challenges of the 1970s would be the same as those confronted at the African–Asian Conference in Bandung fifteen years before. The fight against white supremacy was far from over, and Third World sovereignty needed to be protected against the big powers. This was, he was certain, the only possible foundation for a peaceful future.

But it was no good thinking just in terms of nations and national sovereignty. The Afro-Asians had always wanted the era of empire to be replaced by one of global cooperation. Scanning the papers every day, leafing through the latest political tomes at the weekend, reading the multitude of reports landing on his Swedish teak desk, and learning from countless conversations with people from all over the world, the former schoolmaster was beginning to feel that for the planet as a whole, time was running out.

16 | ONE WORLD

ON A WARM AND sunny mid-August morning in 1969, Thant enjoyed the ride of his life. The astronauts of the Apollo 11 mission had just returned from the moon and the UN Secretary-General was joining them in one of the most spectacular parades of all time.

With as many as four million people cheering from the sidewalks or casting a sea of multicolored confetti from the windows of glimmering skyscrapers along the route, the specially-made, open-top Chrysler limousine, flanked by dozens of police outriders, slowly wheeled its way from City Hall in downtown Manhattan to United Nations Plaza. Over the next three hours, Neil Armstrong, Buzz Aldrin, and Michael Collins waved from an elevated back seat, while in a middle row sat Thant, Governor Nelson Rockefeller, and New York mayor John Lindsay.[1]

Outside UN headquarters, as tens of millions of people around the world watched on television, the Secretary-General, in a sporty striped tie, saluted the "lunar pioneers." The plaque they had left on the moon was inscribed with the words "We come in peace for all mankind." "The words are few," he proclaimed, "but they spell out the common identity of all the inhabitants of this planet and our never-ending search for peace." In reply, Neil Armstrong, addressing the exhilarated crowd of UN staff and diplomats, expressed hope that "we, Citizens of the Earth who can solve the problems of leaving Earth, can also solve the problems of staying on it."[2]

A few months before, Thant had hosted a reception in his office for the Apollo 8 astronaut Frank Borman, who gave him a photo of Earth as seen from the moon with the inscription "as others see us, truly one world." More than ever, we should see clearly that "we are all brothers," the astronaut told the Secretary-General.[3]

Thant searched for spiritual clues about where the planet was heading. He reread old favorites like James Frazier's *The Golden Bough*, a comparative study of religion and mythology, and the Jesuit scientist Pierre Teilhard de Chardin's *The Phenomenon of Man*, with its idea of the Omega Point, where the universe spirals toward a final unification of all things.

In an interview with *Redbook* magazine, Thant said that all the astronauts he had met had emphasized the same thing: that they had come to realize "the unity of the earth and the human community, the indivisible nature of our world." He added his own philosophical spin:

"With our concentration on external, concrete things, we have drifted away from the spiritual realm. We have skyscrapers, microphones, televisions, jets—we are able to travel to the moon . . . but we are still ignorant of the truth about our inner selves. It places us in grave danger."[4]

As he thought more about the planet and outer space, his own country, Burma, was becoming an ever more worrying place. When he had first arrived in New York, Thant had assumed his posting would last only a few years, and that he would return home at the end of his term. But going back to his homeland now seemed doubtful. General Ne Win's Revolutionary Council had shut the country off from the outside world, ended political freedoms, and impoverished a once promising economy. Scores of desperate friends and acquaintances wrote letters pleading for a job at the UN; he wrote back in nearly every case but was only able to help very few.[5]

A new insurgency had also emerged, along the Thai border, headed by Thant's former boss, the ex–prime minister Nu, who was now out of prison and in exile in Bangkok. Ne Win's government suspected collusion between the Secretary-General and Nu to restore democracy, though there was none—only a single private meal in New York. In early 1970, when Thant returned to Burma on holiday, he was cold-shouldered by Ne Win and felt forced to leave after just a couple of days. The Burmese diplomatic mission in New York, the very one he had headed ten years before, ignored his requests to renew his passport. Thant, the champion of Afro-Asian states, was finding himself without a state of his own. As he neared the end of his second term, he was, almost literally, a man without a country.

———

In August 1970, the men of the Apollo 11 mission returned to the UN and presented the Secretary-General with the UN flag they had taken on their space mission, together with a rock from the moon. In the era of Armstrong's "giant leap for mankind," Thant bemoaned the inability of the big powers to take even a "small leap for peace." He told the astronauts that their amazing achievement should remind everyone what "we, as members of the human race, can accomplish on this planet if we are prepared to combine our efforts and work together for the benefit of all mankind."[6]

Thant was ever more convinced that a better future—perhaps human survival itself—rested on a fresh way of thinking and a new planetary consciousness. He was worried for the future of the world. In early 1969, speaking from his raised marble desk at the head of the UN's General Assembly, he had sounded a warning to the assembled delegations:

> *I do not wish to seem overdramatic, but I can only conclude from the information that is available to me as Secretary-General, that the Members of the United Nations have perhaps ten years left in which to subordinate their ancient quarrels and launch a global partnership to curb the arms race, to improve the human environment, to defuse the population explosion, and to supply the required momentum to development efforts. If such a global partnership is not forged within the next decade, then I very much fear that the problems I have mentioned will have reached such staggering proportions that they will be beyond our capacity to control.[7]*

Over the past decade, the United Nations had dramatically expanded its work in many fresh directions. The World Food Programme was established to combat hunger. UNICEF rolled out innovative programs focused on children's educational needs as well as their physical well-being. And the World Health Organization, in a shining example of unprecedented global cooperation, launched a near universal vaccination program to eliminate smallpox.

Much of this was of secondary importance to the US and Europe. But for the states of the Third World, and especially the countries that had recently gained independence, being a respected part of a world organization that focused on the issues important to them, and within which they had an equal voice, was a priceless asset.

Some of the biggest hopes, however, had been dashed. When he was Burmese ambassador, Thant, like other Afro-Asians, wanted the world organization to be a machine powering global economic change. The goal was not aid to reduce poverty, but a fundamental restructuring of the world economic system toward the kind of fairer trade that would make possible rapid industrialization in the Third World. The UN's Conference on Trade and Development (UNCTAD), first convened five years before, was making headway, not least in facilitating discussions between the countries of the South. This may have seemed a pedestrian step to people in London, but not to those in Lagos or Lima, who valued the unprecedented opportunity to craft ideas outside a Western frame, assisted by a Secretariat that was fighting in their corner. At the same time, UNCTAD was failing to produce the transformative dynamic desired. The rich countries of the North had little desire to change a global trade regime skewed to their advantage.

For years, the Secretary-General stressed the interlinked challenges of peace, anti-racism, decolonization, and economic development. Now, a further issue—the protection of the environment—began to take center stage.

A growing influence on his thinking was the pioneering British economist Barbara Ward, who joined the imperative of economic growth in poor countries with the need to protect the environment, into a new idea of "sustainable development." Her book, *Only One Earth: The Care and Maintenance of a Small Planet*, commissioned by Thant, predicted an ecological crisis to come. A similarly determined advocate was Sweden's ambassador to the UN, Inga Thorsson, who suggested a special United Nations conference on the "Human Environment." With the approval of the General Assembly, Thant began plans for what would be the first Earth Summit, in Stockholm.[8]

At the University of Texas, about 150 miles from NASA's Mission Control Center in Houston, the Secretary-General expressed his fear that for the first time in history, mankind was facing "not merely a threat, but an actual worldwide crisis involving all living creatures."[9] He applauded what he thought were the first signs of a new "Earth-patriotism," citing as a recent example the Soviet cosmonauts who had wished their stricken American colleagues on Apollo 13 a safe return to "our native Earth."

Thant also teamed up with the Norwegian adventurer Thor Heyerdahl. Heyerdahl had become famous decades previously for his *Kon Tiki* expedition; he drifted in a raft from South America to Polynesia, to demonstrate that ancient peoples might have done the same. Now he and a multinational crew, which included both Soviets and Americans, were sailing across the South Atlantic in a papyrus-reed boat which flew, with Thant's permission, only the UN flag. The Secretary-General had been interested in Heyerdahl's idea of contact between ancient Egypt and lost pre-Columbian civilizations and wrote to the crew that he was "deeply moved" by their "exciting adventure in human brotherhood."

At his request, the crew also made daily observations of ocean pollution and when back on dry land submitted a report, kicking off an international campaign to ban the dumping of waste oil on the open seas.

In May 1970, at a UN-organized "Conference on Human Survival," Thant expressed hope that mankind were finally coming to appreciate "the overriding reality that [their] one and only habitat is threatened, not by the forces of nature, but by his own negligence and greed."[10] He proposed a new "super agency" to protect Spaceship Earth.[11] And in early

Thant and family with Apollo 11 astronauts Neil Armstrong, Michael Collins, and Edwin Aldrin on the thirty-eighth floor in May 1970.

1971, as he declared the spring equinox Earth Day, he began a tradition of marking the day with the ringing of a "peace bell"—a gift of the Japanese government—just outside the Secretariat building. With Narasimhan and a cheerful-looking American ambassador George H. W. Bush standing behind him, Thant set out what was becoming his credo:

> *It is often said that, in order for mankind to unite and to overcome its wars and divisions, nothing less than an invasion of Earth by Martians would be required. This is no longer true. Humanity will be united by the common dangers we all face: the armaments race and its inherent risks of obliterating all life on earth ... man's endless passion to change the physical and living texture of our planet, primarily for selfish reasons, and often needless consumption; the explosive co-existence of wealth and extreme poverty ... the deterioration of our natural environment.... No wonder that an "Earth Day" has become suddenly necessary to remind us of the fact that our small planet is perishable.*[12]

There was enthusiasm around the possibility of global action on the environment. But around the UN's principal task of preventing war, prospects seemed far gloomier.

In March 1970, Cambodia's longtime ruler Prince Norodom Sihanouk was overthrown in a pro-American military coup. For years, the forty-seven-year-old prince and his neutral kingdom had been pulling off a near-impossible balancing act, staying friends with Hanoi, Peking, Moscow, Paris, and Washington alike. A few weeks later, United States ground forces crossed into Cambodia. The aim was to destroy a shadowy Communist command center in the east of the country, but this "bamboo Pentagon," as it was known to the US military, never existed. Instead, entire rural communities were wiped out or displaced. Peking then unleashed its support for what had been a minor Communist insurgency in Cambodia: the Khmer Rouge.

For nearly two years, since the start of the Paris peace talks in May 1968, Thant stayed publicly quiet on Vietnam in case he might inadvertently harm whatever progress was being made in the confidential discussions. Now, he felt he had to speak out regardless of the impact it might have on his already low standing at the White House. The "one country that had been trying very hard to keep itself neutral," the Secretary-General told the media, "seems now to have been drawn into the conflict." He voiced his concern openly for the first time about the worsening bloodshed in Laos as well as the new war in Cambodia, as a threat not just "for the peoples of Indo-China but for the whole of mankind." The Americans were then backing a right-wing insurgency in Laos and, over these several years, secretly dropping more than two million tons of bombs on the poverty-stricken nation.

In Vietnam, the war had already led to over a million deaths and cost the American taxpayer hundreds of billions of dollars. "It is difficult to visualize," he said, "what advantages the United States and the American taxpayer have achieved by these astronomical expenses both in manpower and money."[13]

A few days later, speaking to journalists, Thant declared that the war in Indochina, "my one preoccupation" since he had become Secretary-General, had become a "colossal horror story, a thousand times grimmer than the grimmest horror story written by man."[14]

Over that spring, protests on American college campuses had mushroomed, especially after revelations emerged of the murder by US soldiers of as many as five hundred civilians in the South Vietnamese village of My Lai, a massacre that included the gang rape and killing of children as young as twelve. After Nixon's announcement of the invasion of Cambodia, a new wave of demonstrations swept the country. On May 4, National Guardsmen, facing three hundred antiwar demonstrators, shot dead four students and wounded nine others at Kent State University in Ohio.

Thant took heart in his belief that the peace movement was stronger than ever, and not just on Vietnam. He told correspondents at the UN that he had "never experienced such a groundswell of public sentiment for peace as there is today. For many weeks and many months my office has been deluged with letters and cables from NGOs, and in particular from young NGOs reiterating their commitment to peace. . . . People all over the world are now fed up with war."[15]

That week, his friend Norman Cousins wrote a piece in the *Saturday Review* entitled "What is Manhood?" Nixon had recently argued, "It is not our power but our will and character that are being tested," and an aide had followed up by saying that the president had to show the world that "America hasn't lost its manhood." Cousins maintained that manhood was not "armed soldiers firing into a crowd of students" or "a powerful nation raining bombs down on the villagers of a small nation"; instead, it was about "maturity, the comprehension born of experience, and the capacity for making moral judgements."[16]

Richard Nixon had little fondness for the UN, but he couldn't be seen to be dismissing its Secretary-General entirely. In July he organized a black-tie dinner at the White House for Thant, featuring a meal of salmon and steak and "mousse en surprise United Nations" and about a hundred guests, mainly big businessmen together with twenty senators and congressmen. Nixon originally meant the event to be "stag" but then invited the actress Shirley Temple Black, who had recently been appointed to the United States delegation to the UN. She sat next to Henry Kissinger, at the former professor's request. White House Chief of Staff Haldeman wrote about the president in his diary that day:

"Had to see U Thant in afternoon, and was pacing back and forth ruminating about Thant and UN. Doesn't think much of either one."[17]

Nixon's toast gave no indication that he was aware of Thant's involvement in the Cuban Missile Crisis or the India–Pakistan war. "Because we have the UN," the president said, "the world has avoided wars, small wars perhaps, yes, but nevertheless wars that otherwise might have occurred." He mentioned nothing about his guest of honor except that in Burma in 1953 "he escorted us through his country" and "was a gracious host."

Toward the end of the dinner, Nixon asked people to speak "about U Thant or anything else they wished." Ralph Bunche, the only other UN official present, praised Thant's "big heart, deep compassion, and broad humanitarianism," and "his remarkable ability to keep his cool in difficult situations." "He's always available as a scapegoat when things don't go well," Bunche continued. "He's used as a lightning rod. I'd like to see him grow furious and angry every now and then. I tell him he ought to cuss somebody, but he didn't take that advice." To which Nixon quickly chimed in, "He can't do it." The discussion having strangely turned to his psychology, Thant felt compelled to respond that for him, "patience, coolness, and being even-tempered" were part of being brought up in a "conservative Buddhist family," with a premium placed on seeing other people's point of view.[18]

Despite Nixon's dismissiveness, the State Department still valued collaboration with the UN Secretariat. That summer, fighting between the Israelis and the Egyptians escalated into a "War of Attrition," with Soviet forces now directly involved.[19] As Kissinger was momentarily distracted by Cambodia and Vietnam, Secretary of State Rogers attempted to make another push for peace in the Middle East. The courtly fifty-seven-year-old lawyer worked well with Thant, Bunche, and Jarring.

Rogers and his Kremlin counterparts came together on a new initiative centered on a ninety-day ceasefire and talks mediated by the UN. Under Soviet pressure, Egypt and Jordan agreed. The Israelis were shocked; they had expected increased American military assistance rather than a fresh peace effort involving the UN. Still, they felt obliged to agree, too. Thant called Jarring to New York and told the press that prospects for peace in the Middle East seemed brighter than at any time since the Six-Day War.[20] The optimism, however, was short-lived. Within a couple of days, the Israelis backed away, saying that the Egyptians had introduced new missiles into the ceasefire area, which Cairo denied.

Behind the scenes, Secretary of State Rogers was being outmaneuvered by Kissinger. The National Security Advisor may have been more sympathetic to Israel, but more important to his thinking were abstract Cold War calculations. The erstwhile academic saw Israel as a valuable chess piece that could check any Soviet advance into the Middle East. Why pressure Tel Aviv before Cairo ejected the Russians? This view was entirely different from that of Rogers and Thant, both of whom based their efforts on the assumption that peace in the Middle East would be good for everyone, the US and the USSR included, and that with peace assured, the Arab states themselves would seek to lessen their dependence on Moscow.

The mood soon turned uglier with a fresh round of hijackings. On September 6, Palestinian militants hijacked El Al, Pan Am, TWA, and Swissair flights from Amsterdam, Frankfurt, and Zurich, all en route to New York. Thant had no truck with terrorist activity and declared it was "high time that the international community put a stop to this return to the law of the jungle."[21] A few days later, a British Airways plane flying from London to Bombay was forced to land in Amman, where two of the other aircraft had been taken as well. All the planes were blown up, with some of the passengers held hostage and others released. Thant noted that the Arab delegates at the UN were as repulsed as anyone. The Security Council met that evening and in one of its shortest sessions ever—seven minutes—condemned the action. That same month, Palestinian militants, with Syrian assistance, unsuccessfully attempted to overthrow King Hussein in Jordan, leading Israel to confront Syria in support of the king.

The Middle East had become an international nightmare and a Cold War powder keg, with the Americans and the Soviets backing opposing sides. This came about in no small measure because UN diplomacy was given short shrift by those like Kissinger who could only view the world in European Cold War terms.

The Secretary-General and the White House were now out of sync across a range of issues. The conflicts in Southeast Asia and the Middle East were by far the most crucial to Washington. For Thant and the Afro-Asians, however, the battle for the future of southern Africa carried at least equal weight. An iron belt of white supremacy had remained intact, stretching two thousand miles from the Atlantic to the Indian Ocean and centered on three regimes: South Africa, Rhodesia (now Zimbabwe), and NATO-armed Portugal (which controlled Angola and Mozambique). Together they ruled over more than 40 million black Africans and cooperated militarily against the liberation movements beginning to gain ground. Facing them were newly independent states like Zambia, who aided the liberation movements as best they could. Attempts by the Afro-Asians to have the Security Council impose sanctions on the white supremacist governments were thwarted by British and American vetoes.

Back in 1962, the General Assembly, with a clear Afro-Asian majority, had passed a resolution labeling the South African system of apartheid a "crime against humanity." The South African government ignored this and over the mid-1960s only quickened the expulsion of hundreds of thousands of people from urban areas to new black "homelands"—crowded, nominally autonomous enclaves within South Africa.

For Nixon, sub-Saharan Africa was a low priority, and the continuation of white domination across the southern (and richest) slice of the continent was of little or no concern. "The Whites are here to stay," suggested one options paper on Africa prepared by Kissinger's National Security Council.[22]

The view from the UN was completely different. Speaking to African leaders in Ethiopia in September 1970, Thant singled out South Africa as a "threat to peace and security," not only for its domestic policy of racial segregation but for its occupation of Namibia, its support for Rhodesia, and its alliance with Portuguese colonialism. In this way, he said, the fights against colonialism and racial discrimination were intertwined.[23] For years, he had stood on the side of African liberation movements, and now he categorized Pretoria's defiance as "the greatest danger" confronting the world body. The United Nations must lead the way in assisting "the peoples of southern Africa in their struggle." The alternative, he warned, would lead to "crippling disillusion."[24]

At UN headquarters, the Afro-Asians, in close cooperation with the Nordic governments (Sweden especially), led the charge, inviting resistance figures like Oliver Tambo of the African National Congress to New York. Thant permitted nongovernmental activists to participate in meetings for the first time, and attended many to demonstrate the personal significance he attached to the future liberation of southern Africa.[25] From his travels to the continent, he was aware of the faith many African governments (perhaps more than any others) had in the UN as the promoter and protector of a decolonized world.[26] He corresponded regularly with African leaders and exchanged ideas almost daily with their ambassadors in New York.

One of these ambassadors was the tough but unfailingly good-humored representative of Liberia, Angie Brooks.[27] Born to an impoverished family, the forty-one-year-old London-educated lawyer had felt the full force of racism when studying on a scholarship in North Carolina, where she refused to take public transportation after once being made to sit at the back of a bus. She had been the West African nation's chief diplomat at the UN for several years and in 1969 was elected president of the General Assembly, only the second woman to hold the position. Often wearing African dress and a colorful turban, Brooks joined Thant in excoriating doctrines of "race supremacy." Together they presided over the UN's International Day Against All Forms of Racial Discrimination, a new annual commemoration of the 1960 Sharpeville massacre in South Africa.[28]

Under pressure, Western governments began to relent. In July 1970, the Security Council at long last imposed an arms embargo on South Africa, with the US, the UK, and France abstaining rather than vetoing the resolution. At the same time, the Secretariat began training refugees from southern Africa in anticipation of the day when they would be able to govern their own countries.[29]

Thant defended his organization's association with armed liberation movements. In Algiers in 1964, he had pleaded for a nonviolent response to continued colonial rule. Now he argued that white supremacists, through "ruthless and inhuman measures of racial segregation," had created "an explosive situation" and by resorting to extreme repression had "closed all avenues to peaceful change."[30]

In mid-September 1970, the Secretary-General moved into high gear with plans for a big event in New York marking the twenty-fifth anniversary of the establishment of the United Nations. Invitations had been sent out six months earlier and nearly seventy heads of state or government had accepted. At Thant's request, his friend the Spanish cellist Pablo Casals would perform a "hymn to peace," with lyrics written for the occasion by the poet W. H. Auden. A grand dinner would follow.

"No dinner up there—this is final!" Nixon informed Kissinger. Instead, heads of government would be invited to the White House. "Let U Thant be one of many!" An added advantage to a dinner in Washington, thought the president, was that he could avoid tiresome encounters with the visiting political leaders he didn't judge significant. Kissinger advised, "You can select them. If you saw the President of Gabon, it would be a bore."[31]

Nixon then decided to torpedo Thant's occasion altogether by scheduling his White House dinner for the same day as Thant's planned address and festival concert. American diplomats tried to blame "faulty co-ordination," but no one at the UN believed it was anything other than a deliberate effort to undermine the Secretary-General's standing.

Several world leaders, especially the US's close allies, attended the White House dinner. Most, not wanting to choose between New York and Washington, sent their regrets to both. One of the few who attended Thant's dinner in preference to Nixon's was India's prime minister, Indira Gandhi. Perhaps in response, no American official was on hand to greet her at JFK airport, and even in Delhi the American ambassador, Kenneth Keating, did not see her off, as is normal diplomatic protocol. He later gave the excuse that a switchboard operator had failed to wake him up on time.[32]

At the event itself, Thant tried his best to heighten awareness of global issues, warning again of an urgent need to protect the environment:

> *As we watch the sun go down, evening after evening, through the smog across the poisoned waters of our native earth, we must ask ourselves seriously whether we really wish some future universal historian on another planet to say about us: "With all their genius and with all their skill, they ran out of foresight and air and food and water and ideas," or, "They went on playing politics until their world collapsed around them."*[33]

The response was far more muted than it might have been just a few years before. The remaking of Thant's image in the Western media was moving full steam ahead. In November, *Newsweek* published a long portrait entitled "U Thant: A Study in Caution." Calling his anniversary event "the biggest social flop of the season," with world leaders heading instead to Nixon's "spotlight-stealing stealing state dinner," the magazine labeled Thant "one of the most publicly lauded and privately belittled figures on the world scene."

A week or so later, Auberon Waugh, in an excoriating attack in *The Spectator*, blamed Thant for the recent Arab–Israeli war and for doing nothing about the war in Biafra. Thant, he wrote, had "raised no hope and fulfilled none"; rather than working diligently, all he had done was "add his little bleat to the wail of discontent from the pre-industrialized nations of the world." Calling his Secretary-Generalship "one of the smaller tragedies of our time," Waugh suggested that a Swede or "even an Austrian, Dr. Kurt Waldheim," might make a better choice in future.[34]

To make matters worse, the newly published memoirs of the UK's recently retired foreign secretary, George Brown, included a mendacious account of the run-up to the Six-Day War. According to Brown, UNEF was a Security Council–mandated "military force"; the Secretary-General had inexplicably not waited for the Council to discuss Nasser's withdrawal request; and even Nasser was surprised by the Secretary-General's rash decision to remove the peacekeepers. All this was false, and Bunche, with his boss's green light, hit back in a letter to *The Sunday Times* (which had serialized the memoir) stating that he was "appalled at the grotesque distortions and misstatements" in Brown's account.[35]

Thant had survived longer than either of his predecessors at the helm of the world organization, but his endurance skills were beginning to elude him. The onetime schoolmaster prided himself on not being a politician, and he had no political team around him. He was forthright and engaging in private but in public tended ever more to read prepared statements or speak in the highly circumscribed language of diplomacy. This enfeebled him, especially in the UK and the US. In an era of Madison Avenue admen, Thant thought little of how to project himself on television, privileging conversations in smoke-filled rooms and seeing little need to take credit for successes, even for his role in the Cuban Missile Crisis.

"I don't like to be disturbed at home," Thant confided to *The New York Times*. "I tell the cable office not to call me before 6:30 a.m., unless there's a war."[36] He was still traveling constantly and otherwise working long days in the office. Occasional swims in his pool at home, perhaps *The Tonight Show with Johnny Carson* in the late evening, and Sundays with his wife and family, including his three grandchildren, were his only relaxation. But even home was not always a refuge. After a series of incidents, including one in which three young men broke into the grounds in the middle of the night and taped onto the house an American flag and a banner reading "Support Our Boys in Vietnam," the UN guards on site were armed with .38 caliber Smith & Wesson revolvers.[37]

Thant had a year left in his second term. There was a wellspring of support, from African governments especially, for him to continue. Washington was determined to see him go. More important was the unfinished battle for the soul of the global organization and the future direction of the world. The die was almost cast.

17 | BOTH SIDES NOW

IN AN ADDRESS TO the General Assembly in October 1970, Thant declared that there was a clear choice facing the United Nations: either there would be no "moral force in this world," no renewed commitment to the UN's founding principles, and no change in the organization's "outmoded procedures and policies," or governments, "especially the mightier ones" could provide the stronger and heartier support necessary for a "just, peaceful and prosperous human community." If the first course was followed, he said, the UN was doomed to become "increasingly irrelevant." But he was confident that "faced with these two alternatives, the good sense of the human race, of *Homo sapiens*, will prevail."[1]

Thant was a realist. From his earliest days at the helm of the UN, he painted a picture of the world he wanted, based on the UN's Charter and the Universal Declaration of Human Rights. It was a view grounded in the Afro-Asian vision of a post-imperial international order. His declaration of faith in *Homo sapiens* was in line with a stream of rhetoric designed to keep alive this vision.

But in his actions he was guided by his calculation, constantly updated, of what the world body—an intergovernmental machine comprised of states rich and poor, authoritarian and democratic—could actually do. And within this calculation was another, narrower calculation: of what the Secretary-General could achieve, not as an advocate making grandiose statements but in a practical way, as the world's preeminent diplomat and peacemaker of last resort.

In early 1971, there was an unambiguous opportunity for peace in the Middle East. Egypt's President Nasser had died the previous September and the new president, Anwar Sadat, was ready to compromise. Nixon didn't want a deteriorating Middle East crisis to cause problems as another presidential election cycle approached. There was a temporary ceasefire. The elements were in place for a deal.

On January 4, Secretary of State Rogers came to New York and informed the Secretary-General that he wanted to back him "in every possible way." Saying that 1971 was "a year of decision," the US's foreign affairs chief reported on his talks with the new UK prime minister, Edward Heath, French president Georges Pompidou, and Soviet ambassador Anatoli Dobrynin.

There was hope, Rogers confided, but Washington shouldn't be "too much out in front." The US wasn't a neutral broker. He thought it would be good for the UN to take the lead. They agreed that Gunnar Jarring's diplomatic effort should be restarted. Thant advised keeping the new ceasefire intact, getting talks off the ground, and only then, when some progress could be announced, convening the Security Council.[2]

Over the following weeks Jarring was hard at work, securing from Tel Aviv and Cairo detailed position papers and meticulously comparing them for Thant and also for Brian Urquhart. The fifty-one-year-old Urquhart was gradually taking over all peacekeeping responsibilities from an ailing Ralph Bunche.[3]

Thant and Rogers remained in regular touch by phone and in person. Much discussion focused on finding the exact words that might satisfy both sides: the Israelis, for example, favored the phrase "observing the ceasefire" while the Egyptians preferred "maintaining quiet."[4]

In early February, the American, French, British, and Soviet ambassadors all proclaimed that they were pleased with Jarring's efforts and publicly endorsed the Secretary-General's appeal for an extension of the ceasefire. The USSR declared that the peace process had reached a "decisive stage."

Jarring then unveiled a proposal designed to achieve "parallel and simultaneous" commitments from both sides. This was meant to overcome Israel's earlier demand for talks before any withdrawal and Egypt's demand for a withdrawal before talks. Under Jarring's proposal, Israel would withdraw to its borders on the eve of the Six-Day War in return for an Egyptian pledge to sign a peace agreement that recognized the Jewish state's right to exist. There would be a demilitarized zone on both sides of the border and freedom of navigation through the Straits of Tiran, all policed by a Security Council–mandated United Nations force.[5] In a confidential assessment, the Pentagon estimated that the multinational force could number 24,000 personnel, including contingents from the US and the Soviet Union.[6]

Anwar Sadat quickly accepted. In Washington, Rogers was positive as well, but in the end Nixon was swayed by Kissinger, who placed little value on any peace effort, least of all one that would give credit to Rogers, his State Department rival. On February 26, Israel formally rejected the proposal, saying that though it "viewed favorably" Egypt's willingness to enter into a peace agreement, "Israel will not withdraw to pre–June 5 1967 lines."[7] Thant then issued a formal report recording Egypt's positive response and Israel's negative response.

The Israelis were furious with Thant and Jarring for publicly putting forward a deal which made peace possible but was not the one they wanted—one in which Israel would keep at least some of the territory seized in 1967. Rogers strongly defended Jarring, who came in for fierce criticism from the Israelis, but Rogers himself was in turn berated by prime minister Golda Meir, who said, "There are certain things beyond which our American friends have to realize we will not go."

Charles Yost, the mild-mannered US ambassador, who had been collaborating closely with Thant and Rogers on Middle East issues especially, was dismissed. Yost wrote that month in *Life* magazine: "There is at the moment a remarkable but probably fleeting opportunity to achieve a peaceful settlement of the Arab–Israeli conflict." The Arabs were ready, the veteran diplomat said, for a permanent settlement with Israel, guaranteed by the big powers. "Why has this not been immediately accepted by Israel? Because the price is the withdrawal from Arab territory conquered in 1967." Israel, Yost said, would only settle for "extensive territorial changes."[8]

Thant sent a handwritten note marked "personal and confidential" to congratulate Yost for his "masterly and courageous" article. "Knowing as I do the extraordinary climate prevailing in many parts of this country regarding the Middle East situation, partly due to ignorance and partly due to set convictions, I am afraid you will be deluged with a flood of critical and even abusive letters and correspondence. I am now sufficiently thick-skinned to bear such an onslaught. I hope you are too.... As a free and liberated man, you are in a far safer position than I am to call a spade a spade. I cannot, *yet*."[9]

Rogers came to the Secretary-General's office soon afterward, accompanied by Nixon's new ambassador to the UN, the genteel former congressman George H. W. Bush. Rogers, who had just been in Cairo, told Thant that his trip had convinced him "beyond doubt" that Egypt wanted peace. Sadat had stressed his desire for Egypt to be "non-aligned" and not "the scene of big-power confrontation." He would accept any security arrangements requested by Israel.[10]

But with Israel (egged on by Kissinger) taking a harder line, a despondent Secretary-General suspended Jarring's efforts, predicting a new war "sooner or later."[11]

Something that did continue, however, were secret attempts by Thant to secure the exit of Jews from the USSR. Many, facing religious persecution, sought emigration to Israel. After being presented by the Israeli ambassador with scores of signed petitions, Thant conferred with the Soviet ambassador, who strongly cautioned him against taking any action.[12]

Thant persisted and established his own channel to the Kremlin through two Russian officials on his staff, Leonid Kutakov and Victor Lessiovski (who was also a clandestine KGB agent). Not even his closest aides—Bunche, Narasimhan, and Urquhart—were informed. Whenever Thant received a petition, he passed it on to Moscow with his implicit approval. In late 1971, he was told by Tel Aviv that four hundred Soviet

Jews, out of the eight hundred who had sent him petitions, had safely arrived in Israel.

The US State Department noted that "for more than a year, United Nations Secretary General U Thant has been making behind-the-scenes representations on behalf of Soviet Jews who wish to emigrate" and that the Soviets, far from finding this inappropriate, had responded favorably to the Secretary-General's confidential appeals.[13] The US government may have been informed about this by the Israelis. Likely they received reports from Lessiovski, too, whom the FBI wrongly believed had become a double agent for them.[14]

Over the previous ten years, only 1,000 Jews had been allowed to leave the USSR; in 1971, the number approached 5,000. The UN was coming under considerable censure in the press for not doing anything about the plight of Soviet Jews, but Thant felt he had to keep his role as discreet as possible.[15]

Thant had now served as UN Secretary-General for nearly ten years—longer than either of his predecessors. Speculation about whether he would carry on for an unprecedented third term was growing. There was nothing in the UN's Charter which limited the time a Secretary-General could remain in office, and Thant was a reasonably healthy sixty-two years old. Third World governments were supportive and some, especially the Africans, according to American ambassador George Bush, were "effusive in their praise." African diplomats were also exploring the possibility of an African Secretary-General but could not agree on a candidate.[16]

Meanwhile, the war in Vietnam was turning decisively against the United States. Fighting intensified in Laos and Cambodia. Washington had already dropped more bombs on Laos than were dropped by all belligerents during all of the Second World War. But Communist forces in all three countries, sensing a final victory, saw no reason to compromise. Kissinger had nothing to show for his efforts in Paris. Thant said little about the Nixon administration's Vietnam policy, but what little he did say was critical. The White House took notice.

John F. Kennedy had wanted to work closely with the UN. Lyndon Johnson, focused on his domestic ambitions, would have been content to do the same if his foreign policy team had concurred and Thant's opposition to military escalation in Vietnam had not come in the way. But Richard Nixon was from the start predisposed against the global body and was the first American president to seek political profit in taking an adversarial stance.

The year before, the UN had put forward plans for new office buildings across First Avenue and asked Washington for its share, which amounted to roughly $20 million.[17] Even this was now difficult. Nixon instructed Kissinger, in case his National Security Advisor needed any reminding, "Don't get too excited about the UN. We've got Bush there and he's on our side. He's not in love with it. If they slapped us in the face, there would be a hell of an American reaction. The liberals and intellectuals say fine, but there are veterans' organizations and . . . and I'd gin them up. There are a lot of people right now who want the UN out of this country. We don't realize how low it is."

Kissinger: "I'm sure it is and deservedly so."

Nixon: "When have they helped us?"

Kissinger: "And when you think of U Thant condemning us in Laos when he's been quiet for eight years about the North Vietnamese there."

Nixon: "And I've been up there twice and they've acted cool and lousy. I'm not going to go there. And go through the hypocrisy about supporting the UN again. It's just hypocrisy."

Kissinger: "I thought the behavior the last time was outrageous when the Secretary-General didn't even have the courtesy to meet you at the door."

Nixon: "I hope they don't get that new building. It hasn't gone through yet, has it?"

Kissinger: "I don't think so."[18]

By this time, George Bush had come to his own conclusions about Thant, with whom he had nurtured an amicable relationship. On being named ambassador a few months earlier, Bush consulted Rusk about Thant and Rusk did not hide his disdain. But Bush didn't fully agree. In his personal diary, he noted, "I find U Thant fascinating. He is obviously against us on the war and things like this, but I must say he impresses me. He is a man totally dedicated to peace." Bush understood that Thant was uninterested in managing the UN's sprawling bureaucracies. "He is a philosopher and not an administrator. The UN desperately needs administration at this critical point but U Thant cannot, will not, does not want to provide it."[19] Bush conferred with Washington. It was clear that President Nixon had no desire to see the Secretary-General continue in his post.

Thant had already made up his own mind. Outside his family, one of the first people he told, in private, was Agda Rössel, with whom had kept up a close friendship since their days together as Burmese and Swedish envoys in New York. They had tried to keep in touch, writing often, but were puzzled when private letters they had mailed by regular post were somehow intercepted. Rössel was now the Swedish ambassador in Prague, and so they resorted to using Swedish embassies to convey their messages. Thant wanted Rössel "to be the first to know" that regardless of any pressure, he would not accept an extension. The main reason, he said, was that he had not been able to take more than two days' rest over the past five years. "There are other reasons of course and I obviously cannot put them on paper," he added cryptically. "All of us at the UN miss you very much."[20]

Thant may have hoped for an unremarkable final stretch in office. Instead, there was a new, blood-soaked conflict, in East Pakistan (now Bangladesh), which also threatened to spiral into a global war. Britain, in carving up its Indian Empire, had created a Pakistan with two halves, West and East Pakistan, a thousand miles apart. West Pakistan dominated the more populous, Bengali-speaking East, as the army was almost entirely officered by Punjabis and other West Pakistanis. In December 1970, an election victory by the East Pakistan–based Awami League had been followed by a vicious army crackdown. Millions were displaced, there were fears of mass famine, and a new movement arose aimed at nothing less than independence for the land of the Bengalis: *Bangla Desh*.[21]

Millions of Bengalis streamed into Assam and other adjacent areas of India, creating a humanitarian emergency of gargantuan proportions, stretching India's already limited food supplies to breaking point. Prime Minister Indira Gandhi assessed the situation as intolerable. Sensing a need to strike against her country's decades-long foe, she ordered the army to begin preparations for a new war. As in 1965, there was every chance that a war between India and Pakistan could draw in India's Chinese foes, as well as the Soviets (who were close to India) and the Americans (who were closer to Pakistan).

There was, however, not a peep from the Security Council. Neither India nor Pakistan favored Council action, nor did any of the big powers. With a chorus of public calls for the UN to "do something," the responsibility for a response, again, fell on the Secretary-General, who had the least power to do anything.

In April, when the crackdown in East Pakistan was first underway, Thant attempted a softly-softly approach, writing a "personal and confidential" letter to Pakistan's president and military chief Yahya Khan which asked his permission to organize emergency assistance for civilians in East Pakistan. The general insisted that "Indian and Western press reports" of killings and widespread destruction were highly exaggerated, so there was no need for aid.[22]

In June, with stories of mass atrocities against civilians by the Pakistani army grabbing headlines around the world, Thant spoke out forcefully, calling what was happening "one of the most tragic episodes in human history."[23] Determined to provide whatever humanitarian assistance was necessary, both to refugees in India as well as to civilians in East Pakistan, the Secretary-General dispatched his High Commissioner for Refugees, the dynamic thirty-eight-year-old Prince Saddrudin Aga Khan, to Islamabad, Dacca, and New Delhi to oversee what he hoped would be the largest aid operation ever. Later, overriding Soviet objections that he was exceeding his authority, Thant assembled representatives of more than two dozen countries to organize emergency funding. If he waited for the Security Council as the Soviets demanded, he lectured their ambassador, he would be waiting another ten years.[24]

He also attempted quiet diplomacy, enlisting the secret help of Malaysia's founding father and recently retired prime minister, Tunku

Abdul Rahman, to kick-start a confidential dialogue between Pakistan and India.[25] In addition, he sent another message to Yahya Khan, warning the Pakistani president that "any developments concerning the fate of detained Bengali leader Sheikh Mujib Rahman will inevitably have repercussions outside the borders of Pakistan."[26] There was little doubt, as in Nigeria, that principles around sovereignty were again being tested in a situation of catastrophic human suffering.

Around midday on June 19, 1971, after complaining of dizziness and extreme fatigue, Thant was driven to the hospital. He had, as always, been working relentlessly fourteen-hour days, six days a week. On the advice of physicians, he took a holiday in the Bahamas, his first time off in more than four years, but after just a few days he was back at the UN. The pressure for public action on the crisis in East Pakistan was growing. That same week, the London *Sunday Times* published an article headlined "Genocide," which relayed accounts of terrible massacres taking place in East Pakistan and brought the unfolding catastrophe more fully into the public eye.[27]

Thant may also have been energized by other news. *The New York Times* had just begun publishing the Pentagon Papers—the secret history of the Vietnam War, commissioned by Defense Secretary Robert McNamara—which exposed, in excruciating detail, the Johnson administration's years of lying to the American public.

With the Secretary-General's approval, at the daily press briefing, his spokesman reiterated Thant's view, made public much to the annoyance of Lyndon Johnson and Dean Rusk six years before, that if the American people had known the truth in 1965, they would have known as well that there was no need for further bloodshed in Vietnam. The spokesman, for the first time, confirmed that the Secretary-General was referring to the talks he had then been trying to broker in Rangoon.[28]

With his attempts at quiet diplomacy unsuccessful and his humanitarian efforts facing innumerable hardships (the UN had never before tried to organize a large-scale humanitarian operation in the middle of a war), Thant pushed for action by the Security Council. He wrote a confidential letter to all the ambassadors on the Council, arguing that "these human tragedies have consequences in a far wider sphere," as they arouse "violent emotions."[29] It was, he argued, "easy to make moral judgements." What was far more difficult was to face up to political and human realities and help the peoples concerned find a way out of their enormous difficulties."

With hundreds of thousands dead, ten million refugees in India, an inadequate international aid response, and mounting fears of famine, public sentiment was running high. The first international benefit concert, "A Concert for Bangladesh," featuring Ravi Shankar, George Harrison, Ringo Starr, and Bob Dylan, was performed in front of an audience of over 40,000 at New York's Madison Square Garden. It raised $250,000 for UNICEF.

Thant conferred with Secretary of State Rogers and George Bush, soon after Kissinger's return from a clandestine mission to Peking, facilitated by the Pakistanis, which paved the way for Nixon's trip a year later. The Americans supported humanitarian action but nothing that might undermine Pakistan's position, genocide notwithstanding.[30] Thant's position was clear: there was no substitute for political accommodation between Pakistan's military government and the Bengali leadership. Otherwise, the crisis in East Pakistan would soon become a "threat to international peace and security." He told Rogers that he might soon invoke Article 99—one of the few powers given by the Charter to the Secretary-General and almost never used—and force an emergency session of the Security Council.[31] But he waited: perhaps aware that with months left in his term he had little strength left to take on American might, perhaps because in his own mind he couldn't square the circle between the shibboleths around non-intervention he and the Afro-Asians had long defended and the sheer scale of the atrocities taking place in the eastern floodplains of Bengal.

Another weighty issue was simultaneously looming over the United Nations: the admission of Communist China. Until then, China's seat had been held by General Chiang Kai-Shek's remnant Kuomintang regime in Taiwan. As Burmese ambassador, Thant had made plain his stance in favor of Peking taking over the seat. Thant was a dedicated anti-Communist at home, but he believed that the UN should be a universal body and this meant including the world's most populous nation. He also thought the People's Republic was starting to open up and predicted that China, then dirt-poor, would likely become "a big power in the next decade, perhaps even a superpower."[32]

For years, successive American administrations had sought to keep the Chinese Communists out of the world organization. Even with Nixon's initial outreach to Peking, there was no shift in policy. But with the Third World in the majority, keeping Taiwan in the UN was no longer possible. On October 26, 1971, after an impassioned debate aired live on American television, the General Assembly voted against Taiwan, whose representatives promptly and unceremoniously left the hall amid scenes of jubilation, with cheers and even impromptu dancing by China's African friends.

In the US, the admission of China only fueled the fire of those looking to disparage the UN. A day after the vote, California governor Ronald Reagan phoned President Nixon and opined, "Last night, I tell you, to watch that thing on television as I did ... To see those, those monkeys from those African countries—damn them, they're still uncomfortable wearing shoes!" Nixon gave a hearty laugh and promptly relayed the remarks to Rogers, adding a line about "cannibals" dancing in the aisles.[33]

A few days later, Thant collapsed in his office and was rushed to the Le Roy Hospital, where he was diagnosed with a bleeding ulcer. This time, he stayed at the former sanatorium on 61st Street for more than four weeks, surrounded by big bouquets of flowers and cards from family and well-wishers around the world. From his hospital bed, he enjoyed episodes of his new favorite show, *Columbo*, about an underestimated detective, with an occasionally mentioned but always off-camera wife, who solves the crime early on but still has to outwit the socially superior villains.

Thant also received a Chinese Communist delegation, the first to come to New York. They had insisted on seeing him in person to present their credentials, and a frail but cheerful Thant obliged. He gave them advice on where to find decent Chinese food in Manhattan before they posed together for the cameras, the Communist envoys in navy blue Mao suits and the Secretary-General in a green and red checked tartan dressing gown and slippers.

By the time Thant was discharged from the hospital, India and Pakistan were at war. With the Security Council deadlocked—the Soviets supporting India and the US and China, in a debut performance, siding with Pakistan—the debate shifted to the General Assembly. On his first day back, the Secretary-General took to the floor and appealed for the protection of innocent civilian lives.[34]

The fighting didn't last long. India won a speedy victory, and Bangladesh was born. The preceding months looked like yet another instance of the UN being unable to come to grips with a devastating conflict.

Just as Thant was checking out of the Le Roy Hospital, Ralph Bunche was checking into the New York Hospital for tests. He had become almost entirely blind and was suffering from kidney failure on top of his other ailments. The preceding summer, he had briefly fallen into a coma, and the Secretary-General had arranged for him to be formally retired so that he and his family could draw a third of his pension as a lump sum. They had no other savings. His wife, Ruth, wrote to Thant, "The children and I want you to know how deeply we appreciate all that you are doing and have done to ease things for us during this difficult period. You couldn't have been more kind, understanding, patient and generous."[35] Bunche had bounced back but now, while in the hospital for tests, passed away peacefully during the night.[36]

Thant had known the day was coming sooner rather than later, but was nonetheless staggered "by the loss of an incomparable friend and colleague." At the General Assembly that day, reading from notes he had just scribbled down and looking up only occasionally, he praised Bunche for his "kindness, humor, and deep compassion," describing his colleague as "an international institution in his own right, transcending both nationality and race in a way that is achieved by very few."[37]

The Nobel laureate's funeral took place two days later, on an unusually warm but windy day, at the Riverside Church in Harlem. It was attended by Thant, Urquhart, Jarring, Bush, Kissinger, Nelson Rockefeller, New York mayor John Lindsay, Bunche's family, and hundreds of friends and former colleagues. Thant and Jarring were among the first to arrive and sat together next to the coffin. Roy Wilkins, a longtime friend and head of the National Association for the Advancement of Colored People (NAACP), said in his eulogy that the United Nations mediator was "a man of peace, not brown, not black, not white, but of the human race."[38]

Thant wrote to Agda Rössel to say that he was feeling better and looking forward to retirement and a "pretty long vacation."[39] World governments, however, were nowhere close to agreeing on a successor. And so, with just weeks to go before the end of his term, representatives of the five big powers, which now included Communist China, gathered in a series of closed meetings at the elegant Park Avenue residence of French ambassador Jacques Kosciusko-Morizet.

The British and the Americans, having already decided they wanted to see Thant go, pointed to the Secretary-General's own statements categorically ruling out any extension, as well as his recent ill health. The Chinese, feeling their way through their first weeks in Manhattan, implied that they would prefer an alternative Third World candidate. The French said they would like to see Thant continue. The Soviets, of similar mind, argued that this was the wish of the vast majority of the UN's membership.

"He doesn't need to be a hundred percent fit as an astronaut," reasoned Yakov Malik, the USSR's balding Ukrainian-born envoy. Perhaps the Charter was flawed, he suggested, and could now include a mandatory "annual vacation." The British ambassador, Sir Colin Crowe, replied that while there was "no doubt he was loved, wise and experienced," Thant had collapsed twice in a year; it would be unfair to force him to continue. Malik argued that the Anglo-Saxons "hated" Thant, which Bush and Crowe strongly denied.[40]

Thant himself was certain about the kind of person he would like to succeed him. At a farewell luncheon with correspondents, he said it should be a person who "looked to the future," was responsive to global public opinion, especially the ideas of young people, and had "an unassailable conviction in the importance of individual human dignity." To protect himself against "the discomfort of perennial, and sometimes unjustified criticism," his successor should also be, Thant concluded, someone with a "a sense of proportion and a good sense of humor."[41]

On December 17, 1971, the big powers agreed on the stony-faced Austrian ambassador Kurt Waldheim as the organization's fourth Secretary-General. Waldheim had been a German Wehrmacht officer in the Balkans during the Second World War, but this may not have been known to any governments at the time.

At the White House Kissinger told Nixon:

"You heard about the new Secretary-General. He is bound to be better than U Thant."

Nixon: "Well, no worse."

Kissinger: "I don't know if we want a strong Secretary-General. If he isn't more favorable to us than the last one."[42]

The Security Council's agreement on Waldheim came on the same day as Thant's retirement party at the Pierre Hotel, with John Lennon and Pete Seeger, where the onetime schoolmaster was honored by the World Federalists as "Planetary Citizen Number One." That week, in a final address to the General Assembly, Thant confided that he felt "a great sense of relief, bordering on liberation."[43] Many formal congratulatory letters arrived, signed by political figures from around the world. There was also a personal letter from one of his first friends at the UN, the Israeli ambassador Gideon Rafael, who was now the head of his country's foreign ministry:

> *My thoughts go back to the days, ten years ago, when we tried . . . to bring understanding between the United States and the USSR missions on the election of the Secretary-General. I do not know how you look at those days in the light of the strain and stresses which your high office has imposed on you for a full decade. . . . Enormous changes have occurred . . . I know that you have never spared an effort to cope with these immense challenges. You have devoted all your strength to the cause of the United Nations.*[44]

In an editorial, *The New York Times* described it as remarkable that in "the poisoned international atmosphere of the sixties," Thant had managed to keep alive at least the hope of future cooperation and "a closer human community." "The wise counsel of this dedicated man of peace," it opined, "will be needed after his retirement."

Thant was leaving the United Nations in what must have seemed a bleak period. In Biafra and Bangladesh, immense suffering had occurred without anything like the needed relief and intervention from the outside world. Thant had been unable to clearly reconcile his defense of state sovereignty with the imperative to protect innocent civilians. The senseless bloodletting in Vietnam continued and had spread to Cambodia. There was no peace in the Middle East; instead, the conflict had spawned international terrorism. The aspirations for global development of ten years previously had largely been dashed.

But from a different vantage point, the United Nations was an extraordinary success. It had become the first truly universal association in human history, with a membership spanning the Earth. Over the past quarter century, the Afro-Asians had inserted themselves into Franklin Roosevelt's dream of a global organization and transformed it into one that belonged as much to them as to the big powers. One of their own had served for more than a decade at the helm of the world body and his voice was their voice, speaking in lofty tones on the future of global collaboration while standing up, as tenaciously as possible, for the sovereignty of newly freed nations. Their perspectives were now seeded at the very core of the United Nations. The die was now cast.

The planet had transitioned, remarkably peacefully, from centuries of domination by a handful of European empires. A nuclear war had been avoided and an era of superpower détente made possible. With the United Nations as a steel frame, all humans now belonged to a single international system, which, despite its flaws and limitations, was dedicated to peace and development. This was not inevitable. And its proper realization may be yet to come.

EPILOGUE

THANT HAD LOOKED FORWARD to his retirement. But he had next to no money saved up and no place to live. He had received a generous income as Secretary-General ($62,500 annually in 1971, not counting benefits like the rented house in Riverdale), but he had spent it all. Some had supported his growing family, with a live-in daughter and son-in-law and four grandchildren. Much more had been expended on entertaining the endless train of Burmese guests, some of whom stayed in the Riverdale house for months, and on the many lunches in his office, including ones with just Bunche, Narasimhan, and a few other top aides, which he paid for himself. He had received considerable prize money, including the $50,000 he received for the Nehru Prize, but in line with UN rules had donated it all to charity.

Luckily, he managed to sell the US rights to his memoirs for the princely sum of $300,000.[1] With the advance for his book, together with a pension lump sum from the UN, Thant paid the deposit on a handsome colonial-style house in suburban Harrison, New York, about a forty-five-minute drive from the city. For Thein Tin, now in her early seventies, there was a meditation room, a glass-enclosed annex with images of the Buddha and views of the Westchester countryside.

The ex–Secretary-General had big ambitions. A few years before, he had set in motion the establishment of a United Nations University, possibly to be located in Copenhagen, and imagined himself as its first rector. He had also been in touch with Chile's president, Salvador Allende, to discuss co-hosting a new development conference in 1972.[2] He had enthusiastically followed plans for the Stockholm Earth Summit and hoped to be part of future environmental campaigns.

For a while, he enjoyed attending dinners in his honor, organized by David Rockefeller, the chairman of Chase Manhattan Bank, Mayor John Lindsay, and other New York luminaries. He spoke on television shows such as *Face the Nation*, and became a senior fellow (not in residence) at an institute in Chicago named after his old friend Adlai Stevenson. At home, he played with his grandchildren, swam in the new pool he had built,

Thant leaving UN headquarters on his last day as Secretary-General in December 1971.

read voraciously, and watched television, including *Columbo* as well as a new favorite, the groundbreaking comedy *All in the Family*, which often poked fun at Nixon and his Vietnam War.

But just over a year later, Thant was diagnosed with cancer. His publisher immediately canceled his book contract. Two operations, to his mouth and later to his neck, were unsuccessful, as was chemotherapy, and he was reduced to a liquid diet. He was also plagued with nightmares that he couldn't swim or that he was drowning in muddy water.[3] He and his family came to distrust the doctors at New York Presbyterian Hospital, and Thant even considered going overseas for a second opinion, as the Soviet government had offered to look after his medical care. But it was too late. After an extremely painful final few months, Thant died in hospital on November 25, 1974, aged sixty-five.

Brian Urquhart ordered flags to be flown at half-staff at peacekeeping missions around the world. And at a special session of the General Assembly, effusive tributes were paid by representatives of all the UN's 132 member governments. Liberia's Angie Brooks remembered Thant simply as "one of the greatest men of our time... a friend, colleague, and brother... a champion of the weak and poor peoples of the earth." Speaking on behalf of all the African states, the ambassador of Upper Volta described the late Secretary-General as "the perpetual embodiment of our fundamental aspirations... in the meeting halls when the fate of Africa was being discussed... we saw him by our side."[4]

At a small Buddhist ceremony in midtown Manhattan, a distraught Thein Tin and family, together with Burmese friends, gathered with a few close colleagues, including Narasimhan and Urquhart. Thein Tin and the other Burmese wept as they prostrated themselves in front of the wooden casket. Thant's body was then transported for the last time to the United Nations where it lay in state in the skylit North Lobby of the General Assembly, the blue and white flag of the world organization draped over the casket, security guards in navy uniforms providing an honor guard and officials and diplomats filing past, some bowing, in a final gesture of respect.

The former schoolmaster's remains were repatriated to Burma, only to be caught up in a deadly political maelstrom. Thein Tin felt too unwell to go, so Thant's daughter and son-in-law accompanied the body. In Rangoon, there was no official reception by the ruling military regime. Instead, thousands of ordinary men and women, in sarongs and leather slippers, lined the nine-mile route from the airport to an abandoned racetrack, where the coffin was housed within a large makeshift tent. There, over the next few days, thousands more came to honor their compatriot.

Simmering anti-government feeling boiled over. On the morning of the burial, a throng of students and Buddhist monks snatched the casket containing Thant's body. Believing that the military junta should have accorded the Secretary-General a state funeral, the protesters ferried his remains to the campus of Rangoon University and declared their intention to build a proper mausoleum for the man they called a national hero. Enormous crowds soon gathered, transforming the funeral fracas into an incipient uprising against General Ne Win's dictatorship. Thant's bewildered family tried to mediate between the students and the authorities, but after four days the talks broke down. At dawn on December 11, bayonet-wielding troops stormed the campus, killing an unknown number of protesters, and seized the casket. That same morning, Thant's remains were interred under six feet of concrete, in the shadow of the city's Shwedagon Pagoda. Days of bloody rioting followed. A small mausoleum was later built around the burial site, which for decades remained virtually neglected, green snakes slithering in the tall grass, ordinary people fearing that any association with the former UN Secretary-General might incur the ire of the ruling generals.

Thant's name soon vanished, with a few exceptions. In April 1975, after Hanoi compelled Washington to accept peace terms far less favorable to the US than what might have been possible a decade before, and as the last American officials were escaping Saigon by helicopter, *New York Post* editor James Wechsler published a piece headlined "The Man Who Knew Too Much." "As the last scenes of collapse unfold in South Vietnam," Wechsler wrote, Kissinger "may prefer to forget what he—and others before him—were told by a wise man whose counsel they obdurately spurned.... What compound of arrogance and ignorance led Dean Rusk, Walt Rostow and finally Henry Kissinger (among other intellects in high places) to assume their judgments about Indochina were superior to those of the thoughtful Burmese Buddhist who served as UN Secretary-General for a decade?"[5]

In the years that followed, there was little if any mention of the Burmese diplomat in histories of the Cuban Missile Crisis, Vietnam, or the Middle East. In the US and the UK, if his name came up at all, it was as a passive Third World bureaucrat who inexplicably or spinelessly withdrew peacekeepers in the face of Egyptian bluster.

In some bizarre ways, Thant was literally airbrushed from history. In 2000, for example, Sheldon Stern, a historian at the John F. Kennedy Library, who had listened to the president's audiotapes, noted that on October 26, 1962, during the Cuban Missile Crisis, National Security Advisor McGeorge Bundy's reference to "the U Thant initiative" was in the mid-1990s transcribed as "the attack thing." Similarly, a mention of "U Thant" by President Kennedy on October 28 was transcribed as "You [unclear]."[6] By the 1990s few people below a certain age had ever heard Thant's name.

Thant's disappearance was partly due to his diminished standing in Washington and London from the late 1960s onward. It was the culmination of relentless attacks that went back to the Congo crisis, his public break with the Americans over Vietnam, and perceptions that he had jeopardized Israel's security. Perhaps to a greater extent, he disappeared because he was an exotic figure from a country most knew nothing about, the odd man out among the Ivy League and Oxbridge-educated personalities of the day.

It's a disappearance that cannot be viewed in isolation, because it's not only Thant who has vanished from sight but the entire story of the Afro-Asians, their friends at the United Nations, and their struggle to bring about global peace and development. There has been a willful amnesia. We live in a world created over the past half century by a perspective that prioritizes military alliances and the globalization of Western-anchored markets, and derides the proponents of peace as idealistic and hopelessly naive. The triumph of this world required the forgetting of an internationalism born in the transition from empire. Thant and his colleagues would have replied that in an age of unmatched technological change, extreme inequality, nuclear weapons, and environmental crisis, their fight for a practical planetary partnership—their fight for a global peace—was not only utterly realistic but essential. They may still be proven right.

AUTHOR'S NOTE

U Thant was my grandfather. I was born in New York when he was Secretary-General and spent my earliest years living with him in Riverdale and Harrison. I have memories of him coming home in his overcoat, briefcase and homburg in hand, swimming with him in the pool, and sitting on the rug in his bedroom watching cartoons on the Zenith TV. And I remember going up to his office on the thirty-eighth floor and meeting the astronauts of the Apollo 11 mission after they returned from the moon. My first trip to Burma was for his funeral in 1974, when I was eight.

In later years, I worked for the United Nations, on peacekeeping missions in Cambodia and the former Yugoslavia, and then at the Secretariat in New York. I saw my grandfather's portrait near the elevators every day, after I had grabbed a morning coffee in the cafeteria. But I never really thought much about his period in the UN. Brian Urquhart, who died only recently, during the Covid pandemic, aged 102, was a far more decisive influence on my career. It was Brian's writings that initially inspired me to join the UN, and it was Brian's exciting counsel that guided me at key turns.

Over the 2010s, when I was living in Burma, I tracked down my grandfather's old house, then a ruin, and helped turn it into a museum and education center, where young people came to learn about global issues. I knew the broad outlines of Thant's life and work but not much more.

Author's Note

In 2021, after a military coup in Burma, I moved to the UK. I thought of writing a book on Burmese history but found myself increasingly drawn to my grandfather's archive, largely (but unfortunately not entirely) declassified and partially digitized. When he died in 1974, my family moved to a much smaller house in New York and gave all his papers, including private records and correspondence, to the UN. As I waded through the notes and documents, I could see that they told a very different story from what I thought I knew. I read through recent publications on topics such as the Cuban Missile Crisis. and could find little or no mention of what I saw in the archive. I decided to write this book, not realizing that my research would open up for me an entirely new perspective on the history of recent times.

I have tried to be as empathetic as possible, drawing on what I know about my grandfather's background and my own experience of living in Burma. Otherwise, I have relied almost exclusively on the wealth of documents in his UN archive and contemporary archives in the US, the UK, and elsewhere, as well as newspapers and other publications from the period and various collections of personal papers. The only exceptions are interviews with my mother, Aye Aye Thant, as well as my own recollections, on his life at home, together with a very few other private papers in my possession. His diaries, except for a few random pages, are nowhere to be found.

ACKNOWLEDGMENTS

I am indebted to the Master and Fellows of Trinity College, Cambridge, for awarding me a Visiting Fellowship over 2021–22. It was during that year that this book was conceived and began to take shape. I am equally grateful to the Master and Fellows of Christ's College, Cambridge, for hosting me as a Distinguished Visiting Scholar over 2023–24, when much of this book was written.

My research was also made possible by the generosity of the UN Foundation. I'm grateful to Elizabeth Cousens and her colleagues at the Foundation for their enthusiastic support.

My heartfelt thanks go to my editor, Alane Mason, at W. W. Norton, for her wise guidance from the earliest stages of this book's development. Thank you as well to YJ Wang for all her assistance during the making of the book and to my copyeditor, Allegra Huston, for her patient attention. At Atlantic Books, I am deeply grateful to Drummond Moir as well as to my editor, Shoaib Rokadiya, for their vital insights and advice.

My special thanks, as always, go to my agent, Clare Alexander, whose friendship and advice have been invaluable.

This book would not have been possible without the expert help of Stephen Haufek, Corinne O'Conner, and Aleksandr Gelfand at the United Nations Archives. I am thankful as well to Under Secretary-General Melissa Fleming and her colleagues in the United Nations

Department of Global Communications, especially Aikaterini Kitidi and Sok Min Seo at the UN Photo Library.

I am deeply appreciative of the help given to me by the teams at other archives and libraries, especially Carrie Tallichet Smith, Alexis Percle, and Chris Banks at the Lyndon B. Johnson Presidential Library in Austin, Texas; Stacey Chandler and Maryrose Grossman at the John F. Kennedy Presidential Library in Boston; as well as the staff at the Library of Congress in Washington, the National Archives in London, and the National Archives in New Delhi.

I'd like to express my warm thanks to Rachel Urquhart, who invited me to read the personal papers of Brian Urquhart in Tyringham, Massachusetts. I'm grateful also to Jennifer Otting for her help in examining the James Wechsler papers at the Wisconsin Historical Society Library; to a Vietnamese historian who prefers to remain anonymous, who conducted research on my behalf at the National Archives Center in Vietnam; to Bjørn H. Vangen at the Norwegian Nobel Institute; to Michael D. Greco at the Miller Center; and to my research assistants, Sophie Lennartsson-Nakamitsu in New York and Holly Sheridan in Cambridge. Thank you as well to Tamara Bradley, who kindly shared photographs in her personal possession.

My special thanks go to Alanna O'Malley at the University of Leiden for our many stimulating conversations on UN history and for organizing an extremely helpful workshop at an early stage of the book's development.

I would also like to recognize the excellent and dedicated staff at U Thant House in Burma for their assistance, especially in locating Burmese-language materials, and for their tireless efforts to build on U Thant's legacy.

I am extremely thankful to Judy Collins, James C. Mitchell, and May Pang for kindly answering my questions about U Thant's retirement party and to Tommy Koh and Lakhdar Brahimi for my interviews with them. Lakhdar's thoughts and reflections on the UN in the late 1950s and 1960s, shared with me at his home in Paris in 2022, guided me in much of the research that followed.

Acknowledgments

I've benefited immensely from the many insightful discussions I've had with friends and colleagues about this book over the past two years. Several were kind enough to read and comment on early drafts. I'd like in particular to mention Jerry Adelman, Jeremy Adelman, Will Atkinson, Susan Bayly, Mats Berdal, Chris Clark, Devon Curtis, William Dalrymple, Richard Drayton, Caroline Dunton, Jeff Feltman, Christopher Goscha, Richard Gowan, Michele Griffin, Christopher Gunness, Andrew Hardy, Poppy Hampson, Elin Jäderström, Michael Keating, Michael Kenny, Guy Laron, Karin Landgren, Tim Knatchbull, Mark Malloch-Brown, Ian Martin, Derek Mitchell, Eva-Maria Muschik, Eleanor Newbigin, Mabel van Oranje, Natasha Pairaudeau, Michael Peel, Andrew Preston, Zeid Raad, Gideon Rachman, Paul Risley, Lisa Roberts, Sophy Roberts, David Runciman, Natalie Samarasinghe, Craig Steffensen, Sujit Sivasundaram, Rory Stewart, Caroline Dunton, Alex von Tunzelmann, and Volker Turk.

I'd also like to extend my thanks to the owners and staff of Pages and Bould Brothers cafés in Cambridge, whose hospitality and endless cups of coffee kept me going over many months of writing.

I am enormously grateful to my mother, Aye Aye Thant, who shared with me her personal memories as well as the private papers and photographs of U Thant in her care. Thank you as well to my son, Thurayn, for our many priceless discussions around the ideas in this book.

My deepest gratitude goes to my wife, Sofia. Her unwavering support, encouragement, and good humor has meant the world to me. This book, and so much more, would not have been possible without her.

NOTES

ABBREVIATIONS

FRUS: Foreign Relations of the United States, Office of the Historian, US Department of State
HAKP: Henry A. Kissinger Papers, Yale University Library
JFKL: John F. Kennedy Presidential Library, Boston, Massachusetts
LBJL: Lyndon B. Johnson Presidential Library, Austin, Texas
RMNL: Richard M. Nixon Presidential Library, Yorba Linda, California

PROLOGUE

1. Sally Quinn, "A Happening for U Thant," *Washington Post*, December 15, 1971; "People," *Time*, December 27, 1971.
2. Brian Freemantle, *KGB* (Little, Brown, 1984), 128.
3. "Handbook for Planetary Citizens," UN Archives S-0893-0006-14.
4. "Farewell Tributes—Luncheon by World Federalists," UN Archives S-0864-0007-11-00001.

CHAPTER 1: NEW WORLD

1. Thant, "Looking Back," unpublished manuscript; author interview with Aye Aye Thant, Westport, CT, July 2023.
2. June Bingham, *U Thant: The Search for Peace* (Knopf, 1966), 229.
3. "New York Hospitality," *New Times* 18 (1962): 8.
4. Charles Abrams, "Stuyvesant Town's Threat to Our Liberties: Government Waives the Constitution for Private Enterprise," *Commentary*, November 1949.

5. Author interview with Aye Aye Thant, Westport, CT, July 2023.
6. "Financial (Personal)," UN Archives S-0890-0004-01-00001.
7. Susan Williams, *Who Killed Hammarskjöld? The UN, the Cold War, and White Supremacy in Africa* (Hurst, 2011), 98–99; Hammarskjöld Commission, Report of the Commission of Inquiry, The Hague, September 9, 2015, ch. 13; JFKL, NSF 310-007-p0002.
8. Author interview with Lakhdar Brahimi, Paris, September 25, 2022.
9. Alanna O'Malley, *The Diplomacy of Decolonisation: America, Britain and the United Nations During the Congo Crisis 1960–1964* (Manchester University Press, 2018), 21; Martin Thomas, *Fight or Flight: Britain, France, and Their Roads from Empire* (Oxford University Press, 2014), 252–54.
10. Mark Mazower, *No Enchanted Palace: The End of Empire and the Ideological Origins of the United Nations* (Princeton University Press, 2009), 62.
11. "Statement at General Assembly," UN Archives, S-0890-0008-09-00001.
12. "The Question of Algeria," December 12, 1960, UN Archives S-0890-0008-08-00002.
13. Thant, letter to Hammarskjöld, December 14, 1960, UN Archives S-0890-0007-06-00002.
14. Author interview with Lakhdar Brahimi, Paris, September 25, 2022; Matthew Connelly, *A Diplomatic Revolution: Algeria's Fight for Independence and the Origins of the Post-Cold War Era* (Oxford University Press, 2002), ch. 4.
15. "Statement to the First Commission, UN General Assembly, Question of Algeria," December 7, 1959.
16. Stephen R. Weissman, *American Foreign Policy in the Congo 1960–1964* (Cornell University Press, 1974), 89.
17. Roger Lipsey, *Hammarskjöld: A Life* (University of Michigan Press, 2013), 513–14.
18. Thant, "Looking Back."
19. Thant, first draft of *View from the UN*, 6, UN Archives S08940-01-000.
20. "Memorandum for the President: Lunch meeting with U Thant, Acting Secretary-General," JFKL, National Security Files 311-001-p0026.
21. "Confidential – Final Report of the Delegation of Burma to the Fifteenth Regular Session of the UN General Assembly," undated, UN Archives S-0890-0007-06-00001.
22. "Confidential Report on the Fifteenth General Assembly, December 1960," UN Archives S-0890-0007-06.
23. Thant, *View from the UN*, 199.
24. "Abba Eban Farewell Dinner" Remarks, May 11, 1959, UN Archives S-0890-0008-09-00001.
25. Thant, *View from the UN*, 7–19.
26. Thant, *View from the UN*, 7.
27. Thant, *View from the UN*, 12.

28. Ramses Nassif, *U Thant in New York, 1961–1971: A Portrait of the Third UN Secretary-General* (C. Hurst and Co., 1988), 8.
29. Ed Kiester, "U Thant of the UN," *Parade*, December 30, 1962.
30. Thant, *View from the UN*, 12–13.
31. Chakravarthi V. Narasimhan, *The United Nations at 50: Recollections* (New Delhi: Konark, 1996), 73–74.
32. Nassif, *U Thant in New York*, 9.

CHAPTER 2: CONGO

1. "International: In the U.S. Tradition," *Time*, December 10, 1945.
2. "Great Eastern Trading, cable to Thant," UN Archives S-0892-0001-01-00001.
3. "Memorandum from Secretary of State Rusk to President Kennedy," January 18, 1962, JFKL, National Security Files, Subjects Series, United Nations (General), January–February 1962, Box 311 (Confidential).
4. O'Malley, *Diplomacy of Decolonisation*, 17–18.
5. "Memorandum from Secretary of State Rusk to President Kennedy," November 11, 1961, FRUS 1961–1963, Volume XX, Congo Crisis – Office of the Historian.
6. UN Archives S-0875-0003-03-00001.
7. Andrew Boyd, *United Nations: Piety, Myth, and Truth* (Penguin, 1962), 146.
8. Ernest W. Lefever, *Crisis in the Congo: A United Nations Force in Action* (Brookings Institution, 1965), 96.
9. UN Archives S-0875-0004-07-00001.
10. O'Malley, *Diplomacy of Decolonisation*, 4.
11. Harold Macmillan, *Pointing the Way* (Harper and Row, 1972), 449, quoted in A. Walter Dorn and Robert Pauk, "Unsung Mediator: U Thant and the Cuban Missile Crisis," *Diplomatic History* 33, no. 2 (April 2009).
12. David Ormsby-Gore, "Oral History Interview," December 3, 1965, JFKL.
13. "The Congo," *Hansard* 651, December 14, 1961; O'Malley, *Diplomacy of Decolonisation*, 127.
14. "Memorandum for the President: Lunch meeting with U Thant, Acting Secretary-General," JFKL, National Security Files 311-001-p0026.
15. Bingham, *U Thant*, 93.
16. "Note to the Secretary-General (Confidential)," UN Archives S-0876-0001-06-00001.
17. "Note to the Secretary-General (Confidential)," UN Archives S-0876-0001-06-00001.
18. Thant, "Oral History Interview," June 23, 1964, JFKL.
19. Thant, "Oral History Interview," June 23, 1964, JFKL.

20. Adlai Stevenson, letter to Thant, January 20, 1962, UN Archives S-0882-0004-10-00001.
21. Eleanor Roosevelt, "My Day," January 22, 1962, Eleanor Roosevelt Papers Project, George Washington University.
22. Sture Linner, confidential note, May 23, 1962, UN Archives S-0875-0002-10-00001.
23. Brian Urquhart, unpublished remarks at Kennedy School of Government, Harvard University, 1994.
24. Bingham, *U Thant*, 9.
25. Interview with Alistair Cooke, March 1962, UN Archives S-0889-0005-06-00001.
26. Thant, *View from the UN*, 26.
27. "To Head the UN, a Gentle Burmese Gentleman," *Newsweek*, November 13, 1961.
28. John McNutt, "U Thant Seen Top Choice for Key Post," UPI, March 21, 1962.
29. "Financial—Personal 72nd Street Apartment," UN Archives S-0892-0009-10-00001.
30. "U Thant and His $6,447 Cat," *New York Herald Tribune*, May 17, 1962; "People," *Time*, May 25, 1962.
31. Bingham, *U Thant*, 53.
32. Tin Maung Thant, UN Archives S-0892-0003-13-00001.
33. "Condolences—Death of Son," UN Archives S-0892-0003-14-00001.
34. Nassif, *U Thant in New York*, 22.
35. "Interview with the Acting Secretary-General in Dublin 14 July 1962," UN Archives S-0889-0005-06-00001.
36. Harold MacMillan, *At the End of the Day, 1961–1963* (Macmillan, 1973), 280–84.
37. Brian Urquhart, *A Life in Peace and War* (W. W. Norton, 1991), 193.
38. "Press Releases—Secretary General," UN Archives S-0891-0002-59-00001.
39. "Plan of National Reconciliation," UN Archives S-0875-0002-07-00001.
40. "United States of America—John F. Kennedy," UN Archives S-0882-0004-02-00001.
41. Thant, *View from the UN*, 60–62.
42. "Statement by Acting Secretary-General U Thant Recorded for Broadcast by Radio Moscow," *Today*, August 30, 1962.
43. Hella Pick, "Opposition to Ceasefire, U Thant Firm," *Guardian*, September 17, 1962.
44. Thant, "Statement by the Acting Secretary-General, Meeting of the Congo Advisory Committee, 12 October 1962," UN Archives S-0886-0001-04-00001.
45. Thant, handwritten note, UN Archives S-0892-0004-05-00001.

CHAPTER 3: MISSILE CRISIS

1. Serhii Plokhy, *Nuclear Folly: A History of the Cuban Missile Crisis* (W. W. Norton, 2021), 28.
2. Plokhy, *Nuclear Folly*, 72.
3. Ernest R. May and Philip D. Zelikow, eds., *The Kennedy Tapes: Inside the White House during the Cuban Missile Crisis* (Belknap Press, 1997), 42.
4. Aleksandr Fursenko and Timothy Naftali, *One Hell of a Gamble: The Secret History of the Cuban Missile Crisis* (W. W. Norton, 1997), 247.
5. Plokhy, *Nuclear Folly*, 2–3.
6. Fursenko and Naftali, *One Hell of a Gamble*, 226–37.
7. Dorn and Pauk, "Unsung Mediator."
8. Thant, *View from the UN*, 155–56.
9. Thant, *View from the UN*.
10. Plokhy, *Nuclear Folly*, 163–71.
11. "Tributes (Cyprus), December 1974," UN Archives S-1076-0015-01.
12. Porter McKeever, *Adlai Stevenson: His Life and Legacy* (Quill, 1989), 524.
13. May and Zelikow, *The Kennedy Tapes*, 241.
14. Nassif, *U Thant in New York*, 20.
15. "Secretary General's statement to the Security Council, 24 October 1962," UN Archives S-0872-0003-04-00001.
16. "Cuba—UN Press Releases," UN Archives S-0872-0002-06-00001.
17. Plokhy, *Nuclear Folly*, 189.
18. May and Zelikow, *The Kennedy Tapes*, 243.
19. May and Zelikow, *The Kennedy Tapes*, 244.
20. Dorn and Pauk, "Unsung Mediator."
21. "Cuba—Correspondence with the USA," UN Archives S-0873-0001-12-00001.
22. Bingham, *U Thant*, 8.
23. Timothy Naftali and Mark Kramer, eds., "The Malin Notes: Glimpses Inside the Kremlin during the Cuban Missile Crisis," *Cold War International History Project Bulletin* (Woodrow Wilson International Center for Scholars), nos. 17/18 (Fall 2012).
24. May and Zelikow, *The Kennedy Tapes*, 263; "Summary Record of the Fifth Meeting of the Executive Committee of the National Security Council," October 25, 1962, 5 p.m., FRUS 1961–1963, Volume XI, Cuban Missile Crisis and Aftermath.
25. Sheldon M. Stern, *The Cuban Missile Crisis in American Memory: Myths versus Reality* (Stanford University Press, 2012), 83.
26. "Cuba—Khrushchev—October 1962," UN Archives S-0873-0001-14-0000.

27. Interview with Joseph J. Sisco by James Sutterlin, Yale University UN Oral History Project, May 18, 1990.
28. "Cuba—correspondence with Castro," UN Archives S-0872-0002-12-00001.
29. Fursenko and Naftali, *One Hell of a Gamble*, 267–68.
30. "Telegram from Fidel Castro to N. S. Khrushchev," October 26, 1962, History and Public Policy Program Digital Archive, Archive of Foreign Policy, Russian Federation, Wilson Center Digital Archive.
31. Plokhy, *Nuclear Folly*, 223–29.
32. Plokhy, *Nuclear Folly*, 266–72.
33. Fursenko and Naftali, *One Hell of a Gamble*, 276.
34. Plokhy, *Nuclear Folly*, 28.
35. "Record of Conversation between Soviet Deputy Foreign Minister Kuznetsov and UN Secretary General U Thant," October 29, 1962, History and Public Policy Program Digital Archive, Archive of Foreign Policy, Russian Federation, Wilson Center Digital Archive.
36. Plokhy, *Nuclear Folly*, 302.
37. Plokhy, *Nuclear Folly*, 10.
38. "Cuba—Cable from Tubman of Liberia," UN Archives S-0873-0001-16-00001.
39. "Cuba—miscellaneous 1962," UN Archives S-0872-0002-14-00001.
40. "Ruth Gage-Colby correspondence," UN Archives S-0872-0003-12-00001.
41. "Cuba—Miscellaneous," UN Archives S-0873-0001-07-00001.

CHAPTER 4: HAVANA

1. NSC Executive Committee record of action, October 29, 1962, FRUS 1961–1963, vols. 10–12, "American Republics, Cuba, 1961–1962," "Cuban Missile Crisis and Aftermath."
2. "Cuba—Notes in U Thant's hand," UN Archives S-0872-0003-22-00001.
3. Nassif, *U Thant in New York*, 33–34.
4. "Cuba – Meeting with Dorticos, Castro, Roa," UN Archives S-0873-0001-03-00001.
5. Tomás Diez Acosta, *October 1962: The "Missile" Crisis as Seen from Cuba* (Pathfinder, 2002), 262–65.
6. Plokhy, *Nuclear Folly*, 74–75.
7. Plokhy, *Nuclear Folly*, 313–14.
8. "Memorandum of Telephone Conversation Between Secretary of State Rusk and the Permanent Representative to the United Nations (Stevenson)," October 31, 1962, FRUS 1961–1963, vol. 11, "Cuban Missile Crisis and Aftermath."
9. Thant, *View from the UN*, 186.

10. "Cuba—Castro Meeting 31 October 1962," UN Archives S-0873-0001-02-00001.
11. "Memorandum of Telephone Conversation Between Secretary of State Rusk and the Permanent Representative to the United Nations (Stevenson)," October 31, 1962.
12. "Cuba—Castro Broadcast—31 October 1962," UN Archives S-0872-0003-10-00001.
13. "Ciphered Telegram from Alekseev to CC CPSU," November 2, 1962, in Naftali and Kramer, "The Malin Notes."
14. "Mr. Wholey," UN Archives S-0892-0009-10-00001.
15. "Telegram from Nikita Khrushchev to Anastas Mikoyan, 11 November 1962," in Naftali and Kramer, "The Malin Notes."
16. Fidel Castro, letter to Thant, November 16, 1962, UN Archives S-0872-0002-10-00001.
17. UN Observation Mission working paper, "Cuba—Miscellaneous—Working Papers," UN Archives S-0873-0001-09-00002.
18. Andrew Boyd, *Fifteen Men on a Powder Keg: A History of the UN Security Council* (Stein and Day, 1971), 177–78.
19. "Thant's Prestige Grows," *New York Times*, November 4, 1962.
20. Sergei Khrushchev, ed., *Memoirs of Nikita Khrushchev*, vol. 3, *Statesman (1953–1964)*, trans. George Shriver (Pennsylvania State University Press, 2007), 283–84.
21. Adlai Stevenson, Hearings before the Subcommittee on International Organization Affairs, Senate Foreign Relations Committee, 88th Congress, 1st Session, March 13, 1963.
22. Gertrude Samuels, "The Mediation of U Thant," *New York Times Magazine*, December 13, 1964.
23. "Cuba—Miscellaneous 1962," UN Archives S-0872-0002-14-00001.
24. "Cuba—Messages from Heads of State and Government," UN Archives S-0872-0002-08-00001.

CHAPTER 5: GRAND SLAM

1. Thant, letter to June Bingham, June 22, 1964, June Bingham Papers, "General Correspondence," Library of Congress.
2. Thant, "Truth and History," in the series "From My School Window," May 1935, June Bingham Papers, Library of Congress.
3. Bingham, *U Thant*, 88.
4. Hans J. Morgenthau, "The New Secretary-General," *Commentary*, January 1963.
5. Henry Kissinger, "Memorandum to Nelson A. Rockefeller," December 26, 1962, HAKP, "Series I. Early Career and Harvard University," Box 152, Folder 15.

6. "Confidential—Courses of action by ONUC over the next few weeks," November 21, 1962, UN Archives S-0875-0002-07-00001.
7. "Memorandum from the Under Secretary of State for Political Affairs (McGhee) to the President's Deputy Special Assistant for National Security Affairs (Kaysen)," FRUS 1961–1963, vol. 20, "Congo Crisis."
8. Kiester, "U Thant of the UN."
9. Bingham, *U Thant*, 5.
10. Indar Jit Rikhye, *Trumpets and Tumults: The Memoirs of a Peacekeeper* (New Delhi: Manohar, 2002), 48.
11. A. Walter Dorn, ed., *Air Power in UN Operations: Wings for Peace* (Routledge, 2014), 17–39.
12. Brian Urquhart, *Ralph Bunche: An American Life* (W. W. Norton, 1993), 357.
13. Dorn, *Air Power in UN Operations*, 17–39.
14. "Reports on the Situation in Jadotville," UN Archives S-0875-0004-09-00001.
15. "Memorandum of Telephone Conversation Between Secretary of State Rusk and Secretary-General Thant," FRUS 1961–1963, vol. 20, "Congo Crisis."
16. "Statements – January 1963 – 30 June 1963," UN Archives S-0886-0001-05-00001.
17. "Kolweizi Is Taken Peaceably by the UN," *New York Times*, January 22, 1963.
18. "Journey's End?," *Harvard Crimson*, January 8, 1963.
19. "A Standby UN Peacekeeping Force," June 12, 1963, UN Archives S-0885-0003-30-00001.
20. "Omar Loutfi Memorial, May 1963," UN Archives S-0886-0001-06-00001.
21. "Letter from the Representative to the United Nations (Stevenson) to Secretary of State Rusk," February 5, 1963, FRUS 1961–1963, vol. 25, "Organization of Foreign Policy; Information Policy; United Nations; Scientific Matters."
22. "Memorandum from Robert W. Komer of the National Security Council to the President's Special Assistant for National Security Affairs (Bundy)," February 7, 1963, FRUS 1961–1963, vol. 28, "Near East, 1962–1963."
23. Urquhart, *Ralph Bunche*, 362–66.
24. "Memorandum for the Record - 11 March 1967," FRUS 1961–1963, vol. 28, "Near East, 1962–1963."
25. John F. Kennedy, "Commencement Address at American University, Washington, D.C., June 10, 1963," JFKL.
26. John F. Kennedy, letter to Thant, July 3, 1963, UN Archives S-0882-0004-02-00001.
27. "Test Ban Treaty Is Signed in Moscow," *New York Times*, August 6, 1963.
28. "Statements – 1 July 1963 – 31 December 1963," UN Archives S-0886-0002-01-00001.
29. TASS News Agency, "U Thant Remarks," August 7, 1963.

30. "Big Four," UN Archives S-0880-0002-02-00001.
31. "Secretary-General's Office Art," UN Archives S-0892-0011-02-00001.

CHAPTER 6: TURN! TURN! TURN!

1. Elsa Maxwell, "Thant Proves a Charming Host at Lunch," *New York Journal-American*, May 2, 1962; UN Archives S-0864-0001-01-00001.
2. "Luncheons, Dinners, Receptions, Volumes I, II," UN Archives S-0864-0001-06-00001.
3. Author interview with Tommy Koh, January 13, 2023.
4. "Alex Quaison-Sackey: The UN's First Black President," *Ebony*, May 1965.
5. J. Anthony Lukas, "UN Not Awaiting Sartorial Revolt," *New York Times*, September 16, 1962.
6. Thomas Buckley, "Head of Protocol at UN Forefront," *New York Times*, April 20, 1962.
7. Phillip Lambro, *Close Encounters of the Worst Kind* (lulu.com, 2006), 45.
8. Lambro, *Close Encounters of the Worst Kind*, 45.
9. "A Summary of Major NASA Launches, October 1, 1958 – December 31, 1979," *KSC Historical Report* (Kennedy Space Center) 1 (July 1980): 175.
10. Ralph Bunche, personal note, September 20, 1963, UN Archives S-0864-0002-05-00001.
11. John F. Kennedy, "Address Before the 18th General Assembly of the United Nations, September 20, 1963," JFKL.
12. "U Thant at the UN," *New York Times*, October 20, 1963.
13. "United Nations We Believe," UN Archives S-0859-0004-07-00002.
14. "Statements – January 1963 – 30 June 1963," UN Archives S-0886-0002-02-00001.
15. "Second Oral History Interview with Marietta Tree," November 10, 1971, JFKL.
16. "Memorandum from the Assistant Secretary of State for International Organization Affairs (Cleveland) to Secretary of State Rusk," FRUS 1961–1963, vol. 25, "Organization of Foreign Policy; Information Policy; United Nations."
17. Thant, "Address at the University of São Paulo, Brazil," August 8, 1962, UN Archives S-0886-0001-03-00001.
18. Anis Chowdhury and José Antonio Ocampo, "The Global Economy since the Second World War through the Lens of the United Nations," in José Antonio Ocampo, ed., *The World Economy through the Lens of the United Nations* (Oxford University Press, 2018).
19. "An Interview with the Secretary-General," *Saturday Evening Post*, September 21, 1963.

20. "Statements – Volume III, 1 January 1963 – 30 June 1963," UN Archives S-0886-0001-05-00001.
21. Martin Daunton, *The Economic Government of the World 1933–2023* (Farrar, Straus and Giroux, 2023), 357–60.
22. "Statements – January 1964 – 31 May 1964," UN Archives S-0886-0002-04-00001.
23. Nassif, *U Thant in New York*, 19.
24. "Algeria – Meeting with Ahmed Ben Bella," UN Archives S-0878-0001-02-00001.
25. "Algeria – Meeting with Ahmed Ben Bella," UN Archives S-0878-0001-02-00001.
26. "Statements – January 1964 – 31 May 1964," UN Archives S-0886-0002-03-00001.
27. Peter Braestrup, "In Algeria Speech, Thant Asks for Shunning of Violence," *New York Times*, February 5, 1964.
28. "Comments on U Thant's visit to Maghreb countries," February 1964, Foreign Office (UK), FO 371/178550.
29. "Conciliation Commission – disengagement," UN Archives S-0874-0001-01-00001.
30. "Meeting held between the United States Party and the Secretary-General regarding Cyprus," June 26, 1964, UN Archives S-0869-0001-02-00001; "Memorandum of Conversation," FRUS 1964–1968, vol. 16, "Cyprus; Greece; Turkey."
31. Boyd, *Fifteen Men on a Powder Keg*, 289.
32. "Une Journée dans le bureau d'U Thant," *Réalité*, 1964.
33. "For United Nations Diplomats, 3 Parties a Night Is All in a Day's Work," *New York Times*, December 13, 1964.
34. "For United Nations Diplomats, 3 Parties a Night Is All in a Day's Work."
35. Larry Bleiberg, "The U.S. Highway that Helped Break Segregation," BBC, March 7, 2022; "Maryland Apologizes to Four African Envoys," *New York Times*, July 12, 1961.
36. "'Incidents' Here Protested at UN," *New York Times*, September 25, 1964.
37. "African UN Aide Denied Housing in N.Y. Twice Because of Race," *Chicago Daily Defender*, May 13, 1963.
38. Wen-yu Yen, letter to Secretary-General, November 1, 1961, in "Appointments," UN Archives S-0892-0001-01-00001.
39. Hernane Tavares de Sá, *The Play Within the Play: The Inside Story of the UN* (Knopf, 1966), 115–18.
40. "Tavares de Sá H," UN Archives S-0852-0004-07-00002.

CHAPTER 7: VIETNAM

1. Nassif, *U Thant in New York*, 14.
2. Thant, *View from the UN*, 58.
3. National Security File, Agency File, "United Nations," vol. 2, Secret, LBJL.
4. "SG Press Conference at London Airport, 23 July 1964," in "Statements – Volume VI, 1 June 1964 – 30 September 1964," UN Archives S-0886-0002-05-00001.
5. Thant, *View from the UN*, 62.
6. Fredrik Logevall, *Choosing War: The Lost Chance for Peace and the Escalation of War in Vietnam* (University of California Press, 2007), 122–23.
7. Ruth Gage-Colby, letter to Thant, August 4, 1964, in "Correspondence – personal," UN Archives S-0892-0004-08-00002.
8. Audio diary and annotated transcript, Lady Bird Johnson, August 6, 1964 (Thursday), Lady Bird Johnson's White House Diary Collection, LBJL.
9. "Memorandum from the President's Special Assistant for National Security Affairs (Bundy) and Samuel Belk of the National Security Council to President Johnson," August 4, 1964, FRUS 1964–1968, vol. 33, "Organization and Management of Foreign Policy; United Nations."
10. "Memorandum of a Conversation, White House," FRUS 1964–1968, vol. 1, "Vietnam, 1964."
11. Audio diary and annotated transcript, Lady Bird Johnson, August 6, 1964 (Thursday), Lady Bird Johnson's White House Diary Collection, LBJL.
12. Thant, *View from the UN*, 63.
13. "State Dinner Honors UN's U Thant," *Washington Post*, August 7, 1964.
14. "Exchange of Toasts Between President Lyndon B. Johnson and the Secretary-General," in "Statements – Volume VI, June 1964 – 30 September 1964," UN Archives S-0886-0002-06-00001.
15. Thant, *View from the UN*, 60.
16. Thant, "Looking Back."
17. "Thant Takes Day to Visit the Fair," *New York Times*, September 24, 1964.
18. Logevall, *Choosing War*, 94–95.
19. "Discussion between Mao Zedong and Pham Van Dong, October 5, 1964," History and Public Policy Program Digital Archive, CWIHP Working Paper 22, "77 Conversations," Wilson Center Digital Archive.
20. Sam Pope Brewer, "UN Chief Urges Account by Khrushchev of Ouster," *New York Times*, October 22, 1964.
21. Jayne Werner and David Hunt, eds., *The American War in Vietnam* (SEAP, Cornell University, 1993), 15; Stanley Karnow, *Vietnam: A History* (Viking, 1991), 348.
22. National Security File, Agency File, "United Nations," vol. 2., Secret, LBJL.

23. "United States of America—Stevenson, Adlai," UN Archives S-0882-0004-10-00001; "Telsum Foundation," UN Archives S-0859-0006-02-00001.
24. O'Malley, *Diplomacy of Decolonisation*, 175.
25. O'Malley, *Diplomacy of Decolonisation*, 179.
26. Urquhart, *Ralph Bunche*, 260.
27. Martin Luther King Jr. letter to U Thant, December 28, 1964, Morehouse College Martin Luther King Jr. Collection 1.1.0.46270, Atlanta University Center Robert W. Woodruff Library.
28. Bingham, *U Thant*, 10.
29. Boyd, *Fifteen Men on a Powder Keg*, 182–83.
30. Narasimhan, *The United Nations at 50*, 114–16.
31. "Stevenson Correspondence," UN Archives S-0882-0004-10-00001.
32. "Personal—Financial—Diet," UN Archives S-0892-0010-28-00001.

CHAPTER 8: ROLLING THUNDER

1. "Telegram from the Embassy in Vietnam to the Department of State," January 6, 1965, FRUS 1964–1968, vol. 2, "Vietnam, January–June 1965."
2. "Memorandum from the President's Special Assistant for National Security Affairs (Bundy) to President Johnson," February 7, 1965, FRUS 1964–1968, vol. 2, "Vietnam, January–June 1965."
3. Logevall, *Choosing War*, 317–19.
4. "United States of America—Stevenson, Adlai," UN Archives S-0882-0004-10-00001.
5. National Security File, Country File, "Vietnam," vol. 28, Top Secret, LBJL.
6. "Memorandum from Ralph Bunche of the United Nations Secretariat," FRUS 1964–1968, vol. 33, "Organization and Management of Foreign Policy; United Nations."
7. "Kennedy, Jacqueline," UN Archives S-0887-0002-16-00001.
8. Walter Johnson, ed., *The Papers of Adlai E. Stevenson*, vol. 8 (Little, Brown, 1979), 701.
9. "SG Press Conference – 24 February 1965," in "Press Briefings, Volume II," UN Archives S-0889-0006-01-00001.
10. Johnson, *Papers of Adlai Stevenson*, vol. 8, 664–69.
11. "Meeting – 27 February 1965," in "Confidential Papers, 1963–1966," UN Archives S-0866-0001-16-00001.
12. "Communications from the General Public," UN Archives S-0871-0006-07-00001.
13. Paul A. Schuette, "King Preaches on Non-Violence at Police-Guarded Howard Hall," *Washington Post*, March 3, 1965.

14. Norman Cousins, letter to Thant, March 24, 1965, in "Norman Cousins," UN Archives S-0887-0001-19.
15. Logevall, *Choosing War*, 371.
16. Johnson, *Papers of Adlai Stevenson*, vol. 8, 732–34, 841–82.
17. "Telegram from the Department of State to the Mission to the United Nations," FRUS 1964–1968, vol. 2, "Vietnam, January–June 1965."
18. National Security File, Files of McGeorge Bundy, SE Asia Regional Development, Confidential, LBJL.
19. "Correspondence with President Johnson," UN Archives S-0871-0001-08-00001.
20. "Memorandum of Conversation," May 12, 1965, FRUS 1964–1968, vol. 2, "Vietnam, January–June 1965."
21. Raymond Daniell, "Thant Warns Continued Ignoring of UN Will End Power to Act," *New York Times*, May 23, 1965.
22. Boyd, *Fifteen Men on a Powder Keg*, 25–26.
23. Boyd, *Fifteen Men on a Powder Keg*, 34.
24. *Hansard*, Wednesday, December 23, 1964, in *The International Situation*, vol. 262.
25. Interview with Ronald Archer Campbell Byatt, 6, Churchill Archives, University of Cambridge; Leslie Glass, *The Changing of Kings: Memories of Burma, 1934–1949* (Peter Owen, 1985), 232.
26. Thant, *View from the UN*, 51–52; "Malaysia – Correspondence," UN Archives S-0884-0012-10-00001.
27. "State Luncheon Files," UN Archives S-0892-0009-06-00001.
28. "Dominican Republic – Secretary-General's meeting with McGeorge Bundy," UN Archives S-0867-0001-08-00001.
29. "Confidential – Meeting with President Lyndon B. Johnson in San Francisco (Opera House) on Friday," June 25, 1965, UN Archives S-0882-0003-11-00001; Thant, *View from the UN*, 68–69.
30. "United States of America – Death of Adlai Stevenson," UN Archives S-0882-0004-11-00001.
31. "United States of America – Death of Adlai Stevenson," UN Archives S-0882-0004-11-00001.
32. "Meeting Held on 8 July 1965," in "Confidential Papers, 1963–1966," UN Archives S-0866-0001-17-00001.
33. National Security File, Agency File, "United Nations," vol. 2, Secret, LBJL.
34. "Paper Prepared by the Assistant Secretary of Defense for International Security Affairs (McNaughton)," FRUS 1964–1968, vol. 2, "Vietnam January–June 1965."
35. Ralph Bunche, personal note, July 28, 1965, UN Archives S-0370-0038-14.

36. "Confidential Papers, 1963–1966," UN Archives S-0866-0001-16-00001.
37. National Security File, Country File, "Vietnam," Lodge Letters to the President, Top Secret: Eyes Only, LBJL.
38. "Proposals Regarding the Situation in Vietnam," in "Secretary-General: Personal and Confidential," UN Archives S-0866-001-07-0001.

CHAPTER 9: KASHMIR

1. "United Nations Military Observer Group in India and Pakistan (UNMOGIP) – incidents reports (Secret)," UN Archives S-0863-0004-19-00001.
2. "Report of the Secretary-General on the current situation in Kashmir with particular reference to the cease-fire agreement, ceasefire-line and the functioning of the United Nations Military Observation Group in India and Pakistan," September 3, 1965, UN Archives S-0863-0003-10-00001.
3. National Security File, Country File, "India," Memos and Miscellaneous, June–September 1965, Secret, LBJL.
4. National Security File, Country File, "Kashmir," vol. 2, September–October 1965, Secret, LBJL.
5. "Secretary-General – trip to India and Pakistan – cables," UN Archives S-0360-0015-16.
6. National Security File, Country File, "Kashmir," vol. 2, September–October 1965, Secret, LBJL.
7. "Secretary-General – trip to India and Pakistan – cables," UN Archives S-0360-0015-16.
8. "Fight for Peace: U Thant," *New York Times*, September 8, 1965.
9. Thant, *View from the UN*, 403.
10. Nassif, *U Thant in New York*, 103.
11. Urquhart, *A Life in Peace and War*, 204.
12. Thant, *View from the UN*, 404.
13. "Secretary-General – trip to India and Pakistan – cables," UN Archives S-0360-0015-16.
14. Richard Salomon, "A Preliminary Survey of Some Early Buddhist Manuscripts Recently Acquired by the British Library," *Journal of the American Oriental Society* 117, no. 2 (1997): 353–58.
15. Carroll Kirkpatrick, "Johnson Encounters Indian with Pakistani Pals," *Washington Post*, September 9, 1965.
16. Urquhart, *A Life in Peace and War*, 203.
17. Urquhart, *A Life in Peace and War*, 205.
18. Thant, *View from the UN*, 405.
19. Sarvepalli Radhakrishnan, *The Dhammapada: With Introductory Essays, Pali Text, English Translation and Notes* (Oxford University Press, 1950).

20. Thant, *View from the UN*, 407.
21. "Secretary-General – trip to India and Pakistan – cables," UN Archives S-0360-0015-16; R. D. Pradhan, *Debacle to Revival: Y. B. Chavan as Defense Minister, 1962–66* (New Delhi: Atlantic, 2013), 273; Russell Brines, *The Indo-Pakistani Conflict* (Pall Mall Press, 1968), 367–69; "Pakistan Frustrates U Thant's Peace Mission," Ministry of External Affairs File No. P-V.304(12)/65, India National Archives PR_000004009528.
22. "Secretary-General – trip to India and Pakistan – ceasefire deadline postponement messages," UN Archives S-0360-0015-17.
23. "Secretary-General – trip to India and Pakistan – Exchange of cables," UN Archives S-0360-0016-01.
24. "Secretary-General – trip to India and Pakistan – cables," UN Archives S-0360-0015-16.
25. "Secretary-General – trip to India and Pakistan," UN Archives S-0360-0015-15.
26. "India – Pakistan – references to the Secretary-General made in Security Council," UN Archives S-0888-0007-03-00001.
27. "Correspondence – personal," UN Archives S-0892-0005-04-00002.
28. "Secretary-General's Reports to the Security Council on Kashmir situation," UN Archives S-0863-0003-11.
29. Boyd, *Fifteen Men on a Power Keg*, 140.
30. "Recording of Telephone Conversation between President Johnson and Ambassador Goldberg," September 18, 1965, Recordings and Transcripts, LBJL.
31. "Vatican – Pope Paul VI," UN Archives S-0882-0005-05-00001.
32. Nassif, *U Thant in New York*, 56.
33. "Visit of Pope Paul VI 1965," UN Archives S-0864-0009-11-00001; "Pope Paul VI correspondence," UN Archives S-0864-0009-20-00001.
34. Narasimhan, *The United Nations at 50*, 129–30.
35. Ralph Bunche, personal note, October 1965, UN Archives S-0370-0038-14.

CHAPTER 10: THE SOUND OF SILENCE

1. "Memorandum from Secretary of Defense McNamara to President Johnson," November 30, 1965, FRUS 1964–1968, vol. 3, "Vietnam June–December 1965."
2. Eric Sevareid, "The Final Troubled Hours of Adlai Stevenson," *Look*, November 30, 1965.
3. "Telegram from Secretary of State Rusk to the Department of State," November 18, 1965, FRUS 1964–1968, vol. 3, "Vietnam June–December 1965."
4. Thant, *Portfolio for Peace: Excerpts from the Writings and Speeches of U Thant, Secretary-General of the United Nations, on Major World Issues 1961–1970* (United Nations, 1970), 15.

5. National Security File, Agency File, "United Nations," vol. 2, Secret, LBJL; "Confidential Papers 1963–1966," UN Archives S-0866-0001-16-00001.
6. "Secretary-General – Vietnam – meetings between SG and Arthur Goldberg – Lyndon Johnson – George Ball," UN Archives S-0370-0045-07.
7. "Confidential Papers 1963–1966," UN Archives S-0866-0001-16-00001.
8. Lan You, "Hanoi's Balancing Act: The Vietnamese Communists and the Sino-Soviet Split, 1960–1965," *Journal of Cold War Studies* 25, no. 2 (Spring 2023): 64–92.
9. McGeorge Bundy, Notes of December 7, 1965, Papers of McGeorge Bundy, LBJL.
10. "Secret – Meeting with Prime Minister Harold Wilson," 16 December 1965, UN Archives S-0866-0001-16-00001.
11. Felix Green, letter to Thant, December 21, 1965, in "Confidential Papers 1963–1966," UN Archives S-0866-0001-17-00001.
12. Lyndon Johnson, letter to Thant, January 15, 1966, in "Correspondence with President Johnson," UN Archives S-0871-0001-08-00001.
13. "Memorandum of Telephone Conversation Between the Under Secretary of State (Ball) and President Johnson," 28 December 1965, FRUS 1964–1968, vol. 3, "Vietnam June–December 1965."
14. Ralph Bunche, personal note, January 6, 1966, UN Archives S-0370-0038-14.
15. "Memorandum from the President's Special Assistant for National Security Affairs (Bundy) to President Johnson," January 3, 1966, FRUS 1964–1968, vol. 4, "Vietnam 1966"; "Secret – Note on the Situation in Vietnam," December 28, 1965, UN Archives S-0866-0001-16-00001.
16. "Summary Notes of the 556th Meeting of the National Security Council," January 29, 1966, FRUS 1964–1968, vol. 4, "Vietnam 1966."
17. "Notes of Meeting," January 27, 1966, FRUS 1964–1968, vol. 4, "Vietnam 1966."
18. Allen Pietrobon, *Norman Cousins: Peacemaker in the Atomic Age* (Johns Hopkins University Press, 2022), 299; "Secret – Notes on the Vietnam Situation," February 5, 1966, UN Archives S-0866-0001-16-00001.
19. "Secret – Note on the Situation in Vietnam," February 9, 1966, UN Archives S-0866-0001-16-00001.
20. Susan Williams, *White Malice: The CIA and the Neocolonisation of Africa* (Hurst & Co., 2021), ch. 39.
21. Vincent Bevins, *The Jakarta Method: Washington's Anticommunist Crusade and the Mass Murder Program that Shaped Our World* (PublicAffairs, 2020), 124–58.
22. Transcript of BBC interview, April 30, 1966, in "Statements – Volume XI, 4 January 1966 – 5 May 1966," UN Archives S-0886-0004-03-00001.
23. "Conversation with Felix Green – 4 January 1966," in "Confidential Papers 1963–1966," UN Archives S-0866-0001-16-00001; Drew Middleton, "Hanoi Said to List Three Terms for Talk," *New York Times*, February 17, 1966.

24. "Secret – Note by Simon Malley on his meeting with Tran Hoai Nam," UN Archives S-0866-0001-16-00001.
25. "Secretary-General Confers with President de Gaulle," in "Statements – Volume XI, 4 January 1966 – 5 May 1966," UN Archives S-0886-0004-03-00001.
26. Ralph Bunche, personal note, March 12, 1966. UN Archives S-0370-0038-22.
27. National Security File, Agency File, "United Nations," vol. 3, Confidential, LBJL.
28. "Necessary Man," *New York Times*, April 30, 1966.
29. "SG Addresses Amalgamated Clothing Workers of America," in "Statements – Volume XII, 6 May 1966 – 6 September 1966," UN Archives S-0886-0004-04-00001.
30. "Mr. Rusk vs. Mr. Thant," *New York Times*, May 26, 1966.
31. "Secret – Notes of Meeting, 2 August 1966," UN Archives S-0866-0001-16-00001.
32. UN Archives S-0370-0045-07; Thant, "Looking Back," 38.
33. "Arthur Goldberg Comes to the Hospital," UN Archives S-0370-0038-01.
34. Urquhart, *Ralph Bunche*, 384.
35. "Notes on a Meeting with Secretary of State Dean Rusk 22 August 1966 – Secret," UN Archives S-0292-0010-11.
36. National Security File, Agency File, "United Nations," vol. 3, Secret, LBJL.
37. "177 Congressmen Ask Thant to Stay," *New York Times*, August 27, 1966.
38. "177 Congressmen Ask Thant to Stay."
39. "Correspondence – Personal," UN Archives S-0892-0006-03-00001.
40. "Secretary-General position – retirement – My statement on retirement," UN Archives S-0855-0005-07.
41. Ralph Bunche, personal note, September 14, 1966, UN Archives S-0370-0038-01.
42. National Security File, Agency File, "United Nations," vol. 4, Secret, LBJL.
43. "The Troubled UN," *Newsweek*, October 3, 1966.
44. Thant, *View from the UN*, 70–71; "Visit of President Lyndon B. Johnson to U Thant," UN Archives S-0866-0001-16-00001.
45. Urquhart, *Ralph Bunche*, 394–95.
46. Ralph Bunche, personal note, December 1, 1966, UN Archives S-0370-0038-01.
47. Thant, "Looking Back," 43.
48. Nigel Nicolson, "World's Middleman: U Thant's Stabilizing Role," *Times of India*, December 14, 1966.

CHAPTER 11: EVE OF DESTRUCTION

1. Christopher Goscha, *The Penguin History of Modern Vietnam* (Penguin, 2017), 357–59.
2. "The Gallup Report," February 8, 1967, in "Correspondence – Personal," UN Archives S-0892-0006-06-00001.
3. "Italian Referendum," in "Correspondence – Personal," UN Archives S-0892-0006-03-00001.
4. "The Gallup Report," February 8, 1967, "Correspondence – Personal," UN Archives S-0892-0006-06-00001.
5. "Correspondence with Permanent Representative of the United States of America," UN Archives S-0871-0001-09-00001.
6. "Vietnam: U Thant—Confidential and Guard," January 6, 1967, Foreign and Commonwealth Office (UK), FCO 15/708: U Thant's peace initiative.
7. "Visits of U Thant, UN Secretary General, to UK: records of meetings," PREM 13/1788, UK National Archives.
8. "Personnel – Bunche, Ralph J.," UN Archives S-0852-0001-10-00001.
9. "Question of Vietnam – Secret," UN Archives S-0866-0001-18-00001.
10. "Interviews – Camera III U Thant," UN Archives S-0864-0012-05-00001.
11. "Secretary-General – personal and confidential," UN Archives S-0866-0001-07-00001.
12. "Editorial Note – 68," FRUS 1964–1968, vol. 5, "Vietnam 1967."
13. "Views and Impressions about the SG from the Chinese and Vietnamese," March 29, 1967, UN Archives S-0866-0001-18-00001.
14. "Views and Impressions about the SG from the Chinese and Vietnamese," March 29, 1967, UN Archives S-0866-0001-18-00001.
15. "Views and Impressions about the SG from the Chinese and Vietnamese," March 29, 1967, UN Archives S-0866-0001-18-00001.
16. "Views and Impressions about the SG from the Chinese and Vietnamese," March 29, 1967, UN Archives S-0866-0001-18-00001.
17. "Personal – notes handwritten and typed copies – United Nations – aide-mémoire of U Thant on Vietnam peace proposals – comments by Bunche," UN Archives S-0370-0039-03.
18. "Transcript of Remarks by Secretary-General at New York Airport 20 April 1967," "Statements – Volume XIV, 1 January 1967 – 30 April 1967," UN Archives S-0886-0005-05-00001.
19. "Recording of Telephone Conversation Between Johnson and Rusk," March 18, 1967, 5:30 p.m., Tape F67.09, Side A, PNO 2, Recordings and Transcripts, LBJL.
20. "Vietnam – Correspondence – 1967," UN Archives S-0866-0001-14-00001.

21. "United States of America – Fulbright, J. W.," UN Archives S-0882-0003-08-00001.
22. Robert H. Estabrook, "Senators, Thant, Scan on Past Peace Moves," *Washington Post*, March 23, 1967.
23. "Jawaharlal Nehru Award," UN Archives S-0864-0012-30-00001.
24. "Secretary-General Confers with Ceylonese Prime Minister, Visits Kandy," UN Archives S-0886-0005-04-00001.
25. "A Warning from U Thant," *New York Times*, May 12, 1967.
26. Thant, "Education in a Changing World," speech at the University of Michigan, March 30, 1967, UN Archives S-0886-0005-04-00001.

CHAPTER 12: GAZA AND THE SINAI

1. "Informal Meeting of Governments Providing Contingents to UNEF – 17 May 1967," UN Archives S-0865-0001-16-00001.
2. Rikhye, *Trumpets and Tumults*, 14–15.
3. Guy Laron, *The Six-Day War: The Breaking of the Middle East* (Yale University Press, 2017), 46–54.
4. Nassif, *U Thant in New York*, 72.
5. "Informal Meeting of Governments Providing Contingents to UNEF – 17 May 1967," UN Archives S-0865-0001-16-00001.
6. "Notes for UNEF Meetings on 17 May 1967," UN Archives S-0865-0001-16-00001.
7. "Notes for UNEF Meetings on 17 May 1967," UN Archives S-0865-0001-16-00001.
8. "Information Memorandum from the Deputy Assistant Secretary of State for International Organization Affairs (Popper) to Secretary of State Rusk," FRUS 1964–1968, vol. 19, "Arab–Israeli Crisis and War, 1967."
9. "Meeting of 18 May with Ambassador Rafael," UN Archives S-0865-0001-13-00001; Gideon Rafael, *Destination Peace* (Weidenfeld and Nicolson, 1981), 139.
10. "Meeting of 18 May with Ambassador Goldberg," UN Archives S-0865-0001-13-00001.
11. Richard B. Parker, ed., *The Six-Day War: A Retrospective* (University Press of Florida, 1996), 139.
12. Nassif, *U Thant in New York*, 75.
13. Nassif, *U Thant in New York*, 76.
14. Brazil, Canada, Ceylon, Colombia, India, Norway, and Pakistan.
15. "Note, 18 May 1967," UN Archives S-0865-0001-13-00001.
16. "Meeting with Ambassador Rafael," May 19, 1967, UN Archives S-0865-0001-13-00001.

17. Laron, *The Six-Day War*, 203–5.
18. "Meeting with Ambassador Ignatieff," May 19, 1967, UN Archives S-0865-0001-13-00001; "Notes on Meeting with Mr. Paul Martin," May 20, 1967, UN Archives S-0865-0001-13-00001.
19. "Notes on Meeting with Mr. Paul Martin," May 20, 1967, UN Archives S-0865-0001-13-00001.
20. "Secret and Personal," May 21, 1967, UN Archives S-0865-0001-13-00001.
21. "Meeting with Ambassador Goldberg," May 20, 1967, UN Archives S-0865-0001-13-0000; "Meeting with Ambassador Goldberg," May 22, 1967, UN Archives S-0865-0001-13-0000.
22. Thant, *View from the UN*, 31.
23. Rikhye, *Trumpets and Tumults*, 50–52.

CHAPTER 13: THE SIX-DAY WAR

1. Thant, *View from the UN*, 233.
2. Thant, *View from the UN*, 234.
3. "Meeting with Foreign Minister of UAR, Cairo, 24 May 1967," UN Archives S-0865-0001-01-00001.
4. "Meeting with President Nasser, Cairo, 24 May 1967," UN Archives S-0865-0001-01-00001.
5. "Memoranda by Maj. General Rikhye re: meeting of U Thant and the Foreign Minister of Egypt and an informal meeting with President Nasser," UN Archives S-0865-0001-02-00001.
6. Nassif, *U Thant in New York*, 79.
7. "Meeting with President Nasser, Cairo, 24 May 1967," UN Archives S-0865-0001-01-00001.
8. "Meeting with President Nasser, Cairo, 24 May 1967," UN Archives S-0865-0001-01-00001; Mahmoud Riad, *The Struggle for Peace in the Middle East* (Quartet, 1981), 20.
9. Rikhye, *Trumpets and Tumults*, 79.
10. Boyd, *Fifteen Men on a Powder Keg*, 201.
11. "Memorandum for the Record – 26 May 1967," FRUS 1964–1968, vol. 19, "Arab–Israeli Crisis and War, 1967."
12. National Security File, Country File, "Middle East Crisis," Miscellaneous Material, Top Secret, LBJL.
13. Laron, *The Six-Day War*, 197.
14. Laron, *The Six-Day War*, 215.
15. Quoted in Boyd, *Fifteen Men on a Powder Keg*, 196.
16. "U Thant's War," *Spectator*, May 26, 1967, in "Supporters of U Thant," UN Archives S-0861-0006-08-00001.

17. Quoted in Boyd, *Fifteen Men on a Powder Keg*, 196.
18. Boyd, *Fifteen Men on a Powder Keg*, 204.
19. Urquhart, *A Life in Peace and War*, 213.
20. Thant, *View from the UN*, 245.
21. Urquhart, *A Life in Peace and War*, 213.
22. "Letters to Mr. Levi Eshkol, Prime Minister of Israel and to President Nasser of UAR," May 27, 1967, UN Archives S-0866-0001-03-00001.
23. "Personal – Notes, handwritten and typed copies – U Thant's appeal to Nasser and Eshkol," UN Archives S-0865-0001-03-00001.
24. "Luncheons, Dinners and Receptions," UN Archives S-0864-0002-07-00001.
25. "Personal – Notes, handwritten and typed copies – U Thant's appeal to Nasser and Eshkol," UN Archives S-0865-0001-03-00001.
26. "Telegram from the President's Special Assistant (Rostow) to President Johnson in Texas," FRUS 1964–1968, vol. 19, "Arab–Israeli Crisis and War, 1967."
27. "Middle East / Near East – withdrawal and United Nations Emergency Force (UNEF)," UN Archives S-0370-0036-10-00001.
28. "Report by the Secretary-General, 26 May 1967," UN Archives S-0888-0004-01-00001.
29. "Secret – Note for the Record, 1 June 1967," UN Archives S-0865-0002-27-00001.
30. "Memorandum for the Record, June 1, 1967" FRUS 1964–1968, vol. 19, "Arab–Israeli Crisis and War, 1967"; Laron, *The Six-Day War*, 279; Parker, ed., *The Six-Day War*, 139.
31. "Telex," June 1, 1967, UN Archives S-0861-0006-08-00001.
32. "Secret – Record of a Meeting held at United Nations Headquarters," UN Archives S-0882-0002-37-00001.
33. "Secret – Record of a Meeting held at United Nations Headquarters," UN Archives S-0882-0002-37-00001.
34. James Reston, "Cairo: Quiet Flows the Nile," *New York Times*, June 4, 1967; see also Joyce Egginton, "U Thant Had No Choice: Middle East Crisis," *Observer*, June 4, 1967.
35. Rikhye, *Trumpets and Tumults*, 100–12.
36. "Kennedy, Jacqueline," UN Archives S-0887-0002-16-00001.
37. "Kennedy, Jacqueline," UN Archives S-0887-0002-16-00001.
38. "Telegram from the Mission to the North Atlantic Treaty Organization and European Regional Organizations to the Department of State, June 17, 1967," FRUS 1964–1968, vol. 13, "Western Europe Region."
39. Felix Kessler, "UN's U Thant," *Wall Street Journal*, July 18, 1967.
40. James Wechsler, "The Ordeal of a Peacemaker," *Progressive*, August 1967.
41. James Wechsler, "An Untold Story," *New York Post*, June 7, 1967.

42. Max Frankel, "'57 Hammarskjöld Memo on Mideast Is Disclosed," *New York Times*, June 19, 1967.
43. Wechsler, "The Ordeal of a Peacemaker."
44. Thant, *View from the UN*, 270–71.
45. "1967," UN Archives S-0865-0002-27-00001.
46. Ralph Bunche, personal note, July 11, 1967, UN Archives S-0370-0039-03.
47. "Secret – August 1967," UN Archives S-0882-0005-08-00001.
48. "1967," UN Archives S-0865-0002-27-00001.
49. "Memorandum of Conversation," June 21, 1967, Dobrynin-Thompson Conversations, FRUS 1964–1968, vol. 19, "Arab–Israeli Crisis and War, 1967."
50. "Interview with Ambassador Gideon Rafael, *Maariv*, 4 August 1967," UN Archives S-0861-0006-08-00001.
51. Urquhart, *A Life in Peace and War*, 215.
52. Ralph Bunche, personal note, June 24, 1967, UN Archives S-0370-0038-22.
53. Ralph Bunche, personal note, January 6, 1966, UN Archives S-0370-0038-22.
54. Ralph Bunche, personal note, January 6, 1966, UN Archives S-0370-0038-22.
55. "McDonald Asks UN to Begin Study of UFO's," *Tucson Daily Citizen*, June 15, 1967.
56. Nicolson, "World's Middleman."
57. Wechsler, "Ordeal of a Peacemaker," *Progressive*, August 1967.
58. Bingham, *U Thant*, 5.

CHAPTER 14: REVOLUTION

1. "316. Editorial Note," FRUS 1964–1968, vol. 5, "Vietnam 1967."
2. "Meeting 20 June 1967," in "Selected Confidential Papers on The Middle East – 1967," UN Archives S-0865-0002-27-00001.
3. Thant, *View from the UN*, 71.
4. Note signed K. M. Wilford 1967, "U Thant's Peace Initiative," Secret and Confidential, Foreign and Commonwealth Office (UK), FCO 15/708.
5. Thant, "The United Nations and the Human Factor," July 30, 1967, UN Archives S-0885-0003-08-00001.
6. "Telegram from the Embassy in Norway to the Department of State," June 14, 1967, FRUS 1964–1968, vol. 5, "Vietnam 1967."
7. "Cyprus – Action by Secretary-General," UN Archives S-0870-0001-19-00001.
8. "Cyprus – Action by Secretary-General," UN Archives S-0870-0001-19-00001.
9. "Kennedy, Jacqueline," UN Archives S-0887-0002-16-00001.
10. "340. Editorial Note," FRUS 1964–1968, vol. 5, "Vietnam 1967."
11. "The Wise Men's Meeting of November 1 and Planning to Stay the Course, November–December," FRUS 1964–1968, vol. 5, "Vietnam 1967."

12. "U Thant Luncheon," January 19, 1968, James Weschler papers. University of Wisconsin, Madison.
13. "United States – Bundy, William P.," UN Archives S-0882-0003-05-00001.
14. "Yogi Confers with Thant," *New York Times*, January 21, 1968.
15. "Visit of U Thant, April 1969: briefing notes," Foreign and Commonwealth Office (UK), FCO 58/265.
16. "Meeting with Consul-General of the Democratic Republic of Viet-Nam – New Delhi – 8 February 1968," in "Vietnam – Confidential Papers – 1967–1968," UN Archives S-0866-0001-18-00001.
17. "Visits of U Thant, UN Secretary General, to UK: records of meetings," PREM 13/3004, UK National Archives.
18. "Visits of U Thant, UN Secretary General, to UK: records of meetings," PREM 13/3004, UK National Archives.
19. "Visits of U Thant, UN Secretary General, to UK: records of meetings," PREM 13/3004, UK Archives.
20. "Recording of Telephone Conversation Between Johnson and Clifford," February 14, 1968, 9:16 a.m., Tape F68.02, Side B, PNO 1–2, Recordings and Transcripts, LBJL.
21. "Notes of Meeting in the Secretary-General's Office – 15 February 1968," in "Vietnam – Confidential Papers – 1967–1968," UN Archives S-0866-0001-18-00001.
22. "Notes on Conversation with Delegate-General of the Dem Rep," February 14, 1968, UN Archives S-0866-0001-18-00001; "Vietnam – notes on Secretary-General – meetings with Lyndon Johnson," UN Archives S-0370-0048-01; Mai Van Bo, *From Geneva to Paris (Political Memoirs - Diplomacy)* (Ho Chi Minh City: Tre' Publishing House, 2002), 123–59.
23. "Lyndon B. Johnson and Robert S. McNamara on 21 February 1968," Conversation WH6802-03-12728, in Kent B. Germany, Nicole Hemmer, and Ken Hughes, eds., *Johnson Telephone Tapes: 1968* (University of Virginia Press, 2014).
24. Transcripts of Meetings in the Cabinet Room, February 21, 1968, LBJL.
25. "Statement by the Secretary-General," February 24, 1968, UN Archives S-0370-0048-02.
26. "Secretary-General's Statement – 24 February 1968," UN Archives 0866-0001-11-00001.
27. "Notes of Meeting," March 26, 1968, FRUS 1964–1968, vol. 6, "Vietnam, January–August 1968."
28. *Public Papers of the Presidents of the United States: Lyndon B. Johnson, 1968–69*, Book 1, 476–82.
29. Lyndon Johnson, diary entry, April 3, 1968, President's Daily Diary Collection, LBJL.

30. "Notes of Meeting," April 4, 1968, UN Archives S-0370-0048-01; "Notes of President Johnson's Meeting with U Thant," Tom Johnson Notes of Meetings, Top Secret, LBJL.
31. "Bunche to Stand In for Thant at Rites," *New York Times*, April 6, 1968.
32. "Vietnam – notes on Secretary-General – meetings with Lyndon Johnson, Richard Nixon and other United States officials," UN Archives S-0370-0048-01.
33. "Telegram from the Executive Secretary of the National Security Council (Smith) to the President's Special Assistant (Rostow) in Hawaii," April 17, 1968, FRUS 1964–1968, vol. 6, "Vietnam, January–August 1968."
34. "Chilly Tone Marks Exchanges Between Johnson and Goldberg," *New York Times*, April 28, 1968; "Choice of Ball for UN Linked to Humphrey," *Christian Science Monitor*, April 1968.
35. Drew Pearson, *Washington Merry-Go-Round: The Drew Pearson Diaries, 1960–1969* (Potomac Books, 2015), 570.
36. "Vietnam – notes on Secretary-General – meetings with Lyndon Johnson, Richard Nixon and other United States officials," UN Archives S-0370-0048-01.
37. "United States of America – Kennedy, Robert," UN Archives S-0882-0004-03-00001.
38. "Security Council Recesses Because of Shooting," *New York Times*, June 6, 1968.
39. "United States of America – Kennedy, Edward M.," UN Archives S-0882-0004-01-00001.
40. "United States of America – Kennedy, Robert," UN Archives S-0882-0004-03-00001.
41. Arthur C. Clarke, foreword to Dan Richter, *Moonwatcher's Memoir: A Diary of 2001: A Space Odyssey* (Carroll & Graf, 2002).
42. Drew Pearson, column, *Washington Post*, June 27, 1967.
43. Garrett M. Graff, *UFO: The Inside Story of the US Government's Search for Alien Life Here—and Out There* (Avid Reader Press, 2023), 212.
44. "Press Briefings – Geneva," UN Archives S-0889-0009-01-00001.
45. Thant, *View from the UN*, 382–83.
46. Nassif, *U Thant in New York*, 306–9.
47. "Statements by the Secretary-General on the war in Viet-Nam," UN Archives S-0871-0002-20-00001.
48. "Ball Says Thant Is Naïve on War," *New York Times*, September 28, 1968.
49. "Vietnam – notes on Secretary-General – meetings with Lyndon Johnson, Richard Nixon and other United States officials," UN Archives S-0370-0048-01.
50. "U Thant: Is Anyone Listening?," *New York Times*, September 29, 1968.

Notes | 341

51. "Notes of Meeting in the Secretary-General's Office," September 30, 1968, UN Archives S-0370-0048-01.
52. Ralph Bunche, personal note, September 30, 1968, UN Archives S-0370-0048-01.
53. "Telegram from the Embassy in France to the Department of State," FRUS1 964–1968, vol. 7, "Vietnam, September 1968–January 1969"; John A. Farrell, "When a Candidate Conspired with a Foreign Power to Win an Election," *Politico*, August 6, 2017; Gene Roberts, "Thieu Says Saigon Cannot Join Talks Under Present Plan," *New York Times*, November 2, 1968.
54. James Wechsler, "Citizen of the World," *New York Post*, November 26, 1974.

CHAPTER 15: BAD MOON RISING

1. "Meeting with President Nixon," September 18, 1969, UN Archives S-0370-0048-01.
2. H. R. Haldeman, diary entry, September 18, 1969, H. R. Haldeman Diaries Collection, US National Archives, Online Public Access Catalog Identifier 7787364.
3. Members of Congress for Peace Through Law, letter, February 12, 1970, in "United States of America – Various Senators and Congressmen," UN Archives S-0882-0005-02-00001.
4. Norman G. Finkelstein, *Image and Reality of the Israel-Palestine Conflict* (Verso, 2003), 151.
5. United Nations Security Council Resolution 242, November 22, 1967, S/RES/242(1967).
6. Hilde Henriksen Waage and Hulda Kjeang Mørk, "Mission Impossible: UN Special Representative Gunnar Jarring and His Quest for Peace in the Middle East," *International History Review* 38, no. 4 (2016): 830–53.
7. Urquhart, *A Life in Peace and War*, 218.
8. "Gunnar Jarring (Special Representative of the Secretary-General to the Middle East) reports," UN Archives S-0865-0001-09-00001.
9. "Gunnar Jarring (Special Representative of the Secretary-General to the Middle East) reports," UN Archives S-0865-0001-09-00001.
10. Thant, *View from the UN*, 302–8.
11. Thant, *View from the UN*, 313.
12. "Press Briefings, 2nd Set Headquarters," UN Archives S-0889-0009-03-00001.
13. Thant, *View from the UN*, 320–23; "Special Representative of the Secretary-General Ambassador Jarring – Confidential," UN Archives S-0865-0002-06-00001.
14. Golda Meir, *My Life* (Weidenfeld and Nicholson, 1975), 243.
15. Thant, *View from the UN*, 328.

16. "1969," UN Archives S-0865-0003-02-00001.
17. "1969," UN Archives S-0865-0003-02-00001.
18. "Introduction to the Annual Report of the Secretary-General on the Work of the Organization," September 1969, UN document A/7601/Add.1, quoted in Joyce Egginton, "U Thant Warns of New Dark Age in Middle East," *Observer*, September 20, 1969.
19. "Israeli Jets Raid Plant Near Cairo," *New York Times*, February 13, 1970.
20. "Ambassador Gunnar Jarring's Mission to the Middle East," UN Archives S-0865-0002-26-00001.
21. John de St. Jorre, *The Brothers' War: Biafra and Nigeria* (Faber and Faber, 2009), 412; Marie-Luce Desgrandchamps, "Dealing with 'genocide': the ICRC and the UN during the Nigeria-Biafra war, 1967–70," *Journal of Genocide Research* 16, no. 2–3 (2014): 281–97.
22. "Biafra: The Mercenaries," *Time*, October 25, 1968.
23. Gemuh E. Akuchu, "Peaceful Settlement of Disputes: Unsolved Problem for the OAU (A Case Study of the Nigeria–Biafra Conflict)," *Africa Today* 24, no. 4 (October–December 1977); "Paper Prepared by the NSC Interdepartmental Group for Africa," FRUS 1969–1972, Volume E–5, Part 1, "Documents on Sub-Saharan Africa, 1969–1972."
24. Thant, *View from the UN*, 95–97.
25. "Press Briefings, 2nd Set Headquarters," UN Archives S-0889-0009-03-00001.
26. "Nigeria," UN Archives S-0884-0013-17-00001.
27. "Nigeria – Nile Goran Gussing," UN Archives S-0884-0014-05-00001.
28. Konrad J. Kuhn, "Liberation Struggle and Humanitarian Aid: International Solidarity Movements and the 'Third World' in the 1960s," in *The Third World in the Global 1960s*, ed. Samantha Christiansen and Zachary A. Scarlett (Berghahn Books, 2013); Michael Aaronson, "The Nigerian Civil War and 'Humanitarian Intervention,'" in Bronwen Everill and Josiah Kaplan, eds., *The History and Practice of Humanitarian Intervention and Aid in Africa* (Palgrave Macmillan, 2013).
29. Akuchu, "Peaceful Settlement of Disputes."
30. "Biafra – meeting with Labouisse," UN Archives S-0878-0001-29-00001.
31. "Meeting with General Gowan – Secret," January 18, 1970, UN Archives S-0878-0001-27-00001.
32. Anthony Lewis, "If Wishing Would Make It So," *New York Times*, January 26, 1970.
33. Robert H. Estabrook, "U Thant: Low-Key Man, High-Tension Job," *Washington Post*, January 4, 1970.
34. "Transcript of Press Conference 17 February 1970," UN Archives S-0889-0009-08-00001.
35. Darius S. Jhabvala, "U Thant – The Select Whipping Boy of UN Rumormongers," *Boston Globe*, February 22, 1970.

36. Winston Berry, "Why the Campaign Against U Thant," *AfricaAsia*, March 16–29, 1970.
37. Lionel Landry, "From Riverdale to Rangoon," *Asia*, supplement no. 3 (1977), 39.

CHAPTER 16: ONE WORLD

1. Joseph Lelyveld, "Surging Crowds Fill the Streets in New York," *New York Times*, August 14, 1969.
2. "Astronauts – Apollo 11," UN Archives S-0885-0001.
3. "Text of Statement by Secretary-General U Thant Welcoming Apollo 8 Astronauts – 10 January 1969," UN Archives S-0864-0005-06-00001.
4. "Redbook Interview 2 September 1969," in "Correspondence – Personal," UN Archives S-0892-0007-04-00001.
5. "Correspondence – Personal," UN Archives S-0892-0007-05-00001.
6. "Text of Statement by Secretary-General U Thant at Presentation Ceremony of Moon Rock – 20 July 1970," UN Archives S-0891-0007-04-00001.
7. "Text from May 1969," UN Archives S-0891-0006-13-00001, reprinted in Donella H. Meadows, Dennis L. Meadows, Jørgen Randers, and William Behrens III, *The Limits to Growth: A Report for the Club of Rome's Project on the Predicament of Mankind* (Universe Books, 1972).
8. L. Joos, "'Only One Earth': Environmental Perceptions and Policies before the Stockholm Conference, 1968–1972," *Journal of Global History* 18, no. 2 (2023): 281–303.
9. Thant, "Human Environment and World Order," *International Journal of Environmental Studies* 1, no. 1–4: 13–17. This article was based on an address Thant gave at the University of Texas on May 14, 1970.
10. "Conference of International Organization and Human Environment – 21 May 1971," UN Archives S-0885-0001-43-00001.
11. "World Federalists," UN Archives S-0883-0026-10-00002.
12. "Earth Day Ceremony 19 March 1971," UN Archives S-0885-0002-17-00001.
13. "Vietnam – notes on Secretary-General – meetings with Richard Nixon," UN Archives S-0370-0048-01.
14. "Thant Deplores Indo-China War," *Christian Science Monitor*, June 13, 1970.
15. "UNCA Luncheon," UN Archives S-0889-0010-01-00001.
16. "The Manhood Game," *Saturday Review*, May 30, 1970.
17. H. R. Haldeman, diary entry, July 10, 1970. H. R. Haldeman Diaries Collection, US National Archives.
18. Marie Smith, "Tipping the Crystal to Mark UN's 25th Year," *Washington Post*, July 11, 1970.
19. William Beecher, "100 Soviet Pilots Reported in Egypt for Flight Duty," *New York Times*, May 14, 1970.

20. Thant, *View from the UN*, 339.
21. United Nations Press Release No. SG/SM/1326, September 7, 1970.
22. "Paper Prepared by the National Security Council Interdepartmental Group for Africa," December 9, 1969, FRUS 1969–1976, vol. 28, "Southern Africa"; "Memorandum from President Nixon to the President's Assistants (Haldeman), (Ehrlichman) and (Kissinger)," March 2, 1970, FRUS 1969–1976, vol. E–5, Part 1, "Documents on Sub-Saharan Africa, 1969–1972."
23. Yassin El-Ayouty, "The United Nations and Decolonisation, 1960–70," *Journal of Modern African Studies* 8, no. 3 (1970): 462–68.
24. "Text from August 1970," UN Archives S-0891-0007-05-00001.
25. Enuga Reddy, "Reminiscences of the International Campaign Against Apartheid – With Special Reference to the United Nations," unpublished manuscript, available at https://www.sahistory.org.za/archive/reminiscences-international-campaign-against-apartheid-special-reference-united-nations-es.
26. "Introduction to the Report of the Secretary-General on the Work of the Organization, September 1970," UN Archives S-0891-0007-06-00001.
27. "The UN's Madame President," *Ebony* 25, no. 3 (January 1970).
28. "Her Excellency Miss Angie E. Brooks," UN Archives S-0856-0002-05-00001.
29. "South West Africa – Namibia," UN Archives S-0884-0019-05-00001; Christian Rogerson, "A Future University of Namibia?: The Role of the United Nations Institute for Namibia," *Journal of Modern Asian Studies* 18, no. 4 (December 1980).
30. "Introduction to the Report of the Secretary-General on the Work of the Organization, September 1970," UN Archives S-0891-0007-06-00001.
31. "Conversation Between President Nixon and the President's Assistant for National Security Affairs (Kissinger)," September 12, 1970, FRUS 1969–1976, Volume VIII, Vietnam, January–October 1972.
32. "India Irked by U.S. Over Visit Protocol," *New York Times*, October 22, 1970.
33. "General Assembly Statement at Commemorative Session, 23 October 1970," UN Archives S-0885-0003-21-00001.
34. Auberon Waugh, "Man in the Muddle," *Spectator*, November 18, 1970.
35. Ralph Bunche, Letter to the Editor, *Sunday Times*, November 1, 1970; George Brown, *In My Way*, excerpt published in the *Sunday Times*, October 25, 1970.
36. Andrew H. Malcolm, "Thant, 8 Years into a Lonely Job Has Hope and No Complaints," *New York Times*, February 3, 1969.
37. "Family," UN Archives S-0892-0003-09-00001.

CHAPTER 17: BOTH SIDES NOW

1. "General Assembly Statement at Commemorative Session, 23 October 1970," UN Archives S-0885-0003-21-00001.
2. "Notes on Meeting between Secretary-General U Thant and Secretary of State Rogers," January 4, 1971, UN Archives S-0865-0003-04-00001.
3. "Gunnar Jarring (Special Representative of the Secretary-General to the Middle East) reports," UN Archives S-0865-0001-10-00001.
4. "1971," UN Archives S-0865-0003-04-00001.
5. "1971," UN Archives S-0865-0003-04-00001.
6. "Minutes of a Senior Review Group Meeting," FRUS 1969–1976, vol. 23, "Arab–Israeli Dispute, 1969–1972."
7. Thant, *View from the UN*, 346–47; "Aide-Mémoire – 15 February 1971," in "Gunnar Jarring Reports," UN Archives S-0865-0001-10-00001.
8. Charles Yost, "Last Chance for Peace in the Middle East," *Life*, April 9, 1971.
9. "United States of America – Yost, Charles W.," UN Archives S-0882-0005-01-00001.
10. "Record of the Meeting with Secretary of State Rogers," May 17, 1971, UN Archives S-0865-0001-10-00001.
11. "1971," UN Archives S-0865-0003-04-00001; Gershon Shafir, "The Miscarriage of Peace: Israel, Egypt, the United States, and the 'Jarring Plan' in the Early 1970s," *Israel Studies Forum* 21, no. 1 (Summer 2006): 3–26; Finkelstein, *Image and Reality*, 138.
12. "1970," UN Archives S-0865-0003-03-00001.
13. "Action Memorandum from the Assistant Secretary of State for European Affairs (Hillenbrand) to Secretary of State Rogers," May 11, 1971, FRUS 1969–1976, vol. 13, "Soviet Union, October 1970–October 1971."
14. Freemantle, *KGB*, 128.
15. Thant, *View from the UN*, 351–52; "Selected Confidential Reports on the Middle East 1970," UN Archives S-0882-0003-02-00001.
16. "Telegram from the Mission to the United Nations to the Department of State," May 10, 1971, FRUS 1969–1976, vol. 5, "United Nations, 1969–1972."
17. "Memorandum from the President's Assistant for National Security Affairs (Kissinger) to the President's Deputy Assistant for Congressional Relations (Timmons)," June 25, 1970, FRUS 1969–1976, vol. 5, "United Nations, 1969–1972."
18. "Kissinger Telephone Conversations, Mar. 30, 1971," Nixon Presidential Material, UK National Archives.
19. George H. W. Bush, *All the Best, George Bush: My Life in Letters and Other Writings* (Scribner, 1999), 146.
20. "Correspondence – Personal," UN Archives S-0892-0008-02-00001.
21. Thomas W. Oliver, *The United Nations in Bangladesh* (Princeton University Press, 2016), 4.

22. "Selected Confidential Papers on Indo-Pakistan Conflict – April – August 1971," UN Archives S-0868-0001-03-00001.
23. "Transcript of Press Conference by Secretary-General – 3 June 1971," UN Archives S-0891-0007-15-00001.
24. "Secretary-General's Meeting with Representatives of Governments – Confidential, 13 August 1971," UN Archives S-0863-0001-08-00001.
25. "Selected Confidential Papers on Indo-Pakistan Conflict – April – August 1971," UN Archives S-0868-0001-03-00001.
26. "Indo-East Pakistan notes (correspondence between the President of Pakistan and the Secretary-General)," UN Archives S-0868-0001-04-00001.
27. Anthony Mascarenhas, "Genocide," *Sunday Times*, June 13, 1971.
28. Henry Tanner, "UN Aide Confirms '65 View of Thant on Vietnam War," *New York Times*, June 17, 1971.
29. "Memorandum by the Secretary-General to the President of the Security Council – 20 July 1971," UN Archives S-0863-0001-10-00001.
30. Gary J. Bass, *The Blood Telegram: Nixon, Kissinger, and a Forgotten Genocide* (Knopf, 2013), 56–87.
31. "Memorandum from Secretary of State Rogers to President Nixon," FRUS 1969–1976, vol. 11, "South Asia Crisis, 1971"; "Notes on Meeting in Secretary-General's Office," August 9, 1971, UN Archives S-0868-0001-03-00001.
32. "Press Briefings – 2nd Set Headquarters," UN Archives S-0889-0009-03-00001.
33. "Richard Nixon and Ronald W. Reagan on 26 October 1971," Conversation 013-008, RMNL; "Richard Nixon and William P. Rogers on 26 October 1971," Conversation 013-012, RMNL.
34. Eric Paces, "UN Assembly, 104-11, Urges Truce," *New York Times*, December 8, 1971.
35. "Bunche, Ralph J.," UN Archives S-0852-0001-08-00001.
36. Urquhart, *A Life in Peace and War*, 224.
37. Thomas A. Johnson, "Tributes Are Led by Thant and Nixon," *New York Times*, December 10, 1971.
38. "Bunche as 'Idealist and Realist' Mourned by Thant and Wilkins," *New York Times*, December 12, 1971.
39. "Correspondence – Personal," UN Archives S-0892-0008-01-00001.
40. "Telegram from the Mission to the United Nations to the Department of State," December 7, 1971, FRUS 1969–1976, vol. 5, "United Nations, 1969–1972"; "Telegram from the Mission to the United Nations to the Department of State," December 10, 1971, FRUS 1969–1976, vol. 5, "United Nations, 1969–1972."
41. "The Role of the Secretary-General – 16 September 1971," UN Archives S-0891-0013-05-00001.

42. Telephone conversation transcript, December 22, 1971, HAKP, Part III, Series IV, December 17–23, 1971, MS2004.
43. "The Liberation of U Thant," *New York Times*, December 29, 1971.
44. Gideon Rafael, letter to Thant, December 23, 1971, Thant personal papers.

EPILOGUE

1. "U Thant – Office of Special Political Affairs 1972–1975," UN Archives S-1076-0015-01.
2. "UNCTAD – correspondence and clear cables – 1971," UN Archives S-0290-0004-06.
3. Thant, "Looking Back."
4. "U Thant – Office of Special Political Affairs 1972–1975," UN Archives S-1076-0015-01.
5. James Wechsler, "The Man Who Knew Too Much," *New York Post*, April 19, 1975.
6. Sheldon M. Stern, "What JFK Really Said," *Atlantic*, May 2000.

IMAGE CREDITS

4	AP Photo/Marty Lederhandler
15	Thant Myint-U
29	UN Photo
36	Thant Myint-U
67	UN Archives
78	Thant Myint-U
89	UN Photo
105	Thant Myint-U
107	UN New York
127	UN Photo
173	Thant Myint-U
247	White House photographer, Yoichi Okamoto
267	UN Photo
278	UN Photo
306	AP Photo

INDEX

Abdullah (Sheikh of Kashmir), 151
Acheson, Dean, 61, 104, 238, 245
Adebo, S. O., 106
Afro-Asian states
  arms control and, 43, 92
  Bandung Conference, 14–15, 100
  Biafra conflict and, 267, 269
  Chinese UN admission and, 299
  Cold War and, 43, 167
  Congo Crisis and, 19, 29, 30, 31, 38, 39, 87, 126–27
  Cuban Missile Crisis and, 49, 65–66, 76
  Declaration on the Granting of Independence to Colonial Countries and Peoples and, 14–15
  global vision of, 14–15, 76, 120, 167, 255, 264, 271–72, 289, 309–10
  historical invisibility of, 309–10
  Israel and, 20
  revolutionary change in, 82
  Six-Day War and, 207, 264
  solidarity dissipation, 178–79, 207
  southern African white supremacy and, 283, 284
  support for United Nations, 76
  Thant's appointment as Acting Secretary-General and, 21, 22, 24
  Thant's entertaining and, 96
  Thant's ongoing connections with, 237–38, 271
  Thant's policy speeches on, 81
  Thant's second term decision and, 179
  on Third World economic development, 14, 100, 101, 276
  turmoil within, 129
  UNEF withdrawal and, 202
  UN membership, 14, 15, 162–63
  Vietnam War and, 120, 133–34, 138, 172
Aldrin, Edwin, 278
Alekseev, Alexander, 68, 73
Algeria, 16, 21, 22, 101–2, 104, 265
Allende, Salvador, 306
Alsop, Joseph, 219
Amachree, Godfrey, 106–7
Amer, Abdel Hakim, 211, 216
Amit, Meir, 223
Anderson, Elizabeth, 137
Anderson, Rudolf, 70–71
Andrei Gromyko, 99
Angola, 102, 265, 283
Apollo 11 mission, 273–74, 275, 278
Arab-Israeli conflict
  Arab states Khartoum summit (1968), 257
  Big Four negotiations (1969), 260, 261, 262, 263, 264, 290
  Egyptian-Israeli relations, 257, 259, 291
  hijackings, 259–60, 282
  Jarring mission, 258–59, 260–61, 263, 265, 290–92

Arab-Israeli conflict (*continued*)
  occupied territories, 257–58, 261, 262, 263–64, 291–92
  ongoing violence (1969–70), 259–60, 261, 263–64
  Palestinians and, 259, 260, 261
  Rogers initiative, 281–82
  Security Council Resolution 242, 258, 259, 260
  Soviet Union and, 257, 260, 281–82
  Suez Crisis, 17, 198
  Thant's appointment as Acting Secretary-General and, 23
  Thant's views on, 262–63
  Thant as UN ambassador and, 20
  UNEF, 103
  UN observers, 230, 259
  War of Attrition, 281–82
  See also Six-Day War
Arab states
  Khartoum summit (1968), 257
  Thant's appointment as Acting Secretary-General and, 22–23
  Thant as UN ambassador and, 20
  See also Arab-Israeli conflict
Arkadev, Georgy, 27
arms control, 15, 43, 91–92
Armstrong, Neil, 273–74, *278*
Auden, W. H., 285
Aung San Suu Kyi, 158

Baez, Joan, 3
Ball, George, 53, 252
Bandung Conference (1955), 14–15, 100
Bangladesh Liberation War (1971), 295–96, 297–98, 303
Bay of Pigs, 46
Belgium
  Congo Crisis and, 28, 30, 38–39, 125, 126–27
  Vietnam War and, 240–41
Belgrade conference (1960), 18
Ben Bella, Ahmed, 102, 138, 139, 265
Ben-Gurion, David, 20
Benjamin, Robert, 95
Bérard, Armand, 22
Berlin crisis, 18, 40–41, 43
Bernstein, Leonard, 3

Berry, Winston, 270–71
Bhutto, Zulfiqar Ali, 152, 153, 154, 156, 159–60
Biafra conflict, 264–71, 267, 269, 286, 303
Black, Eugene, 143
Black, Shirley Temple, 281
Blacklock, Josephine, 231
Boland, Patrick, 16
Borman, Frank, 274
Borneo, 141
Bradley, Omar, 246
Brahimi, Lakhdar, 16
Brezhnev, Leonid, 55, 123, 167, 177, 241
Brinkley, David, 118
Brooks, Angie, 284, 307
Brown, George, 241–42, 287
Brown, Pat, 118, 142
Brynner, Yul, 124
Buddhism, 34–35, *105*, 154, 156, 195, 250, 281
Bull, Odd, 212, 227, 259
Bunche, Ralph, *29*
  antiwar movement and, 195
  Arab-Israeli conflict and, 281
  civil rights movement and, 126
  Congo Crisis and, 33
  death of, 300–301
  health issues, 183, 231, 290
  Indo-Pakistani War and, 153, 157–58, 159, 160
  Jarring mission and, 258
  JFK assassination and, 99
  JFK UN General Assembly address (1963) and, 98
  Johnson administration and, 139
  King assassination and, 248
  Six-Day War and, 208–9, 216, 218, 219, 222, 224, 231
  Thant-Johnson Vietnam War discussions and, 246, *247*
  Thant's dependence on, 174, 271, 300
  Thant-Senate Foreign Relations Committee meeting and, 194
  Thant's entertaining and, 96, 97, 180, 305
  Thant's Nobel Peace Prize nomination and, 162
  as Thant's peacekeeping chief, 26–27

as Thant's political advisor, 88, 91, 103
Thant's second term and, 177–78, 183, 184, 187
Thant state dinner and, 281
Thant's UFO fascination and, 231
Thant's Vietnam War international diplomatic mission and, 243, 244
Thant's Vietnam War press conference (1967) and, 186
Thant's Vietnam War stand-still truce proposal and, 191–92
2001: A Space Odyssey and, 250
UNEF withdrawal and, 200, 201, 202, 203, 204, 205, 221, 229, 230, 287
UN twenty-fifth anniversary and, 143
US-Hanoi negotiation initiative and, 130, 183
Vietnam War and, 114, 116, 118, 136
Yemen Civil War and, 90–91
Bundy, McGeorge
Cuban Missile Crisis and, 51, 54, 55
Vietnam War and, 115–17, 119, 131–32, 167–68, 169–70
Yemen Civil War and, 90
Bunker, Ellsworth, 89–90
Burma
Cold War and, 18–19, 24
political struggles, 108, 129, 274–75, 308
post-independence civil war, 28–29, 242
Thant's burial and, 307–8
Thant's childhood in, 77–78
Thant's visit to (1964), 108–9
US military assistance to, 135, 136, 145
Bush, George H. W., 278, 292, 293, 294–95, 298, 300

Cambodia, 256, 279, 293, 303
Canada
UNEF withdrawal and, 205, 206, 207, 221, 224
Vietnam War and, 111, 122, 123
Caradon, Lord (Hugh Foot), 140, 216, 257
Casals, Pablo, 285
Castro, Fidel
Cuban Missile Crisis escalation threats, 49, 58–59
Cuban Missile Crisis speech, 70, 72–73
gift to Thant, 96
Soviet military assistance and, 46
Thant's Cuba trip and, 62, 63, 66–68, 67, 69–71
Central Intelligence Agency (CIA), 181, 182, 236
Chen Yi, 188
Chiang Kai-Shek, 298
China
Bangladesh Liberation War and, 300
Cultural Revolution, 187
Indo-Pakistani War and, 149, 150, 159
nuclear test ban treaty (1963) and, 91
Soviet relations with, 121, 123, 133, 167, 177
Thant's successor and, 301
UN membership, 19, 298–300
US relations with, 298
See also Chinese role in Vietnam War
Chinese role in Vietnam War
Burma invasion, 240–41
escalation and, 187, 188
Hanoi-Chinese discussions, 121–22
military aid to Hanoi, 146
Sino-Soviet relations and, 121, 123, 133, 167, 177
Thant-Johnson discussions on, 116, 117
Thant's international diplomatic mission (1968) and, 240–41, 244
Thant's outreach, 139
Thant's stand-still truce proposal and, 190–91, 192
Three Point Proposal and, 175
US policy and, 145
Chomsky, Noam, 238
Chou En-lai, 8, 121–22, 190–91
Church, Frank, 1, 193
Churchill, Winston, 9
Clark, Joseph, 192
Clarke, Adele, 64
Clarke, Arthur C., 250
Cleveland, Harlan, 83–84, 116, 130, 131, 135
Clifford, Clark, 238, 242
Cohen, Samuel, 137
Cold War
Afro-Asian states on, 43, 167
Arab-Israeli conflict and, 282, 283
arms race, 46

Cold War (*continued*)
　Bandung Conference on, 14–15
　Bangladesh Liberation War and, 296
　Burma and, 18–19, 24
　Cuban Missile Crisis and, 76
　détente possibilities, 76, 260
　Indo-Pakistani War and, 149
　Kissinger on, 82–83, 282, 283
　non-aligned states and, 18
　Thant's appointment as Acting Secretary-General and, 5, 18
　Thant's policy speeches on, 81–82
　UN establishment and, 13
　Vietnam War and, 112–13
　Western international interventions and, 173
　See also arms control
Collins, Michael, *278*
colonialism, 13, 14–15, 16, 81, 112, 268
　Burma, 78
　Indo-Pakistani War and, 147
　Nigeria and, 265
　See also decolonization; racism/white supremacy; southern African white supremacy
"Concert for Bangladesh, A," 298
Congo Crisis, 28–34
　Burmese position, 19
　Hammarskjöld and, 11, 17, 28
　Stanleyville rebellion, 125, 126–27
　Thant-JFK discussions, 43
　Thant-Khrushchev meeting and, 42
　Thant's negotiation attempts, 33
　UN exit strategies, 88, 103
　United Kingdom and, 28, 30–31, 38, 125, 126–27
　UN peacekeeping operation (ONUC), 30–31, 34, 68, 83–84, 85–86, *89*
　UN Security Council resolution on, 29–30
　U Thant Plan (federalization), 38–39, 83, 88
Cordier, Andrew, 17, 21, 60
Cousins, Norman, 2, 3, 4, 138, 170–71, 180, 271, 280
Cousteau, Jacques, 1, 3
Cranston, Alan, 256
Cripps, Stafford, 80

criticisms of Thant
　Biafra conflict and, 268–69, 286
　racism and, 228, 236, 270–71
　Six-Day War and, 219–20, 223, 227–28, 229–31, 232–33, 286, 287
　See also US relationship with Thant
Cronkite, Walter, 118, 245
Crowe, Colin, 301
Cuba
　Bay of Pigs, 46
　Che Guevara assassination plot, 127–28
　See also Cuban Missile Crisis
Cuban Missile Crisis, 43, 45–76
　appreciation for Thant, 75
　escalation threats, 58–59, 60–61
　Ilyushin bombers, 74
　international responses, 63–64
　JFK bombing/invasion proposals, 46–47
　JFK speech, 48
　missile site dismantling, 68–69, 71, 72
　non-aligned states and, 49, 50–51, 57, 65–66, 67, 76
　perceptions of JFK's inexperience and, 45–46
　reconnaissance photographs, 47, 56, 57
　Thant Plan (missiles for non-invasion), 51–52, 55, 58, 59–60, 61–62, 68
　Thant's appointment as Secretary-General and, 75
　Thant's call for shipment halt, 53–57
　Thant's Cuba trip, 62, 63, 64, 65–72, 67, 73
　Thant's historical invisibility and, 6
　Thant's mediation, 73, 75
　Thant's policy speeches on, 81–82
　U-2 spy plane incident and, 60
　UN presence proposals, 68, 69, 70, 71, 74
　UN Security Council meetings, 48, 49, 51–53, 56–57
　US aerial reconnaissance, 47, 56, 57, 60, 63, 65, 70–71, 72, 74
　US blockade, 47, 48, 49, 52, 53, 58, 63, 72, 74
　US missiles in Turkey and Italy and, 46, 47, 59–60, 61, 62
Cyprus, 103–4, 237
Czechoslovakia, 251–52

Index

Dalai Lama, 3
Daley, Richard, 114–15
Dangeard, Alain, 189, 194
Dayan, Moshe, 206
Dean, Patrick, 96
decolonization
   Afro-Asian global vision and, 14–15, 120, 167, 255, 264, 265
   civil wars and, 28–29, 265
   Congo Crisis and, 84
   India, 81
   ongoing struggles, 265
   revolutionary change and, 82
   secessionist movements and, 39, 267–68
   Thant on, 16, 39, 285
   Zambia, 84
   See also colonization
de Gaulle, Charles, 17, 112, 175, 188–89, 243, 245
dependency theory, 101
Derwinski, Edward, 137
Dirksen, Everett, 219
Dobrynin, Anatoly, 60, 61, 62, 290
Dominican Republic, 142, 144
Dood, Chris, 30
Dorticós Torrado, Osvaldo, 67, 69
Douglas-Home, Alec, 91–92, 112, 219
Dubček, Alexander, 251
Duke, Angier Biddle, 114
Dylan, Bob, 298

Earth Day, 278
"East-West Relations and the United Nations" (Thant), 81–82
Eban, Abba
   Big Four negotiations and, 261
   hijackings and, 259–60
   occupied territories and, 262
   Six-Day War and, 208, 213, 217, 219, 220, 228–29
   Thant's friendship with, 20
Ecker, Frederick, 9
Egypt
   Cuban Missile Crisis and, 49, 52
   Thant's appointment as Acting Secretary-General and, 23
   Thant as UN ambassador and, 20
   UNEF withdrawal request, 197–99, 201–7, 208, 209, 212, 213, 221, 223, 224
   Yemen Civil War and, 89, 90, 201
   See also Afro-Asian states; Arab-Israeli conflict; Six-Day War
Eisenhower, Dwight D., 19, 45–46
Elizabeth (queen of England), 37–38
environmentalism, 276–79, 286
Eshkol, Levi, 199, 206, 217, 219, 220, 221, 226
Estabrook, Robert, 269
Ethiopia, 138, 265

Falle, Sam, 103
Fanfani, Antonio, 211–12
Fatah, 260
Faure, Edgar Jean, 127, 133
Fawzi, Mohammed, 23
Fawzy, Muhammad, 197–98, 214
Federenko, Nikolai, 96, 120, 125, 160, 167, 216, 230
Fleming, Ian, 124
Forman, Milos, 251
France
   Arab-Israeli conflict and, 260
   Biafra conflict and, 265
   colonialism and, 16, 22
   Congo Crisis and, 30
   Hammarskjöld and, 17
   Indochina and, 112
   nuclear test ban treaty (1963) and, 91
   nuclear testing, 15
   protests (1968), 250
   relationship with Thant, 104–5
   Thant's 1964 visit, 112
   Thant's appointment as Acting Secretary-General and, 22, 23
   Thant's successor and, 301
   Vietnam War and, 112, 116, 144, 170, 175, 188–89, 243, 245
Frazier, James, 274
Frederick, Pauline, 181, 186
Frye, William R., 134
Fulbright, William, 91, 115, 171, 177, 192, 193
Fuller, Buckminster, 3
Furnivall, J. S., 80

Gagarin, Yuri, 99
Gage-Colby, Ruth, 64, 73, 114
Gandhi, Indira, 195, 241, 286, 296
Gandhi, Mohandas, 81, 85, 126
Garcia Inchaustegui, Mario, 67
Gardiner, Robert, 33–34, 86
Genocide Convention, 16
Ghana
   Congo Crisis and, 19, 30, 87
   Cuban Missile Crisis and, 49, 52
   military coup, 172
   Thant's appointment as Acting Secretary-General and, 21, 22
Gheorghiu-Dej, Gheorghe, 52–53
Ginsberg, Allen, 238
Glass, Leslie (U Hman), 140–41
Glenn, John, 43
Goldberg, Arthur
   appointment of, 145–46
   Indo-Pakistani War and, 159
   occupied territories and, 257
   papal US visit and, 161
   resignation of, 248
   Six-Day War and, 203, 205, 208, 219
   Thant's retirement and, 1
   Thant's second term decision and, 177–78, 183
   UNEF withdrawal and, 203, 205
   Vietnam War and, 169, 171, 174, 243, 246, 247, 248
Golden Bough, The (Frazier), 274
Goldwater, Barry, 111, 114, 124
Gore, Albert, 193
Goulert, Joao, 95
Gowan, Yakubu, 268
Grace (Princess of Monaco), 124
Greece
   Cyprus and, 103–4
Greene, Felix, 168, 174, 193
Gromyko, Andrei, 23, 55, 75, 91, 92, 125
Gross, Ernest, 229–30
Guevara, Che, 127–28
Gueye, Youssouf, 106
Gulf of Tonkin resolution, 114, 119, 131

Haessler, Lucy, 137
Haile Selassie I (Emperor of Ethiopia), 138, 265, 266, 267, 269
Haldeman, H. R., 256, 281

Hammarskjöld, Dag
   Arab-Israeli conflict and, 261
   Bunche and, 27
   communication style of, 34
   death of, 11–12, 17–18, 162, 266
   press relationships, 35
   superpower mediation and, 48
   UNEF and, 202, 229–30
   UN headquarters and, 97
   UN Secretary-Generalship and, 16–17, 23, 26, 28, 34, 173
Hammerstein, Dorothy, 1
Harmel, Pierre, 241–42
Harriman, Averell, 117, 169–70, 248
Harrison, George, 298
Hassan II (king of Morocco), 101
Hatfield, Mark, 256
Ha Van Lau, 189–90, 191, 193
Hayworth, Rita, 124
Hearst, William Randolph, 95
Heath, Edward, 290
Helms, Richard, 223
Heyerdahl, Thor, 3, 277
Hillary, Edmund, 3
Hinchingbrooke, Viscount (Victor Montagu), 31
Hiroshima/Nagasaki bombings, 111, 114
Hoare, Michael "Mad Mike," 125
Ho Chi Minh
   Democratic Republic of Vietnam founding and, 112
   fading influence of (1967), 188
   Thant as chief adviser to U Nu and, 9
   Thant communications with, 168–69, 174, 182–83, 193
   Thant's estimate of, 116
   US-Hanoi negotiation initiative and, 120, 121
   on US "peace offensive," 170
Hoffman, Abbie, 238
humanitarian crises, 265, 268–69, 276, 297–98, 303
Humphrey, Hubert, 91, 92, 254
Hussein (King of Jordan), 223, 226–27, 228, 261–62, 282
Hynek, J. Allen, 250

Ignatieff, George, 202, 205
"Imagine" (Lennon), 4

Index | 357

India
  Bangladesh Liberation War and, 295–96, 298, 300
  Cuban Missile Crisis and, 49, 63–64
  decolonization, 81
  Thant's appointment as Acting Secretary-General and, 22
  UN twenty-fifth anniversary and, 286
  Vietnam War and, 195, 241
  See also Indo-Pakistani War
Indonesia
  Congo Crisis and, 84
  Malaysia and, 133, 141
  military coup, 173
  Papua New Guinea and, 33, 39, 267
  Thant's appointment as Acting Secretary-General and, 22
Indo-Pakistani War, 147–60
  Jawaharlal Nehru Award for International Understanding to Thant and, 195, 305
  origins of, 147–48
  summit proposal, 157–59, 160
  Thant's appeal, 148–50
  Thant's mediation mission, 150–58
  UN observers, 160
  UN Security Council ceasefire resolutions, 150, 159
International Control Commission (ICC), 122
International Red Cross, 63, 72, 268
Iran, 149, 151
Iraq, 20, 223
Ireland, 38
Israel
  Soviet Jewish émigrés and, 292
  Thant's relationship with, 20, 220
  US commitment to, 257
  West Bank settlements, 264
  See also Arab-Israeli conflict; Six-Day War
Italy, 250

Jahn, Gunnar, 162, 182
Jarring, Gunnar, 258–59, 260–61, 263, 264, 281, 282, 290–92, 300, 301
Jarvis, Jacob, 256
Jhabvala, Darius S., 270
Johnson, Lady Bird, 115, 117, 119

Johnson, Lynda Bird, 142
Johnson, Lyndon B., and administration, 43
  Bunche's relationship with, 139
  civil rights and, 114–15
  Congo Crisis and, 125
  Cyprus and, 104
  Gulf of Tonkin resolution and, 114, 119, 131
  Harriman negotiation proposal, 142–43
  Indo-Pakistani War and, 148, 149–50, 155, 159
  international interventions and, 142, 172, 173
  JFK assassination and, 100
  Johns Hopkins Vietnam War speech, 139–40
  nomination withdrawal (1968), 246
  papal US visit and, 160–61
  "peace offensive," 169–70, 171
  Pentagon Papers on, 297
  relationship with Thant, 129, 134–36, 144, 145, 146, 159, 166, 176, 207, 228
  Six-Day War and, 207, 208, 218–19, 223, 228
  Thant's second term decision and, 178, 182–83
  Thant's Vietnam War international diplomatic mission and, 242–45
  Thant Vietnam War discussions, 115–19, 142–43, 246–47, 247
  UNEF withdrawal and, 203, 205–6
  UN twentieth anniversary and, 141–42
  Vietnam War Canadian communications and, 123
  Vietnam War seven-state meeting proposal and, 133–34, 135
  Vietnam War stand-still truce proposal and, 192–93
  Vietnam War Three Point Proposal and, 175–76, 178
  See also US-Hanoi negotiation initiative; US Vietnam War military engagement
Jordan
  Palestinians and, 259, 282
  Six-Day War and, 223, 226–27, 228

Kashmir. *See* Indo-Pakistani War; Kashmir UN observation mission
Kashmir UN observation mission, 103, 147

Kaunda, Kenneth, 84, 265
Keating, Kenneth, 286
Keita, Modibo, 63
Kennedy, Edward, 177
Kennedy, Ethel, 249
Kennedy, Jacqueline, 1, *127*, 133, 161, 226, 238
Kennedy, John F., and administration, 19, 20
  assassination of, 99–100, 249
  Bay of Pigs and, 46
  Berlin crisis and, 41
  Congo Crisis and, 30, 31, 32–33, 43, 83
  Indonesia and, 33, 39
  relationship with Thant, 20, 39, 75
  space exploration and, 43, 98
  UN General Assembly address (1963), 98–99
  UN funding and, 27
  world peace speech, 91
  Yemen Civil War and, 89
  See also Cuban Missile Crisis
Kennedy, Robert F., 60, 61, 62, 192, 249
Kent State shooting (1970), 280
Kenya, 14, 138, 265
Kenyatta, Jomo, 138, 265
Khan, Mohammed Ayub, 148, 152–53, 154–55, 156–57, 160
Khan, Yahya, 296, 297
Khin Kyi, 158
Khrushchev, Nikita
  Berlin crisis and, 40–41
  Cuban Missile Crisis and, 45, 52–53, 54, 58–60, 62, 70, 73, 74
  Eisenhower meeting proposal, 19
  nuclear test ban treaty (1963) and, 92
  overthrow of, 122–23
  Thant as chief adviser to U Nu and, 8–9
  Thant meeting (1962), 39–42
  Thant's 1964 Moscow visit and, *107*, 112
  Thant's appointment as Secretary-General and, 75
  Thant's policy speeches on, 81
  on UN Secretary-Generalship, 21
  Vietnam War and, 120, 167
King, Coretta Scott, 3, 126
King, Martin Luther, Jr.
  assassination of, 247–48, 249
  decolonization movements and, 84
  Nobel Peace Prize, 105
  Six-Day War and, 223
  Thant's meeting with, 126
  Vietnam War and, 137–38, 195
Kissinger, Henry
  Arab-Israeli conflict and, 263, 282, 283, 291, 292
  Bunche's death and, 300
  Cold War and, 82–83, 282, 283
  Nixon election and, 255
  Nixon UN General Assembly speech and, 256
  Paris Peace Talks and, 254, 256, 293
  southern African white supremacy and, 283
  Thant state dinner and, 281
  UN twenty-fifth anniversary and, 285
  US relations with China and, 298
  US relationship with Thant and, 294
  Vietnam War and, 281
Kony, Mohammed El-, 200, 201, 203, 204, 208–9, 221–22, 223
Kosciusko-Morizet, Jacques, 301
Kosygin, Alexei
  accession to power, 123
  Cuban Missile Crisis and, 55
  Indo-Pakistani War and, 160
  Six-Day War and, 228
  Thant's second term decision and, 177
  Vietnam War and, 132, 167, 241
Krohg, Per, 51
Kubrick, Stanley, 250
Kutakov, Leonid, 292
Kuznetsov, Vasily, 55, 58, 62, 63, 73, 75

Labouisse, Henry, 268
Lambro, Phillip, 98
Landry, Lionel, 271
Laos, 139, 145, 293
Latin American states, 101
  See also non-aligned states
League of Nations, 25, 224
Lebanon, 103
Le Corbusier, 25
Le Duan, 193
Lee Kuan Yew, 237–38
Lemay, Curtis, 143
Lemieux, Lucien, 209, 211

Lennon, John, 1, 2, 4, *4*, 302
Lessiovski, Victor, 2, 57–58, 292, 293
Lewis, Anthony, 269
Liberia, 284
Lie, Trygve, 162
Lindsay, John, 273, 301, 306
Linner, Sture, 34
Linowitz, Sol, 124
Lippmann, Walter, 1, 132
Lodge, Henry Cabot, 118, 119, 146, 238
Lorning, Edith, 64
Loutfi, Omar
  appointment as Thant's chief political advisor, 27
  Cuban Missile Crisis and, 48, 49, 65, 66, 68, 69, 76
  death of, 88–89, 174
  Thant's appointment as Acting Secretary-General and, 23
  as Thant's close colleague, 12, 20
  Thant as UN ambassador and, 12
Loves of a Blonde, 251
Loy, Myrna, 2
Lumumba, Patrice, 11, 17, 28

MacMillan, Harold, 31, 38, 52, 95
Maharishi Yoga, 239–40
Mahasi Sayadaw, 37
Mailer, Norman, 238
Mai Van Bo, 144, 242, 243, 248
Malawi (Nyasaland), 14
Malaysia, 133, 141
Malik, Yakov, 301
Malinovsky, Rodion, 46
Malley, Simon, 174
Malraux, André, 175
Mandela, Nelson, 265
Mansfield, Mike, 131, 177
Mao Tse-tung, 8, 120, 121–22, 167
Marin, Miguel, 66
Martin, Manuel, 69
Martin, Paul, 111, 123, 206
Mau Mau massacres, 14
Maxwell, Elsa, 95
McCain, John, 48
McCarthy, Eugene, 193
McCloy, John J., 71–72, 73, 75
McDonald, James E., 232

McGovern, George, 177, 256
McHenry, William H., 64
McNamara, Robert
  resignation of, 239
  Six-Day War and, 217, 223
  Vietnam War and, 119, 131, 165, 167–68, 169, 170, 239, 243, 297
Meir, Golda, 20, 22, 261, 262, 291
Menuhin, Yehudi, 3
Meredith, Burgess, 2
Meulemeester, Pierre de, 97
Middle East. *See* Arab-Israeli conflict
Mikoyan, Anastas, 55, 73, 75
Miller, Arthur, 3
Mokhtar, Eiz-El-Din, 198
Mondale, Walter, 256
Morgenthau, Hans, 82
Morocco, 101
Morozov, Alexander, 55, 56
Moses, Robert, 120–21
Mountbatten, Lord (Louis Mountbatten), 158
Moyers, Bill, 134, 139
Mozambique, 265, 283
Muskie, Edmund, 256
Myint-U, Tyn, 42
My Lai massacre, 280
Myrdal, Alva, 182

Namibia, 265, 284
Nan Thaung (Thant's mother), 77, 79, *105*
Narasimhan, C. V.
  appointment as Thant's *chef de cabinet*, 27
  Che Guevara assassination plot and, 127–28
  Cuban Missile Crisis and, 47, 61, 76
  death of Thant's son and, 37
  Earth Day and, 278
  Six-Day War and, 230
  Thant's death and, 307
  Thant's dependence on, 174
  Thant's entertaining and, 96, 180, 237, 305
  Thant's Nobel Peace Prize nomination and, 162
  Thant's second term decision and, 182
  Thant's Vietnam War press conference (1967) and, 186

Nasser, Gamal Abdel, *15*
  criticisms of Thant, 231
  death of, 290
  Indo-Pakistani War and, 149
  Six-Day War buildup and, 206, 209, 211–12, 214–16, 217, 218, 221, 223–24
  Thant's appointment as Acting Secretary-General and, 22
  UNEF withdrawal, 201, 202, 203, 204, 207, 213–14, 224
  Vietnam War and, 138
  Yemen Civil War and, 89
Nassif, Ramses
  Cuban Missile Crisis and, 65, 69
  Czechoslovakia invasion and, 251–52
  death of Thant's son and, 37
  Indo-Pakistani War and, 150
  Six-Day War and, 211, 212, 217
  Thant's appointment as Acting Secretary-General and, 23–24
  UNEF withdrawal and, 200, 203, 204
National Association for the Advancement of Colored People (NAACP), 301
Nehru, Jawaharlal, *15*, 19, 63–64, 81, 130, 207
Nesterenko, Alexei, 218, 231
Netherlands, 33, 39
Ne Win, 108, 131, 274, 308
Nguyen Cao Ky, 171
Nguyen Hoa, 241
Nicaragua, 128
Nicolson, Nigel, 184, 232
Nielsen, Sievert, 162
Niemeyer, Oscar, 25
Nigeria-Biafra conflict, 264–71, 286
Nimmo, Robert, 147, 148, 149, 156, 159, 160
Nixon, Richard, and administration
  Arab-Israeli conflict and, 260, 261–62, 263, 291, 292
  Cambodia bombing, 256
  Cambodia invasion, 279, 280
  election of, 251, 254, 255
  Nixon UN General Assembly speech, 256
  southern African white supremacy and, 283
  Thant's retirement decision and, 295

Thant state dinner, 280–81
  UN twenty-fifth anniversary and, 285
  US relations with China and, 298
  US relationship with Thant and, 264, 285–86, 294
  Vietnam War and, 255–56
  Vietnam War military engagement, 255–56
Nkrumah, Kwame, *15*, 22, 30, 87, 138, 149, 172, 207
Noel-Baker, Philip, 181
non-aligned states
  arms control and, 92
  Belgrade conference (1960), 18
  Cuban Missile Crisis and, 49, 50–51, 57, 65–66, 67, 76
  Indo-Pakistani War and, 149
  military coups and, 172–73
  Six-Day War and, 230
  Thant's appointment as Acting Secretary-General and, 22
  Thant's policy speeches on, 81
  Vietnam War and, 112, 138, 172
Noronha, Reggie, 85, 86
North Atlantic Treaty Organization (NATO), 104, 175
Northern Rhodesia. *See* Zambia
Norway, 38
Nu, U, 8, 22, 274–75
nuclear arms, 15, 18, 43, 91–92, 111, 207
  See also arms control
Nyerere, Julius, 125, 265

Ojukwu, Chukwuemeka, 266, 269, 270
Olav (king of Sweden), 38
Onassis, Jacqueline Kennedy. *See* Kennedy, Jacqueline
Only One Earth: The Care and Maintenance of a Small Planet (Ward), 277
Ono, Yoko, 1, 2, *4*
ONUC (UN Congo peacekeeping operation), 30–31, 34, 68, 83–84, 85–86, *89*
Organization of African Unity, 266
Ormsby-Gore, David, 31
Orwell, George, 80

Pachachi, Adnan, 20
Pakistan. *See* Bangladesh Liberation War; Indo-Pakistani War

Palestinians
  Jarring mission and, 259, 261
  Jordan revolution attempt, 282
  ongoing violence (1969–70) and, 259–60, 261
  Thant on, 260
Pandit, Vijaya Lakshmi, 13
Papua New Guinea, 33, 39, 267
Paris Peace Talks (1968), 248–49, 252, 254, 256, 293
Paul VI (Pope), 160–62
Pauling, Linus, 3, 223
Pearson, Drew, 248, 250, 252–53
Pearson, Lester, 99, 111
Peck, Gregory, 118
Pell, Claiborne, 256
Pentagon Papers, 297
Peter, Paul, and Mary, 119
Pham Van Dong, 121, 123, 188
Phenomenon of Man, The (Teilhard de Chardin), 274
Platz, Hannah, 66
Pliyev, Issa, 58, 59, 62
Po Hnit (Thant's father), 77, 79
Pompidou, George, 175, 290
Portugal, 265, 283, 284
Prague Spring (1968), 251
Prebisch, Raul, 101
Prem Chand, Dewan, 85, 86
Preto, Luis, 63

Quaison-Sackey, Alex, 12, 48, 96–97, 106, 127–28, 127, 133
Quinn, Sally, ?

Rabin, Yitzak, 213, 217
racism/white supremacy
  Afro-Asian opposition to, 14, 283, 284
  Biafra conflict and, 265–66, 269–70
  Chinese UN admission and, 299
  Congo Crisis and, 28, 31, 126–27
  criticisms of Thant and, 228, 236, 270–71
  Hammarskjöld's death and, 266
  nuclear arms and, 111
  southern Africa, 14, 102, 265, 283
  Thant's Algerian speech on, 102–3
  Thant's position as Secretary-General and, 130

UN diplomats and staff and, 9, 41, 106–8
  UN establishment and, 13
Radhakrishnan, Saravepalli, 154, 156, 158, 195
Rafael, Gideon
  criticisms of Thant and, 231
  Six-Day War buildup and, 208, 217–18, 222
  Thant's relationship with, 220
  Thant's retirement and, 302
  UNEF withdrawal and, 201, 203, 206
Rahman, Sheikh Mujib, 297
Rahman, Tunku Abdul, 296–97
Rapacki, Adam, 188
Reagan, Ronald, 299
Reston, James, 224
Rhodesia, 265, 283, 284
Riad, Mahmoud, 204, 212, 213
Rikhye, Indar Jit, 29
  background of, 85
  Congo Crisis and, 34, 85, 86
  Cuban Missile Crisis and, 47–48, 61, 65, 66, 68, 69, 72, 76
  Six-Day War and, 212, 213, 214, 216, 224, 225–26
  UNEF withdrawal and, 197–99, 200, 201, 203, 209
Rivers, Mendel, 186
Roa, Raul, 66, 67, 69
Rockefeller, David, 306
Rockefeller, John D., 1, 180
Rockefeller, Nelson, 1, 3, 95, 273, 300–301
Rogers, William
  appointment of, 255
  Arab-Israeli conflict and, 260, 263, 290, 291, 292
  Bangladesh Liberation War and, 298
Rooney, John, 239
Roosevelt, Eleanor, 20, 33
Roosevelt, Franklin D., 13, 303
Rössel, Agda, 16, 63, 97, 174, 295
Rossides, Zanon, 50
Rubin, Jerry, 238
Rusk, Dean
  arms control and, 91, 92
  British views on Vietnam War and, 186
  Bunche's relationship with, 139
  Congo Crisis and, 86–87

Rusk, Dean (*continued*)
   Cuban Missile Crisis and, 47, 50, 52
   Indo-Pakistani War and, 149–50
   Johnson's White House dinner for Thant and, 118, 119
   relationship with Thant, 90, 145, 166, 176, 207, 228, 236, 253–54, 294
   Six-Day War and, 217, 218
   Thant-Johnson Vietnam War discussions and, 116
   Thant's second term decision and, 178
   UNEF withdrawal and, 203
   UN funding and, 27
   US-Hanoi secret negotiation initiative and, 117, 130–31, 133, 135, 166, 168, 183, 236
   Vietnam War military engagement and, 167–68, 170, 253
   Vietnam War San Antonio formula and, 244
   Vietnam War stand-still truce proposal and, 192, 193
   Vietnam War Three Point Proposal and, 175–76, 178
Russell, Bertrand, 64, 80

Sadat, Anwar, 200, 290, 291, 292
Saddrudin Aga Khan, Prince, 296–97
Salaam, Saeb, *15*
Salisbury, Marquess of (Robert Gascoyne-Cecil), 31
Saudi Arabia, 89
Saw Lwin, 43
Schlesinger, Arthur, 32
Seaborn, J. Blair, 122, 123
Seeger, Pete, 1, 3, 302
Sellers, Peter, 124
Serling, Rod, 124
Sevareid, Eric, 144, 165–66, 168
Seydoux, Roger, 188, 189, 192
Shankar, Ravi, 298
Sharif, Omar, 124
Sharkaway, Ibrahim, 197, 199
Shastri, Lal Bahadur, 138, 148, 150, 156–57, 160
Sidney, Hugh, 246
Sihanouk, Norodom (Prince of Cambodia), 22, 256, 279

Sinatra, Frank, 97, 98
Sisco, Joe, 218–19
Sisco, Joseph, 56
Six-Day War (1967), 196, 199–231
   Afro-Asian states and, 207, 264
   beginning of, 224–25
   buildup to, 206, 207–9, 211, 217–18, 221–23
   criticisms of Thant and, 219–20, 223, 227–28, 229–31, 232–33
   early signs of, 199–200
   progress of, 226–27, 230
   territorial results of, 227, 230
   Thant Egypt mission, 208–9, 211–17, 219
   UNEF vulnerability and, 224–26
   UNEF withdrawal, 197–99, 201–7, 208, 209, 212, 213, 221, 223, 224, 228–29, 287
   UN General Assembly emergency session, 228–29
   UN observers, 230
   UN Security Council and, 207–8, 216–17, 218, 222, 227, 230
   US policies, 218–19
Slim, Mongi, 9, 12, 22, 35
Smuts, Christian, 13
Snow, C. P., 3
South Africa, 14, 102, 265, 283–84
southern African white supremacy, 14, 102, 265, 283–85
Soviet Union
   Arab-Israeli conflict and, 257, 260, 281–82
   Bangladesh Liberation War and, 300
   Berlin crisis and, 18, 40–41
   Biafra conflict and, 265
   Chinese relations with, 121, 123, 133, 167, 177
   Congo Crisis and, 11, 17, 39, 42
   Czechoslovakia invasion (1968), 251–52
   Eisenhower-Khrushchev meeting proposal, 19
   Hammarskjöld and, 17
   Indo-Pakistani War and, 148, 149, 150, 158, 160
   intelligence, 2, 120, 292
   Jewish émigrés, 292–93

Khmer Rouge and, 279
Khrushchev overthrow, 122–23
nuclear test ban treaty (1963) and, 91–92
nuclear testing, 18
Six-Day War and, 205, 221, 228, 230
space exploration and, 99
Thant-Khrushchev meeting (1962), 39–42
Thant's 1964 Moscow visit, *107*, 112
Thant's appointment as Acting Secretary-General and, 21, 22, 23
Thant's appointment as Secretary-General and, 75
Thant's attitude toward, 40
Thant's second term decision and, 177
Thant's successor and, 301
UN funding and, 123, 125, 130, 132–33
on UN Secretary-Generalship, 21
US Dominican Republic intervention and, 142
US-Hanoi negotiation initiative and, 120, 123, 132
Vietnam War and, 112, 123, 132, 136–37, 167, 177, 241, 254
See also Cold War; Cuban Missile Crisis
Sow, Adam Malick, 106
space exploration, 43, 98, 99, 273–74, 275, 278
Spock, Benjamin, 195
Starr, Ringo, 298
Steiner, Rolf, 265–66
Steingart, June, 37
Stern, Sheldon, 309
Stetsenko, Igor, 69, 72
Stevenson, Adlai
  appointment of, 19–20
  Congo Crisis and, 31, 32–33, 83–84
  Cuban Missile Crisis and, 48–49, 50, 52, 54, 56–57, 61, 71–72, 73, 74, 75
  death of, 144, 165–66, 174
  entertaining and, 105
  Johnson presidency and, 100
  nuclear test ban treaty and, 91
  Thant-Johnson Vietnam War discussions and, 114, 116, 117
  Thant's appointment as Acting Secretary-General and, 23

  Thant's entertaining and, 97, *127*
  UN twentieth anniversary and, 142
  US relationship with Thant and, 20, 90, 136, 144
  Vietnam War seven-state meeting proposal and, 133–34
  See also US-Hanoi negotiation initiative
Stewart, Michael, 151, 186–87
St. John, Jill, 98
Suez Crisis (1955), 17, 198
Sukarno, *15*, 22, 84, 172, 207
Sulzberger, Cyrus, 219
Suslov, Vladimir, 120, 125, 136–37
Sweden, 284
Syria, 282
  See also Arab-Israeli conflict; Six-Day War

Taiwan, 120, 298, 299
Tambo, Oliver, 284
Tanganyika Concessions, 28
Tanzania, 265, 266
Tavares de Sá, Hernane, 65, 108
Taylor, Maxwell, 131, 132
Teilhard de Chardin, Pierre, 274
Tereshkova, Valentina, 99
test ban treaty (1963), 91–92
Thant, Aye Aye (Thant's daughter), 8, 42, 171, *173*
Thant, Tin Maung (Timmy) (Thant's son), 8, 36–37, *36*, 109
Thant, U, *36*
  acclaim for, 1–2, 5
  appointment as Acting Secretary-General, 21–24, 26–27, *29*
  appointment as Secretary-General, 75
  Bandung Conference and, 15
  Buddhism and, *105*, 154, 195, 233, 250
  as candidate for Secretary-General, 18–20
  championing of Third World states, 5–6, 276
  as chief advisor to U Nu, 8–9
  childhood of, 77–79
  communication style of, 34
  controversy surrounding, 5
  daily life, 179–80
  death of, 307–8

Thant, U (*continued*)
  death of son Timmy, 36–37, 109
  dress habits, 97
  early civil service career, 4–5, 8–10
  entertaining, 95–96, 105–6, *127*, 180, 237–38, 305
  with family, *173*
  fragile prestige of, 129–30
  global vision of, 76, 100, 120, 167, 250–51, 271–72, 273–74, 275, 289, 309–10
  health issues, 125, 126, 128, 297, 299, 301
  historical invisibility of, 6, 308–9
  isolation of, 173–74
  Israeli views of, 261
  Jawaharlal Nehru Award for International Understanding, 195, 305
  with Khrushchev, *107*
  Maharishi Yoga and, 239–40
  marriage of, 8
  media relationships, 35–36, 220, 287
  meditation habit, 45
  memoirs of, 305
  Muslim heritage of, 154
  Nobel Peace Prize nominations, 162, 182
  on nuclear testing, 15
  office of, 92–93
  with ONUC chiefs, *89*
  Organization of African Unity and, 266
  papal US visit and, 160–62
  passive image of, 269
  personal philosophy of, 34–35
  policy speeches, 81–83
  political orientation, 80–81
  racist vilification of, 270–71
  retirement decision, 293, 295
  retirement of, 1–3, *4*, 6, 295, 301, 302–3, 305–7, *306*
  Riverdale residence, 42–43
  on secessionist movements, 267–68
  second term decision, 176, 177, 178–84
  self-education, 80
  on southern African white supremacy, 283–84
  space exploration and, 43
  spiritual search and, 239–40, 274
  successor decision, 301–2
  teaching career, 4, 7–8, 79–81
  team appointments, 26–27
  travel of, 111–12
  UFO fascination, 231–32, 250
  as UN ambassador, 7, 9–12, *15*, 18–20
  university education of, *78*, 79
  US popularity of, 185
Thein Tin (Thant's wife), 36, 278
  Burma visit, 189
  death of son Timmy, 36–37
  entertaining and, 171, 180
  marriage of, 8
  Riverdale residence, 42–43
  Thant's death and, 307
  Thant's early career and, 9–10
  Thant's retirement and, 305
  Thant's second term decision and, 179
Third World economic development
  Bandung Conference on, 14, 100
  failure of, 276
  Thant's belief in, 5–6, 15–16, 100–101
Third World states. *See* Afro-Asian states; non-aligned states; Third World economic development
Thomas, Helen, 246
Thorsson, Inga, 277
Tito, Josip Broz, 149, 230
Toynbee, Arnold, 3
Tran Hoai Nam, 174
Tree, Marietta, 106
Tshombe, Moïse
  death of Hammarskjöld and, 17
  detention of, 86–87
  Katanga secession, 28
  military situation and, 85–86
  prime ministership plan, 125
  Thant's negotiation attempts and, 33
  threats to Thant and, 266
  Union Minière and, 39
  UN Security Council resolution on Katanga secession and, 29–30
  U Thant Plan and, 38, 83, 88
Tubman, William, 63
Tuchman, Barbara, 220
Turkey, 103–4, 149
2001: A Space Odyssey, 250

UFOs, 231–32, 250
UN Emergency Force (UNEF), 103, 200

Hammarskjöld memo on, 229–30
Six-Day War beginning and, 224–26
withdrawal of, 197–99, 201–7, 208, 209, 212, 213, 221, 223, 224, 228–29, 287
UNICEF, 268, 276, 298
Union Minière du Haut Katanga, 28, 30, 38–39
United Arab Republic (UAR). *See* Egypt
United Kingdom
   Arab-Israeli conflict and, 260
   Biafra conflict and, 265
   colonialism and, 13
   Congo Crisis and, 28, 30–31, 38, 125, 126–27
   Cuban Missile Crisis and, 52
   Indo-Pakistani War and, 147, 148, 149, 151, 159
   international interventions, 172
   Labour government UN support, 140
   Malaysia and, 141
   nuclear test ban treaty and, 91–92
   racism/white supremacy issue and, 103
   Six-Day War and, 223–24
   Thant's 1964 visit, 112
   Thant's audience with Queen Elizabeth, 37–38
   Thant's relationship with, 140–41
   Thant's second term decision and, 180–81
   Thant's successor and, 301
   US Vietnam War "peace offensive," 169–70
   Vietnam War and, 138, 141, 168, 186–87, 241–42
United Nations (UN)
   Afro-Asian membership, 14, *15*, 162–63
   apartheid and, 283, 284–85
   Apollo 11 mission and, 275
   Bandung Conference on, 14–15
   Chinese membership, 19, 298–300
   Chinese view of, 120
   death of Hammarskjöld, 11–12
   Declaration on the Granting of Independence to Colonial Countries and Peoples (1960), 14–15
   environmentalism and, 276–79
   establishment of, 13
   funding issues, 27, 123, 125, 130, 132–33, 136, 294

   Goldberg as US ambassador to, 145–46
   humanitarian programs, 268, 276, 297–98
   International Day Against All Forms of Racial Discrimination, 284
   JFK assassination and, 100
   JFK's world peace speech on, 91
   New York headquarters of, 9, 25–26, 41
   racism and, 106
   Security Council Resolution 242, 258
   social hierarchy and, 97–98, 105–6
   Thant's colleagues in, 12, 16
   Thant's global vision and, 14–15, 100, 120, 167, 250–51, 271–72, 289
   Thant successor decision, 301–2
   twentieth anniversary and, 141–42
   twenty-fifth anniversary, 285–86
   2001: A Space Odyssey and, 250
   US public support for, 124
   Vietnam War lack of authority, 119–20
United Nations Conference on Trade and Development (UNCTAD), 101, 276
United States
   Bangladesh Liberation War and, 300
   Biafra conflict and, 265
   Cambodia invasion, 279–80
   Congo Crisis policy, 28
   Congo Stanleyville intervention and, 125, 126–27
   Cyprus and, 104
   Dominican Republic intervention, 142, 144
   Indochina and, 112
   Indonesia and, 33, 39
   Indo-Pakistani War and, 148, 149–50, 159
   international interventions, 130, 142, 172, 173, 279
   JFK-Thant Congo Crisis discussions, 43
   nuclear test ban treaty (1963) and, 91–92
   ONUC support and, 30, 31, 83–84
   Six-Day War and, 206, 207, 217, 218–19
   Thant-Kennedy Congo Crisis discussions, 32–33
   Thant's successor and, 301
   Thant as UN ambassador and, 19–20
   UNCTAD and, 101

United States (*continued*)
UNEF withdrawal and, 203, 205–6
UN funding and, 27, 123, 132, 136, 294
See also Cold War; Cuban Missile Crisis; US relationship with Thant; US Vietnam War military engagement; Vietnam War
Universal Declaration of Human Rights, 16, 289
UN Secretary-Generalship
ambiguity of powers, 17
appointment process, 20–21
Hammarskjöld and, 16–17, 23, 26, 28, 34, 173
Khrushchev on, 21
limitations of, 255, 289–90
superpower mediation and, 48, 76
Thant's boldness, 83, 87
"UN We Believe," 124
Urquhart, Brian
Bunche's death and, 300
Congo Crisis and, 38, 85
Czechoslovakia invasion and, 252
Indo-Pakistani War and, 150, 151–52, 153, 155, 156, 159, 160
Jarring mission and, 258, 290
Six-Day War and, 211, 219, 231
on Thant's communication style, 34
Thant's death and, 307
UNEF withdrawal and, 200, 201, 205, 221, 230
US-Hanoi negotiation initiative (1964)
Canadian communications to Hanoi and, 122, 123, 124
Frye article on, 134
Hanoi-Chinese discussions, 121–22
Pentagon Papers and, 297
possible locations for, 131
Rusk and, 130–31, 135, 166, 168, 183, 236
Sevareid's knowledge of, 144, 165–66, 168
Soviet role in, 120, 123, 132
suggestions for, 116, 117
Thant-Johnson discussions, 142, 183
Thant-Senate Foreign Relations Committee meeting on, 194

Thant's initial approach to Hanoi, 120
Thant's public verification of, 134–35
US lack of response, 121, 122, 128, 130–31
US military engagement and, 131–32
US rejection of, 132–33
US relationship with Thant and, 133, 134–36, 166
US relationship with Thant
Arab-Israeli conflict and, 264
Biafra conflict and, 264–65
Congo Crisis and, 84
Cuban Missile Crisis and, 75, 84
Johnson election and, 129
Johnson White House dinner and, 118
Papua New Guinea and, 39
Rusk and, 90, 145, 166, 176, 207, 228, 236, 253–54, 294
Schlesinger on, 32
Thant-Kennedy meetings (1962), 32–33, 43
Thant's appointment as Acting Secretary-General and, 23
Thant's historical invisibility and, 309
Thant's opposition to Vietnam War and, 5, 146
Thant's relationship with Stevenson and, 20, 23, 32, 144
Thant's second term decision and 176
UN twenty-fifth anniversary and, 285–86
US-Hanoi negotiation initiative and, 133, 134–36, 166
Yemen Civil War and, 89–90
US Vietnam War military engagement
Cambodia bombing, 256
combat troop deployment, 128, 138, 139, 165
disengagement (1968), 245–47, 252, 254
Hanoi's Four Points and, 140
Johnson advisors discussions, 167–68, 170
1966 escalation, 177
1967 escalation, 236
1967 recommitment, 238–39
Nixon drawdowns, 255–56
"peace offensive" and, 169–70, 171

San Antonio formula and, 238, 241, 244
search and destroy operations, 165
Tet Offensive and, 240
Thant-Johnson discussions, 143
Thant's protests against, 146, 186
US-Hanoi negotiation initiative and, 131–32
US public opposition and, 165, 171, 176, 190, 191–92, 195, 235–36, 238, 240, 245–46

Valera, Éamon de, 38
Vietnam War
  British views on, 138, 141, 168, 186–87
  Cambodia and, 256, 279, 293, 303
  Canadian communications, 122, 123, 124
  China and, 116, 117, 121–22
  end of, 308–9
  escalations, 165, 185, 187–88, 236
  French back channel, 188
  Gulf of Tonkin resolution, 114, 119, 131
  Hanoi's Four Points, 140
  Johnson's Johns Hopkins speech, 139–40
  Laos and, 139, 145, 293
  My Lai massacre, 280
  nuclear arms and, 111
  origins of, 112–13
  Paris Peace Talks, 248–49, 252, 254, 256, 293
  Pentagon Papers, 297
  Polish back channel, 170–71, 188
  Sino-Soviet relations and, 121, 123, 133, 167, 177
  Six-Day War and, 207
  Soviet assistance, 120
  Tet Offensive (1968), 235, 240
  Thant-Hanoi communications, 168–69, 174, 182–83, 241
  Thant-Ha Van Lau discussions, 189–90
  Thant-Johnson discussions, 115–19, 142–43, 246–47, 247
  Thant-Mai meetings, 144
  Thant's ceasefire proposal, 139
  Thant-Senate Foreign Relations Committee meeting, 193–94
  Thant's Geneva Conference proposals, 113, 116, 145, 172, 175, 190
  Thant's international diplomatic mission (1968), 240–45
  Thant's international travels and, 112
  Thant's Nobel Peace Prize nomination and, 162, 182
  Thant's press conference (1967), 186
  Thant's rhetoric on, 176, 186, 236–37, 249, 252–53, 279–80
  Thant's second term decision and, 178, 181
  Thant's seven-state meeting proposal, 133–34, 135
  Thant's South Asia tour and, 194–95
  Thant's stand-still truce proposal, 190–93
  Thant's Three Point Proposal, 174–76, 178, 183, 186
  Thant's views on, 166–67, 168, 186, 194
  US antiwar protests, 165, 171, 176, 190, 195, 238, 249–50, 252, 280
  US goals, 145
  US "peace offensive," 169–70, 171
  US public opposition to, 137–38, 195–96, 235–36, 240, 245–46
  US public support for, 185–86, 190
  US San Antonio formula, 238, 241, 244
  See also Chinese role in Vietnam War; US-Hanoi negotiation initiative; US Vietnam War military engagement
Vonnegut, Kurt, 3

Wagner, Robert, 2
Waldheim, Kurt, 287, 302
Ward, Barbara, 2, 3, 276–77
Waterhouse, Charles, 28
Waugh, Auberon, 286–87
Webb, Beatrice, 80
Webb, Sidney, 80
Wechsler, James, 228, 229, 239, 254, 308–9
Wells, H. G., 80
Westmoreland, William, 240

Wexler, Jacqueline, 2
Wheeler, Earle, 170, 218
White, William S., 137
white supremacy. *See* racism/white supremacy
Wholey, William, 35–36, 73–74
Wilkins, Roy, 301
Wilson, Harold
   Indo-Pakistani War and, 148, 149
   Six-Day War and, 223–24
   Vietnam War and, 138, 140, 141, 168, 186–87, 242–43
Women's International Strike for Peace, 64, 73

Wood, Natalie, 32
World Federalist Movement, 2–3, 4
World Food Programme, 268, 276
World Health Organization, 276

Yemen Civil War, 89–91, 103, 201
Yen, Wen-Yu, 107–8
Yost, Charles, 83–84, 130, 131, 136, 260, 291–92
Yugoslavia, 18, 49

Zambia, 84, 265, 266, 283
Zimbabwe, 283
Zorin, Valerian, 49, 52, 55, 57